The Prophet and the Presidents

Other books by Gilbert M. Valentine

W. W. Prescott: Forgotten Giant of Adventism's Second Generation (2005)
The Struggle for the Prophetic Heritage (2006)

The PROPHET and the PRESIDENTS

GILBERT M. VALENTINE

PACIFIC PRESS® PUBLISHING ASSOCIATION
NAMPA, IDAHO
OSHAWA, ONTARIO, CANADA
WWW.PACIFICPRESS.COM

Cover design by Gerald Lee Monks
Cover design resources from Pacific Press® Publishing Association Art Vault
Inside design by Aaron Troia

The author assumes full responsibility for the accuracy of all facts and quotations as cited in this book.

You can obtain additional copies of this book by calling toll-free 1-800-765-6955 or by visiting http://www.adventistbookcenter.com.

Library of Congress Cataloging-in-Publication Data:

Valentine, Gilbert M.
The prophet and the presidents : Ellen G. White and the processes of change, 1887-1913 : a study of Ellen White's influence on the administrative leadership of the Seventh-day Adventist Church / Gilbert M. Valentine.
p. cm.
ISBN 13: 978-0-8163-2485-9 (pbk.)
ISBN 10: 0-8163-2485-9 (pbk.)
1. White, Ellen Gould Harmon, 1827-1915. 2. General Conference of Seventh-day Adventists—Presidents—History—19th century. 3. Seventh-day Adventists—Government—History—19th century. 4. General Conference of Seventh-day Adventists—Presidents—History—20th century. 5. Seventh-day Adventists—Government—History—20th century. I. Title.
BX6154.V225 2011b
286.7'3209—dc22

2011011370

11 12 13 14 15 • 5 4 3 2 1

DEDICATION

To my former parish, the Castle Hill Seventh-day Adventist Church in Sydney, Australia, which continues to demonstrate delightfully and lovingly what it means to be the body of Christ.

CONTENTS

FOREWORD

The Prophet and the Presidents—an intriguing title, and a topic largely overlooked in Seventh-day Adventist history. Yet the story of the interaction between the spiritual gifts of prophecy and administration holds many valuable insights for the church in the twenty-first century.

As to the nature of the gifts, that of General Conference president is easier to define than that of prophet. By constitutional mandate the president is elected by a General Conference in session and functions as the denomination's chief executive officer and spiritual leader. That is clear enough. But explaining the role of prophet is much more difficult. Most people think of a prophet as one who foretells the future, but in both the Bible and Ellen White's experience, foretelling is a minor aspect in a prophet's work. Closer to the truth is the concept of "forth-telling." In that sense a prophet serves as a spokesperson for God. In the Old Testament, a "forth-teller" signified one who spoke for God and interpreted God's will.[1] In that sense, Gerhard von Rad points out, the "messenger formula" is the most characteristic form of prophetic speech.[2] Ellen White would have had no problem with that insight—the title she preferred for her calling was "the Lord's messenger,"[3] although she tended to refer to her messages as "testimonies."

But such pedestrian approaches to a definition certainly fail in capturing either the dynamism or the complexity of the prophetic office. Abraham Joshua Heschel helps us a bit when he notes that a "prophet is a man who feels fiercely" about the burden that God has "thrust . . . upon his soul."[4] And John Goldingay is even more helpful in capturing the complexity of the biblical role of prophet when he writes that "a prophet shares God's nightmares and dreams, speaks like a poet and behaves like an actor, is not afraid to be offensive, confronts the confident with rebuke and the downcast with hope, mostly speaks to the people of God, is independent of the institutional pressures of church and state, is a scary person mediating the activity of a scary God, intercedes with boldness and praises with freedom, ministers in a way that reflects his or her personality and time, [and] is likely to fail" in some of his or her prophetic undertakings. While noting that no prophet manifests all those characteristics, Goldingay points out that individual prophets exhibit most of them.[5]

The biblical prophets, of course, did not perform their role in a vacuum. To the contrary, they were in constant contact with God's people as they presented God's messages. Their purpose in that interaction was to advise, encourage, and confront Israel's administrative leadership. Heschel highlights what he calls "the separation of powers" between the roles of king and prophet. The king "must reign according to the will . . . of God," while the prophet was to advise and confront the ruler with the message of what God's will was.[6]

Thus in the Bible we find Israel's leaders going to the prophets for advice, and the prophets going to them to give counsel from God and even to rebuke them when necessary. Some of that rebuke could be quite pointed, as when Nathan confronted David with the words "thou art the man" in the aftermath of his affair with Bathsheba (2 Samuel 12:7). The ministries of such prophets as Elijah, Isaiah, and Jeremiah reflect constant interaction with the kings (i.e., the administrators) of their day, often in conflict mode.

We see the same in Adventist history. Ellen White, in her role of God's "messenger," was in regular contact with the denominational leaders as they sought to guide Adventism according to God's will. As in the Bible, at times the relationship was pleasant and harmonious, while at other times it was difficult and confrontational. Ellen White's relationship with George I. Butler during the 1888 era exemplifies just how difficult it could become. Not only did Ellen White refuse to be manipulated by Butler's presidential power plays, but she had to confront him repeatedly in regard to his misguided notions and the poor spirit he displayed.[7] Given the fact that leadership in all of its flavors must of necessity be strong-willed and opinionated, it is only natural that conflicts would arise. When it comes right down to it, in terms of leadership and the prophetic gift, Adventist history has the same basic dynamics as does the history portrayed in the Bible.

It is that picture that Gilbert Valentine helps us see more clearly in his path-breaking

The Prophet and the Presidents—especially during the period extending from 1887 through 1903. Adventist historians have been quite avid in writing about the theological and organizational developments of that era, but they largely have neglected the creative tension that operated between Ellen White and those responsible for administering and leading the organization during those same years. Thus Valentine's book is an important one as the church seeks to understand better the meaning of a modern prophet not only as that prophet influenced its past but also its present.

In closing, I should note that Valentine's book is at the forefront of a new genre of Adventist historiography: serious studies dealing with the complex relationships between Ellen White and her contemporaries. Most Adventist history has treated the topic merely as an aside to biography or the history of the church. Jerry Moon, in his PhD dissertation entitled *W. C. White and Ellen G. White: The Relationship Between the Prophet and Her Son,*[8] signaled the new direction. Similar doctoral studies are currently underway in the United States and Australia regarding her relationship to her husband and to James Edson White, her oldest surviving child.

Valentine's volume is of the same genre, but it is more ambitious in scope. It provides important understandings for a church still undergoing the process of history and the ongoing relationship between prophetic guidance and administrative responsibility in a world that is different than it was in Ellen White's lifetime, yet surprisingly the same in many of its dynamics. Because of both the differences and the likenesses, *The Prophet and the Presidents* is of crucial importance to the Seventh-day Adventist Church in this century.

George R. Knight
Rogue River, Oregon

INTRODUCTION

For seventy years, from the age of seventeen until her death at eighty-seven, Ellen G. White (1827–1915) was actively involved in initiating, shaping, and developing the Seventh-day Adventist Church. The Adventist community recognized and accepted her as one manifesting a genuine prophetic gift.[1] The church initially emerged in the late 1840s as an informal charismatic fellowship motivated and characterized by its intense eschatological expectation and distinctive observance of the seventh-day Sabbath. In its early years it had little need of church organization or structure, but beginning in 1863 the group adopted a formal and legal organizational structure that later spawned numerous loosely organized branch organizations, related institutions, and other parachurch entities. At the turn of the century, these entities were integrated more tightly into what became a strongly centralized church structure. The process involved radical organizational adjustment and gave rise to significant leadership tensions resulting in damaging defections and losses and the potential for major schisms.

Church members early accorded Ellen White an important, though informal, leadership role in the movement based on her demonstration of an extraordinary charisma—a giftedness involving insights and understandings that she understood as coming from beyond herself.[2] The failure of William Miller's predictions of an immediate return of Christ in 1844 and the consequent keen disappointment experienced by his followers had led to a splintering of Miller's movement. Numerous visionary experiences at this juncture guided Ellen White into an expanding public ministry that nurtured and unified elements of the disappointed and fragmented Millerite believers into a cohesive and enduring movement. Over a period of time, the group developed a consensus acknowledging that while some of their biblical interpretations had been mistaken, neither their central conviction nor the reality of their spiritual experience had been ill founded or delusional. During this early period, unusual physical phenomena accompanied many of Ellen White's vision experiences. Some fellow Adventists found these troubling, but many others regarded them as affirming, and thus most Adventists conceded her a pivotal role in the emerging movement. The practical relevance of her public and private counsel, her emphasis on the importance of the ethical life, her gifted preaching, and her "confirmation" of doctrinal understandings verified the genuineness of her charisma manifested through her visionary experiences.[3] And perhaps most important, her messages and ministry gave meaning to the religious experience of her fellow spiritual travelers. Her remarkable personal journey, and the deep and powerful self-perception of a particular calling as a messenger to her chosen community, underscored this ministry. The manifestation of this unique and extraordinarily influential charisma, exercised as it was in a helpful and timely way, provided a foundation for her community to place a continuing confidence in the legitimacy of her giftedness. In turn, such recognition helped the emerging community to develop a deeper understanding of itself and its mission.[4] The charismatic legitimacy extended to Ellen White by her community thus strengthened over time and reinforced and validated her leadership role.

Not everyone who observed Ellen White, of course, was convinced of the legitimacy of her charismatic experiences. Numerous dissenting voices murmured at various times—and not just at the fringes of her ministry. At times, even some of her closest colleagues expressed concern over what they saw as inconsistencies in her statements and perspectives. Such perceived inconsistencies, coupled with her inevitable human foibles, raised questions about the authority of her charisma in the minds of some. Thus her ongoing legitimacy periodically faced challenges and tests.[5] The most significant dissent tended to gather around the exercise of her leadership as she interacted with those in administrative or other leadership roles. Occasionally, conflict occurred at the interface between her function and the personal ambitions of members within institutional or administrative leadership. In this environment, with its intense focus on the immediacy of administrative problems, the scarcity of financial resources, and an inability to see issues in a larger context, tensions escalated between Ellen White and other prominent leaders. Generally, at such times, past experience and the acknowledgment of the overall value of her role as an arbitrator in disputes was sufficient to provide for continued confidence—but not always. Their inability to resolve tensions led some prominent colleagues to reject her gift. In the long term, however, and for the mainstream of the church, the positive value of her role as leader, arbitrator, and guide validated the legitimacy of her distinctive function. She continued to receive affirmation of and confidence in her gift.[6]

During her seventy years of involvement with the Adventist movement, Ellen G. White personally attended the majority of the general meetings (later called General Conference sessions) of the church.[7] Her unique and perceptive insight into spiritual matters, her practical Christian counsel and advice to individuals, her timely intervention in the organizational affairs of the life of the developing church, and the spiritual authority of her extensive writing provided more than sufficient evidence to the church's expanding membership that her gift was not only a genuine prophetic one, but that it was a major boon to the community. Many recognized that her continuing influence and authority in the movement kept it focused on its mission, strengthened it, and enabled it to become the substantial and still expanding community it is today.

Ellen White never accepted an official position or an elected leadership role or administrative office in the church.[8] Although recognized as a significant leader in her community, her employment status with the General Conference was that of a "worker" and she received the equivalent of a minister's salary. By the 1880s, her employment role was defined as that of a "writer" supplemented by general pastoral duties. In 1887, in recognition of her ministerial role, the General Conference voted her credentials as an ordained minister, but the status was accorded without any formal ceremony of ordination.[9] Nor was she attached by way of pastoral assignment to any particular congregation, although she did respond to invitations by the formal organization to locate her labors in specific fields for various periods of time.[10] Mrs. White exercised her influence and authority among the formally elected leaders of the Adventist community in an informal manner. She achieved this through her personal relationships and interactions with the officially appointed leadership of the organization, augmented by her letter writing, counseling, and preaching. Later, her articles and books and other communications enabled her to have a wider influence with the broad membership of the church. This study asks whether Ellen White consciously reflected on the process of how she should exercise this informal, and somewhat tangential, leadership role or whether the exercise of the role occurred intuitively. To what extent did she evaluate and choose or reject various methods that might enhance her influence or make her ministry more effective?

In spite of the fact that Ellen White held no elected office, she was nevertheless intensely interested in the structural and organizational aspects of the community's development. In particular she was concerned with the quality and appropriateness of those chosen to lead the organization. During the fifty-two years of her involvement with the church following its adoption in 1863 of legal status and a formal central organizational structure, she worked closely with the eight men who at different times and for varying periods were elected to serve as the officially appointed leaders of the movement.[11] Although she did not accept election to an official position in the church herself, she was intimately acquainted with most, if not all, of those in the church's highest leadership ranks.

From the earliest period in the denomination, the election process for the position of General Conference president and other senior officials of the organization involved the appointment of a nominating committee at a duly called session of the General Conference. Sessions convened annually at the beginning and then changed to a biennial election pattern in 1889. In 1905, the denomination adopted a four-year term of office. Since 1970 the term has been five years. Of the thirty-eight regular sessions of the General Conference held during her lifetime, Ellen White made special efforts to be present at most, missing the meetings only when she was in Europe or Australia. Her advanced age and uncertain health prevented her from attending the 1913 session, held just two years before her death.[12]

These sessions of the General Conference were essentially meetings of delegates representing the constituent state conference organizations and associated parachurch entities. The nominating committee usually consisted of individuals selected on the basis of a recommendation by the incumbent president, who was called upon to "name" the standing committees of the session early in the proceedings. The nominating committee would meet during the session and would bring a slate of potential officers to the floor for approval by a simple majority of delegates. If delegates were unhappy with the nominations, they could vote to refer the names back for further consideration by the nominating committee. Thus the system avoided extensive personal and potentially embarrassing discussion on the floor of the session and minimized party politicking and campaigning.

Ellen White is recorded as having attended General Conference sessions as an appointed delegate from the earliest period. She thus had a formal right to speak in discussions on the floor during session meetings and to vote on the various motions made. Also she participated at formal sessions by being invited to present devotionals or to preach at the regular worship services. Often the session would invite her to address specific issues being discussed by delegates. She appears never to have participated formally as an elected member of a nominating committee, although evidence indicates that at times she received specific requests for advice on possible candidates. Clearly she was interested in the outcome of the nomination-election process. But did she ever attempt to influence the process for the purpose of achieving a specific outcome? How involved was the "prophetic gift" in determining who should exercise the "gift of leadership" in the church? Given the extent of her interest in the elected leaders of the Adventist movement and the level of her interaction with them, the question arises: To what extent was she involved in the selection and appointment of those who served as leaders? Did she participate in their removal or replacement? How did her informal, charismatically based authority within the community interact and relate to the usual democratic processes of election and appointment? In what ways—if any—did her informal, charismatically based authority interface with what we might view as the more prosaic exercise of the administrative gift or the apostolic gift? Which of the gifts should take preeminence in matters involving conflict? Exploring these questions is a primary focus of the present study, and answers are suggested through the unfolding narrative and discussion.

In 1913, in a Bible study presentation at the General Conference session of that year, W. C. White, son of Mrs. White, attempted to help his colleagues and his critics understand the interaction among the various spiritual gifts. His attempt at setting out an understanding occurred in the context of the approaching end of his mother's ministry. She would die in 1915. It was an important issue, but it was fraught with inherent tensions. White linked his discussion of the topic with an attempt to inform the delegates more broadly about the way Ellen White produced her books and how her literary assistants helped her. He suggested that the role of spiritual leadership and administration should be understood to be embraced in the gift of apostleship. But he firmly believed that "the sacredness of the apostolic gift can best be taught without any effort to tear down confidence in the gift of prophecy." Nevertheless, some misunderstood and heavily criticized him.[13] Following his unsuccessful attempt to educate the larger community, White commented in a letter to A. G. Daniells, president of the General Conference, that he, White, was "fully in harmony" with "the effort that should be made to emphasize in the minds of our people the sacredness, the authority of the apostolic gifts." He had repeatedly said to his colleagues that he thought the subject "could not be perfectly understood without a better understanding of all the gifts in the church," and he wished that others would give Bible studies from that perspective. Employing an allusion to the leadership arrangements in the time of Jesus, White commented, "For a long time I have been praying the Lord to take the burden that for years has rested upon Mother and place it upon the seventy elders." In addition, he wished to assure his colleagues that they had his sympathy and his prayers "in their effort to build up and strengthen the apostolic gift, and all the other gifts in the church." W. C. White and those in leadership felt that it was very important for the health of the church that there be a fuller understanding of the role and interaction between the gifts.[14] This study seeks to understand more fully the interaction of the various spiritual gifts of leadership in the life of the church highlighted by the questions raised by W. C. White. It attempts to address and to explain such issues and provide a more adequate understanding of Ellen White's work.

Both the wealth of material and the constraints of space have suggested that the present study focus on the three General Conference presidents who served during the latter years of the nineteenth century and through the turn of the new century, with a particular emphasis on the sixteen-year period between 1887 and 1903. The men involved are Ole A. Olsen (1888–1897), George A. Irwin (1897–1901), and Arthur G. Daniells (1901–1922). These presidents served following the death of Ellen White's husband, James White, in 1881. The early presidencies of John Byington, John Andrews, and the first term of George I. Butler, as well as that of Ellen White's husband, James White, lie outside the focus of this study. The fact that in many of the early years, leadership roles were overlaid by close family relationships makes that period a less clear area for study. Furthermore, an understanding of the most desirable leadership pattern for the denomination took time to evolve, and during the early years the varying concepts and styles advocated often reflected the personalities and temperaments of the various proponents as much as they did clear biblical, theological reflection.

Before James White's death in 1881, for example, he had been elected president of the General Conference more than ten times. It has been well documented that his autocratic management style, strength of personality, and native entrepreneurship achieved a great deal in building up the movement.[15] But, unfortunately, such a leadership style also often strained relationships between White and his colleagues. Even when he wasn't in office, the strongly opinionated James White remained a predominant leadership figure. Between the years 1874 and 1876, when George I. Butler served as General Conference president, tensions over what "leadership" entailed became acute. Butler's resignation in 1876 was a direct result of conflict over the nature of leadership and his difficulty in relating to James White, who, although out of office, still acted in large measure as a de-facto president.

For obvious reasons, Ellen White's interaction with administrative leadership was more tangled when her husband was the president. Complicating the formal relationship was the spousal relationship and the inevitable blurring of roles (at least from James's perspective) that Ellen White exercised as both spouse and prophetic voice. Differentiating between the two roles was not always successful. The closeness of family relationships also complicated the short presidency of J. N. Andrews.[16] After James's death, however, Ellen White's involvement with the appointment and removal of presidents comes into better focus. Her influence in the election processes of the church became more formal and remote and thus more readily analyzed.

A further reason for focusing on the latter period is that although Adventists established the overarching General Conference in 1863, it was not until the mid- to late-1880s that growth of the church led to the development of a more complex structure. Beginning in the mid-1880s, the role of the General Conference president began to take on more the nature of a leader of a team of administrators. His associates were responsible for distinct areas of activity, such as education, home missions, and publishing. The early 1890s saw the creation of major organizational sub-units designated as "districts." These were later organized as "unions" of state conferences with their own financial and legal constitutions. Under this arrangement, supervision of the local, largely state-based, conferences was no longer the direct responsibility of the General Conference. Moral suasion and influence replaced executive action and supervision in this arena. The responsibilities of the General Conference president had, however, become more complex. Now he functioned as a team leader for a broadening array of General Conference associates and union conference presidents. The role continued to evolve yet further. While the radical changes in organizational structure had been largely settled by 1903, the church did not, of course, cease to develop, and it adopted minor adjustments in structure post-1903. During this period, Ellen White continued to interact with church leadership up until the time of her death in 1915. Chapter 10 will extend the discussion beyond the period of particular focus to survey the final years of Ellen White's relationship with General Conference president A. G. Daniells and her involvement in the various issues of his presidency and his re-election to office.

By the mid-1890s, during the presidency of O. A. Olsen, Ellen White began to give critical attention to the General Conference associates as well as to the president. While she had strongly advocated the development of a broader presidential staff to lessen the demands made on the office of president, she was not reluctant to counsel a president for relying on associates whom she believed were ill-suited to their tasks. Such focus created uncomfortable dilemmas for the presidents, who were often hamstrung by the non-availability of suitably qualified and experienced alternative individuals. They were also constrained by the fact that these associates had been elected through formal democratic procedures. Presidents thus had to follow due process if they were to consider replacing a colleague. They could not simply ignore proper electoral processes. Changes, if needed, could not be effected simply by the counsel they received from Ellen White.

The administrations of O. A. Olsen and G. A. Irwin witnessed a pattern of Ellen White criticizing the elected team of associates. This continued in Daniells's administration, although during this time she communicated her criticism and counsel through her son, W. C. White. He, in turn, maintained the practice with subsequent administrations.[17]

A study of the relationship and engagement between the charismatic authority of Ellen White and the formal administrative authority of the elected leadership is valuable, because it illuminates, and therefore facilitates, a better understanding of the numerous leadership conflicts in the church during the 1890s and into the first decade of the new century. Such conflicts mostly centered on the allocation of resources, which were scarce, and the determination of priorities for investment and development as the church went through a period of rapid expansion. The various parties sought to influence the church leadership and budget managers in the General Conference treasury, seeking funds to pursue their work—each trying to justify that their area of need had higher priority than the others. Sometimes the jousting was fierce. This conflict often manifested itself over the allocation of resources for work in Australia versus that in England or for work in the southern United States versus that in Africa or Europe. The competition involved both monetary resources and skilled personnel.[18]

Ellen White keenly felt the lack of financial resources when she worked in Australia in the 1890s. During this period, she struggled with stress and anxiety that periodically manifested themselves through a number of physical symptoms. These, in turn, would surely have affected her perception of the problems at headquarters as well as her feelings of frustration, exasperation, and anxiety about them. Such circumstances help us understand the frequency of the sometimes strong language that she employed at this time in her communications with denominational headquarters.

In order to have an adequate grasp of the relationship between the prophet and the presidents, it is necessary to consider some of the difficulties involved in the publishing program of the church around the turn of the century. Therefore, this study also attempts to throw light on the complexities involved in the development of the church's publishing branch during that troubled period. The interaction between Ellen White and the General Conference presidents often concerned issues related to publishing activities. Tensions arose at the intersection where her work as a writer in the church met the actual business of publishing and printing. This was mostly because she sought to establish a unique relationship with her publishers not available to other authors. She felt the need to retain control over both the content and the circulation of her works, yet at the same time wanted free access to the church's marketing networks. The circumstances were unusual to say the least. She assumed the financial responsibility of preparing the printing plates for her books and retained ownership of them, stating that her arrangements needed to be unique because she was concerned about possible constraints being placed on her influence by anyone unfavorable toward her writings. More important, to do otherwise would perhaps make her vulnerable to pressure to dilute the messages that God's people needed to receive.[19] Such constraints, she maintained, would compromise her charismatic influence and authority, as indeed, would also any attempt by her to publish her own work independently. The authority of self-published material could not be as great as that printed by a recognized publishing house. However, this approach created significant management problems for the publishing houses themselves. It disrupted and complicated planning for the release and circulation of other books as conflicts emerged over what products needed to be given priority.

Publishing was an expensive business both for the publishing houses and for Ellen White. It was not always easy to cover basic production costs, let alone generate sufficient surplus funds for a livelihood. Ellen White understood the need to control expenses and ensure surpluses in order to support her charitable and development projects. Therefore, access to marketing networks and enthusiastic distribution by colporteurs (then called "canvassers") were critical. On numerous occasions she was not timid about directing publishing house management regarding which books should or should not be published and at what price. She also indicated what kind of books should be subsidized and what should be done with company surpluses. The publishing house managers, however, felt that *they* needed to be able to decide whether they should subsidize the loss on one book by the profit on another. It seems clear that some publishing house managers considered that Ellen White's intervention into the decision-making processes made their task difficult. Did such managers perceive her as meddling in their roles?

Sometimes, as she sought to give urgency to the need to resolve problems, she presented her intense concerns about the problems of book marketing and circulation as issues of the highest moral principles. Many of the issues, however, were time and circumstance specific. They included, for example, her vigorous opposition to wage differentials between institutional employees, arguments for specific percentages for book royalties, and concerns about marketing policies. Today, the church may have abandoned these policies for good reason, even though she ardently advocated them at the time and couched her arguments in terms of universal ethical principles. Again, this study attempts to throw light on the perplexing circumstances the publishing program faced at the turn of the century and provide a context for interpreting and understanding Ellen White's involvement in these problematic areas. (Chapter 11 also provides a broader context and interpretive framework for understanding the intensity of feeling over some of these issues.)

In many respects, piecing together the story is like weaving a tapestry. At one level, the story explores the detailed stitching as well as tracing out each colorful thread that forms the warp and woof of the richly textured fabric that is Adventism's past. At the same time, as the story emerges, we need to stand back, to gain perspective, to make sense of the larger patterns that have appeared over time. Both tasks are necessary in the quest for understanding and developing an appreciation of how Providence led and shaped the Adventist movement.

It is important to note that this is a believer's study. It is not an attempt to discredit or demean the function of Ellen White's charisma that contributed so much to the survival and growth of Adventism and to the molding of its distinctive shape. Rather, it is an endeavor to grasp and appreciate the dynamics of the interaction of the "gift of administration" and the charisma of the "gift of prophecy" in the church's formative years. It may even help to provide a basis for understanding how that interaction should function today. This study helps put to rest the "myth of the inflexible prophet" and confirms George Knight's observation that Ellen White's charismatic leadership and approach to problem solving was characterized both by flexibility and pragmatism, while adhering to broad guiding principles. It also confirms Barry Oliver's observation that her flexibility grew out of a central focus on mission.[20]

The interaction between the prophet and the various presidents illustrates the principle that changed circumstances require a modification of approaches and action plans. It also indicates that the urgency of present mission opportunities, the duty of pastoral care, and the duty of meeting human need takes precedence over other competing priorities. Recognizing the principles supporting this pragmatic approach to leadership provides us a way of interpreting problematic particulars. How to explain, for instance, the prophet condemning a certain course of action as unethical ("highway robbery") in one set of circumstances, and then half a decade later seeing no ethical dilemma in advocating and endorsing the condemned practice in a different set of circumstances?[21] It should not surprise us to find that Ellen White, like each of us, experienced a mix of conflicting emotions as she encountered problems and disappointments in her spiritual journey. Nor should it puzzle us that these conflicting emotions would give rise, at times, to conflicting statements of intent or point of view. For example, we should not be shocked that in her frustration and disappointment with the church leadership she could express the view that she would never return to America, and then later state that she would return. She might at one moment resolve in her mind and in her discussions with friends that she would write no more personal letters because they created too much misunderstanding. Instead, she would confine herself to preaching and oral delivery. But then, a short time afterward, she would simply resume writing such letters. Thinking out loud, as it were, in some of her correspondence or expressing how she felt about something at a particular moment might inevitably result in inconsistencies, but that would not be abnormal either. We need a more adequate construct than just concluding that such things consequently invalidate the exercise of her charisma. Standing back from the historical tapestry suggests otherwise. We, therefore, need a larger frame of reference to understand the pattern of Providence at work in the life and ministry of a person who, like anyone else, experienced the usual range of emotional ups and downs, joys, and disappointments. Every person in his or her own way is a bundle of inconsistencies.

The present study and the story it uncovers has reinforced the convictions of this author that we have much yet to learn about the richly textured dimensions in which Providence has led in the development of the Adventist movement. The story unfolded here illustrates this more clearly. The appreciation of these brightly hued patterns underlies the continuing conviction that the Spirit of truth, uniquely manifested in the ministry of Ellen White, still leads the Adventist community. The church's continued growth through the years since she interacted with its leadership would seem to be a clear evidence of the ongoing blessing of the Spirit. It is hoped that this study will help enrich the understanding of new generations of Adventists and deepen their appreciation of Ellen White's work.

While the pages of this volume tell the story of struggles and of joys as well as pain and sorrow in the development of the church, in a very real sense the pages themselves emerged through the mists of a difficult journey of pain and loss. I am indebted to many friends and colleagues in the church for their encouragement and assistance in bringing this project to completion. Two research grants from Asia-Pacific International University (then Mission College) in Thailand enabled the location, collection, and processing of materials. I gratefully acknowledge this assistance. The university administration also generously provided long-term research and writing time and accommodated some extended absences away from campus at a very difficult time when my late wife Gail needed extensive medical treatment. I will be forever grateful for the generous understanding and support of Warren Shipton, Mack Tennyson, Bill Townend (board chair), and the secretariat personnel at the General Conference. Barry Oliver and Barry Hill of the South Pacific Division have also been gracious in facilitating difficult transitions, and I am deeply grateful to them.

Merlin Burt and the staff of the Andrews University Heritage Room were generous and ever courteous in providing advice and access to materials. The same is to be said for Janice Clark, Patricia Chapman, and the staff of the Loma Linda University Heritage Room. John Skrzpaszek and Marian de Berg at the Avondale Ellen G. White Research Center were always willing to facilitate the study with ready responses to my requests for assistance to materials. Tim Poirier of the White Estate in Washington, D.C., was unfailingly courteous and helpful with his guidance in the quest for sources. I also highly value his numerous thoughtful suggestions for corrections and clarifications on reading the completed manuscript. Bert Haloviak, director of Archives and Statistics at the General Conference, not only provided helpful access to materials that I requested but knew where else to look. He is truly every researcher's companion and friend, for he genuinely shares the joy and excitement of discovery and values new insights. His suggestions on the first four chapters of the manuscript provided helpful feedback and valuable additional sources.

Arthur Patrick read a first draft of the material, excitedly encouraged me in the project, and provided suggestions for shaping the theme. His sensitivity to the issues and his pastoral passion for leading the church to a more adequate understanding of the mystery and the marvel of Ellen White's charismatic role in the shaping of Adventism have been a source of continuing inspiration and encouragement. My good friend and discussion partner, Rick Stone, provided valuable pointers on writing style and ideas for thematic development. And my mentor, George Knight, read the first several chapters and provided invaluable initial feedback on structure and appropriateness of material. His eye for detail in reviewing the final manuscript was most valuable. Jerry Moon also made structural suggestions concerning the manuscript and aided in the removal of some blemishes. A college classmate and friend, Murray Chapman, at the time the ministerial director for the New South Wales Conference, read the manuscript and offered numerous suggestions for clarification and adjustment. His pastoral concerns and perspectives were a valuable guide in my desire to address the subject in a pastorally helpful way. Doctor Percy Harrold, long experienced in church health administration, also read the manuscript and provided insightful feedback for dealing with the subject pastorally. His careful eye for detail and suggestions concerning clarity and appropriate expression, I have valued very much. Russell and Helen Schulz not only continued to encourage me in the project but also brought clarity through our many discussions of the topic. They challenged ideas both old and new, and Russell has an excellent eye for grammar and spelling. Doctor Kendra Haloviak of La Sierra University, whom I am now delightfully blessed to call my wife, read the completed manuscript, and I am deeply grateful for her eagle eye for punctuation, smoothness of expression, and for her especially helpful suggestions for better integration of the themes of the book. I am also deeply grateful for the valued input of Gerald Wheeler, who did the primary edit of the book, and for the experience and wise advice of David Jarnes, who helped bring the book to completion. It should go without saying, but needs to be reiterated anyway, that the author is nevertheless responsible for any flaws in expression, errors of fact, or inadequacies in interpretation of the material.

Other valued supporting and understanding friends contributed to the completion of the project whose names cannot go unmentioned. Trevor Roy and Norma Rosenhain generously made available their apartment at Manly, with its wondrous views of the ocean and a distant horizon that gave me opportunity not only to gain perspective but also to find peace and healing even if wellness was not possible during the difficult early stages of Gail's illness. The early chapters of the manuscript took shape there. And thanks are due to my good pastoral friend and colleague Lyell Heise, who helped make important connections when life and its problems seemed overwhelming. John and Marla Matthews of Berrien Springs graciously hosted me during an extended research visit to Andrews University and encouraged the project. Sue Scharffenberg, provost at Washington Adventist University, and her administration generously provided accommodation and concerned care during a research leave in Washington, D.C. Mary and Bert Haloviak provided a refuge for writing in a corner of their home in Beltsville, Maryland, and Mike and Helen Pearson of Wokingham in the U.K. likewise made room in their home and in their hearts for me during the final writing stages. And Gail, what can I say? Your beauty, bravery, and trust throughout the terrible twists and turns in the painful struggle with your illness during the writing of this project, was a life-enriching inspiration. You shared the joy and stimulation of new insights and understanding, and you lovingly encouraged your itinerant Kiwi in every step of the long journey. Although you did not live to see the project completed, you were the one who made it possible. A thank you is not nearly enough, but I thank you deeply and the good Lord, who I know, lovingly keeps you.

Because of space limitations, I have tried to keep referencing as brief as possible while at the same time providing the essential information for those who wish to check a source or an interpretation or pursue further inquiry. References in the endnotes generally follow the same order in which they are referred to in the text.

The majority of unpublished sources used in the research for this book can be found in the General Conference Archives, the special Ellen G. White Collections in the Loma Linda University Library and in the Heritage Room at Andrews University or at the offices of the Ellen G. White Estate in Washington, D.C. Space limitations have precluded the providing of specific details about the location of documents. Fortunately, in recent times the catalogue details for both incoming and outgoing correspondence in the Ellen G. White Estate collections are available online through the services of Loma Linda University and can be accessed at http://www.whiteestate.org/search/collections.asp.

CHAPTER 1

The PROPHETS and POLITICS: SCRIPTURAL PRECEDENTS

"Have you not heard that Adonijah, the son of Haggith, has become king, and our lord David knows nothing about it?" Nathan whispered to the surprised Bathsheba as he explained the palace coup that had just taken place in Jerusalem. "Let me advise you how you can save your own life and the life of your son Solomon," he went on as he elaborated on the seriousness of the military situation and the threat it represented to Solomon and probably to himself and undoubtedly to the security of the young kingdom. Nathan carefully plotted a diplomatic maneuver with Bathsheba. She immediately was to go to the aged King David in his room with instructions to report the insurrection and ask him if he had authorized the ascension of Adonijah. And she needed to be worried, realizing that after David's death, both she and Solomon would be "treated as criminals," if the succession to the throne went in any other direction.

"While you are still there talking to the king, I will come in and add my word to what you have said," the prophet explained. He would remind David of his pledge that Solomon would be given the succession. The strategy worked. David was able to intervene, aborting the attempted coup by Adonijah and his supporters and thus avoiding civil upheaval and huge potential loss of life. The prophet Nathan was an experienced political adviser.[1]

The Old Testament frequently presents the informal charismatic prophetic role as being closely involved in the process of appointing personnel to civil or administrative leadership roles. For example, Scripture records that Samuel in his prophetic role was directly involved in the significant social and political development of Israel as it moved from what John Bright describes as an "amphictyonic tribal league" type of societal organization to a more politically cohesive nation-state under a monarch.[2] The Philistine crisis brought on by the rise of the neighboring military aristocracy and the failure of Israel's tribal organization to cope with its ambitions posed a serious dilemma. In the scriptural account, Samuel, as prophet, participates not only in identifying the appointed person for leadership (the anointing of Saul) but also in the framing of the constitutional arrangements for governance, setting out the rules for the kingship (see 1 Samuel 10:1, 25). Later, Samuel again directly identified and authorized Saul's successor through his anointing of David (see 1 Samuel 16:3). As already noted, Scripture also presents the later prophet, Nathan, as being closely involved with the uncertainties concerning the succession of the throne at the end of David's life. Through careful and diplomatic political participation, Nathan initiated a process that ensured the avoidance of civil war by uniting the various factions of the priesthood, the military, and the royal family. Just how much of a personal stake he may have had in bringing about the ascension of Solomon to the throne is not clear, but it certainly had a political dimension (see 1 Kings 1).

Later prophets who had various roles in the royal succession included Ahijah, the prophet of Shiloh (see 1 Kings 11:29), who anointed Jeroboam and spoke of the breakup of the kingdom; Shemaiah, who counseled Rehoboam not to engage in civil war with his northern ethnic neighbors (see 1 Kings 12:22); Elijah, who anointed Jehu as the successor to Ahab (see 1 Kings 19:16); and Micaiah, the son of Imlah (see 1 Kings 22:14), who advised Jehoshaphat and Ahab on military strategy and predicted the downfall of Ahab's dynasty. As the monarchy established itself more securely as a form of government with strong dynastic rules of succession, the prophets were less involved in identifying and anointing candidates for national leadership. Nevertheless, they still counseled the monarchs on issues of leadership and national policy and provided spiritual guidance more broadly to the populace (for example, see 2 Chronicles 36:15).

The Chronicler's interpretative summary of the fateful events leading up to the Babylonian captivity makes clear that prophets still played a significant role in national life, but a general resistance to their messages had developed. For example, Zedekiah, the last king of Judah, is reported as one who "did not humble himself before Jeremiah the prophet, who spoke the word of the Lord" (2 Chronicles 36:12). But even beyond the monarchs, the leaders of the priests, the community leaders (the nobles), and the people themselves are reported as despising the words and scoffing at the messages of the prophets until "there was no remedy" (verse 16).

In New Testament times, the discussion of leadership of the people of God moves away from civic administration and the political issues directly relevant to the nation-state arena. Instead, the focus shifts to the role or function of spiritual leadership within a community of faith no longer defined by ethnic or geographic boundaries. The Christian church is a community or a fellowship of the Spirit. Leadership in the church is understood in the context of gifts that function within the body of the church to ensure that the body lives and achieves its objectives and purposes. Although the New Testament employs numerous other complementary metaphors to describe the nature of the church as a spiritual community, the body metaphor is probably the dominant motif, and the concept of gifts and servant leadership the most common theme.

Beyond the concept of the body and the extended use of terminology to describe leadership functions such as elders, bishops, and deacons, we actually find very little information in Scripture about the specific organizational structure of the community, which leads many to conclude that the early church was very egalitarian. In consequence, various Christian groups through the centuries have adopted different forms or mechanisms of organization depending on the historical period and cultural context in which the group emerged.

The New Testament identifies the role of the prophet as one among numerous gifts such as those of apostleship, ministry, deaconship, teaching, administration, and leadership. The role of the prophet in the New Testament church appears to have a more subdued function and status than that accorded to prophets in Old Testament times. The New Testament contains no record of direct, specific prophetic involvement in the process of identifying and sanctioning community leadership or of the distribution of the other gifts in the church.[3] In the community of the church, the appointment of leaders to positions or functions of leadership involves either apostolic designation, such as in the case of John Mark, Titus, or Timothy, or recognition by local house churches of the presence of leadership gifts in their midst. Prophets in the church at Antioch, however, did participate in the assigning and sanctioning of Saul and Barnabas for a particular mission task—the first missionary journey through Cyprus and southern Turkey (see Acts 13:1–3). It is not clear who these prophets are, because the biblical author includes them in a general list along with teachers. Furthermore, Scripture reports nothing else about the specific ministry of these prophets in Antioch, and we find no mention of their role in the planning and decision making concerning the second or the third missionary tour involving the sharp contention between the two leaders over the role of John Mark.

The New Testament does, however, give evidence of the creative tension between the roles of the gift of prophecy and the gift of apostleship or the gift of administration. In the report of the fateful return of Paul to Jerusalem sometime between A.D. 56 and 58, a prophet named Agabus from one of the Christian communities in Judea dramatically appears in Caesarea to give a dire warning on the outcome of Paul's mission plans.[4] The prophet Agabus had previously visited the church in Antioch and had warned of a period of famine and of the general distress affecting the church in Judea (see Acts 11:27–30). On that occasion, the church's favorable response to the intervention of the prophet resulted in a large offering being taken to assist the poor in Judea. The offering became an important instrument of church unity at a time of growing tension between the new Gentile churches and Palestinian Christians. Delivered by Paul and Barnabas, the offering not only brought practical help to the afflicted believers in the famine-stricken areas in Palestine, but it served a significant strategic purpose of forming stronger ties of fellowship linking mother and daughter communities.[5]

The second occasion of Agabus's recorded involvement with Paul occurred at the home of Philip the evangelist in Caesarea, where Philip's four daughters are reported as also having the gift of prophecy (see Acts 21:8–11). On the basis of a dramatically acted-out warning given by Agabus, Paul's colleagues and the local Tyrean believers offered counsel and advice to the apostle in an attempt to persuade him that it was questionable wisdom to proceed with his particular mission strategy at that time. According to William Neil, "Paul chose to disregard their advice not to go to Jerusalem presumably because he put more trust in the guidance he was himself being given by the Spirit to make Jerusalem his goal."[6] Besides, did not Paul also claim to have not only the gift of apostleship but other gifts of the Spirit as well (see 1 Corinthians 14)? Because of the apparent contradictions here, the passage has given rise to a number of interpretations. Some exegetes suggest that the Tyrean believers misread the prophecy of Agabus as an implied warning for Paul not to continue his pilgrimage.[7] Others note that Luke can hardly mean that Paul was deliberately disobedient to the will of God or that the Spirit was mistaken in the guidance given. Most note, however, that at the least, the record in Luke is simply not clear. But could Agabus's warning been intended to prevent the catastrophe? Could there have been another more appropriate time for Paul to proceed to Jerusalem? Did he have to go there at that specific time and under those particular circumstances? Was Agabus's warning designed to indicate that Paul could consider other ways and means of accomplishing his mission? The biblical record does not indicate what issues were involved in the discussions that Paul's colleagues had with him. But as John Polhill notes, the incident "provides an excellent example of that sort of interchange within the Christian community between conflicting understandings of God's will."[8] Beyond the seeming conflict in the Spirit's direction, Paul seems to have based his determination to proceed with the plan in spite of the warning on his own convictions about how to understand the will of God in the situation. Does the dispute indicate a creative tension between the gift of apostleship and the gift of prophecy? Paul's colleagues eventually gave up their attempt to dissuade him from his plan and resigned themselves to what they felt was the larger will of God.

The gift of prophecy as manifested in the life of Ellen White functioned profitably as counselor to Adventist Church leadership, guiding church leaders through many periods of difficulty, helping the church to maintain its distinctive sense of self-identity, and keeping it focused on its gospel mission. As I have noted elsewhere, on various occasions in the church's development the gift functioned as a spiritual referee among competing theological or administrative viewpoints and perspectives. On other occasions, such as during the 1890s, it served as a valuable check on executive authority and the tendency in some leaders to exercise their leadership role with "kingly power."[9] Similar to what we may observe in the functioning of the prophetic role in biblical times, on numerous occasions Ellen White's role also operated in a state of prophetic tension with administration.[10] The charismatic authority of the prophet stood over against institutional authority as it was embodied in various organizational structures. The gift of prophecy, in a certain sense, almost inevitably stands in tension with the gift of administration. Creative conflict in this sense is not bad but rather is good for the church.

The present study will focus specifically on how Ellen White related to the process of identifying, electing, or removing formally appointed leaders of the movement. What kind of authority or power did she have when it came to the appointing of individuals to spiritual leadership? What kind of influence was she able to exert and what methods or approaches were available for her to use in exerting her influence to bring about change or achievement of the ends desired? Our study shall explore this aspect of her work and discuss it within the context of concepts of power and authority utilizing the theoretical framework of concepts and insights from the discipline of organizational behavior.

CHAPTER 2

SPIRITUAL LEADERSHIP as "POLITICAL" SKILL

"Unless some action is taken to appoint someone to provide assistance to Elder Butler to lessen the burden on him, I shall not lift my hand to vote him to be the President." Ellen White was emphatic as she participated in an important floor discussion among the delegates at the 1888 General Conference Session in Minneapolis. The topic of discussion was the introduction of administrative changes relating to the role of the General Conference president. Without added staff to take some of the responsibilities and to lighten the workload expected of the president, his health would completely break down. And it would be the same for anybody else appointed to the position.

As it happened, Butler was not reappointed to the presidency at that session, and it is not known whether Ellen White needed to carry out her stated intention to abstain from participating in the ballot. But many delegates were upset that Butler was not re-elected. In the end, the presidential position did not receive any assistance—perhaps because it was not clear how to determine effectively what duties could or should be delegated. But then Ellen White had only one hand to raise on the issue, anyway. Thus in the final analysis, her vote on this issue counted only as one. But her speech and her statement to the delegates was a very telling exercise of influence. Was she aware of what she had said, or was it a spur-of-the-moment thing?

Very much conscious of her unique ability to influence people and events in the church, Ellen White regarded herself as having a duty to do so, because her insights and her messages were not her own. She, and the church, understood them as coming to her through a prophetic impulse, a "burden" from the Lord, mediated through her by the Holy Spirit. Along with the insights and messages was the conviction that the messages were vitally important in the spiritual life and development of the church or of the individuals to which they were directed. The methods she adopted in order to communicate her insights and to exercise her influence effectively were very intentional and required careful thought. Many of them directly involved communicating with and influencing the church's leading administrators, the General Conference presidents, to take a particular course of action. Is this kind of influence "political" in a right and proper sense, one that also reflects how the prophets in Old Testament times interacted with their national leaders?

Ellen White's life and work as a leader was inextricably and deeply linked with the Adventist Church as an organization. In many ways it was her life. She not only helped establish the church, but it was an organization to which she gave all her energy and thought and care. Mrs. White was entirely committed to ensuring its welfare, nurturing its growth, and seeing it fulfill its mission. This chapter will discuss three related perspectives on her role as a gifted, charismatic spiritual leader in the Adventist Church. The approach will be first to briefly review contemporary concepts of leaders and their behavior and role in organizations. The reader should keep in mind that at certain points this part of the chapter may seem a little more theoretical than the later sections of the chapter as well as succeeding chapters of the entire study. It is important, however, to take the time to understand what we now know about the way organizations function and behave and what researchers have discovered about the various kinds of skills that leaders have and the way they use them to be successful in their organizations. Such insight will give a deeper appreciation of Ellen White's unique contribution to her church in her role as a charismatic and gifted leader. Persevering with this section will provide the reader with a helpful framework in which to understand her leadership role and the legitimate and perfectly appropriate behaviors that she adopted to influence others. It will also equip the reader with terminology and concepts that will help to interpret many of the fascinating episodes in her leadership experience in the church. Readers who find the material a little more prosaic may be tempted to skim these pages (although they will miss some valuable insights). But they could move on to the second theme of the chapter, which will discuss Ellen White's awareness of negative "political" behavior in an organization, her assessment of it, and her reaction to it. The last part of the chapter will document and illustrate how Ellen White was quite conscious of the various ways in which she could exercise her leadership influence within the organization that was the focus of her life work.

On the one hand, Ellen White exercised her leadership role intuitively in a spiritual sense, understanding that it was the direct impulse of the Spirit of the Lord that prompted her, often spontaneously, to respond to or intervene in a situation. This was the biblical and theological paradigm through which she understood her experience and her work. On the other hand, still within this same paradigm, on many other occasions she gave careful thought and reasoned consideration to the particular way in which she might approach a situation. On these occasions she would consider the manner or the time or the place in which she might convey the information she needed to communicate. Such consideration could be from a pastoral and human relations perspective without the sense of a direct instruction of the Spirit. Most of the time, however, as a whole person through whom God had given this special spiritual gift, she did not differentiate between the two approaches, for she lived her entire life in the Spirit. At the same time—and at all times—she was very much aware of the particular ways available to her by which she could exercise her influence. Not only intentional and insightful about the strategies she would use, she reflected on them and their effectiveness. She understood that her ability to influence others in the organization was not only a sacred trust, but also that it needed protecting and managing wisely and carefully.

In the latter part of this chapter the reader will learn about the various specific ways in which Ellen White chose to exercise her influence both intuitively and often in a spontaneous manner as if she were on autopilot in her interactions. In this way she was very much like us in our interactions with people. But at other times, in order to be an effective leader, she had to be thoughtful, consciously taking time to deliberate in her choice of strategies. In this sense she could not avoid her influence being "political," but in the very best of meanings.

Ellen White's extensive correspondence and the records of her close involvement with the leadership of the Seventh-day Adventist Church reveal a woman with a remarkable clarity of self-understanding and a highly perceptive insight into human nature. Her letters and manuscripts introduce us to someone valued for the depth of her spiritual insight and understanding and who was actively sought out for her timely and practical spiritual advice. They also reveal an individual who was both awed and humbled by the unique and unpredictable experiences she encountered through the charisma she possessed and which her community identified as a spiritual gift, the gift of prophecy. At the same time, she was also respected for her skill in personal and social relationships, her ability to articulate her thoughts, and her effectiveness in exerting her influence on others. This was true even though at times she encountered significant resistance to her spiritual authority within the community. How Ellen White related to such opposition and how she sought to be effective in exercising her influence is instructive. She was a person whom contemporary students of the science of leadership would recognize and describe as having high levels of social skill, emotional intelligence, and what in social science terms would be described or identified as political skill.

A social psychology perspective

The relatively recent development of organizational theory and the related study of the way organizations behave clearly help to explain many of the social dynamics at work in all manner of organizations, religious ones included. Organizational behavior as a field of study located in the broad discipline of social psychology throws much light on the social dimensions involved in all kinds of groups and institutions. Much of the literature, of necessity, focuses on the nature of leadership and seeks to understand the exercise of power and influence by the leaders of organizations. This field of enquiry is important because it offers a valuable perspective by which we are able to understand some of the important personal dimensions involved in Ellen White's successful and highly influential leadership role in the Seventh-day Adventist Church through the exercise of her special charisma.

Recent studies of effective leadership behaviors in organizational contexts have highlighted the significance of social skills and have sought to understand their nature.[1] Such research has suggested that social skills may be conceptualized as alternate forms of intelligence—practical or emotional intelligence rather than just intellectual intelligence.[2] Ellen White did not benefit from an academic education beyond the age of nine, but she certainly had the ability to learn from life and to benefit from the teaching experiences that Providence brought her way. From this perspective we could describe her as having high levels of practical and emotional intelligence.

According to Frederick Mintzberg, a noted researcher in leadership studies, successful leaders in an organization not only have an authority or a basis of power for their exercise of influence, but they have the ability to exercise their influence astutely and with intelligence.[3] Recent research has attempted to define this astuteness more precisely, distinguishing it from other social skill characteristics. Such astuteness enables a leader to be effective in resolving differences, assisting people to move toward consensus, and making compromises when necessary, thereby achieving desired goals. This skill develops through maintaining extensive networks of relationships and personal ties in the organization that a leader can mobilize as situations allow and then draw on to promote collective action. Effective leaders behave in an engaging manner and inspire confidence, trust, sincerity, and genuineness.[4]

Viewed through the prism of these studies, we can see Ellen White as possessing high levels of "political" skill that she used effectively in her relationships with other church leaders and with the church membership generally. While such a skill may be viewed as a natural, normal part of the ebb and flow of human relations, the skill set has particular relevance to understanding behavior within an organizational context. The concept of this skill provides a helpful construct for understanding the ability of a leader to know intuitively what to do and how to execute it in a convincing manner.

To suggest that Ellen White had high levels of both this "political" skill and of social skills is not in any sense to overlook the special spiritual dimensions of her work or to suggest that it was of limited human origin. Without doubt, the church accepted her leadership as a spiritual one rooted in both a clear self-understanding and in a conviction on the part of her fellow believers that God had gifted her with insights and information from beyond normal sources for the spiritual development and guidance of the community of faith. Study of her life and writings reveals that the exercise of this spiritual gift occurred in unique ways with impulses and intervention frequently beyond her choosing. Such are the mysteries of Providence attendant upon the communication of ideas and information through the Spirit.

At the same time, from a human dimension, she functioned in discussion groups, in church business sessions, and in planning groups as an effective spiritual leader with great people skills that enabled her to exercise leadership with varying levels of success within a complex social group. Seeking to understand the social and organizational dimensions of her leadership, as this study does, is not to downplay or diminish the providential dimensions. Nor is it a tactic to find ways of discounting the helpfulness and value of her ministry. She was well aware of such a negative strategy when she complained in 1888 that some of her colleagues "did not seem to see beyond the instrument" (referring to herself) and thus fell into a pattern of finding reasons to resist her counsel and advice.[5]

Rather, in exploring the socio-political dimensions of her leadership, a broader and deeper appreciation of what a believer sees as the working of Providence becomes possible. The perspective of organizational behavior theory drawn from the field of social psychology allows helpful insights into these aspects of her role as we seek to understand the dynamic of her leadership and her interaction with those administrators in the church who had been elected to exercise influence alongside her through the more formal roles of executive leadership.

In a technical sense, the ability of one person to influence the behavior of others and particularly their appointment to leadership in an organization may be defined as political influence. In this sense, from the perspective of organizational behavior, politics is a neutral activity that needs to be seen in a positive way. Within this context, it is simply a way of describing the normal organizational decision-making process. Employed this way, the term has a respectable meaning and a legitimate use. Influence seeks to resolve conflicts and uncertainty or to achieve consensus and make decisions that otherwise might be stalemated or unsolvable. We will discuss the exercise of influence as politics in its technical sense, and the nature of authority and power in organizations in the following pages.

Viewed in this technical sense, it is clear that Ellen White utilized her influence and authority and made her counsel available for what we may describe as legitimate "political" purposes. Her influence functioned as part of the dimension of decision making in the denomination. In terms of overall common purpose and mission, Adventist Church leadership has been clearly focused and has functioned in unity. Ellen White's role in helping the church to maintain this unity of purpose has often been remarked upon as one of the outstanding contributions of the exercise of her prophetic gift.

On the other hand, even though there was clear consensus on overall objectives and mission, on numerous occasions in the development of the Adventist Church a marked diversity of viewpoints on what methodology to use to achieve these common objectives has existed among the organizational or institutional leadership or at the level of subsidiary units such as state conferences.[6] On such occasions, as when many felt that an organizational restructuring was necessary during the 1890s, there was a sharp lack of consensus. The specific model of organization considered best to adopt was not clear, and the church vigorously debated various approaches. Leadership reflected a distinct lack of common ground. Union conferences were created in 1897 and the independent service organizations, such as the Sabbath School Association and the Educational Association, were subsumed under the authority of General Conference management in 1901, but that didn't clarify what shape the church would take in the future. Regarding issues such as the allocation of personnel and financial resources (handled through the Foreign Mission Board during the 1890s) and a fair and equitable distribution of tithes and offerings (debated during the 1901–1903 period) and the adoption of proper terminology and appropriate role descriptions for senior church leadership positions (1901–1903), the information and input available, even from Ellen White, was often ambiguous. However, leadership still needed to resolve the issues in an efficient manner. Under these circumstances, "political" processes clearly came into play. Strategies and approaches employed to persuade others to change their minds or to adopt a common view, as well as the use of influence to achieve consensus among diverse opinions, are all by definition "political." Such approaches and strategies, as discussed and defined below, were clearly evident in the church's decision making and were not only inevitable, but they were clearly legitimate and effective as vehicles within the church organization for solving problems. When the process is open and remains focused on the best and most desirable outcomes for the organization, such activities remain positive. But when employed for personal ends and goals they become dysfunctional and damage an organization and its process of decision making. During the major periods of change in the church, politics of both kinds were evident, and Ellen White, if she felt called to exercise her influence in any effective sense at all, had to do so within this context.

Influence as "politics"

F. R. Ferris and his research colleagues at Florida State University point out that recent leadership studies of the dimension of effective leadership indicate that it combines social awareness with the ability to communicate well. Those with such skills possess a keen sense of social astuteness and an understanding of people, along with a fundamental, intuitive conviction that they can help shape the outcomes of interactions with others in an organization. Such leaders are able to leverage social capital for the purpose of resolving differences, assisting people to move toward consensus, and reaching appropriate compromise in areas of conflict so as to gain desired goals. This is achieved through maintaining extensive networks of relationships and personal ties in the organization that they can mobilize as situations allow, thus promoting collective action. The leader who is skilled in this way is able to coalesce, rather than polarize, various organizational constituencies. This, in turn, enables a person to create a synergy among a range of interpersonal behaviors, generating an interpersonal dynamic that enables one to develop and leverage social capital to promote common goals.[7] Such skill enables a leader to exercise power in an organization.

Management literature often describes power as a personal characteristic, and management studies seek to provide insight into the process of how one person influences another. Power is an intangible concept and difficult to measure. In organizations, however, power is normally the result of much more than mere personal characteristics. Organizations, even religious organizations, are large complex systems that often involve thousands of people. Church organizations are often complex, with distinctive characteristics, because they comprise a group of paid employees who work closely with teams of non-paid volunteers. As organizations, they involve an extensive division of labor, forcing them to adopt complex processes for the equitable allocation of resources and the exercising of responsibility and accountability. Christian believers maintain that we should not view the church as just another organization. It is, rather, a dynamic spiritual entity, a spiritual community, a creation of the Spirit of God. Its members are linked in spiritual ways, and its various functions are regarded as the work of the Spirit through the exercise of gifts and abilities. This cannot be denied either at the congregational level or in the various structures that link congregations together.

But even with an organizational ethos rooted strongly in the idea of a community of the Spirit and undergirded by the fundamental concepts of spiritual stewardship and servant leadership, we nevertheless still find a hierarchy of tasks in the organization regardless of who performs them. Some positions are more influential than others because of their access to greater resources or simply because their role is more central in the organization. Organizational power in a church organization reflects the larger relationships of these various positions, both horizontal and vertical. Such power is vested in the position, not the person. As with a commercial entity or an institution such as a school or a hospital, a church also bestows authority on individuals to preside and to lead. The various nuances of leadership roles are not actually exclusive to one kind of organization or another.

If we think broadly of power as the ability of one person to influence the behavior of other people in an organization in order to bring about a mutually desired outcome, authority is narrower in scope. Authority is vested in organizational positions, is voluntarily accepted by subordinates, and flows down vertically in the hierarchy of an organization. Generally, authority is exercised only in a downward direction or along the chain of command. The power exercised through the authority of a leader generally derives from four sources: his or her formal position, expertise, control over resources, and the regulation of decision parameters and premises and network centrality.[8]

When it comes to the decision-making process within an organization, researchers have identified two basic approaches. Many organizations prefer what we may term "rational processes" for making major decisions. Considered by most managers to be more reliable and objective, this approach to decision making is effective when the organization clearly defines its goals, identifies and understands the various alternatives, and selects the choice with the highest probability of achieving the desired outcome. It is desirable where there exist reliable information systems, centralized power, a norm of optimization, uniform values across the various groups within the organization, little conflict, and an orientation toward efficiency.

An alternative avenue to decision making is the political approach. Politics, like power, is an intangible concept and difficult to measure. But if we can define power as the ability to influence the achievement of desired outcomes, then politics is the actual behavior used to exercise that influence or power in order to reach those goals. Popular understanding, however, often regards politics as self-serving behavior employed to attain favorable outcomes.

Richard Daft reports that surveys of leaders of organizations reveal that most managers or leaders have a negative view toward politics and believe that political behavior more often hurts an organization than helps it achieve its goals. At the same time, they acknowledge that political behavior is common to practically all organizations, that it occurs at upper levels more often than at lower levels, and that it usually arises in specific situations involving such things as structural change or when significant uncertainty exists in the organization or there is disagreement about choices and objectives. Dan Madison reports that many view politics negatively as self-serving behavior because it often may involve activities not sanctioned by the organization and is usually perceived by people as incorporating deception and dishonesty for the purposes of individual self-interest.[9]

In its technical sense, however, we can define politics as a natural organizational decision-making process with a respectable meaning and a legitimate use. Politics occurs as a natural process for resolving differences among interest groups wherever negotiation and bargaining are required to overcome conflicts and differences of opinion and to build coalitions for the purpose of joint decision-making processes. From the perspective of organizational theory, politics in this sense is a neutral activity that one can use in a positive way. In this approach, leaders employ influence to resolve conflicts and uncertainty or to achieve consensus and make decisions that otherwise might be stalemated or unsolvable. Disagreement and conflict are normal in settings in which information may be ambiguous and often incomplete. Groups engage in the push and pull of discussion to decide goals and reach decisions based on the information that is available.

In reality, neither the rational model nor the political model fully characterizes the decision-making process in any organization. Each approach surfaces at one time or another, depending on the particular organizational environment and context and or the kind of issues being addressed. The rational model may apply best to organizations in stable environments with well-understood technologies but may be quite inadequate in the face of significant uncertainty and ambiguity of information, when the usual rules do not work or when past experience is not available or not relevant. Whenever an organization contemplates structural change, for example, or when it plans a substantive shift of personnel or when the allocation of resources is being decided, there are inevitable political dimensions and activities involved in the decision-making processes even in religious organizations. We frequently witness such legitimate and positive political approaches in decision making within Adventist organizational settings—for example, at General Conference sessions. They may surface in the denomination at times of structural change or during the selection of key personnel for important roles. Such activities may build consensus through informal discussions outside of formal meetings, or they may involve developing trust and confidence in relationships between groups with conflicting interests as part of a legitimate attempt to facilitate mutual understanding and willingness to work together for common objectives. In addition, such political activities may include the expanding of networks through reaching out to groups that disagree or that share other perspectives, as well as the co-opting of dissenters for the purpose of achieving cooperation. Other strategies will seek to control the boundaries of a decision through sequencing the order of an agenda in order to best use the available limited time; to build better understandings about decisions through focusing information on relevant problems or issues; and through enhancing legitimacy and expertise by the use of external consultants or personnel with specific expertise in the area of conflict.

Political processes are involved when leaders make their preferences explicit. An assertive proposal may be accepted because of the lack of any better alternatives. And an explicit proposal will often receive favorable treatment because other alternatives are ambiguous and less well defined. The tone adopted by leaders in their communications about a proposal will also help shape the effectiveness of their influence. They may intentionally and strategically adopt a certain tone, or it may surface subconsciously. Leaders in every organization employ such strategies to forward the interests of the organization and to assist it in the decision-making process.

Ellen White and the tone in her exercise of influence

The extensive correspondence and manuscript files left by Ellen White reveal a wide range of writing reflecting a variety of emotional styles. Some manuscripts are quiet, homiletic, or pastoral, drawing out spiritual lessons from biblical passages and giving them an application to current problems. Some letters reflect a writing style that is very matter-of-fact, almost brisk—for example, hastily written ones that ask questions or provide information may exhibit little emotional warmth. Others are warm and cordial, with irenic language, sharing personal information, and offering advice or counsel with a persuasive pastoral tone. Yet other letters reflect a high level of emotional involvement, deeply passionate with concern and anxiety about situations. This latter category of letters frequently exhibits extensive hyperbole or overstatement, sometimes having strong irony and expressions of exasperation or frustration, and are often laced with dramatic emphasis. Such correspondence indicates Ellen White's state of feeling on a particular issue and the intensity with which she viewed a situation or the gravity of a particular problem.

She was quite self-aware about this and often noted the fact that she frequently became very wrought up about a situation. Her endeavors to exert her influence in the church on such occasions often involved a style of language that she sometimes described as being written with a "very strong spirit." On numerous occasions she comments that she was aware of her heightened state of anxiety about a problem and that her writing reflected this, and also, at times, that it could lead to misunderstanding or misinterpretation of the things she said. Mrs. White realized that this had occurred, for example, in 1893 at the time of a religious revival in Battle Creek that led many to make plans for leaving the city for missionary work elsewhere.[10] Several factors help to explain this kind of writing and assist in understanding the human emotions that underlay her unique work.

During some periods of her life, Ellen White would feel a particular burden or anxiety for the welfare of the cause that she loved and had been called to serve. During these periods, such as the 1890s, for example, she apparently suffered significantly from insomnia. When awake, she would worry intensely about the situation in Battle Creek or in other places where wrong attitudes and practices were occurring in the church. After many months when she was able to sleep only two or three hours a night and not catch up on the lost sleep during the daytime because of her workload of speaking or writing, did the situation she was thinking about at Battle Creek come to be perceived as somewhat larger than the actual reality? Ellen White worried about this possibility herself and at times tried to stop her mind from churning over the problems at Battle Creek. She was aware that such anxieties could affect her. This is not to deny, of course, that the attitudes and practices she protested were real and dangerous problems. In the end, her messages of warning were productive, but in her trying to achieve the change, was such a pattern of dramatically stating the problem really effective in itself? Did it help to achieve the desired outcomes or actually delay them?

Another branch of social psychology throws light on this dimension of Ellen White's leadership. Researchers such as John Gray, who have explored the differences in communication patterns and social interaction responses between males and females (particularly as they manifest themselves in many marriage relationships), have observed that in general males prefer to seek solitude and mull matters over by themselves. Then they often try to approach discussion of the issues in a cool, detached sort of way devoid of emotions, focusing on fixing the problem through practical suggestions. On the other hand, females characteristically express their concerns and feelings in absolute terms and often employ hyperbole when offering assessments, because the basic content of their communication involves feelings, especially those of anxiety or concern. Part of the intent of such communication is a desire to express the depth of their emotional response to a problem and the level of anxiety they experience because of it, something that others need to hear and understand. The specific informational content being referred to or described has been filtered through an emotional screen, and that must be recognized and acknowledged. As a result, the recipient or listener must interpret such hyperbole within its emotional context.

In light of this perspective, the question arises: To what extent might some of Ellen White's communication have been more effective, more influential, and have attracted less opposition had she used more moderate language? Is this an example of where her oft-repeated counsel concerning the need to consider time and place when interpreting her writings becomes relevant? Some of her correspondence was clearly time-bound, and this factor must be taken into account in arriving at a proper understanding of her intent.

A fuller discussion of these issues regarding the particular color and dynamic of her writing in the 1890s and the problematic issues complicating church development that called them forth appears in chapter 11, "A Hermeneutical Paradigm for Understanding Ellen White in the 1890s."

The marked range of style in her correspondence indicates that she consciously used a variety of approaches in the process of exerting her influence in the denomination. The styles varied depending on the individual to whom she was writing, the nature of the problem being addressed, and her own emotional involvement in the situation as well as her feelings about the possible outcomes. In this process she demonstrated that she had intuitive people skills and was socially astute in the best sense. It was these skills that helped to make her an effective leader. Mrs. White was well aware of the negative impact of self-serving political activity and how such activity diminished the effectiveness of leadership.

Positive politics: Principles from the case of Dr. Maxon

Ellen White recognized and wrote about the negative impact of self-serving approaches to political activity within the church organization. The case of Dr. Maxon provides a good case study for illustrating the downside of such activity. In the late 1880s, an unpleasant dispute arose between certain organizational units over the allocation of personnel resources. Apparently, an inducement had been used to secure an employee from another institution. When the matter came to her attention, Mrs. White, who was in Europe at the time, became involved in the dispute and gave very direct counsel about the danger of such inappropriate and unethical methods. "I believe in open square work in dealing with one another in large interests and small interests," she wrote to Dr. Maxon in 1887. She counseled that it was not wise to accept an appointment to leadership when the circumstances looked as if the decision-making process had been conducted in an underhanded manner. "All should be conducted on honorable, square, noble principles. . . . To try and save our own feelings, to avoid censure, to conceal facts and pursue an underhanded course, or even a course that appears not quite straight forward, is not after God's order in any case. It is the custom and fashion of this age, but it is not the fashion of Christ, and is not meeting God's standard of righteousness."[11]

Dr. Maxon and his physician wife had been trained at some expense by Dr. John Harvey Kellogg to work at the Battle Creek Sanitarium. In 1887, they resigned from the sanitarium. They had received a request to labor in New York in mission work and to develop health-reform principles. Maxon was evidently unhappy that Kellogg had not given him adequate opportunities for promotion at Battle Creek, and he felt inclined to accept the invitation to serve in mission work.[12] Then promptly after his separation from the Battle Creek program, Dr. Maxon was offered the position of leadership at a proposed new sanitarium in Ohio. It seems that R. A. Underwood and Stephen N. Haskell, leaders of the New England Conference, planned to start another sanitarium in that state, perhaps without seeking wider counsel from their church colleagues. The proposed sanitarium would have apparently operated in direct competition with the Battle Creek program. Ellen White had not heard about the proposal and in the absence of any clear information was not at all in favor of it.

In order to secure the services of Dr. Maxon as head of the proposed institution, reports had been circulated that Haskell had called him to serve in "missionary work" in New York. But this was really just "a blind." Dr. Kellogg considered the situation to be definitely deceitful. Ellen White was sorry that the manner of Dr. Maxon's leaving his employment with the Battle Creek Sanitarium "left upon Dr Kellogg's mind the impression that Elder Haskell did not work fairly and frankly in this. I am afraid that he [Haskell] did not take a wise course." If the Maxons were to accept the invitation to Ohio, "the impression will certainly prevail that the object that was presented before the committee for you to go to New York to labor was a mere blind, and will put a very bad appearance upon the motive which led Brother Haskell in particular to urge this movement. It would create a state of feeling that the Lord alone could see the after results," she added.[13]

Mrs. White had become convinced that the conference committee had been duplicitous. Taking the matter "as it stands," she wrote to Maxon, "I do not like the way in which they are trying to bring you to connect with that institute. It looks too much like the secretive work of the enemy rather than the open, frank, noble work of Christian commandment-keepers."[14] She felt that if the Maxons were acquainted with this "undercurrent working to separate them from the San and a false reason was presented as a blind that they were to work in the mission," it would be "a fraud," and could not "be called by any other name." In her view, "it was a sin in the sight of God," and "any attempt to gloss it over" would only deepen the guilt "of those who connived it." "Christians can afford to be fair," and "open as the daylight to deal with one another as brethren," she asserted. Observation of the golden rule is paramount in all such organizational relationships.[15]

In order to depoliticize the problem, Mrs. White raised the idea of the couple going to St. Helena in California instead of to Ohio or New York, but in an open and transparent way. "I do not want to do anything without laying the whole matter before you. Let us unselfishly counsel together, for we are interested in the same work, and these institutions are God's instrumentalities to the same work—to relieve the suffering, to advance reform."[16] She later explained to the administrators at the Health Retreat at St. Helena her open strategy and set out the case for having the Maxons join the staff in California. She had sent copies of her correspondence to all the parties in order to ensure that everyone knew what was happening.

"Now I did not wish to give the least occasion for the doctor [Kellogg] to be tempted that we were getting Dr. Maxon and his wife to unite with the institution in California unless I could have the evidence that he would be in perfect harmony with the plan. If I frankly laid open the matter before him, I thought he would not feel that we wished to take any underhanded course. I laid the matter plainly open before him that we meant to make a success of the Retreat. By the letter of which I sent you a copy, you will see what I said."[17] She indicated that she had received a telegram from Kellogg indicating his consent to the idea.

According to Dr. Maxon, their part in the process had been quite innocent and straightforward, and as far as they understood, it was thus also the case with the others involved. Ellen White later commented, "I accept your explanations and I am glad indeed that there was no occasion given to Dr. Kellogg to think that there was underhand working in the removal of both of you from the San." But the episode served to draw out from Ellen White a clear statement on the dangers of self-serving political activity within the organization.[18] The episode also clearly illustrates that she understood the value of open communication as an important principle in helping ensure the effectiveness of her exercise of influence.

Ellen White's strategies for exercising influence

During her life of leadership and service, Mrs. White went to thousands of meetings. Among the most important were the regularly scheduled General Conference sessions. She generally made sure she attended them whenever she could. If she did miss any, it was because she was either serving overseas at the time or because of her advancing age.[19] Occasionally, she would also go to the annual council meetings of the church, which involved a smaller group of officers and institutional leaders. At General Conference sessions, she would exercise her influence through her role as a featured speaker or preacher. On these occasions, she would also address general spiritual themes and sometimes speak specifically on the particular issues being discussed by delegates, as she did in 1888 on the matter of the election of G. I. Butler as president, the incident cited at the beginning of this chapter. At the 1888 Minneapolis session, Ellen White gave nearly twenty addresses on the issues under debate and followed closely the business sessions as the attendees discussed and adopted resolutions and actions.[20] She was not usually involved in the subcommittee activity at General Conference sessions but would frequently participate in the discussions from the floor on the current policy issues being debated. Frequently, she would read prepared manuscripts addressing specific issues. One could consider them as position papers that would set out general directions and the principles that the delegates needed to consider in making decisions. Often she would have sent such manuscripts to delegates and to church leaders prior to the session, and the documents would even help to set some of the agenda. Apart from these general meetings, however, she was rarely involved in the executive committee processes or board meetings of church entities. She generally attended committee meetings only on rare occasions when invited to give counsel on particular issues or problems. For example, while visiting camp meetings in the Northeast in 1889, she reported that she spent several hours in an "important council" in New York with church leaders from the region.[21]

More frequently, leaders from the General Conference and other church administrators would seek her out at session or camp meeting time or at her home to consult with her about particular problems developing in the church. They would explain the problems, and Ellen White would be "drawn out" to give advice about how to handle the situation. The basis for the advice was usually insights that she had received about previous similar problems or light divinely given her about the particular problem at hand. Sometimes the advice was based on general biblical principles but given a timeliness and a context that proved enormously helpful to the presidents in resolving complex or delicate issues.

Ellen White was an effective, clear, and forceful speaker. Her ability to persuade her audience was considerable although not always successful, as at the 1888 General Conference Session, significant resistance to her arguments for openness and for allowing younger preachers to be heard on their new ideas surfaced.

After the adoption of the new union conference organizational structure in 1901, Ellen White, as strength and time allowed, also attended these union session meetings to preach and speak on issues as they came up for discussion. When particularly important issues were either on the informal or the formal agenda, she sometimes went out of her way at significant travel cost and investment of emotional energy to attend and exercise her influence. On other occasions when union sessions convened nearer to her place of residence, she would attend as a guest speaker.

Another effective way of exercising her influence in the church was through her attendance at the regular annual camp meetings of the church held at the local conference level. On these occasions she was able to directly address her ministerial colleagues as well as the membership of the church rather than just its administrative leadership. Her use of such opportunities to bring about unity of purpose and unity of belief was highly effective. Visiting churches or local institutions for preaching and counseling was also a regular part of her work routine. Sometimes this would be just a Sabbath visit, but often it would consist of a series of revival or week of prayer meetings at a particular church or institution. The exercise of influence at this level was effective in solving problems at a local or institutional level and in building confidence in her work and in the special nature of her gift and in her as a person.

In addition to her speaking, Ellen White exercised her influence through the things she wrote. Much of her writing consisted of articles for church periodicals and magazines or manuscripts for book publication. But perhaps the most direct and forceful way she was able to spread her influence in the church was through personal letters. Depending on the particular context and on the need, her letter-writing activity was one of the most effective means of influencing the development of the church. She addressed many of her letters to leaders, and at times she complained that they did not consult or correspond with her enough on their plans for church development. Much of her correspondence also involved efforts to influence conference and union presidents, or the leaders of denominational institutions such as colleges, publishing houses, or hospitals. The largest proportion of her correspondence went to people in prominent church leadership positions.

Many of the scores of hours she devoted to writing each month involved personal letters. (On an average day when not traveling and speaking, she could spend eight or nine hours writing letters or manuscripts.) Many letters provided news—particularly to family members and close colleagues. Others shared information about personal activities and church developments with the General Conference presidents. Through these letters she maintained strong channels of communication. But many of the letters she wrote specifically to give advice and counsel about the need for changing behavior and attitudes or about decisions that had to be made. As previously noted, her letters varied in tone. Some were warm, friendly, even chatty, in which she presented general information about church and family life. Others were more formal and polite, with a matter-of-fact tone, making some request on a business or family or personal matter. Yet other letters were passionate and direct, often with highly critical comments focusing on emerging problems, doubtful or misguided decisions, or the emergence of wrong attitudes and the necessity for behavioral or attitudinal change. This latter category of letters were termed "testimonies" to reflect their direct spiritual concerns. The adaptation and editing of such letters and manuscripts for publication in book form for wider readership in the church later broadened their circle of influence. Eventually, Pacific Press® published nine volumes of such letters and manuscripts, comprising approximately 4,900 pages of densely printed material.[22]

Ellen White was also very intentional about how she wrote and circulated such "testimony" letters in order to maximize their effectiveness. This exercise of influence called for careful forethought. Commonly she would send such a letter directly to the individual recipient. Frequently, however, she would also share copies of it with other church leaders or with colleagues of the addressee or would address it to a number of individuals.[23] This enabled those involved in a specific situation to know exactly what she was saying to people on particular issues. Another purpose was to increase pressure on an individual to adopt the changes recommended or to extend the arena of accountability of the person concerned. She adopted this strategy with some of her letters sent to O. A. Olsen during the 1890s.[24] The leaders of the Adventist community understood and accepted that their leadership was in a special sense collective and communal and that they must have a spiritual accountability to each other. Circulating letters and providing copies of letters to a group of colleagues was an accepted and effective way to enhance such accountability. Maintaining people "in the loop," as communication theorists today would express it, not only keeps them informed on important information but lets other people know that they have been informed and therefore hold them accountable for that part that might apply particularly to them.

Sometimes Ellen White would send a letter to a close colleague of the individual and ask the colleague to read the letter to the individual. Occasionally, she might even instruct the colleague not to provide a copy to the individual, because she was not sure what use the person might make of the letter should they resist the counsel or react negatively to what it said. On other occasions she would send a letter addressed to several persons but through a primary addressee who may have been the major subject of the letter and who was then to forward it on to the larger group.[25]

Other times she would dispatch a letter to a group of church leaders, either broadly to "The Brethren," "The Brethren in Battle Creek," "The Brethren in Ministry," or "To the Men Who Occupy Responsible Positions in the Work." Such letters usually circulated judiciously to a small circle, and selected recipients would often pass on or copy the material for their colleagues.[26]

Another effective method involved dispatching a letter to a president along with other manuscripts with a request that he have the material read publicly to his administrative colleagues or perhaps publicly to members of the executive committee or to the board if the matter involved an institutional board of governors. This could be quite embarrassing for the president or for his colleagues if the letter mentioned names, as they sometimes did when she objected to certain behaviors or to decisions that she felt were incorrect. As one could imagine, to fulfill such requests was not easy and required the grace of humility, considerable spiritual strength, and a sound sense of self-esteem. In Ellen White's view, the ability to confess to a mistake in public and to adopt an attitude of humility and submission was an essential quality of a Christian leader. To neglect to read a letter to colleagues, whether deliberately or through oversight, could often bring further rebuke. For example, in the 1890s, President O. A. Olsen received letters and manuscripts from Ellen White just prior to her departure for Australia that she wanted him to read at an appropriate time to his fellow conference committee members and colleagues on the board of management for the publishing house. The material made personal references with some strong statements about several individuals. Olsen, perhaps because of his busyness, forgot to share the material, or more likely, could not bring himself to use it in such a direct manner and thus sought to adopt a less confrontational approach. Mrs. White considered it a major neglect of duty, and it elicited severe remonstrations from her.[27]

Sometimes, Olsen, as a recipient of such a request, would read appropriate selections of material from the letters or manuscripts in a general meeting or public forum but omit those portions that might identify specific individuals. Ellen White regarded the practice of passing over embarrassing or difficult or painful material as a neglect of duty that would result in further rebuke.[28]

On occasion she would rely on the judgment of others to determine the best time to deliver a letter or a message. "I wrote to you because light came to me from God," she explained to Homer Salisbury, manager of the Bible Echo publishing house in 1898. "I sent that light to W. C. White so that he could bring it in when it was thought best."[29] To Uriah Smith and A. T. Jones in 1898, for example, she sent a letter that was to be read to A. R. Henry. Later she wrote to the two men suggesting that "you had best not read that letter to him until I shall write him again, and try to reach him." But then she added, "If you think the letter is timely, that he should have it now, I trust to your judgment." Likewise, in 1900, she entrusted President George Irwin with copies of letters she had written to J. H. Kellogg with the instruction that he was not to divulge the contents to anyone else or to make copies of the letters. She explained that the reason she forwarded him the correspondence was so that he might know the nature of her communication with Kellogg and that should further problems develop, he might know how to respond. It would appear that she did not directly inform Kellogg that she was sharing the correspondence with Irwin, but he probably knew from past experience that the correspondence was being circulated among a circle of readers.[30]

Ellen White was aware of the ethical implications of the public disclosure of people's names in material that she wrote. For example, in 1896, a church member's name inadvertently appeared in print in an unfavorable light in the *Review and Herald.* "I learn that you have been offended and would naturally hold me in a measure responsible," she wrote to the woman concerned, a Mrs. Anderson who lived in Melbourne. "I ask you to pardon me for the share I have had in this unfortunate occurrence. I will try hereafter to give my correspondents directions so explicit that nothing of the kind shall occur again."[31] And if such a thing ever did happen again, we have no record of it. Publishing program leader and sometime church financier, Archibald R. Henry, about whom Ellen White had a number of highly critical things to say in the mid-1890s, also objected to her mentioning of names in letters that she circulated to others and threatened to initiate a lawsuit for libel in 1898. He was later persuaded to drop the matter. Generally, however, although at times uncomfortable with the directness of this approach to community spiritual accountability, church leaders accepted the strategy, and it proved to be an effective method for her to employ her influence.

Clearly, Ellen White understood the process of exercising her influence in the church and the value attached to her ability to do so. It was a trust that required careful stewardship and management. From one perspective, when she experienced the prophetic impulse to address an issue, she was overwhelmed with a sense of having to speak out regardless of the consequences—part of the "burden" she experienced in her work. On the other hand, she also had a clear and deeply felt self-understanding that she was under a sacred duty to guard and protect her influence in the church. She felt responsible to use it in such a way as to extend and continue her ability to persuade others over time. Mrs. White understood the tension between the two convictions. The responsibility to protect and preserve her ability to continue to guide the church led her to be careful about the misuse of her influence, especially in areas and issues that might undermine her credibility and standing with her colleagues.

It was this motivation that made her generally unhappy with the practice of individuals selecting short phrases, sentences, or paragraphs from her letters or manuscripts for the purpose of trading on her influence and advocating a particular position against the feelings or decisions of other leaders. First, she was not sure that such selections were wisely used or indeed relevant to the particular matter to which they were being applied. And second, she felt that the practice could result in unfairly pressuring a colleague or forcing the will or the conscience of a fellow minister. For example, in 1901 she remonstrated with her publisher son, Edson White, over his use of some selections from letters she had written him to get A. G. Daniells and R. M. Kilgore to accept his particular point of view with regard to publishing policies in the South. Neither Daniells nor Kilgore had apparently seen what Ellen White was supposed to have said to Edson. They both felt he was unfairly trading on her authority to achieve a particular outcome with which in good conscience they could not agree. Both Daniells and Kilgore had immediately written to Ellen White herself, asking her to send the instruction to them "at once" if there was any "light in reference to the points" that Edson had quoted from her letters.[32] She felt awkward, embarrassed, and trapped when it came to such predicaments. In her plea to Edson to back away from such an embarrassing strategy, she accepted that in unusual or extreme circumstances such a practice might be justifiable (she cited occasions such as during the late 1890s when there was substantial malpractice by publishing houses). But even then it was a dangerous procedure, unless she herself could be present to understand the issues in the debate and then give counsel as to which lines from her letters might be applicable. But in Edson's case, on this occasion, it was not justifiable, because circumstances had changed since she had written the material, and now more responsive management and new General Conference leadership was in place. Furthermore, it seems that Edson had received these letters inadvertently and she had not intended for him to see them. She had taken out of her satchel some material that she did plan to give him. But at the same time, "I must, by mistake, have given you that which I did not mean should fall into the hands of you or anyone else." In this situation, Ellen White was embarrassed and worried about the effect it might have on her influence. "It hurts me," she wrote. Edson should not quote pre-1901 statements, "words which I wrote prior to the conference" as if they were absolutes.[33]

The episode also highlights how jealously she guarded her influence and how difficult the task was sometimes, particularly when it involved close members of her family. "In the name of the Lord, I charge you," she wrote Edson, "not to make the burdens resting upon me doubly hard to carry." Regarding his conflict with Daniells and Kilgore, she counseled him that "the less you try to control matters, the better will be your influence." In particular, she stressed, "you must not, my son, use my name in such a way that you will come in between the people of God and your mother's influence to weaken that influence in any respect." She explained that there was a danger that in his zeal and ardor he might not only hurt his own influence but also hers, "so that in a crisis, as at the General Conference," she would not be able to do the work that she felt God had spared her life to do. Ellen White was very conscious of the need to protect and enhance her ability to exert influence.[34]

While the problem of misplacing confidential documents did not happen often, it could be damaging when it did. Managing the flow of correspondence could be difficult at times, and sometimes she might write letters but then hold on to them. Others were occasionally inadvertently sent to the wrong recipient. Anna Ingels, for example, in 1896, received a letter intended for George B. Starr. The woman quickly returned it after realizing it was not meant for her. On another occasion, in 1908, letters that were delayed for a reason did not eventually get sent even though Ellen White or her helpers thought that they had been, and thus Mrs. White felt free to quote from them or to circulate them to others in the meantime. Such a mix-up naturally gave rise to hurt and misunderstanding.[35]

During the period of the Kellogg conflict she had to guard her influence especially carefully. Conflicts over reorganization and the assigning of personnel made it a highly sensitive time. In 1902, for example, in the midst of one particularly complex conflict over the struggling Southern Publishing Association, a document reporting conversations with Ellen White inadvertently circulated that had the potential to make matters much worse and also to undermine her credibility and influence. The issue involved removing the publishing house leader, W. O. Palmer. She reported that on this occasion she had instructed her assistant, Clarence Crisler, *not* to give a copy of the transcript of her interview with Palmer to A. G. Daniells. Crisler had apparently misunderstood and had passed it along to Daniells anyway. But she "did not wish this report to come before anyone." After the interview, Ellen White had come to realize that what she had said in the discussion was ill informed. "I had not a clear knowledge of facts that made it safe to make such statements," she reported to Daniells. "The statements that I made must not be held but retracted." The realization that she had misunderstood the situation caused her considerable agony, but her letter to Daniells explaining the situation reached him in time to correct the situation.[36]

While letters, manuscripts, and transcripts of her oral counsel were a common way of exercising her influence in the church, she had other, sometimes more immediate, approaches that she also used. One very direct and very persuasive method involved the investment of her personal financial resources. Ellen White was a most generous individual and invested readily of her personal means (almost to a fault) to help a wide variety of causes and to meet human need. She would assist people in difficult economic circumstances, sponsor students through college, help to pay ministers' salaries when the local conference was short of funds, and contribute to the building of new churches and institutions among numerous other activities. But she had to depend largely on the royalties from her book publishing to support such charitable activities. Through some of the projects she was able to bear considerable influence in the development of a new institution by investing her own personal resources in it even in the face of opposition from officially appointed leadership. Such contributions helped to overcome skepticism or resistance from other church leaders who were either not persuaded of the wisdom of the venture or of the time or place for initiating it. She secured a personal loan to invest in the establishment of the Avondale School at Cooranbong, in New South Wales, Australia, for example, which helped get the project started when others were less sure that it was the wisest place to build. In a similar way, she invested in the Loma Linda enterprise and in a number of other healthcare institutions in California. Ellen White would also exercise her influence on such occasions by working to secure other investors in a project. At times, such drive and determination inevitably created tension between her and those charged with administrative and financial responsibilities in the church as a whole.

This approach to using her influence was frequently effective in situations in which timing meant everything. Ellen White's close involvement in major building projects at critical stages could not only be very direct and personal but also quite autocratic. Recent academic study of leadership has identified a number of specific "styles" of leadership, such as lassez-faire, democratic, and autocratic, but concludes that there is no one "best" style. Effective leaders need to be flexible enough to adopt different approaches as demanded by each situation. Mrs. White understood this principle intuitively in the exercise of her own authority and influence in the denomination. For example, on one occasion midway during the construction of a new dormitory at Avondale in 1897, when the building committee had determined to construct a building of only one story because of extremely tight budget restrictions, she overruled the decision. After walking onto the building site, surveying the work, and discussing matters with the contractor, she directed that he proceed immediately with the second story regardless of the additional cost. She thus countermanded the decision of the responsible committee. But she was determined in this instance that the venture would succeed and that faith needed to be exercised that the required funds would become available. On this occasion she was prepared to back her confidence and underwrite the expense with her own personal resources if necessary to ensure that the building was big enough to begin with.[37]

On another occasion she found herself in conflict with a determined builder, Metcalfe Hare, about the location of the proposed Avondale church building on the new college property. Hare argued in what apparently was his usual dogmatic manner that the structure should be situated close to the other school buildings. Ellen White was just as determined in her view that it should be located in a more public location on the main road about one kilometer from the central campus. Her letter on this occasion was vigorous and frank in expressing her point of view. In league with Haskell, and sweeping aside the seemingly reasonable arguments to the contrary, she persuaded the school board to reserve land out by the main road. Hare was outflanked. He was not consulted thereafter on the building plans, and furthermore the administration bypassed his college-operated sawmill in the ordering of lumber for the project.

When things needed to be done in a hurry, she knew how to exert influence sufficient to overcome inertia and opposition.[38] To adopt this approach too frequently, however, could seriously detract from her leadership. Furthermore, matters were not always perhaps so ultimately inconsequential as the location of a campus church building. When she encountered resistance to her influence on more important matters she had to give careful thought as to how to respond to it.

Clearly, she regarded the challenge of the responsibility of exercising her influence in the church as a spiritual trust. She had to take care to ensure that nothing diminished her credibility and impact. How did she respond when it became clear that her influence was not working? What approaches did she have available when the opposition to her ministry and leadership appeared to be direct and deliberate? Above all, how did she react to deliberate, intentional resistance?

During the late 1880s and through the 1890s, Ellen White experienced mounting opposition. As already noted, it arose largely in response to the rapid development and expansion of the church and the natural tensions arising from the competition for limited resources and the lack of adequate organizational structures to cope with the growth. The temperature of conflict during this period became quite elevated. Ellen White's language became increasingly more forceful as she sought to overcome the resistance to her influence during this period. The extended discussion in chapter 11 notes Arthur White's observation, as well as those of other denominational historians, that the period of the late 1880s and 1890s could arguably be considered the most critical period of administrative and political development in the church. Ellen White's relationship with the General Conference presidents and other top-tier church leaders during this time was an intense one. I will explain the reasons for this in chapter 11 and suggest a context for understanding them. The period illustrates well many of the various approaches that she adopted in the exercise of her influence to achieve desired outcomes for the church.

Another way she responded to the opposition to her authority was simply to withdraw. When difficulties and misunderstandings arose between her and the church administrators in Battle Creek over marketing policy for her publications and the amount of royalty she should receive, it appeared to her that some leaders in the publishing branch were intentionally attempting to restrict her influence by limiting the circulation and marketing of her books. She protested the practices adopted and eventually withdrew from the Review and Herald, either with the intention of undertaking the publication and marketing of her books herself or seeking other publishing houses more willing to deal with her on what she considered a fair and equitable basis. In the end, such a strategy was not practical, but at least she seriously considered it and made initial plans to implement it (see chapter 11.) She believed the conflict about marketing policy resulted from the desire of some individuals to deliberately resist and minimize her influence in the church.

Another method she adopted on at least one occasion was to advise a senior colleague, Charles Jones, the manager of Pacific Press®, to refuse to comply with a directive from the General Conference committee because she believed it to be wrong. The dispute on this occasion concerned initiatives from publishing leaders in Battle Creek to consolidate the church's publishing houses under one organization in order to achieve economies of scale and minimize the unhealthy competition developing between the publishers. Ellen White felt that such a policy would result in unacceptable levels of control over the content of books, restrict freedom of expression and the contributions of individual authors, and lead to a general loss of a vital service. She advised Jones that he should feel quite free—in fact, it was his duty—to refuse to cooperate with or comply with any orders from Battle Creek on the matter.[39]

Sometimes she sought to withhold resources from opponents. When she differed with John Harvey Kellogg, for example, and struggled to exercise her authority in order to keep the church united and focused on its central gospel mission rather than being turned aside into a preoccupation with and concentration on social work, she adopted an effective strategy of writing well-timed testimonies to Irwin and other church leaders to prevent Kellogg's access to church resources and funds for his rebuilding project in Battle Creek. "The testimonies have closed up his way of getting means from our people for the building of his tower," she reported to G. A. Irwin.[40]

At times Ellen White considered absenting herself from important meetings. In 1888, she decided on what Arthur L. White suggests was a "pre-determined course of action." If she perceived a spirit of disregard for her counsel in follow-up sessions of the General Conference she "would lay it out in clear lines" before the leaders, "show them the sinfulness of their course and with decided testimony turn the current if possible. If I could not succeed," she wrote, "then I would withdraw myself from the meetings, for I am afraid to be in such gatherings."[41]

On occasion, she used the prospect of such a boycott as a means of applying pressure. For example, in 1897, she felt very "aggrieved" that no one had sought her advice on the appointment of a principal for the new Avondale school. The board had chosen a young Australian graduate of Battle Creek College, H. Camden Lacey, whom Ellen White considered to be totally unsuited to the role. Furthermore, Lacey had discomforted the senior spiritual leader on campus, Stephen N. Haskell, so much that she feared Haskell would resign. No one had sought her judgment or her opinion on the selection, "but as sure as Elder Haskell leaves I shall leave also," she wrote.[42] Given her financial situation at the time it is not clear where she might have gone, but nevertheless, she had made her point. It was a heavy use of her influence, and it worked. The board soon replaced Lacey. Her ultimate use of this strategy of withdrawal would have been to pull back from the denomination completely. She never publicly expressed such a possibility, but faced with immense opposition to the exercise of her charisma in 1888, she pondered, in one of her darkest moments, whether "another coming out" might eventually become necessary.[43]

Also she might shift her attention away from those who resisted her to others who might be more responsive. "If the ministers will not receive the light," she said at an early morning talk to the delegates at the 1888 General Conference Session, in which she took care to have her remarks taken down in shorthand by her secretary, "I want to give the people a chance; perhaps they may receive it." She had not spoken so bluntly before. "God did not raise me up to come across the plains to speak to you and you sit here to question His message and question whether Sister White is the same as she used to be in years gone by." She knew she was in a difficult situation, but she was determined. "I don't expect that my testimony is pleasing, yet I shall bear it in God's fear."[44] In 1890, she chose not to attend the General Conference session. "I do not expect to be at your General Conference," she informed Olsen. "I would rather run the other way."[45]

In both 1897 and again in 1899, she turned down invitations to travel back to the United States to be at biennial General Conference sessions. She had, of course, valid reasons for not coming, such as some unfinished projects in Australia, the expense of journeys to America, as well as the increasing difficulty at her age (she had just turned seventy) of making extended journeys. Nevertheless, she took pains to point out to church leaders that her decision to remain in Australia was a deliberate protest against their slowness in adopting needed reforms and changing attitudes. The painful memory of "the terrible siege" she had experienced in 1888 and 1889 with so few to help her remained with her "as a warning," she reported to Olsen. She had learned, she said, that she could accomplish tenfold more by her pen in Australia than by her actual presence in America. In this instance, absence was apparently effective.[46] For a spiritually sensitive administrator such as O. A. Olsen, who was more often than not the recipient of her pointed messages, it was also a difficult strategy to live with.

Ellen White was very much aware of her unique ability to shape people and events in the church. She regarded herself as having a duty to do so, for she did not see her insights and her messages as her own. Rather, she understood them as a prophetic impulse, a "burden" from the Lord, mediated through her by the Holy Spirit. Along with the insights and messages came the conviction that the messages were vitally important for the spiritual life and development of the church. Through the pulpit and in personal conversations, with her pen, through her purse, and by her direct action she had learned what methods worked well to ensure the effectiveness of her ministry in supporting the spiritual development of the church. Mrs. White carefully thought through each approach, using not only common sense but also a perceptive understanding of human nature. And when viewed in the light of more recent studies in social psychology that help us to grasp the dynamics of the way that organizations function and how leaders act in them, we are able to understand how many of the methods she chose to use proved to be so effective in facilitating her influence. As she explained on one occasion when she was defending her need to have her son W. C. White help her in sending out letters and manuscripts and determining when and how to do so, such responsibility required mature wisdom and judgment, and she believed that God had blessed Willie with these gifts.[47]

Having the right leaders in place was also vitally important for the spiritual welfare and the life of the church. In particular, how did Ellen White exercise her influence in having suitable administrators elected to serve as president of the denomination? This question we shall now explore in more detail.

CHAPTER 3

OLE ANDRES OLSEN: A RELUCTANT PRESIDENT (1888–1893)

"Have you thought of Elder O. A. Olsen?" Ellen White asked the chairman of the nominating committee. She had accepted an invitation to counsel with its members about the best person to replace George I. Butler as president of the General Conference.[1] The committee had apparently been caught by surprise at Butler's withdrawal, having assumed that his re-election was a foregone conclusion. But in the light of his unexpected and very late decision not to stand for re-election, the committee found itself nonplussed and apparently without a list of suitable backup names. Butler had notified the delegates seven days after the start of the session that for health reasons he would not be available. According to R. T. Nash, who happened to be nearby at the time, the nominating committee chair asked him to get Ellen White from her rented boarding-house room close to the church and escort her to the small, round tent where the nominating committee was meeting, adjacent to the large dining tent.[2]

Butler had been too sick to travel to Minneapolis to attend the Bible Institute held during the week prior to the General Conference session, and ill health also kept him away from the opening of the session itself. The highly respected Stephen N. Haskell was requested to act temporarily as chair in his place. Then, five days into the session, Butler sent a letter announcing that his health had improved. The delegates felt encouraged enough to hope that the status quo would continue.[3] But two days later Butler reluctantly realized that the effect of prolonged stress on his health was not going to be quite so easily repaired and decided enough was enough. He had not the strength of mind or body needed to keep going.

Because they had fully expected that Butler would continue to serve in spite of his poor health and the illness of his wife, the members of the nominating committee at first did not know what to do. After all, the changes adopted in the church's administrative structures twelve months previously provided for three new additional senior administrators—one for education, one for home missions, and one for foreign missions—and this initiative, to a marked degree, had lifted much of the burden off the president. Though W. C. White had argued at the 1887 session that the workload on the president had increased enormously and seemed to be doubling each year because of the rapid expansion of the church, many had assumed that the new system would make life much less onerous for Butler. But the demands on the president had continued, and the cumulative stress of thirteen years in the leadership role finally proved too much. The second issue that made the task of the nominating committee a perplexing and difficult one arose from the reason that Butler had been experiencing such discomfort during the previous twelve months. An intense theological conflict had erupted, causing particularly high stress levels for the president, and the conflict was badly polarizing the delegates at the 1888 session. Butler's conservative supporters had regularly kept the absent president informed of the state of play in the discussions, and he had rallied them with a telegram urging the conference to stand by the old theological landmarks. The president's own strongly partisan role in the conflict, his reactionary attitudes, and the poisoned atmosphere of rumor and conspiracy that had been generated all finally proved too much. The rugged and normally robust Butler had decided he could not cope with it anymore.

So tense had the atmosphere become at midpoint through the meetings that even Ellen White felt tempted to return to California. She felt keenly the criticism of her role and the openly manifested lack of confidence in her counsel and her ministry. Perhaps it would be best to leave the quarrelling men to their own designs, she had reasoned with herself. But on second thought, and after prayer and reflection, she had finally determined to stay and meet the challenge head on. In spite of the situation, she felt that she had enough influence with the delegates to effect a change.[4]

As George Knight notes, Ellen White had already insisted that President Butler include theological issues on the agenda of the Ministerial Institute that would precede the 1888 General Conference Session. It was this stance that seems to have particularly raised Butler's anxieties to a debilitating level. The president had worked hard to keep the controversy off the church agenda. From his perspective, the new ideas being agitated by two young pastors, Ellet J. Waggoner and Alonzo T. Jones out in California, were just plain dangerous. They would perilously undermine the church's central traditional teaching on the Sabbath and its united stance on prophetic interpretation. Furthermore, they would also undermine Ellen White's own influence because, he argued, she had already said several years earlier that the idea being propounded by Waggoner and Jones about the interpretation of Galatians was theologically incorrect. Furthermore, back in February 1887, she had written to Jones and Waggoner with some cautions. The letter was a rebuke for making the theological disagreements a public matter, and she had sent Butler a copy of it.[5]

Unfortunately, the president had mistakenly interpreted the letter as a confirmation of his own position and had gone on to aggressively publish his own view of the disputed issues in the *Review and Herald.* His misuse of her February letter clearly upset Ellen White, and in April she penned a letter of rebuke to Butler and to Uriah Smith, who was both editor of the *Review* and secretary of the General Conference.[6]

Her words caused them to smart. Butler should not have used her letter to Jones and Waggoner as a weapon against the younger men, she pointed out. But now that he had gone public with the issues in his own articles, then it was only fair that the two younger men have their views published and discussed in the planned pre-session Ministerial Institute meetings. Not persuaded that it was safe to do so, Butler was still reluctant to have the issues publicly aired, and W. C. White, in the lead-up to the Institute, had to write to persuade him of the need to be fair and open. As George Knight observes, Ellen White, sensing Butler's reticence, deliberately chose to exercise her influence to outflank the president's resistance. In early August of 1888, she jumped into the debate about the proposed pre-session Ministerial Institute with a carefully planned letter that she sent to all the delegates. In it she gave a rousing call to "search the scriptures," since truth could "lose nothing by close investigation." And in a direct allusion to the stance adopted by Butler and Smith, she protested, "We are not to set out stakes, and then interpret everything to reach this set point." A mentality that relied too much on authority of leadership and Adventist tradition was dangerous. "Pharisaism" was to be set aside and "all assumptions and preconceived opinions" were to be "thoroughly tested" by Scripture.[7]

Ellen White's actions left Butler no choice but to follow her counsel. He announced in the last issue of the *Review* in August that the upcoming Ministerial Institute would explore the debated issues. But he did not at all like being pressured in such a way. The more he thought about it, the angrier he became. On October 1, he penned a thirty-nine-page, strongly emotional letter to Ellen White complaining of her betrayal of him and of the meddling by her son W. C. White. He regretted that he had not dealt more strongly with the two young Californian "fledglings" and their out-of-line theology. Now he could see a clear conspiracy emanating from California that threatened traditional Adventist teaching. He sent off a series of telegrams to the delegates, urging them to "stand by the old landmarks." Ellen White received his lengthy missive as she arrived at the Institute, just a day before the meetings were to start. "We are in for it," she wryly noted to her daughter-in-law after she had read Butler's letter.[8]

On Wednesday morning, October 24, the seventh day of the session, the troubled proceedings were "suspended" and Butler's letter informing the committee of his unavailability for reappointment or "bearing any more heavy responsibilities" was read to a somber assembly of delegates.[9] If he had not withdrawn, it seems quite clear that Butler would have been re-elected. But Ellen White approved Butler's decision to step down. In hindsight and in the light of the difficulties he had recently caused, it had not been too soon, she thought. Humility had departed from the aging administrator, she noted, and she guessed that in the days ahead, his case would be difficult to handle. Again, confiding to her daughter-in-law after the event, she noted regretfully that Butler had already been in office "three years too long." He had come to think of himself as "infallible," and "a sick man's mind" unfortunately had had a "controlling power over the General Conference Committee and the ministers have been the shadow and echo of Elder Butler about as long as it is healthy and for the good of the cause."[10] But this was in hindsight and in spite of the fact that she had evidently supported his re-election by exercising her vote at the session the previous year.

Six years later, reflecting on the 1888 leadership crisis, W. W. Prescott concurred with her view about the timeliness of the change. It is interesting to note, however, that with the passage of time the change was apparently being interpreted more as a deliberate strike against Butler. Some, at least, perceived what had happened as a removal rather than a voluntary stepping down. Prescott did not attend the 1888 session and may not have been acquainted with the detailed sequence of events. But he commented to Olsen that in his view, Butler's administrative style had been as much a problem as was his attitude to theology. It had seemed "almost necessary," the professor observed, "to have Eld. Butler removed from his position at the head of the work on account of his unwillingness to associate others with him who could share the burden. His course was delaying and cramping the work."[11]

But at Minneapolis, midway through the session, the selection of a replacement had become a highly sensitive matter. The question was no longer simply who might be qualified in experience and in sound judgment to take Butler's place. Now it was a matter of who would be acceptable to the groups who were so widely and sharply divided on theological grounds. Who would be able to unite the two parties? Who was available who would not be perceived as being allied in some way with one group or the other? The theological factionalism among the delegates had spilled over into the wider arena of church life and had significantly politicized the election process as a whole—not just the elections of the General Conference officer group itself, but also of the membership of the various institutional boards and subsidiary organizations.

The membership of the executive committee became a hotly disputed issue, with several attempts made from the floor of the conference to try to ensure that Butler, as the guardian of the status quo, did not get entirely left out. The inclusion of the name of W. W. Prescott in place of Butler on the executive committee, for example, met vigorous resistance and then finally went in Butler's favor by a knife-edge margin of forty to thirty-nine in the polling that took place on October 31, the last day of the General Conference session. It was a highly polarized body of delegates that left Minneapolis for their home districts.[12]

According to Nash's account, in her recommendation of the forty-three-year-old Olsen to the three-member nominating committee, Ellen White acknowledged that he was not present at the session. In itself, however, that was a major advantage. Others would perceive him as being neutral in the discussions. He had not come to the General Conference session, in fact, because he was still laboring in Christiana, Norway's capital, where he was conducting evangelistic meetings and overseeing the development of the church in Scandinavia.

No intimation of grooming

In spite of the fact that from the perspective of hindsight Ellen White was glad that Butler had not been reappointed, we do not find even a hint in her correspondence prior to the session that she favored any particular alternative candidate. There appears to be no intimation of her grooming someone else, no clue in her letters to others to suggest it was time for a change, no expression of dissatisfaction. Furthermore, even though there existed a significant groundswell of dissatisfaction with her role at the conference and some mild opposition toward her from some older ministers because of her support of open discussion of the disputed theological issues, nevertheless the delegates still sought and respected her counsel in the presidential election process. We know that the session considered at least one other name. Six months after the session she recalled that some delegates wanted to put forward William Ostrander as a possible candidate. Ostrander was a pastor from Michigan who, during the previous term, had served as president of the Colorado Conference. When members of the committee asked her about Ostrander, she expressed great surprise at the "blindness" of the delegates. In her view, Ostrander was "unbalanced in mind, little less than [an] insane man." What she meant by this, apparently, was that he had a problem with domestic violence. "This man was even dangerous in his home in his insanity . . . for his wife has told me in regard to it." The only thing really in his favor was that he was "fully in the confidence of Elder Butler." But that was not a factor that carried any weight with Ellen White. As she saw it, the delegates were so wrought up about the theological issue of the law in Galatians that they "had no sense to discern his [Ostrander's] true condition."[13] It is not known what other names the nominating committee or Ellen White might have suggested.

She had become more closely acquainted with Olsen and his work just prior to the General Conference session. The previous year she had been a delegate with him both at the large Michigan camp meeting and at the General Conference session in Oakland, California, where they both had spoken about denominational progress in Europe.[14] Mrs. White had seen Olsen taking an increasingly public leadership role at General Conference session meetings and was aware that he had served as a member of the General Conference executive committee since 1883, when it first expanded from a membership of three to five. He had been the president of the Minnesota Conference at the time.[15]

On a more personal level, she had worked closely with Olsen in numerous settings in Europe. For example, she had sat together with him in lengthy and delicate personal counseling sessions with J. G. Matteson over Matteson's problematic leadership style and roles. The thoroughness and careful planning that Olsen had put into the first ever camp meeting in Norway (held at Moss, forty-two kilometers south of Oslo in June 1887) had greatly impressed her. His earlier evangelistic work in the town there had succeeded in drawing "a class of people who can represent the truth in Norway."[16] They had both shared the preaching at the camp meeting and then again several days later at the first tent meetings ever held in Sweden.[17] She had appreciated the leadership style Olsen had demonstrated in the fifth European Council on Missions that had immediately followed the Moss camp meeting. After the camp meeting and the council at Moss, Ellen White had been a guest in Olsen's home for several days. Then shortly afterward they had voyaged together on the same ship out of Liverpool, England, back to the United States.[18]

Several months earlier, her son W. C. White had also been impressed with Olsen's leadership skills at the 1886 European Missionary Council. Even though the tall American-educated Norwegian had just recently arrived in Scandinavia, he took time to understand "the run of things" before he began to speak. And, White noted, Olsen was careful but thoughtful and very articulate in the speeches he made. "I tell you," White commented to Butler, "Bro. O. A. Olsen was a pillar of strength" and did "good work." Although he was slow to take hold because this was the first council he had attended in the region, "when he did speak it was to the point." W. C. White clearly noted to himself and his mother that Olsen as a leader was well worth watching.[19]

Ellen White had also previously watched Olsen from a more distant perspective. She had itinerated around the camp meetings in what came to be known as the western district of the United States in the late 1860s and occasionally during the 1870s and had undoubtedly come into contact, at least casually, with the quiet and deeply spiritual Norwegian who served as conference president in the area.[20] It had been a time when Olsen was accumulating experience and developing his administrative gifts in local conference leadership.

Olsen had entered conference leadership rather early in his ministerial career. He had first been elected as a conference president in 1874 when at age twenty-nine, just one year after his ordination to full-time ministry, he received an invitation to head his home conference in Wisconsin. Butler commented that being of Norwegian birth was a distinct advantage for Olsen in his new role. The Wisconsin Conference had eight churches of Norwegians and Danes, and Butler regarded it as important that "there should be close union of those of different tongues."[21] One two-year term in the role of president, however, persuaded Olsen of the urgent need for further education, and he had taken himself to Battle Creek for a year of study under Goodloe Harper Bell. Upon returning, he served for another four years as president of the Wisconsin Conference (1877–1880), and then with his name becoming more widely known, was invited to serve as president of adjacent conferences: Dakota (1880–1882), Minnesota (1882–1884), and Iowa (1885).[22] The numerous Scandinavian communities that had settled on the prairies had particularly appreciated his ministry, and he had been successful in establishing many new churches. Thus in 1885, when the General Conference needed someone to guide the struggling work recently opened in northern Europe, it had turned to Olsen and requested that he take leave from his administrative duties and assist John G. Matteson for a time both in Christiana and Copenhagen.[23]

Although he was born in Norway, Olsen had immigrated to the United States with his parents when he was five years of age and thus thought of himself as American. His family had settled in Wisconsin at Oakland Town, on rich farmland about forty-two kilometers west of Milwaukee. The whole family had become Adventists in 1858 when Ole Olsen was thirteen years of age. He had enjoyed only limited post secondary schooling by taking winter terms at Milton College, a Seventh Day Baptist institution not far from his home. But he enjoyed dairy farming better than studying and had accumulated enough capital to purchase his own farm by the time he married at age twenty-three. But farming alone did not seem to utilize his full potential or provide satisfaction of soul, and about the time he married he ventured into lay preaching at his local church. Then as he developed confidence he received a ministerial license and became associated with summer evangelistic tent programs not far from home, preaching on a part-time basis. In 1871, at the age of twenty-six, he found good success with his own first independent evangelistic campaign and shortly thereafter sold his farm to enter full-time ministry. Two years later the denomination ordained him at age twenty-eight.

Although Olsen had spent only a short time in congregation-based pastoral activities, he saw its importance and seems to have continued his involvement in pastoral and congregational ministry at the local church level even while serving as president. His passion for the spiritual development of his church members remained a life-long concern. During his eleven years in local conference leadership he also accumulated leadership skills. His ability to relate across cultural barriers, tolerate differences in culture and custom, and accept people with, and in spite of, their differences became characteristic of his ministry and constituted a distinctive strength. On the other hand, this part of his background, it would seem, also created difficulties for him in some other areas.

We see Olsen's diplomatic skills and his ability to live with a significant level of ambiguity illustrated in the way he related to the role the denomination asked him to accept when he went back to Scandinavia in 1885. As the president of a local conference, his duties and the line of his responsibility were clear. But they were less so in the role he undertook in Europe. At first, J. G. Matteson feared that the church had sent Olsen from America to replace him and "put right all the things that Matteson had done wrong." Ellen White had to assure Matteson's wife that "this was not to be so: Elder Olsen had come to help him, not to replace him."[24] As Mrs. White saw it, Olsen had come "to take hold with Brother Matteson, and Brother Matteson with him, and they can thus help each other in carrying forward this work." The church in Christiana and the publishing program there had serious problems, and Olsen "is greatly needed," she reported to Butler.[25] Olsen was the kind of leader who did not need an official position or title to be effective. He became involved in evangelistic and pastoral activities and served as a consultant in the various council meetings. Within twelve months after his arrival in the field, he had expanded the Norwegian church outside of Oslo and organized the new congregations into a new conference of which he was then appointed president and which was accepted into the General Conference at the 1887 session.

Olsen was enjoying his work in Scandinavia. Serving as General Conference president appears to have been the farthest thought possible from his mind, almost as far, it seems, as it was from the mind of the committee when it was first obliged to sit down and consider alternatives to Butler. After the vote, it took almost six months before the decision could be implemented and Olsen could arrive in Battle Creek to assume the office.

It was, in fact, some time after the Minneapolis meeting that word of the surprising invitation apparently got through to Olsen that he had been elected. He had noted very briefly in his diary that he had "received word from the brethren" that he had been appointed. His busy schedule left him no time to write any other reflections or even to note his feelings about the news, although after digesting what he had learned about the theological turmoil in the States, he was willing to express himself. For the moment, though, he was too preoccupied with the immediate needs of the work at hand. Public meetings, Bible studies, and establishing a new congregation clearly took priority, and he could not easily just walk away.[26]

Olsen's inability to return to the United States until early summer the following year posed a problem. In the interim, it was first intended that S. N. Haskell serve as acting president, but shortly after the session, which concluded November 3, the executive committee requested W. C. White to take the reins until Olsen was able to assume the office.[27] Five months later, Olsen again noted tersely in his diary: "Leaving today for America to take up duties at the General Conference." The comment seems almost nonchalant. But Olsen was not unaware of what awaited him.[28]

The newly appointed president was not overly impressed with his new assignment. And as he thought about the perplexities associated with it, neither was he too confident in his ability to cope with the challenges. "It is indeed unfortunate that the General

Conference has come to this that such a poor stick as I must be chosen as its president," he commented to W. C. White sometime after he had received word of the appointment. In fact, the very idea somewhat distressed him. "It fills me both with grief and disgust if I may so express it," he confided to White. He clearly approached the new challenge with considerable apprehension and would have much preferred to have been doing something else.[29] W. C. White had earlier briefed him on the "peculiar" features of the 1888 session, which White conceded he "could not understand." On the other hand, those "features" he thought he could grasp were "not very pleasant to write about." His mother was clearer in her description. She confided to her daughter-in-law that the controversy at the session had been "the hardest and most incomprehensible tug of war we have ever had among our people."[30] Trying to bring harmony to the theologically divided church would need to be Olsen's highest priority. The conspiracy theory conjured up by William Healey asserted that W. C. White and his mother, together with the two young western church leaders, Jones and Waggoner, were plotting to take over the denomination's theology, and this view had circulated among many leaders prior to the conference. It had resulted in significant misunderstanding and had led to a large number losing confidence in Ellen White.[31] While the rumor had no basis in fact, nevertheless Ellen White's support and endorsement of E. J. Waggoner and A. T. Jones cast doubts on the validity of her charisma in the eyes of leaders such as Uriah Smith, George Butler, and a number of state conference presidents. They had understood from her previous pronouncements on the major point at issue—the question of what particular law Galatians 3:24 referred to—meant that the matter had been resolved and was no longer negotiable. How could she now say something different? Olsen would have to be a bridge-builder.

"As I contemplate returning to America, in answer to the call of the General Conference," Olsen wrote in the *Review,* "my feelings are beyond description." He was not sure at all that he was the right person for the task and felt "most unworthy."[32] When he arrived in Battle Creek ready to take up duties on May 7, 1889, Ellen White was out of town, attending ministers' meetings in Kansas and camp meetings in the surrounding conferences. He would not have the opportunity to meet her in Battle Creek until six weeks later. But he understood the needs of the hour, and besides getting quickly caught up in administrative matters, he gave substantial time to supporting her intensive endeavors to bring about harmony and agreement among church leadership. He threw himself into leading ministers' meetings, spoke frequently at church and conference revival meetings, and participated in weeks of prayer in order to help reduce the tensions. Also he focused on trying to achieve reconciliation between the church's senior leaders, with a view to rebuild confidence in Ellen White's ministry. Nine months later, she observed that Olsen had been "giving excellent talks . . . right to the point." She was glad that "Brother Olsen stands well, firm, and free and boldly on the right side."[33]

Olsen received his first recorded letter from Ellen White three months after he took up the reins of office. It was a short, inconsequential note asking him to pass on a message about her unavailability to accept a speaking appointment and to help make other arrangements.[34] In the succeeding eight years, through the next four elections, she would send him at least eighty-two personal letters. Some of these were very painful, others highly encouraging. In addition to the personal letters, he received numerous circular type letters with multiple addressees, along with many manuscripts dealing with problems emerging in the church and which provided pastoral guidance. Olsen, on the other hand, although in regular contact with W. C. White, apparently did not have occasion to write his first letter to Ellen White until two years later on the eve of her departure to Australia.[35]

In contrast to Butler's style of leadership that tended to be much more autocratic, Olsen by nature was a much more cautious and consultative administrator, careful to take counsel from colleagues. One of Olsen's major challenges would be to assemble the right team of associates and counselors. But the harsh reality was that in his first term he had to live and work with the personnel already elected, many of whom were opinionated, hard-headed leaders, and in succeeding terms, to a large degree, he was obliged also to work with whoever was available. Without trusted colleagues available with whom to counsel, he was not always sure of himself. And when his associates were away from denominational headquarters, he felt the burden heavily. "I tell you, I feel pretty lonely here many times," he wrote to W. C. White. "I have none of the brethren around that I used to counsel with so often. It makes a wonderful difference in the work and the situation."[36] By nature Olsen was able to accept people with their differences and was willing to work with their strengths, realizing that each person on the team would need to make up for the weaknesses of the others.

Reorganizing for efficiency

Olsen was also very mindful of the stress and work overload that had burned out Butler and ruined his health. The denominational organization was beginning to become rather cumbersome. By 1885, there existed at least five quasi-independent parachurch organizations allied with, but not subject to, the General Conference—all of which replicated the governance, administrative, and electoral processes of the General Conference itself. These included the International Sabbath School Association, the International Tract and Missionary Society, and three separate independent organizations set up to manage the publishing, health, and educational programs. Several of the parachurch units also had counterparts at the state conference level. The denomination expected the president of the General Conference to be involved in all of them. It was a broad responsibility for which to care. Modern leadership theory would say the "span of control" was too wide. Olsen had participated in the debates at the 1887 General Conference Session that had strongly urged that the workload of the president be lightened by the appointment of administrative assistants. He had, in fact, been the chair of the resolutions committee that had introduced the recommendation and had heard W. C. White defend the appointment of a corresponding secretary to care for the ever increasing clerical duties and the innumerable reports that regularly came in to the president's office. According to W. C. White, the rapid growth of the church in the recent past meant that the workload of the president was "doubling every year." Also he had listened to his mother report that she had been "burdened with this matter a great deal for some time," and Olsen had heard Mrs. White insist to the conference in 1887 that she would "not lift her hand" to vote in favor of Butler's re-election unless the denomination provided additional help for the president.[37] Thus he had warmly supported the initiative to appoint an administrative assistant in 1887 (designated as a recording secretary) as well as three other individuals assigned to serve as secretaries to coordinate and share the administrative load. Although, as it turned out, none of these additional positions were full-time salaried ones; the people simply added their new duties to their existing full-time assignments. Being aware of the problem and knowing how to fix it were two different things. Olsen had already tried, unsuccessfully, to solve it.

A committee he had chaired had framed the resolution of protest about the "overburdening" of the General Conference president in 1887. "With the cares and responsibilities of the State Conferences and local institutions," the resolution read, the state of things resulted in "endangering his [the president's] health and drawing his attention from the general work." The intention of the proposed resolution (number 17), had been to find or create some mechanism that would operate between the many state conferences and the General Conference that would ease the burden of direct administrative responsibility between the state conferences and the General Conference, thus allowing the General conference president more time for general oversight. Although Olsen, Ellen White, Butler, W. C. White, and six other conference presidents debated the resolution at "considerable length," the delegates finally rejected it.[38] Why they did is not clear. Did the local conferences fear being orphaned? Would such an action suggest a fracturing of the organic church unity? Was there simply not enough time for proper discussion before the end of the conference? Perhaps a more positive and practical formulation for the resolution would have had better success than simply expressing a negative protest about the problem of overload.

Olsen was glad, however, to hear that delegates to the 1888 session at least had approved an initiative to divide the North American conferences into four large geographical "districts," each under the general supervision of a member of the General Conference executive committee. The incoming president agreed with this plan and, in fact, he claimed to White that he had been thinking of the same idea himself even before he read the report from the session.[39] At least it would be a start toward easing the overload. The following year Olsen was re-elected as president at the last of the annual meetings of the General Conference. At the same time he shepherded through the session an action to expand the number of districts to six, with a redrawing of the geographical boundaries. Delegates were happy with the experiment thus far. District superintendents served as liaisons between the conferences and the General Conference, attended camp meetings, and kept the General Conference informed about issues of wider significance. The districts, however, were still informal arrangements with no administrative or legal authority. But the creation of the district entity at least enabled a reduction in the frequency of General Conference sessions. Sessions would now convene only every two years. Districts would have regional council meetings in the alternate years.[40]

Another proposal floated at the 1889 session was to appoint "secretaries" at the state conference level to oversee and coordinate the activities of each of the parachurch agencies. In this way they would be drawn into the conference structure. Although delegates vigorously debated the proposal, agreement somehow eluded them. In the end, even the record of the various comments and arguments made during the discussion was expunged from the minutes. It seemed to the parachurch agencies themselves to be a very threatening concept. Perhaps, also, some delegates had said some strong things that they did not want on the public record.

The idea of "departments" within the conference structure also lost traction because it looked too much like the parallel proposal to consolidate the entire publishing program of the church under one corporation and management. Ellen White opposed the latter, arguing that regional publishing houses must be able to maintain their identities. The idea of conference departmental secretaries operating within the conference structure would eventually become the essential structural design of the church, but not until eleven years later in 1901.

At the next General Conference session in 1891, Olsen proposed strengthening the district council through the appointment of full-time administrators and granting the districts the legal right to hold property, but the idea still seemed too threatening, and again he met resistance. It went back on the shelf. The evolving of a formal intermediate administrative level eventually called a "union conference" and located administratively between the General Conference and the local conferences was a slow and painful process for the church in America. It was easier to develop, test, and refine the concept in the church's mission fields outside the United States than in the homeland. Eventually, administrative developments in Europe, South Africa, and Australia gave the church confidence enough to make changes at the center. In the meantime, work pressures on the president increased, as did congestion and administrative inefficiency in church decision making—largely because of the cumbersome structure and the particular nature of the church's centralized form of governance.

The impact of overwork on Olsen's health came into close focus eighteen months after he had assumed the presidential role. He lost his younger brother Edson to tuberculosis in mid-1890. Ellen White had written him at the time, reporting on a visit she had had with the younger Olsen in Colorado. She confirmed that tuberculosis had done its work and that Edson was "beyond human skill" and would not live much longer.[41] W. C. White's wife, Mary, also died of tuberculosis at the age of thirty-three at about the same time. John Matteson, who was also suffering from the disease, would perish from it three years later. Olsen was aware of the need to guard his own health. But he found the demands of office were incessant and the stress of dealing with strong-minded, determined individuals and complex difficulties to be wearing in the extreme.

About the time his brother died, approximately nine months prior to the 1891 General Conference Session, Olsen apparently first learned how strongly Ellen White felt about the apparent reluctance of some church officials and publishers to actively promote the circulation of her revised 1888 edition of *The Great Controversy*. Her sense of deep injustice at the way the publishing house and others had handled the matter returned again and again to demand his attention during his presidency. It came to color much of the way Ellen White viewed other events and how she regarded the people involved, most of whom were individuals with whom Olsen had to work closely. The episode loomed large for Ellen White for a number of reasons. She had personally gone deeply into debt in order to get the book revised (the $3,500 she spent on it represented about five years of her annual salary), and thus she needed a good return from royalties in order to pay down her debt. Also, she believed that the church greatly needed the book and that it would be a powerful evangelistic aid for growing the church membership. She had counted heavily on income from royalties in order to underwrite her further literary projects and to provide resources for her denominational development program in Australia. Furthermore, she saw behind the resistance to the promotion of the book a deliberate strategy of opposition to her role in the church—an attempt to minimize her influence—which she regarded as being orchestrated particularly by those who had fought the emphasis on righteousness by faith at Minneapolis and during the year or two afterward. The failure by the book committee and the publishers to promote the volume had forced her deeper and deeper into embarrassing debt. Her loans on the book carried an interest rate of 7 percent. With her inadequate level of income, she could not meet even her household operating expenses.

In a letter to Olsen in June 1890, Mrs. White asked him to help resolve the problem and to promote the book at any camp meetings he attended. She went on to explain the background to the quarrel from her perspective, mentioning that she had lost much sleep worrying about the problem and that it had burdened her "beyond expression." It particularly disturbed her that in spite of the fact that she had invested money for the purchase of the book plates herself, and then, in addition, had paid for the publication costs of the book, the publishing and book distribution people had "shoved" a cheaper book (*Bible Readings*) out into the market in its place. The experience had seriously tempted her to bypass the denominational publishing system entirely and instead sell her books at the camp meetings herself. Getting Frank Belden and Captain Eldridge at the Review office to change their minds on the decision to give priority to *Bible Readings* in the market was useless. In fact, she felt that she could "as much as talk to a stone."[42] Even longtime friend, C. H. Jones, manager of Pacific Press® out in California, felt he had to follow suit in complying with the general policy that only one subscription book must be in the field at a time. But in doing so, Ellen White alleged, Pacific Press® had "violated their solemn promise to me." She interpreted such betrayal in the severest terms and quoted Scripture against the men: "Judgment is turned away backward and justice standeth afar off" (Isaiah 59:14). "I have often quoted this as representing the course of the false shepherds," she pointedly asserted to Belden two years later, "but I never expected to make an application of it to the treatment I myself received among our own people."[43]

Much of the problem she ascribed to former president George Butler's lingering and malicious influence since the Minneapolis conference. He "has been at the foundation of it all, but he makes no confession and writes in the paper as though he were all right," she complained to Olsen. In fact, both Butler and *Review* editor Uriah Smith, she alleged, had been "scattering seeds of doubt and unsettling the confidence of the churches" in her testimonies. Both men, it is true, were struggling with evidence that, in their minds, seemed to cast doubt on Ellen White's authority. The cognitive dissonance they experienced tempted both of them to deny, or at least to modify and restrict, the validity of her charisma. She found herself having repeatedly to vindicate and validate herself to secure the support of her fellow church leaders. Mrs. White had to press with all her powers "against the prejudice, unbelief, false statements and misrepresentations" until it almost gave her a nervous chill just to think about it. "I refuse to live in this way any longer," she declared and stated that she would "not much longer wait for my brethren in positions of trust to do their duty." Nor would she let the matter rest. If the church administration allowed her "to carry this burden longer in this way" she would certainly know that God could not be leading both them and her. It was one or the other; no compromise. The matter had troubled her mind hundreds of times. "What am I to do, Elder Olsen?" she pleaded. "I have no rest, day nor night, in spirit."[44]

The problems and struggles of the publishing program and the personal conflicts mixed up with it were not easily fixed. They burdened Olsen throughout his presidency and became increasingly more complex. The frequent protests from Ellen White over the issue intensified and finally led to Olsen withdrawing from a leadership role. But even during the first year or two of his term in office he experienced the uncomfortable heat that these issues generated.

In July 1890, Mrs. White sent Olsen another letter with an enclosed testimony for the church along with a request that he read it at the Ohio camp meeting and at other conferences. The testimony protested the continuing theological resistance to the new gospel emphasis by Waggoner and Jones and opposed those who used the tactic of labeling it "fanaticism" or "heresy." The testimony contained personal rebukes to some of the

Ohio leadership that she intended to be made public in the Ohio reading. With prophetic conviction, she intended another version of the end-run around resistant church leaders by naming them and appealing over their heads, as it were, to the church membership. Olsen could erase the personal references if he saw fit to use the letter at other camp meetings. "I will leave that with you," she suggested.[45]

Confronting colleagues in leadership and working to bridge the wide chasm between the differing parties was emotionally draining work for both Olsen and her. As the long dark days of the Michigan winter of 1890 advanced, Olsen's courage retreated. Swamped by anxiety and overwhelming duties, he began to sink under a pall of discouragement, his self-confidence wilted by the biting wind of continual conflict. Ellen White found it necessary to cheer him up as he approached the 1891 election. "Be of good courage," she urged. The Lord "can and will make you efficient, but you must have faith. Do not be depressed." He was not to "mourn in secret" because of the "unfaithfulness" of his colleagues in leadership. There was "no call for despondency and misapprehension," she gently chided, although later she herself struggled with the same feelings.[46]

Following the intense three weeks of dawn-to-late-night meetings of the 1891 General Conference Session in Battle Creek, Olsen felt he simply could not keep up with the pressure nor cope adequately with the increasing complexity of the problems arising from the church's growth. "You complain of not being able to do one half of what you ought to do," Ellen White responded in a letter to him three months after the session. But "is not this because there are so few [others] doing anything?" she inquired. Olsen should not continue to work "on the high pressure plan." He was to "put down the brakes" and give himself periods of rest. "You have no right to draw from the bank until the last farthing is withdrawn," she urged. "Leave a deposit my brother." The president was somehow to find ways to "unload."[47]

Finding suitably qualified assistants to share the burden would certainly help. But where were reliable and experienced individuals? And besides, much of the problem was systemic, arising from the inherent structure and nature of the organization itself rather than simply reflecting the personal weaknesses of leaders. Administrative and legal issues constantly flowed up from the state conferences and institutions. Power was concentrated in the hands of too few. Strong, opinionated voices could easily prevail. If the voices were untrustworthy, there was danger. Already, in 1891, Ellen White had begun to lose her confidence in the decisions of the General Conference boards and committees. In her mind, they could not necessarily be regarded as "the voice of God" correctly guiding the church with decisions and policies that would be safe to follow.[48]

In September 1891, Ellen White had finally accepted, reluctantly, and with much apprehension, an assignment to go to Australia at the request of the General Conference. But in hindsight she felt that it was a mistake. She came to see it as a decision that had been manipulated by the hands of a few individuals.[49] During her darkest days of discouragement in Australia a few years later, she blamed Olsen's weakness for not seeing and standing up to the machinations of his associates.

Following the 1891 session, Ellen White became increasingly disturbed at the kind of colleagues that Olsen was obliged to rely on so extensively in his work. The General Conference Association, as a legal holding body, had been reorganized at the General Conference of 1891 to embrace not only the General Conference assets but the interests of the church's publishing enterprises and other institutions as well. Its membership had been expanded to twenty-five, and in some ways it was even more powerful than the General Conference executive committee itself. Former banker Archibald R. Henry, who headed up the large Review and Herald publishing enterprise, chaired the association and became a dominant voice in its management. General Conference treasurer Harmon Lindsay, who shared many of Henry's ideas, admired his financial skills and supported his marketing and business strategies.

This may have been the first, but it was not to be the last time that Ellen White or her son W. C. White found fault with the team of associates serving around or under the General Conference president. It was a pattern that occurred regularly through the coming years. For example, she would lodge complaints and develop a distrust of some of George A. Irwin's associates in the late 1890s, and in the early part of the new decade, Arthur G. Daniells's team came in for criticism. And around 1908, the same problem developed with some of Daniells's later associates. In the 1930s, W. C. White continued the pattern and laid serious criticisms against those surrounding General Conference president C. H. Watson. Olsen and Irwin were not quite sure how to deal with this lack of confidence in their colleagues. On the other hand, both Daniells and Watson felt able to reply to the charges and diplomatically defend those who had been elected to work with them in the senior administrative team.[50]

"To correct the existing evils"

Late in 1891, just before going to Australia, Ellen White left a number of manuscripts with Olsen with instructions for him to read them to his colleagues "in order to correct the existing evils." She meant for him to present the material formally to his assembled boards and committees. For some reason, Olsen neglected to do this—either for lack of time or not sensing their importance or perhaps even wishing to avoid the unpleasantness of confrontation. He addressed the problems identified by Ellen White in a more indirect way with his co-workers, apparently thinking that he could reduce the post-1888 tensions with a diplomatic and pastoral approach. Thus, instead of reading the materials publicly to his colleagues, he studied them himself and dealt with the principles and their application in his general talks and sermons, hoping to correct the wrongs by talking with his colleagues about the general principles. Also, he took steps between 1892 and 1897 to issue, on a limited basis, some of the material as a twelve-pamphlet series titled *Special Testimonies, Series A* for his colleagues in leadership and the pastorate. Later he explained that his associates were men with whom he had no choice but to work. It was true that they were a fragmented team. But they had, nevertheless, been elected by their various constituencies, and he felt that by reaching out to them and bridging the gap through his pastoral ministry he could bring them into harmony. But this proved more difficult than he anticipated. During late 1892 and through 1893, the theological tensions lingering from Minneapolis continued to sour the working relationships among the leaders of the various church enterprises in Battle Creek. And Olsen's lengthy absences from headquarters did not help. He was away from Battle Creek for three months at a time in both 1891 and 1892 and for almost six months during the latter part of 1893. During these periods, he relied heavily on his education secretary, Professor W. W. Prescott, to serve as acting chairman of the executive committee and keep things functioning.

Such was the attitude of some senior church leaders during this period that they were inclined to interpret revivals and periods of spiritual renewal in the college at Battle Creek and in the local church, for example, as "mere excitement." Prescott felt the problems could not be ignored, although Olsen's absence made it difficult. The professor reported that he considered it necessary to undertake extensive personal pastoral labor with individuals such as Uriah Smith, A. R. Henry, Harmon Lindsay, and J. H. Kellogg. His objective was to try to reconcile differences, reduce alienation between various colleagues, and bring about spiritual renewal. This involved trying to persuade A. R. Henry of the need for change and perhaps even for a public confession. Some progress occurred as the men "talked things over in the plainest way going over the whole ground beginning with the Minneapolis meeting." Prescott detected "a new spirit in the work." But some individuals found it hard to do things differently.[51]

Because Olsen "did not follow the directions" in 1891, Ellen White pointed out later, the problems "went on accumulating in their objectionable features" until they had assumed "an aggravated character." Not until mid-1894, it seems, did she learn that he had not read the materials either publicly or directly to his colleagues in 1891, something that she regarded as a major lapse. "Here you failed to do your duty as President of the General Conference," she wrote. She was distressed that he had chosen to not speak "decidedly" but had preferred a softer pastoral approach. Because his handling of the matter was "such a feeble protest," she pointed out, the "wrongdoers" had cause to think that "he was with them." She did not want Olsen to assume that she was "in harmony with your course in these things." In fact, she asserted, those involved should have been "separated from the work both for their own soul's sake and for the sake of the cause."[52]

After Ellen White learned that Olsen had not publicly read the 1891 materials, she took things into her own hands and forwarded a copy of her 1894 rebuke of him to the circle of leaders around the president. She did not want him to have to bear all the responsibility, she said, and "therefore I will send this to others who should understand the situation, and help you." Of course, it also increased the pressure on Olsen and made him more publicly accountable. He would live to regret his oversight.

Coping with the stream of correspondence and manuscripts from Ellen White and knowing just how to deal with it all was at times a challenge for Olsen. He commented to W. C. White in February 1892 that he was glad for the stream of letters, but it seems they were beginning to reinforce his well-established feelings of inadequacy as much as they offered encouragement. "I almost fear that she gives me more attention than I ought to have, I mean by writing so much; but I assure you it is highly appreciated. It seems just what I need at this time."[53] Olsen's sense of failure had begun to intensify well before he received the 1894 letter of rebuke. The year 1892, in particular, would be a dark one for the president.

In March, Olsen had endured ten days "closely confined continuously" for a series of committees and boards from "early morning until late at night."[54] And then he also had constant travel to various places with lengthy counseling needed to meet the demands of the state conferences. He found it extremely stressful and lamented to Ellen White two months later, "I am much perplexed about myself. My strength and ability are not equal to the demand. I come so far short in every matter that it is hard to keep up courage at times." He knew he had to unload some of his duties, but that would require additional personnel. "It is not enough that I have a stenographer," he noted. Rather, he needed a good administrative assistant. "I must have a person that is more than a stenographer," an individual "of some experience and a man of good sense and some ability."[55] By June, his gloom had deepened. Yes, he deeply desired to be able to change things, "to take heed to it all," he replied after receiving further letters of advice. But he acknowledged that one of his greatest difficulties was that "I do not know how to do what I so much desire to do."[56] Olsen recognized that he needed to change if he was to survive. But again, much of the problem was systemic. Knowing what should be done and actually being able to do it were two quite different things. Boards and committees tended to have minds of their own. Working things through the system was not easy. "It is many times very difficult for me to do even that which I know to be right."[57]

Serious discouragement overwhelmed him again by September. He felt imprisoned by circumstances, unable to effect any change and unable to extract himself from the constant demands of the urgent and the necessary in his office. Things seemed to be getting beyond control. On top of this, the lack of spirituality he perceived in the congregations burdened him. Ellen White's frequent and strongly worded letters to the denomination about its spiritual lethargy bothered Olsen. As president he felt personally responsible. In September, she wrote again to him in an endeavor to hold up his hands. "I hope that you will not permit anxiety concerning the neglect of duties of the church to so cloud your mind that you will fail to look steadfastly to Jesus." Although the church had great deficiencies, she noted, "you cannot make one soul clean." The president should not "suffer this event or that event" to "confuse and startle" him. It was best to "look above the whirl of daily occurrences." "We cannot expect that everything will move along smoothly." Olsen was to do what he could but was not to "worry." "I know that a heavy burden rests upon you," she encouraged, and she pledged that "we will try and bear it with you, though we cannot be upon the ground," meaning that she would have liked to have been in Battle Creek beside him. She knew that he felt "intensely" over the matter, but she also realized that "you cannot make those who will not place themselves in the channel of light, stand where they may reflect the glory of God." Again she observed that he could not "always be in the din of battle" and still preserve his strength. Olsen was "not immortal," and his health would not "bear constant strain." He needed to have periods of rest. Mrs. White was seriously worried that he would break under the pressure. "You may weep my brother, but ever hold through your tears the sunshine and the rainbow of promise. In the name of Jesus, I beseech you to rest."[58]

In spite of the encouragement from his pastoral and prophetic mentor, crisis after crisis seemed to erupt in Battle Creek, and by the end of 1892, Olsen was absolutely sure that he did not want to continue as president. He was approaching a nervous breakdown. In despair he indicated to Ellen White that it was time for the church to look for someone more effective to take on the role of General Conference president.[59]

The prospect of Olsen pulling out alarmed her. She wrote back, this time in a strong pastoral counseling mode, acknowledging that his load was too heavy. "The responsibilities which you have borne should be shared by three men," she asserted. "One man is not physically or mentally capable of overseeing and doing so large an amount of work as you have tried to do. You have done too much."[60] At the same time, she indicated that she understood his discouragement. "Do not write bitter things against yourself; do not charge yourself with being an unfaithful servant or betraying sacred trust. You tremble and fear because after all your labor there seems to be so much left undone." Understanding both his longing "to lay off the great responsibility" and his feelings of failure and inadequacy, she sought to build up his self confidence. "You are un-reconciled to the smallness of the largest gifts which you can lay on the altar for Christ . . . you bemoan the imperfect service." But, she remonstrated with him, "God has given you your talents. He has chosen you to bear responsibilities, not because you had a thorough education, not because you were an orator, or a man of brilliant intellect; He chose you because through his Grace you walked humbly with God and manifested faithfulness in that which is least." Now she urged him not to waste valuable time "lamenting the opportunities you never had," because "the Lord knew all about this matter when he selected you for the work he has given you to do."[61]

It was the lack of suitable alternative leaders that apparently really alarmed Mrs. White. "Where is the man that you could, that you would dare, put in your place?" she asked. Who could he trust? "You have difficulty in finding even a man to act as an assistant, one on whom you can depend to do humble service," she asserted. If it was so hard "to find a man to stand by your side, I ask you," she challenged, "where is the man to stand in your place?"[62] Olsen must not consider stepping down. Rather he should select someone to assist him. She said that she had been shown that this should be done just as it should have been done for Butler when he had been president. The church needed to think carefully about succession planning. If it did not have suitable individuals to take on this critical role, then "there must be decided efforts to educate and train the best kind of talent." But it was clear, she declared, that "we cannot release you until some one shall be raised to take up the work."[63] Olsen was to remain bound to the duties of his office for at least one more term. Three months later, at the February 1893 session which met in Battle Creek, Olsen was re-elected without dissent.

Ellen White's role in the appointment of church leadership at this session, as in 1888, was very direct, even though behind the scenes. Because of her absence from the session on this occasion, she was not a formal delegate or a member of the nominating committee. But distance clearly did not negate her influence. Even from Australia, she was able to have a significant influence on the process and the outcome of the General Conference election. But although the delegates were happy to vote Olsen back into office, they did not like his plan to delegate administrative authority to the General Conference districts. That would have to happen somewhere away from headquarters, it seemed, if the idea was ever to get off the ground.

Olsen's journey to the South Pacific in the latter part of 1893 helped stabilize his emotional resources for a while and also gave him opportunity to better understand the Whites' circumstances. Olsen had been urged to go out to Australia in the months after the 1893 General Conference Session to help establish the concept of a new administrative unit for the church in Australia. W. C. White had proposed the establishment in Australia of some "ecclesiastical body to stand mid-way between State and Colonial Conferences and the General Conference." The proposal meshed with Olsen's own plan to give greater powers and responsibility to the district superintendents in the United States in some sort of "District Confederation of Conferences."[64] Thus Olsen was present for the launch, but it still didn't make it any easier to introduce reform in Battle Creek.

CHAPTER 4

FOUR MORE YEARS of STRESS for OLE OLSEN (1893–1897)

If problems had discouraged the tall, bearded Norwegian in 1892, they were dwarfed beside those that emerged following his re-election as General Conference president in 1893. Such problems provide an important context for understanding the difficulties Olsen encountered in his leadership. They also provide background for understanding Ellen White's own experience, her increasing disillusionment with Olsen, and her heightened frustration, anxiety, and agitation over the general state of affairs at church headquarters. It was her direct pressure that influenced Olsen's eventual resignation from the presidency.

In 1893, a severe economic recession lasting for four years hit the United States and many other countries. By mid-1894, denominational revenues plunged sharply. Harmon Lindsay, treasurer for the General Conference Association, who was also caring for Ellen White's personal American-related business matters while she was away in Australia, reported that the decline, bad as it was by August 1893, would undoubtedly worsen in the coming year. It did. And by 1895, circumstances still had not improved, with church officials noting that the "great financial depression" was causing "a great scarcity of money." For another two years, the drop in church offerings continued to create extreme financial perplexity for church leaders. Lindsay's own personal situation, he said, was typical of many. Although he had given substantial offerings in the past, his ability to contribute to the cause had been sharply curtailed as his personal finances were tied up in real estate, and he was falling behind in the struggle just to pay the interest and taxes.[1] The economic downturn caught the church unprepared.

When the recession struck, the church was already committed to significant and costly institutional development, expansion into many new mission territories, and increased numbers of support personnel for its overstretched General Conference staff. For example, the General Conference payroll tripled between 1893 and 1895. The church found itself floundering in an unrealistic fiscal fantasy land. In some ways, money seemed plentiful. But that was because church members, not trusting the banks, were lending money to the denomination, assuming it would be a safer place in which to deposit their savings. But the expenses of the entire General Conference operation were much greater than its income, and the church was hard pressed just to pay its interest on the loans. Denominational headquarters had not yet adopted a process of advance annual budgeting in order to anticipate expenses. Olsen would not introduce such a system until 1895 and then only as a way of coping with the crisis.[2] By that time it was too late. Although some efforts had been made to conserve resources, by mid-1896 General Conference secretary L. T. Nicola reported that the treasury was empty. The church could not pay its creditors and clamped a freeze on sending out new personnel.

Earlier malfeasance on the part of some senior church officials did not improve the image of the General Conference. L. C. Chadwick, for example, embarrassed his fellow administrators and contributed to a loss of confidence in church leadership through his shady financial dealings. A relatively recent Adventist convert, Chadwick had rapidly advanced to leadership of the Tract and Missionary Society and to membership of the Foreign Mission Board. In 1891, he had embarked on a lengthy world junket that extended well into 1892.[3] Substantial financial irregularities were later discovered, and by early April 1893, Chadwick left denominational employment to work for the Baptists. General Conference treasurer W. H. Edwards later called the trip an escapade that had cost the church $4,000[4]—an amount that could have employed a minister for almost six years.

As a result of the economic crisis, denominational publishing houses also faced financial dilemmas due to declining book sales. Publishing house managers put the squeeze on authors by reducing royalty payments in an effort to contain expenses and make their enterprises more financially viable.

In late 1893, economic collapse struck Australia. The lack of financial resources both from the General Conference and from local sources created intense anguish for Ellen White and her colleagues, who were already struggling with grinding poverty in their efforts to start new work in the antipodes. Culture shock, ill health, family crises, and periods of discouragement compounded her problems. On the personal level, life became particularly stressful for Ellen White at this time. For example, back in Colorado, William Walling, who was married to her niece, filed a civil lawsuit against her for the wrongful alienation of the affections of his two daughters. Some years earlier the two girls had gone to live in the White home and had become very attached to Ellen's side of the family. The settlement of the case involved negotiation and the intervention of Harmon Lindsay—and finally a cash settlement. According to Lindsay, the case was "mischievous" and without substance. Walling was "a desperate character," verging on being insane, and simply wanted to extract satisfaction from Mrs. White. Nevertheless, the case produced a great deal of unwelcome distress and anxiety.[5]

Closer to home, the stress of overwork and financial anxiety was also taking its toll on W. C. White, who, during this period, went through an extensive period of burnout. His mother referred to it as brain fever or "brain weariness." It caused Ellen White much anxiety. In early 1894, White had suffered a low-grade fever for many weeks and had become lethargic and withdrawn. "He is now in a condition which causes me decided alarm," his mother noted to Olsen in mid-1894. If Olsen had felt "free to express some appreciation of his work," Ellen White wrote, it might well have cheered her son. It certainly would not have done "the least bit of harm," she lamented. Although she knew that the General Conference must look hard at containing its expenses, she nevertheless felt provoked that Willie had been "cut down in his wages" by two dollars per month. She was deeply distressed that his financial embarrassment would now be perpetuated. As it was, he was borrowing money from his mother to meet day-to-day expenses and was burdened by trying to pay off a mortgage at home in the United States. Mrs. White wrote so that Olsen could "enlighten" his board "as to the real situation, as, in your position, it is your privilege and duty to do."[6]

By now, her own personal financial situation was desperate. Because of her prominent role in leadership, she felt she could not simply turn away the constant stream of visitors who came to her home. This had led to the need to put up a tent in her yard to accommodate and entertain them at considerable personal expense. She had purchased used furniture from auction rooms. As a further economy measure, she had to discontinue buying butter and even dispense with the very occasional meat dish just to make ends meet.[7] For various reasons, the keenly anticipated repayment of a sizeable $20,000 loan she had made earlier in the United States, and which in 1894 she desperately needed, was not forwarded to her. The disappointment more than "grieved" her. She was absolutely "indignant." With head aching and heart burning she reported that at night she "would walk the room in her distress and agony." Sleep eluded her as her mind refused to switch off and her thoughts apparently recycled themselves around and around in her head.

In her darkest moments, as she reviewed the messy details of her conflict with church publishers over the publishing and marketing of *The Great Controversy* and the financial distress this had caused her, she felt that the Review and Herald officials had deliberately and malevolently set out to hurt her. "Have I not every reason to believe if they could manage to place me in trying places they would do it?" she challenged Olsen. "They have done it." The hurt was deep, and her frustration at times led her to contemplate various avenues that might be open to her. What if she were to send to the Review and Herald office *all* her expenses involved in preparing the many articles she wrote for the church paper? "I have thought I would hunt up . . . expenses," she reported. Surely that would demonstrate how serious her situation was. But then on reflection she decided that it was not worth the effort. "I will not take the trouble. God knows the whole history. I am sick and disgusted with the management of those things."[8]

Then, just at her lowest point in mid-1894, Ellen White read a two-part article in the *Review* that she perceived as unnecessarily negative. Written by W. H. Littlejohn, the articles were critical of some of the early Millerite excesses in the 1840s, and she saw a danger that they could undo much of the work of evangelism and faith building into which she had poured herself during the past two difficult years in Australia. The foreign colonies, with their underlying suspicion of anything American, had not been easy fields in which to work. Furthermore, she had been pushing hard to get Avondale established. She had found it exceedingly difficult to overcome the inertia of the local membership. Some church members thought that she had been rather extreme in forcing the project. If they read Littlejohn's articles about excesses of the Miller period, would they become discouraged in their outreach? Littlejohn seemed to her to be totally undermining her work. How on earth could the editors at the *Review* "have so little discernment," she lamented? How could they so easily give "us as a people into the enemies' hands?" From her perspective, on the front lines of the battlefield, the articles represented a "most terrible betrayal of our cause." If the people at the *Review* were prepared to print such matter, they should "be discharged, whoever they may be."[9] From the perspective of her distress, such behavior on the part of an employee of the church fell into the category of gross misconduct.

For several weeks after reading the articles, Ellen White remained so discouraged that she became totally disabled, "passing through such agony of mind" that she scarcely knew whether she "should live or die."[10] In the darkness of those cold, wet winter months as she worried about her desperate financial plight, she lamented the fact that she had agreed to come to Australia at all. How could the unspiritual Battle Creek leaders have sent her to Australia to suffer like this? She certainly would not visit Africa or Europe again. "I am not willing to go at the voice of the Conference unless I see my own way clearer [*sic*] to do so," she declared to Olsen, the president. But neither did she want to return to America. She would remain where she was until "further orders from the Lord" would come "to bid me how to move." In addition, she seriously considered retiring from the work. Was she not sixty-six years old already? Perhaps it was time now for her to cease receiving income from the General Conference and be truly independent. Then she could be "entirely free from all responsibility" and be able to "move independently of every man and power." Her husband had always warned her, she reflected, that she should "beware of men in high places." She "must not be bound," he had urged. How could she continue to receive direction from administrators in Battle Creek who were giving clear evidence that they had not been converted?[11]

The coalescing of these circumstances seemed to reach a peak during the latter half of the 1890s and created an agonizing Gethsemane experience for Ellen White. Her experience provided the prism through which she viewed the troubles of the church as a whole and the failures of those involved in particular. The inadequacies of the organizational systems at the center of the work seemed all the more marked. In these episodes she saw in stark and frightening outline what might become of the church if things were to continue as they were. With heightened apprehension and anguish, she sensed the possibility of dramatic consequences. These circumstances constituted the crucible out of which she wrote many of her frequently pointed, direct letters to Olsen and others in General Conference leadership. The dark hues of possible calamitous consequences occasioned the use of more impassioned language than usual. (A more extensive discussion of the general issues of this time period appears in chapter 11.)

During 1893 and 1894, Olsen traveled to the South Pacific as part of a four-month trip around the world to better understand and advise the rapidly growing worldwide Adventist program. His itinerary also took him to South Africa, the United Kingdom, and continental Europe, but did not include Asia or South America. The time he spent in the South Pacific enabled him to experience firsthand the challenges that Ellen White and her colleagues faced in growing the church in Australia and New Zealand. The visit also gave him opportunity to counsel with Ellen White and W. C. White about how best to handle the problems at Battle Creek. But in spite of the counsel, he found on his return to Michigan by mid-1894 that the problems seemed to be no easier to solve. Certainly the demands of office had not disappeared simply because he had been absent from Battle Creek. In order to bring himself up to speed on developments that had taken place in his absence, Olsen asked W. W. Prescott to meet him when he landed in California. The five-day journey together across the country to Michigan would give the two men time to plan and strategize about how best to address the many problems and move the work forward. Olsen could sense that the problems were becoming more serious.

During this period, some decisions Olsen presided over as president clearly caused major unrest in Australia and also made life difficult elsewhere in the church. In 1892, for example, senior management executives at the Review and Herald, such as Archibald Henry, Frank E. Belden, and Clement A. Eldridge, had been voted significantly higher salaries, bringing them into line with other local publishing businesses. But this resulted in them receiving almost double the wages being paid to other employees in the church. The injustice of such "exorbitant" remuneration deeply disturbed Mrs. White. She protested to Olsen, "You saw the evil that was at work, yet you did not move as one in your position ought to have done." He should have protested the increases rather than consenting to them. Money spent in this way on personnel in Battle Creek, in her view, deprived desperately needy fields such as Australia of funds. It was not good stewardship. The possible effect on other aspects of the denominational program also alarmed her, and she labeled the initiative a gross "injustice" and a "deep wrong" that "God does not wink at." The fact that she succeeded in having the decision reversed meant that those involved developed hostility toward her. Henry, Belden, Eldridge, and others, she reported "have not had kindly feelings toward me because they were deprived of these large wages."[12] The fallout from the remuneration issue had a serious impact on the ability of the Review and Herald to find capable leadership.

Ellen White had been "much distressed" to the point of disgust that her nephew Frank Belden and his associate, Captain Eldridge, had resigned from the publishing house because of the wage issue. Their vacancies were extremely difficult to fill. Though roles are not always clearly based on job titles, in effect, Belden served as sales manager and Eldridge as production manager at the Review and Herald. In Ellen White's view, such a response from Belden indicated that he was only a "time-server." If they could pull out of the work and "drop it so easily," both men had revealed that they were "not men that can be depended upon." On the other hand, Ellen White noted pointedly, individuals such as her late husband, James, who had started the publishing program, "could not be bought and sold." He would not have sold his soul just for a larger pay packet.[13]

The action of the Review and Herald board in designating F. S. Russell to replace Belden did not do anything to build her confidence in its judgment. She was astonished "at the blindness manifested" in such an appointment. It was not "according to the order of God." Individuals who had "never surrendered themselves to the control of the Spirit of God" were "not to be placed in positions of holy trust."[14]

If Olsen had only "discerned the evil more clearly and had acted decidedly" when the wage differential idea was first proposed, the problem would not have become as large as it had, she chastised him in mid-1894. She lamented the fact that "constant suspicion, jealousies and evil surmisings" in the hearts of his financial colleagues were standing in the way of their own spiritual advancement as well as "providing a decided hindrance" to her ability to carry out her mission. It made her work difficult. The administrators at the Battle Creek publishing house should recognize that she had "a connection and an experience with the work that not one of them have." Because she did not have their "sympathy," or "the faith and confidence" of some of those who sat on Olsen's councils, she noted, she did not think that she should therefore "feel under restraints which they wish to impose."[15] Olsen clearly felt caught in the middle.

In the light of Archibald Henry's negative reaction and attitudes, Ellen White thought it not wise for Olsen to proceed with his plan to travel to Europe in late 1894. At that time, Henry was the leader of the Review and Herald publishing house. She was "much depressed at the thought" and decided that although she would not discourage the General Conference president from his intended trip, she must "warn" him of the danger. "I have been pained at my heart as I have seen the great demand you have for Bro. Henry. I can see no light in it. God wants unselfish, just men, whose judgment is not swayed by feeling, men who will not make decisions under a perverse spirit."[16]

If only Olsen could have somehow changed the system or transformed his associates, the work would have become much simpler. But he could not find a quick answer. "I see very plainly that I must take another course than I have in the past if I shall be able to hold out as I ought to," he confided to W. C. White. It was an anxiety to him to "know how to properly relate myself to the work." He sensed that Willie White would understand his dilemma because he himself faced something of the same challenge. "One of my greatest difficulties is to get away from a large amount of detail work that must be done by somebody." But someone still had to do it, even if there was no one competent enough or mature enough to whom to delegate it.[17]

A STRONG LETTER OF REBUKE

By late 1894, as the next General Conference session loomed on the horizon, Olsen seriously began considering again whether he should step aside. A strong letter of rebuke addressed to him personally, along with a highly charged testimony to leadership in general, had arrived from Ellen White at the end of December. She had actually written the testimony in August at a time when she had been feeling intensely about the developing situation in Battle Creek, but she had obviously felt apprehensive about sending it then and so had waited. Developments in late 1894 troubled her further, and with prophetic foresight she began to see where things might eventually end up if the current situation continued. As a result, she cast her interpretation of developments and her accompanying warnings in the kind of highly charged language used by eighth-century B.C. Old Testament prophets such as Amos.

After reading her letter, Olsen clearly began to conclude that it was time for him to step down. And he realized, learning from his oversight in 1891, that he should in no way avoid sharing the letter publicly with his colleagues in leadership. Ellen White had addressed it to all of them, but she had sent the letter to Olsen. In the dying hours of 1894, with the General Conference session just weeks away, he called an urgent meeting of all available personnel from the Review and Herald board, the Battle Creek College board, the sanitarium board, the General Conference Association executive committee, as well as some pastors. Then he read aloud to them the general testimony as well as the letter addressed to him personally. "We had a very solemn meeting," he reported a day or two later, and at the close of the meeting "a few spoke in response to the testimony." He stated that he thought "everyone had some sense of the gravity of the situation. I trust that the Lord will not give us over to ourselves . . . and that we may be enabled to see and understand the will of the Lord as it is our privilege.[18]

The personal letter to Olsen stung, and as he read it and re-read it again and again, he was sure that Ellen White was suggesting that it was time for him to go. He indicated that he understood himself well—at least he thought he did—as he acknowledged to her his receipt of the letter. "I am fully aware that my failures and shortcomings are very great, and many times it is difficult for me to keep up my courage." Furthermore, he acknowledged that although he had "a most earnest desire to serve the cause of God faithfully" according to whatever ability God had given him, "in the midst of all this I have failed greatly in doing my whole duty." As a result, he realized that he was "utterly unworthy for the position of responsibility" that he held and that he "lacked in executive ability in many ways." Aware of his defects, he had sought the Lord and made earnest efforts to remedy them "as far as I know how. . . . I am glad that God remembers that I am but dust." But he feared that his deficiencies were too great. "The achievement of what I ought to be seems almost insurmountable."[19]

Still mulling the letter over the next day, he dictated one to W. C. White in which he indicated that in light of the letter from Ellen White, he could see the writing on the wall. The coming General Conference session "may see fit to relieve me from the office of President, and choose some other one." He noted that he would be more than relieved should that happen. In his mind, finding a suitable replacement would not now be a problem. "It would seem to me that there is no one as well prepared for the position as yourself," he suggested to the forty-year-old White. Willie's closeness to his mother and the much better understanding that he would therefore have of what she wanted done at General Conference headquarters would be a distinct advantage. White would be in a stronger position to implement his mother's counsel. Olsen was content, however, to "trust that the Lord will guide and direct in this matter to His own glory."[20] Although on the surface his response might seem to convey an attitude of "I can't do what is necessary, so you come and do it yourself," such an interpretation would not be in keeping with his character. Olsen genuinely thought that W. C. White would have a better understanding of his mother's intentions and therefore have a clearer idea of how to implement them.

As it turned out, however, Olsen found himself returned to office in 1895 despite everything. In submitting his name, C. H. Jones, the nominating committee chair, reported that his committee had given the names submitted "careful and prayerful consideration." He asserted that "the help of God had been sought and experienced." Before the conference voted on his name, Olsen took the opportunity to point out to the delegates his "deficiency" and that he had urged the nominating committee "to consider this matter most seriously." The position of president, he said, "required largeness of mind to a degree that he felt he did not possess," and it had been pointed out to him that his work was defective in his "not disposing the burdens and labor upon others." Therefore he wanted the session to "act intelligently" and asked to be excused. Could he not be "placed in a position in connection with the work where he could better serve the cause"? Prescott replied that "if he knew of any one else who could as well bear these burdens and do this work," he would suggest the name as a substitute, but there was none. Others spoke in the affirmative, and then a prayer for guidance was offered before the vote was taken. There was not a word of criticism, and Olsen was elected unanimously.[21]

Some days later he reported to Stephen Haskell, who had remained in South Africa, that he was both surprised and disappointed at the turn of events. Those nominated were all elected, he recounted, "without any criticism whatever. I think they received a very general approval, more-so than for several years in the past." "I should have been exceedingly glad to have been released," he opined, "for I never felt such a dread of taking up the responsibilities of the General Conference as at the present time. Of course I shall aim to do my best, but even then there will be so many mistakes and shortcomings."[22]

The following month Olsen found time to write to W. C. White again. "You see I am again placed at the head of the Conference," he reported. "But I never accepted this position under so many misgivings as at the present time." Again he asserted that he would have been quite happy "to have been released from the responsibility, and some other one better fitted than I could have carried it." Not a day passed that he did not "mourn" over his "many lacks." He reiterated to White that he felt he did not have "the largeness of mind" or "the quickness of understanding" so necessary for one occupying the position. Nor did he have the necessary "thorough knowledge of every branch of the work," observing that "with the growth of the work these things are become more and more so." His unfamiliarity with technical detail bothered him, since he lacked knowledge of the techniques of printing, the legal niceties of marketing and publishing administration, and the intricacies of health-care administration. All of these issues were being made more complex by the rapidly evolving corporate law system in America. Never before had he gone to a General Conference session "with so many misgivings, and with such an intense anxiety for the result of the work that should be done." His deepest concern, however, seems to have been that even though he might desire to have certain personnel appointed in order to implement the ideals that Ellen White advocated, ultimately the delegates were the ones to make the choices, and he had to work with whomever they (or the stockholders in the case of the institutions) might elect. As Olsen noted to W. C. White, he found "that in connection with the work, are men of strong minds and with great powers of expression, and that many times their influence and judgment prevail in matters that are not for the best." In addition, he was aware that even at the General Conference session, the appointment of personnel and the decisions taken were often probably less than ideal. "May the Lord forgive our mistakes and errors, and bless that which has been transacted, according to his mind and will."[23] Henry and Lindsay were still active in denominational affairs. Because church leadership could not find anyone else with the competence to fill the role, Henry was still manager of the Battle Creek publishing house and had also been elected to numerous other subsidiary roles. He was a trustee of Union College, treasurer of the Seventh-day Adventist Medical Missionary and Benevolent Association and thus a member of its executive committee, a member of the Seventh-day Adventist Educational Society, a trustee of the General Conference Association, and a member of the International Tract Society. Clearly, the nominating committee valued his expertise. Lindsay, as General Conference Association auditor, was less heavily involved. Olsen thought that placing the publishing program directly under General Conference administration instead of having it as an independent entity should, at least, help improve accountability and control.[24]

Ellen White, however, could not understand how such people as Henry and Lindsay could still be serving after all that she had said prior to the session. In October of the previous year, she had declared that "the same men are not to compose your boards year after year. Changes should have been made long ago." She certainly would not assent to Olsen's proposal that Henry visit denominational projects in Australia. Mrs. White asserted that "the Lord has a controversy" with both Henry and Lindsay, "yet Elder Olsen treats them as representative men."[25] Influencing things so that the right kind of personnel would get appointed to office was proving to be extraordinarily difficult. "I am troubled for you, my much respected brother," she wrote to Olsen in May, just two months after the 1895 session had concluded. "I am bowed down with anguish of spirit, for the situation is become [*sic*] more and more perplexing." Acknowledging the systemic nature of the problem, she stated that she felt that, to a large degree, the management of finances was being "conducted on wrong principles," and "the condition of things" was binding Olsen's hands and "hindering the work." She understood that, given the circumstances, he feared to exercise his judgment "lest there be an explosion." Quite explicitly she stated, "The two men who have been especially associated with you should, in their present spiritual condition, have no part in planning and carrying forward the work of God in any of its various lines." As a result, she believed that "it is time that there was a change."[26] But whether she mailed the letter at this time or later is not clear. Earlier she had expressed a reluctance to send the counsel, because she knew there was no one to help Olsen even if he were to take a stand against the problem people.

Ten days later, from Tasmania, where she had just attended her forty-one-year-old son's marriage to twenty-one-year-old May Lacey, Ellen White felt the need to write to Olsen to clarify his apparent misinterpretation of her November letter. He had read it as an indication that he should step down. "I had no other idea than that you would be selected as President of the General Conference," she wrote. "Both Willie and myself understand your perplexities and difficulties." But it was her intense desire that Olsen would "not allow any man's judgment" to "control" him." She conceded that the November letter might have hurt Olsen. It had, in fact, been difficult for her to write as she had, she recalled. She had "nothing but the most tender, pitying sympathy" for him, and she addressed him cordially as "my brother." "It has been hard for me to give the messages that God has given to me for those I love," she continued, "and yet I have not dared to withhold it." In order to do so, she said, she had to make her face as "flint against the faces of those who set themselves so stubbornly to carry out their own way and to pursue their own unrighteous course."[27] It appears that she did not think Olsen was becoming one of the stubborn ones. Rather, she referred to what his associates were doing. But if the General Conference president could not see the harm caused by the "precept and example" of the two financiers, "I cannot hold my peace."

Olsen had been warned. He needed to act. But how? That was the question. To be in Battle Creek was inevitably to have to work closely with people such as Harmon Lindsay, the longtime treasurer of the Review and Herald and of the General Conference (1888–1893), and Archibald R. Henry, chair of the powerful General Conference Association and manager of the Review and Herald—people who had very prominent roles in church affairs. Lacking confidence in his own financial skills, Olsen found himself having to lean on both Henry and Lindsay. They had both been reappointed to leading institutional roles; both were successful entrepreneurs and good financial managers. As Richard Schwarz points out, Henry's skill had turned the Review and Herald from a losing printing business into one that now generated welcomed surpluses. Henry also understood the local legislative environment and had valued expertise in numerous legal issues the church faced, as well as in the practical details of institutional management. The denomination called upon him to give estimates on institutional development projects, and he had oversight of the church's relationships with the railway companies that provided subsidized train travel for church employees. On the other hand, it seems that Henry operated a number of private commercial enterprises on the side and had come to think principally in terms of profits and losses, seeking to wring advantage out of every transaction. Furthermore, he had a forceful, sometimes abrasive, personality and could readily dominate discussion in a committee. His influence was not such as to encourage the spiritual fruits of humility, generosity, patience, and meekness.[28] According to Ellen White, Henry and Lindsay had lost their spirituality, and their introduction of contemporary commercial philosophy and practices into denominational affairs was damaging the church. Unfortunately, as the nation's economic troubles bit deeper and the church's financial perplexities worsened during 1895, Olsen found himself having to depend even more heavily on the two men. As Schwarz observes, if Olsen had possessed a more forceful personality he might have profited by their sound financial knowledge while avoiding their "clever" deals and their commercial emphasis.[29]

A month later, Ellen White tried a softer approach with the perplexed president. Speaking "in confidence as a mother would speak to her son," she wrote about her fears for Olsen. He needed to avoid other individuals besides the two financiers. It was not safe for him to have to depend on those who were "not in a living connection with God." She could not understand him. "What reason do you have for putting so much dependence on A. R. Henry, Leroy Nicola [the General Conference Secretary], and others I might name?" she enquired.[30] "I fear and tremble for the souls of men who are in responsible positions in Battle Creek," she wrote. "I know that the enemy is using men who are in positions of trust, and who are not consecrated to the work and who know not what manner of spirit they are." She was becoming increasingly frustrated and worried about the drift of things in Battle Creek and Olsen's seeming inability to turn things around. "Wake up, Bro. Olsen, wake up," she pleaded with him.

Why was it so hard for Olsen to make the changes she had suggested? In September she wrote again, more urgently this time. "The present state of things has continued long enough," she protested. However, in one respect, Ellen White reflected, she was not sorry the problems had become so pronounced. At least the problems would enable Olsen "to better discern their true character before some other agent shall come in to preside over the conference in your place. I now beg of you to arise in the name of the Lord, and he will help you retrieve the errors of the past."[31] Was Ellen White suggesting that Olsen was about to let the devil himself take over the presidency of the General Conference? Or was she just advising him that if he did not do something to remove the problem associates in his administration, he himself would be replaced? Olsen was not sure. But it was clear that his association with individuals whom God was not leading was now becoming dangerous. "You accept as sound, the propositions of men who in some things start you on a wrong track." Just giving "sanction" to these propositions, gave them "authority and power."

Ellen White was seeing the future in increasingly darker hues, and Olsen sensed that life was becoming even more complicated and stressful. But what was he to do? How was he to take a strong stand and yet work with the existing organizational processes that regulated administration? Should he call a special session of the General Conference and hold new elections for the officers? Could he implement an impeachment process for failure of spirituality? Should he reconvene the stockholders meetings for the publishing company and the educational society that owned the college in Battle Creek and have the boards appointed again on the basis that Ellen White had identified some members as unsuitable for office? For that matter, how could he even state the reasons?

After the 1902 fire destroyed the Review and Herald publishing plant, George A. Irwin noted the difficulty of working with the church's institutions, because of the way that they were structured. "As you know," he wrote to Eugene Farnsworth about the relocation of the publishing house, "it is still a stock company and controlled by those who hold shares of proxies, so it is difficult to predict at this date what will be done." The direction of the company, where it would move, how it would do its work—all would "depend altogether upon the vote of the stock-holders."[32]

In October, Ellen White wrote Olsen yet again in even stronger terms. "I have now no words of sufficient force to describe the situation that has been steadily carried forward," she declared in frustration. As for the new book committee at headquarters that had just turned down Prescott's manuscript on the subject of the law and the Sabbath, it was so far from knowing what was of value and what was not, that she would not for a moment consider placing with it any book she might write. The committee had declined Professor Prescott's pamphlet manuscript titled, "The Law in Christ," because it supposedly contained "fundamental error." But she had heard him preach the very same subject and the very same theme at the Melbourne campground and knew that what he had taught was gospel truth. The book committee, in its blindness, was "following in the paths of Rome," she declared. Having the General Conference take over the Review and Herald Publishing Association "does not relieve the situation at all."[33]

Olsen, too, was wearying of the conflicting expectations being placed on him. Earlier in April 1895, when W. C. White had complained about the excessive length of time it was taking to get important actions approved through the Foreign Mission Board and the General Conference Association, Olsen had defended himself. He had not long before returned from an important but lengthy itinerary that had given him vital insights about the needs of the denomination and had helped him in processing important decisions at the General Conference. In fact, he noted, "for a long time" he had been "on the go continuously." It had been considered mandatory by his colleagues and by W. C. White and his mother that he make himself available to visit institutions and new fields and attend important meetings in the many state conferences, both to give counsel on problems and to study the development of the work in new areas. On the other hand, he argued, "It is impossible for me to do justice to the many lines of work and be traveling continually." The reason he had not been able to get things through the General Conference Association or the Foreign Mission Board in a reasonable manner was simply a lack of time. "To come before a board and start a question which has not received much careful thought or preparation" meant that the matters would not "receive justice under ordinary circumstances."[34] The members of the boards themselves were "all exceedingly busy men," occupied with the duties of their primary roles, he pointed out. To reach the right decisions on important issues, things needed to be thought through carefully first, and that required consultation. He could do it if he did not also have to travel so much. "I am much of the time unfit for doing justice to many of these important questions from the tremendous brain weariness that I have been laboring under," he conceded.[35]

The exasperation and irritation in Olsen's reply is noticeable. He was not sure how much to write to keep W. C. White informed. The General Conference president had written "a good deal" he thought, although it was "only a small portion" of what he might have. In this new term, Olsen had determined that he could not meet the overwhelming demands and that he would simply not travel as much. As a result, he reported to White that he had "taken a pretty firm stand on the matter not to be asked to be continually on the go." Instead, he needed to be able "to stop for a while, and digest that which I have gathered up." Only in this way could he adequately review "the plans, and study the workings . . . and bring these matters before the different Boards for decisive action."[36]

Compounding the problems for Olsen in late 1895 was the fact that one of his more dependable local associates, General Conference education secretary W. W. Prescott, had left Battle Creek for what became a ten-month visit to Australia and South Africa.

Prescott's experience thus far had been limited to a college presidency and education supervision within the United States. Both Olsen and W. C. White felt that broadening Prescott's experience would benefit the church. It would seem that Olsen may have been grooming Prescott for wider responsibility. Was he thinking of a possible successor? It was a good strategy. But on the other hand, Prescott's absence from Battle Creek exacerbated the difficulties arising from the weaknesses evident in Olsen's leadership team.

In early January Olsen wrote to Ellen White, asking whether she would consider returning to America. "It must be time for you to come nearer to the center of the work," he suggested, acknowledging that he was not able to get rested and that "perplexity and difficulty" continued until he was feeling "as it were, overwhelmed."[37]

Three weeks later he wrote to W. C. White, discussing the same problem. Intensely desirous of doing the right thing, Olsen had sent a letter to some of the leading administrators outlining the current difficulties. He also forwarded to them copies of the testimony addressed to them that had come from Australia. He asked W. C. White to inform his mother and W. W. Prescott of his actions so that they could be "fully conversant with all my moves." It was important that they were singing from the same page if the outcome was to be harmonious. Again, he lamented that due to the continual pressure of work he did not feel in any "fit condition to deal with intricate matters." And some matters were exceedingly delicate. The increasingly complex requirements for legal incorporation in Michigan and in other states and the implications these had for denominational institutions presented other problems. "Many times" Olsen did not consider himself prepared "to dare to touch some of these matters, feeling myself so utterly unfit to deal with them properly."[38]

Engineering a change

If Olsen could not adequately deal with such matters nor prevent the drift toward adopting contemporary business policies and practices in the church, who could? And how would the denomination implement such a change? Several months earlier, Ellen White had written that she did not want Olsen to have to bear all the responsibility, "therefore I will send this [letter] to others who should understand the situation, and help you." She assured him she would "watch and pray."[39] But that approach in exercising her influence had not seemed to work effectively. Mrs. White feared that the adoption of secular business philosophy and shoddy employment practices in the Review and Herald publishing house were beginning to permeate and pollute the whole of the church organization. It just had to be stopped. In March of 1896, she wrote possibly her most forceful letter to Olsen, clearly outlining the problem areas.[40] He received the letter on April 21 as he returned home from a series of appointments in the southern United States. The letter, along with some accompanying manuscripts, brought the crisis to a head. Immediately, the president again called a meeting of prominent administrators and the board of the Review and Herald and read the testimony to them. He met with the members of the group many times and had personally gone over the material, reading and re-reading the letters and manuscripts, trying to bring out the principles and understand the mistakes he and others had been making. As a result of these consultations, a new institutional board was elected. Olsen felt that he could say on behalf of its members "that there is a disposition on their part to do that which is the will of God, according to their best understanding."

The March letter reinforced for Olsen what he had known within himself for some time. As he read it, he realized that further leadership of the General Conference was not for him. Three days later he replied to Ellen White that "it seemed very clear" to him now "that the Lord does not want me to occupy my present position after the next General Conference, and that some other one should be selected to foll [*sic*] this position."[41] It was not that he "would shirk from any duty, or responsibility." He would be prepared to render assistance "in any place that may be called for," but in view of what she had said "some years ago about the time presidents should serve and in view of the magnitude and growth of the work . . . in every part of the world," and his "inadequacy to meet these things," he was sure it was the Lord's will for someone else to "take the place."

Olsen could think of no one so well qualified as W. C. White, he said in a letter to Mrs. White. Thus he felt free to "mention these things in just the way I do," because he realized the depth of her "intense anxiety for the work and her general knowledge of the situation." Writing to her, he said, "as mother in Israel," he realized that he could "appreciate only in small measure, the burdens, cares, and the perplexities" that she carried. These things "weigh you down and throng your mind continually." Furthermore, he knew that he had "failed greatly in appreciating the situation in all its bearings." It wasn't because he had lacked interest. He didn't want to offend her, nor did he want be misunderstood by trying to justify the situation, but he lamented that he could not write out everything he felt in order to "present every phase of the question so that the one reading it will not be misled." While he had much in his mind and heart, he could present things "only in the most fragmentary manner."[42] He "desired so much" that she consider attending the next General Conference session as well as W. C. White. "It will be a most important meeting," he concluded and signed himself, "your unworthy brother in Christ," a closing that he now used in almost every letter.

The previous day Olsen had also written to W. C. White, suggesting that he plan to come to the United States early, two or three months prior to the next session. Only with that amount of time, Olsen argued, could White prepare "to do justice to the meeting" and secure the outcomes they all desired. Olsen clearly informed W. C. White about his decision. "I have no idea that it will be my duty to serve as the President of the General Conference any longer." It was obvious to him that it was the Lord's will that "some other one should now be selected to bear this burden." And while, he said, it was not for him "to make any suggestions as to who should take the position," he proceeded to do just that. As he looked around for possible replacements (as he had also done two years earlier), he reported that he could see no one so well fitted to the situation as W. C. White himself. It seemed quite clear to Olsen that "it would be the Lord's will that you should be in a position to accept the responsibility at the time of the next General Conference." He was sure Willie would have the hearty cooperation of all the leadership. As W. C. White and his mother considered these questions they should give such an option "the most serious attention." While some might think it "all unnecessary for him to mention it in this way," Olsen nevertheless "felt it was right to express to you my feelings and convictions freely." Of course, the president did not "feel it proper to say this to everybody." So far, not only had he remained silent about it, but he would continue to do so. But he felt that it should be White's privilege to understand Olsen's feelings "and to appreciate the situation in its fullness." Although he believed that Ellen White would have additional light from the Lord on these matters, he still was "firmly of the conviction" that it was the Lord's will that there should be a change.[43]

In her March letter, Ellen White had been highly critical of Olsen's continuing reliance on Henry and Lindsay and of his assent to the strategies being adopted to resolve the financial situation in the Battle Creek publishing house as well as in the wider church. In April, she declared that the publishing house was under a deadly "malarious influence." There had developed "a confederacy" that was resisting her advice and counsel. "A spirit is and has been at work to make of none effect the voice of reproof and warning."[44]

A month later, her language and the tone of rebuke became even more dramatic. The publishing house, she declared, needed to be "purified from the buyers and sellers." It should no longer be "a den of thieves and money changers." In the institution "Christianity is sick, and needs a physician." And she also implicated the General Conference. Apparently referring to the powerful General Conference Association chaired by Henry, she alleged that the leaders were dismissing "the Holy Spirit from their Counsels, and then, under the power and name of the General Conference, they invent regulations through which they compel men to be ruled by their own ideas and not by the Holy Spirit."[45] They had adopted principles, she said, that "should never have seen the light of day." Then in a dramatic flourish of rhetoric to give force to her point, she added, "The illegitimate child should have been stifled as soon as it breathed the first breath of life."[46]

As General Conference president, Olsen held ultimate responsibility, and she personalized the responsibility for the church's failures. "The very position you have taken with these men in concocting plans to relieve the financial embarrassment, has made you in some respects a weak man," she noted pointedly. The denomination had no need of "crafty inventions to sustain the cause of God," she went on. "We need no unjust dealing. Let the Lord breathe upon his work the spirit of the heavenly principles, and it will live." Whatever strategies leadership might invent, nothing would "justify the violation of truth or a disregard for the rights of humanity."[47] Ellen White was still smarting over the enforced reduction of her own royalty rates and the close, sharp dealings the publishing house had with other authors.[48]

Still personalizing the responsibility, she wrote to Olsen that she had no confidence in "your" book committee. The business principles it employed were not "such as God can sanction." Moreover, Battle Creek's policies were spreading. C. H. Jones was being influenced to follow them. "In both houses [Pacific Press® and Review and Herald] a course has been pursued that is not fair and noble."[49] Olsen should have spoken up at the very first, but a "mist" had come over his eyes. On the one hand she was sympathetic. "We know that you have been placed in a very trying position." But on the other hand he could not excuse himself. "We know also that you have signally failed in some things." It was true that much of the problem was systemic and intractable. Olsen had to work with colleagues that others had appointed. But according to Ellen White, that was not enough to excuse his course of action. "You have tried to make yourself believe that this was the only thing you could do." But the truth was that he saw "little the extent and the necessity for the change which the Lord calls for." Ellen White was "more surprised" than she could express at his "failure to discern that God has not set up these men." The "new order of things" should have alarmed him "for it had not the sanction of heaven."[50]

It was now clear to Olsen that this was all too much for him, and it produced in him a spiritual crisis. It seemed quite clear to him that Ellen White was directly saying it was time he left office.

In her reply, which crossed with Olsen's earlier letter of response, she did not attempt to persuade him to rethink his decision to step aside. Rather she wrote in sympathy, but also reflected on the damage caused by his inability to bring about change in the organizational practices entrenched at the church's center. "I feel very deeply for you, my brother," she told him. "I hardly know just what I ought to send you." She had communications which she had written but had held for one or two years, thinking they ought not to be dispatched until "some one could stand" by his side "who could clearly distinguish Bible principles from principles of human manufacture." But it seems that no such person had come forward. Mrs. White was sorry that Olsen had not been able to implement her suggestions for change and that he had not regarded the warnings "as of sufficient value to be heeded."[51] It seems that Olsen did sense the seriousness of the situation, but figuring out how to change the system and how to override the regular electoral processes was difficult. It appears that at this time Mrs. White may have forwarded to Olsen a number of the letters and manuscripts she had written earlier and that he received them near the end of June. On the last Sabbath of that month, Olsen did not attend church with his local congregation in the Battle Creek Tabernacle. Rather, he spent the day quietly at home in Bible reading and prayer and re-reading a number of the communications he had received from Ellen White. For him, it was a spiritual crisis. As he reflected on his years in office, he was sure he had done what he thought was best under the difficult circumstances. He knew what was needed, but how to do it, given the structures then in place, was more than he could manage. It was not within his gifts or abilities. As he meditated and prayed and sought forgiveness for his failings, he was assured of his peace with God. At the end of the day, he penned to Ellen White a two-page handwritten letter of confession and despair. "I have greatly failed in everything," he wrote. "I can see nothing good. Every effort and work is sadly marred and cursed. O what miserable work I have made."[52]

Olsen tried to analyze what had gone wrong. "I have suffered much confusion of mind because of over-taxation and weariness," he noted, and had "acted on important questions when the brain was utterly unfit for clear thinking. No more fit for its task than a horse would be to win a race after having exhausted all its reserve strength on a long journey." He was deeply sorry that he had "done a great wrong to the work, to God, whose mouthpiece I was to be" and also to himself, "in not refusing to act under such circumstances." With the help of God he would watch these things more in the future. "I am so sorry," he concluded the letter, "that I have added so much to your care, your perplexities. I hope this too may be forgiven. . . . I felt after reading over a number of the letters this morning, I wanted to again express my feelings and desires."[53]

Having received his statement of resignation, Ellen White was not about to let Olsen simply bide out his time in office. In the remaining six months until the General Conference session he needed to accomplish specific things. "I want you to make it your first business to investigate . . . every man in that [Review and Herald] office; and to make it your special business to inquire of the youth who are employed there, in regard to their work." He was to "open his eyes wide to see what needs adjustment and correction." The treatment of the apprentices demanded urgent attention. She believed that the situation was so bad that she herself would not "under any consideration," send a child of hers "to learn the printer's trade under the present discipline and management in the several rooms."[54] Although she wrote the letter of instruction on May 26, 1896, and addressed it personally to Olsen, it was not until more than a year later, on July 25, 1897, that a committee of investigation began its work. The committee submitted its report to the institutional board fifteen days later. Why it took a year to implement the directive is not clear. But it is also not clear when the letter was sent or when Olsen actually received it.

Ellen White's instructions about removing Henry and Lindsay from office were also quite specific. But the church had no impeachment process and no system to deal with removing influential people from office in midterm. It was not simply a matter of Olsen being able to summarily dismiss a treasurer or the president of the Association or the manager of the Battle Creek publishing house. Boards had to make those decisions. And surely, Olsen must have reasoned with himself, Ellen White did not intend that in pursuing justice for some and rectifying wrongs, that the church should deny the treasurer and general manager the right to justice and a proper hearing. Normal practice would involve, at least, giving them an opportunity to reply to the allegations against them. Olsen was fully aware of these complications.

He had attempted to replace the two men at the end of 1895. He called the Review and Herald board together and read the testimony from Ellen White. Did Henry willingly resign or was he dismissed? It is not clear. But at a meeting of the publishing house stockholders in February, Lindsay secured the reappointment of Henry to the board of management of the Publishing Association by the careful use of proxy votes. Lindsay defended his action to the meeting. That led to an uproar among the stockholders who were aware of Ellen White's assessment of Henry. Olsen had to convene another meeting the next day to have the matter reversed.

The hubbub from the forced removals continued to reverberate around Battle Creek. On March 9, Olsen again called a meeting of the "leading brethren" and publishing house board members and read the additional testimonies he had been receiving from Australia. "The testimonies . . . have been faithfully placed before him [A. R. Henry] and the spirit of resistance which he showed at the first, has to a large degree left him. . . . Faithful work is being done with brother Henry," he reported to Ellen White. The General Conference Association met on March 9. At this time, Olsen was able to persuade Henry to tender his resignation from the executive committee. It was accepted, and a committee was appointed to nominate another person to the position. Olsen reported that in connection with the resignation, "the reasons for such a move were freely talked over."[55] It was not an easy or comfortable process in spite of his diplomatic efforts in trying to soothe Henry's feelings. The following year, Henry filed a civil suit against the General Conference alleging that Ellen White's letters about him that Olsen had circulated were libelous and had heavily damaged his reputation in Battle Creek. The Review managers filed a counter suit alleging misappropriation of funds, prompting further litigation by Henry claiming that he had been vastly underpaid during his fifteen years at the Review. Independent arbitrators determined that Henry had indeed been underpaid, but the Review declined to pay, and relationships became publicly acrimonious. In 1899, in an attempt at reconciliation, then-president G. A. Irwin invited Henry to attend the General Conference session at which a number of leaders asked his forgiveness for treating him in an un-Christlike way. This appeared to remove the hostility.[56]

It was not easy, however, to find competent and suitable people to replace Henry and Lindsay. Not until the end of 1896 did Olsen report to W. C. White that he had at last been able to secure the appointment of W. C. Gibson to the publishing association board and as secretary of the General Conference Association.[57] And despite having gone through the extremely painful process of replacing these two key figures, what had been accomplished? To achieve the sweeping change in values and philosophy that Ellen White seemed to be demanding, Olsen was sure that wider changes were needed. "You mention the names of Henry and Lindsay," he wrote to Ellen White in December, "yet it seems to me that merely removing these men would not accomplish the desired reformation. In studying the matter somewhat, it has occurred to me that a general change involving several persons and positions might be a step in the right direction." It was the only way that he could see of achieving a "break in certain combines."[58]

Securing a replacement

Having received Olsen's notice in April that he would not make himself available again for leadership of the General Conference, Mrs. White next set about trying to create a readiness for change among the church's administrators. She needed to prepare the church members and leadership to expect it. Furthermore, she wanted to make it clear that achieving the right outcomes as a result of such change was imperative. This was a highly sensitive task, since she did not want to undermine Olsen's authority or totally destroy his future usefulness to the denomination, and it would require the exercise of her pastoral gifts. At the same time, however, she did not want the status quo to continue, either. She knew that there were still many leaders who struggled to have full confidence in her counsel or who, at least, had difficulty understanding just how to implement it. Realizing that she must move carefully, she began to write to individuals in leadership who she thought could support change in the right direction when it came time.

For example, in August of 1896, she wrote to A. O. Tait, who was an assistant editor for Uriah Smith and whom she evidently considered a loyal supporter. "I have not written you much," she reflected about the recent past, "because I knew that that which I should write you would only increase your burden and intensify the painful feelings you must have, while there is no hope that you can in any way relieve the situation." She reported that she had written Olsen much about the situation. After telling Tait that she felt very sorry for the General Conference president and that Olsen had written back to her, thanking her for the "timely letters," she observed that he had "not acted upon the light." Mrs. White could not fully understand him. "The case is a mysterious one."[59]

In her letter to Tait, she alluded to the fact that she recognized that there were structural problems with the organization and that attempts had been made to try to fix things by taking steps toward re-aligning the denominational framework. But in her view such modifications seemed only to make matters worse. She described the organization as in "a sickly diseased state of things." But she stated to Tait that she was sure Olsen had given "unmistakable evidence that he does not regard the testimonies which the Lord has seen fit to give his people as worthy of respect or as of sufficient weight to influence his course of action." He had "ventured on, directly contrary to the light which the

Lord has given him" which had confused his "spiritual discernment" and placed him "in relation to the general interest" as an "unfaithful steward." As a result, she was "distressed beyond any words my pen can write." She was also concerned that she had not received any letters of response from A. R. Henry or Harmon Lindsay, which suggested to her that they did not respect her enough to reply. The leadership needed a total spring cleaning. "Many of the men who have acted as counselors in board and council meetings need to be weeded out," she asserted. "Other men should take their places." It was strong criticism, and what she wanted Tait to do with it she did not state. Evidently, she felt the need to build support for the case against Olsen and the need to find someone suitable to replace him.

In August 1896, Ellen White penned a general manuscript to church leaders on the same theme of the necessity for change. But it seems that the manuscript was not copied or circulated to key leaders until December—just two months before the session.[60] The manuscript commented on the systemic problem that made leadership so difficult for Olsen. "The president of our General Conference has been left to gather to himself burdens which God has not laid upon him, and the things that he has tried to do, could not be done wisely and well. The men he has connected with himself have been in character and principle, entirely the opposite of that which the Lord has specified." But the problem was broader than just the General Conference. "Many of the presidents of the several conferences do not answer the measurement of God." Without the molding influence of the Holy Spirit "they are unfit for the work, and should be dismissed." She urged replacement of presidents on a wide scale. "If the men who now bear responsibilities will not do it [follow God and His laws in their administration] then it must be committed to others." Much of the problem she saw as still flowing from the attitudes of suspicion and doubt manifested in 1888.

It seems evident that some conference presidents were still struggling with how to process reports and information that had come to them that, in their minds, tended to invalidate Ellen White's role and prophetic gift. She understood that quite a few had boldly stated that "they would not receive the testimonies." "In triumph they have declared," she reported, ". . . that many of our most responsible men have lost faith in the messages coming from Sister White." She regarded such individuals as part of "a strong confederacy."[61]

As Ellen White both saw it and experienced it from her situation in the South Pacific, the role and activities of the General Conference had become extended and some things had been made "unnecessarily complicated." As a suggested remedy, she advocated the idea that the church must avoid "one man rule" and that the organization might require more than just one individual to head up the administration as "president," if things were to be cared for efficiently. (Attempts to implement this idea later caused considerable confusion, and eventually it had to be abandoned.) She also proposed, in a radical challenge to the traditional nominating committee system, that in order to ensure that the leadership chose the right associates, "the president of the General Conference should have the privilege of deciding who shall stand at his side as counselors." Had Olsen been able to do so, it would have helped ease, at least partially, some of his difficulties. "He had the privilege to at least express his preference as to the men who should be his counselors . . . but a strange blindness came over him."[62]

It is interesting to note Olsen's response to the large amount of correspondence and manuscript material from Australia that arrived on his desk in August, 1896. He read it all "with care," but it clearly discouraged him further. Although the General Conference president was thankful for all of it and accepted its contents "heartily," he still felt grieved at "how greatly" he had come short in the work he had been given to do and resolved that he would act upon it "to the best of his ability." In the light of what he read, he now thought he saw and "understood some things" that he had not grasped before and was sorry that he had been so "blinded." Humiliated and ashamed, he acknowledged that he had "never before felt so unfit and so utterly incapable of moving forward and doing the work that needs to be done." Though "surrounded with exceedingly great perplexities," he did "want to do what is right . . . and I do want to be a faithful man that God may be honored and his work advanced." At times he felt so overwhelmed that he felt "there is but little hope for my future improvement." But he was resolved not to cast away his confidence.[63]

Olsen wanted to make it clear to Ellen White, however, that he had not been deliberately willful in his resistance or in the difficulties arising from the kind of colleagues around him. "When you speak of the underlying principles that have actuated some of these moves, I can truly say that I have not knowingly had any selfish purpose in my action as far as I know. But I can readily see that because of my blindness I did not see the bearing that certain things would have upon individuals and the work."[64]

In October, when yet more letters from Australia about the need for change arrived in Olsen's Battle Creek office, he took the opportunity to share them with the committee and board members attending the annual end-of-year council. They produced a good response, "a spirit of solemnity" and a "cementing together in union and in love." In the light of what had been sent, he now better understood Ellen White's references to the "Minneapolis spirit" and could see the danger that an apparently still unrepentant George Butler down in the south continued to face. He was beginning to feel more confident about there being a better atmosphere for the next General Conference session planned for early 1897.

Reflecting on the deep, dark waters that had threatened to "completely swallow" him during the previous several months, Olsen reported that he had passed through "an experience different from anything that I have ever had before." He wanted Ellen White to know that he had "always had the fullest confidence in the work of the message, and in God and his word. I have always accepted the Spirit of Prophecy, believe its position in the church, and cherished the instruction." But in the pointing out of his failures, he had "gained an experience" that he had not had before. As a result, he had taken the matter to God, had "expressed it to the brethren," had sought the Lord's pardon, and had "felt that acceptance of his love." In response, he had organized revival meetings with the church elders and leaders and with the managers and foremen of the Review office as well as other more general meetings. Olsen believed that there was a readiness now to "receive the testimony of the Spirit of God as never before." And on behalf of the General Conference committee and the members of General Conference Association, he could assure Ellen White "that we will do all in our power to second your efforts, and make your work as pleasant as possible."[65] It seems that the issues that had been a barrier to unity and progress had been resolved.

In her final letter to Olsen as General Conference president in 1896, Ellen White assured him that the Lord "understands all about the mistakes of the past," and that He would help him. Olsen had done a "sad work," but he should take care not to "repeat it." In later years, she continued to find herself haunted by Olsen's inability to confront the powers in Battle Creek. Late in 1897, as she was recounting matters to I. H. Evans, she observed that Olsen had "rejected" the trust given to him in reading manuscripts to his boards. Later, however, before sending the letter out, she changed the word "rejected" to "neglected." The change was significant. She wanted to be careful to note that the problem was one of weakness rather than an act of resistance.[66]

Lamenting the fact that it had been Olsen's unwillingness to demonstrate courage against the political maneuvering in 1891 that had led to her being sent to Australia, she recalled that she had written to him at that time, telling him that it was God's design that she should stand side by side with him, to counsel, advise, and move with him. If he had said, "I must have you, or I dare not fill this position," she would have answered the call. She suggested that had he realized then that he could not bear the responsibilities by himself, she would have returned from Australia, but he had not recognized his need. Thus "the Lord's ways were miscalculated and overlooked."[67] Such reflection after the event and in the light of subsequent developments illustrates again the inherent tension between administrative responsibility and the prophetic charisma. Ellen White clearly thought that she should have had a stronger role in the central leadership. But in any event, she would certainly not attend the 1897 General Conference Session with attitudes being as they were. W. C. White would come, but she would stay in Australia.

Finding a replacement for Olsen

In the months after receiving Olsen's April letters indicating that he would not continue in office, W. C. White and Ellen White each gave thought both to the process and to the candidates to replace him. The level of Ellen White's involvement is noteworthy. She was absolutely sure that her son was *not* the one for the job, even though Olsen thought so. Willie's role was to assist her with her publications. Besides, it seems that with diplomatic input from Prescott who was visiting Australia at the time, she had become more aware of the difficulties that her son had fallen into as president of the New South Wales Conference. W. C. White was, in fact, not a strong administrator; neither was he very competent as a financial manager. To return to Battle Creek to experience again the criticism and suspicion he had suffered in the years following 1888 was not at all to be considered, she argued. On the other hand, Professor Prescott, the General Conference education secretary and former president of Battle Creek College, was a definite possibility.

Prescott's powerful Christ-centered preaching in Australia had impressed both Ellen White and her son. His deep spirituality, literary and scholarly abilities, and his executive talents had also had a favorable impact on them. W. C. White had apparently regarded Prescott as a backup candidate for Olsen for some time. In response to Olsen's April letter, Willie recalled some things his mother had said five years earlier at the time of the 1891 session. She had made some remarks, he said, "about Bro Olsen and Prescott working together that made a strong impression on my mind." He recalled that "since that time whenever you have spoken of being relieved from the burden, my mind has turned to Bro. W. W. Prescott as the one whom the Lord was preparing to take the

Presidency of the General Conference, whenever the time came for you to have a season of release." His recent re-acquaintance with the professor, he commented, "has left me with a settled conviction that God is preparing him for some such work." At the time that Prescott was leaving Australia to return to America in mid-1896, W. C. White had indicated to him what he might need to prepare for. "You may be called upon to take more general responsibility in the work after the next General Conference session."[68] In fact, it seems that Prescott's extended visit to Australia and South Africa in 1895 and 1896 was not just to help the developing church in those regions. It would be a "most excellent thing" for the enlargement of Prescott's own experience, White had noted. It was clear that Prescott was being groomed for higher office.[69]

A day or two after receiving Olsen's April letter, Ellen White was so anxious about what was happening—and was likely to happen—in Battle Creek that she talked directly with Prescott about her feelings. She related that both Prescott and W. C. White endeavored to "dissipate her fears" and "presented things in as favorable light as possible." Their efforts, however, proved counterproductive. Instead, their calming assurances alarmed her even more. "If these men cannot see the outcome of affairs, I thought, how hopeless the task of making them see at Battle Creek." The realization struck her heart "like a knife."[70]

On the occasions when she spoke with Prescott about the problems in Battle Creek, she had sometimes done so in such severe terms that she had actually frightened him. After all, he was also a member of the very boards and committees that she so strongly criticized. But she felt confident that Prescott could help change things. She confided to him that she did not feel free to talk to W. C. White about these sensitive matters, because he was not in a position to be able to change anything.

In light of such discussions, Prescott decided it would be much safer for him at the next General Conference session to take an appointment away from denominational headquarters. He was also receiving copies of the letters and manuscripts that Ellen White was sending to Olsen and a wider circle of leading administrators. From what Prescott knew about the management systems that church leaders had inherited and developed, and about the difficulties these had given rise to throughout the denomination—as well as the perplexities that the boards and committees faced—he felt that he did not want to be "caught up again" in such a setting. "I feel that I cannot go back to the old regime and bind myself up with the same management any longer."[71]

Ellen White, on the other hand, had come to a firm conviction that Prescott would probably be the best candidate to be the next General Conference president. Just as he was leaving Australia to return to the United States, she indicated this to him in correspondence now lost.[72] As noted previously, W. C. White had also mentioned the possibility to the professor in order for him to prepare his mind to accept it. Of course, the outcome of nominating committee discussions and the wishes of delegates could not be predetermined. And this time Mrs. White was not going to be in America; thus she would be unavailable to the nominating committee should it wish to consult with her as it had at the time of the last change in the General Conference presidency. However, W. C. White was planning to attend.

It would have been unwise of Ellen White to have lobbied openly or to have stated publicly outside of the committee her recommendation for the person she thought it should ask to fill the position. That would have made the work of the session and its committees redundant and would have been improper in the extreme. Thus Prescott did not know how much to make of statements about his taking Olsen's place, but they were direct enough to cause him to start "thinking anew." He had "serious dread" about returning to America "to take up again, the work of Boards and Committees," and in light of the circumstances he did not feel at all that he was "prepared to accept such a responsibility." "I shall be glad of your counsel," he wrote to Ellen White from South Africa en route home. But she refused to offer any specific indication that he would be nominated. She sought to prepare his heart and mind for leadership, but she also realized the limits of her influence in such matters. She simply replied that he would know "what was duty" when the time came and that times of necessity were God's opportunities.[73]

However, Ellen White continued to send correspondence and manuscripts to Prescott, urging upon him the responsibility of trying to effect the much needed changes. Would he take the initiative in pushing reform and try to implement structural changes in the organization? Would he please find a way to ease the growing tensions in the church and help to solve the accompanying spiritual crisis? Prescott's response was to throw up his hands almost in horror. For some years, he had been seeking to implement reforms she had advocated in the education program at Battle Creek College. That had been a very difficult, slow, and dangerous process that had produced explosive reactions.[74] Prescott had become highly unpopular with his faculty and others in Battle Creek, although Olsen, close colleagues, and the church membership generally held him in great respect. "What can I do?" he asked despairingly in his response to Ellen White. He was sure the eschatological "shaking time" had come and things would collapse into chaos. However, he did give consideration to some possible alternatives in reorganizing the administrative systems and sent them to Ellen White for review and comment. She seems to have regarded them with favor and elaborated on the principles in reply. In response to her pleas, Prescott eventually assured her that when the opportunity came to initiate reform, he would exercise "whatever influence" he might have.[75] He complied with Olsen's request that he return to the United States in adequate time to be able to help plan agenda materials and prepare for the upcoming session. Thus Prescott arrived in Battle Creek in December, six weeks prior to the start of session proceedings.

As expected, Olsen was not re-elected at the General Conference session. It assigned him, instead, to direct the church in Europe. He spent a year in South Africa before taking up that assignment. But Ellen White's hopes for Prescott's appointment were disappointed. The outcome left her surprised and, it seems, chagrined.[76] The 1897 General Conference Session turned into a major debacle; its electoral processes fell apart, and key appointments were resolved only on the last day and from the conference floor. It was a session long remembered as one of the most difficult the denomination had experienced, highly charged as it was with confusion, uncertainty, and political overtones. In the end, Prescott was too much of a controversial figure to be elected as president, and the session passed him by.

CHAPTER 5

GEORGE A. IRWIN: A WAR VETERAN From the SOUTH

(1897–1899)

Civil War veteran turned Adventist pastor George Irwin did not go to the 1897 General Conference Session at Union College (Lincoln, Nebraska) with even the remotest expectation of becoming the denomination's next president. Although he had served as a district superintendent for two years, he was, in fact, an Adventist leader of very short and limited experience. But by the end of the session he was the new president. He was as surprised as were most others. This chapter will seek to explain how Ellen White's hopes for a different outcome from the election were disappointed and how a relatively inexperienced Adventist leader found himself elevated to the church's highest office. It will also explore how the new leader related to Ellen White and her emphatic letters of the 1890s. Her prophetic role in relationship to the new president's administrative style will also become clear.

Born in 1844 and raised on a farm in Ohio, George Irwin had forgone the benefit of a high school education when he volunteered to serve as an enlisted soldier in the Civil War. He had seen intense military action at Vicksburg (1863) and fought under General Sherman in numerous other battles across the southern states before being captured by Confederate troops. Then, while a prisoner of war at Andersonville, he had become a Christian at age twenty-one from reading Richard Baxter's *The Saint's Everlasting Rest,* given to him by a friend. After finishing out the war in the harsh conditions of Camp Libby near Atlanta, Georgia, Irwin was mustered out of the army in 1865 and immediately joined the Congregationalist Church, then later transferred his membership to a Methodist congregation nearer his home. The following year, at age twenty-two, he had married and established his own farm. During the next two decades as a Methodist, he had developed into a prominent leader both in his local farmers' organization, The Grange, and in the local temperance and prohibition movements.[1]

Irwin's conversion to the Seventh-day Adventist cause came in 1885 when he was forty-one years of age. Along with his wife and fifteen-year-old son Charles, he attended a series of evangelistic meetings held in the local schoolhouse built on a corner of the family farm, land which Irwin himself had donated for the purpose. After thinking about Adventist teachings for some twelve months, the Irwin family made its momentous decision to link up with the Sabbath keepers when a new team of evangelists came to conduct meetings the following year, this time in a neighboring town.

Two years after his conversion, Irwin received an invitation to pastor a small cluster of churches in the district near his home, and then during a troubled period among the congregations in Ohio, the state conference had chosen him to serve as its president. Eugene Farnsworth, who, with O. A. Olsen, was on the campground in Ohio at that time (1889) helping to deal with "the rather peculiar situation of things" in the conference, later recalled the circumstances of this first administrative appointment for Irwin. According to Farnsworth, "Brother Irwin was not a preacher; he was just a farmer." But Olsen and Farnsworth had observed him in action on the campground, and both agreed that Irwin would be the best choice from among the available ministers. Olsen had observed wryly that "the man that can pull off his coat and drive tent stakes all day will make a pretty good president." Farnsworth reported that "the only thing we knew about him was that he was all over the campground, looking after everybody and everything. It was that circumstance that placed him where he was."[2] Although he had no theological training or college study of any kind, Irwin was obviously blessed with strong spiritual gifts of pastoral and administrative leadership.

After Irwin had spent six years in Ohio learning the ropes of leadership and honing his people skills, his fellow administrators perceived him as ready to command a larger ship. Thus in 1895, he moved to Chattanooga, Tennessee, to serve as superintendent of District 2. A regional consultation mechanism rather than an administrative unit, it comprised nine southern state territories. But the appointment placed him on the General Conference executive committee and introduced him to wider church issues.[3] Overall, Irwin had participated in denominational work for a little less than a decade prior to the 1897 General Conference Session, and his pastoral and administrative experience had been rather narrow and limited. Ellen White was surprised at his appointment to the church's highest office and at first thought of him as but a "stripling" in experience. The action of the General Conference session of 1897 seems to have startled Irwin himself. It certainly turned out quite unexpectedly for him.

For W. W. Prescott, who went to Nebraska with "considerable anxiety," the session also turned out unexpectedly. In fact, as he recounted later to Mrs. White, his "experience at the Conference" was "very peculiar."[4] The 1897 General Conference Session was indeed unusual in numerous ways.

To start with, scheduling a General Conference session at Lincoln, Nebraska, in the heart of the midwestern Corn Belt instead of in Battle Creek was itself a novel concept. But the idea made good sense to Olsen, who had suggested it to W. C. White twelve months earlier. The denomination had established Union College in Lincoln, Nebraska, just seven years earlier, and it had good accommodation facilities. Railroad connections were excellent, and Adventists had become well known in the city. Holding a session there, Olsen argued, would be good for public relations. There would be the strong likelihood of attracting good press coverage if they met in Lincoln, and thus the session could also have a significant evangelistic impact. The town had some respected and widely read newspapers. Olsen figured that many of the reports from delegates "would find their way into the secular papers, and would be very interesting and profitable reading to thousands of people, and they might receive information with reference to this work and the truth of God for this time in a way that has not been opened to them before."[5] As it turned out, local newspapers certainly gave good and sustained coverage to the event with many substantial and detailed reports. Unfortunately, the headlines were not always of a nature that would make the church feel comfortable. But then the session itself, in truth, was not an altogether comfortable experience either.

Circumstances being what they were, convening the meetings in Nebraska presented logistical difficulties for the editors, proofreaders, and printers of the regular *General Conference Daily Bulletin.* The editor noted that he could not guarantee the same level of dispatch and freshness as might be possible in Battle Creek, but he did promise to "convey a faithful report of the various meetings, not only of the matters transacted, but of the spirit and interest that attends them."[6] As the chaotic events of the session unfolded, the *Bulletin* succeeded rather well in capturing the confusion, anguish, and anxiety as well as the spiritual intensity of the delegates. Reporters from the local newspapers, who were clearly sympathetic, also logged daily reports. They complement the information provided in the official bulletin and reflect, in perhaps a more unvarnished way, the real atmosphere of at least some of the meetings. The session and its difficulties made it into the headlines repeatedly. "From Prayer to Scrapping" read one uncomfortable header. "Sent Back for Revision" declared another that reported frankly on the hot opposition aroused by the nominating committee's report. According to modern marketing doctrine, even bad news is good news in terms of profiling the name of an organization, but in the end headlines in the local Lincoln newspapers may not have been the kind of media coverage Olsen had hoped for.

But, then, he had not known quite what to expect of the session anyway. Certainly he had been rather apprehensive about it as well as very sorry that Ellen White had not traveled from Australia to attend it. And he was not at all sure of what the outcome would be. Stephen N. Haskell, pioneering in South Africa, had anticipated a serious crisis and, like Mrs. White, had deliberately chosen to stay away. Prescott would have liked to avoid attending as well, but neither she nor Olsen would let him.

The conference session and its attendant meetings went down in denominational history as one of the longest, most confused and difficult sessions ever from an organizational perspective. It consumed the energies of the executive committee members and the leading administrators for all of a month and a half. The pre-session Institute meetings together with the formal session itself occupied delegates for twenty-eight long days.[7] Although Ellen White did not attend the meetings, her influence clearly permeated the entire proceedings. The delegates participated in long sessions of intense study and reflection on her many relevant letters and manuscripts. They sought to understand and to respond to her pointed criticisms and pondered long just what changes she was calling for and how to implement them. For example, the ten-day pre-session Institute set aside an hour each day for the public reading and study of her letters and manuscripts, and public readings continued during the session itself. Another daily meeting of similar length focused on reading and trying to understand how to apply her counsels on education. In midsession, an unscheduled, spontaneous, day-long meeting for study, prayer, and testimony reading replaced scheduled business. It concluded with a long session of confession and prayer. Debate and vigorous discussion and disagreement over leadership, organizational structure, and even session voting and appointment protocols snarled the passage of regular business for days.

Commenting on the impasse, the *Nebraska State Journal* observed that the delay in the nominating committee's report "practically blocks the wheels of all other business of the conference, since every other committee's work to a greater or less extent depends upon who are chosen to fill the important positions."[8] Both the *Daily Bulletin* and the newspaper commented on the lack of progress. The newspaper reporter observed at one point toward the end that it was difficult to say much "in reference to the proceedings," because the conference in fact "did not do very much proceeding."[9] Without knowing what kind of structure to adopt, the delegates had no clear understanding of what leaders to recommend.

Ole A. Olsen had not indicated in any formal public statement to the session that he would not stand again for office, but it apparently had become widely known that there would, indeed, be a change in leadership at the session. In his rather upbeat report at the opening of the session, Olsen gave a positive assessment of the rapid development that had taken place in the church in spite of the financial depression that had "brought many perplexities upon those who bear responsibilities." In an aside, he noted that "references to the universally prevalent 'hard times' have become so common as to be almost tedious." Then in a tangential way he acknowledged the background to the anticipated change in leadership and his desire not to continue as president. "Failures and mistakes in the work of God may generally be attributed to defects of character, or to a lack of knowledge of God's will which it is our privilege to possess."[10] Both had been specific problems for Olsen.

But the broader problem of administration in general was also an agenda issue. Ellen White's recent and repeated criticism of the quality of leadership appeared to call for a wholesale spring cleaning in the organization. She saw the leadership problems as widespread. "Many of the presidents of the several conferences," she asserted, "do not answer the measurement of God." The "malaria" of unbelief had infected many leaders. "If the men who now bear responsibilities will not do it [follow God and His laws in their administration] then it must be committed to others."[11] Troubles from the Adventist colleges concerning educational philosophy, the role of the Bible in the curriculum, and the appointment of educational personnel also spilled into the agenda for discussion on the floor and, according to Prescott, generated many "delicate" moments. In the end, the nominating committee did not know whether it was required to elect one president or three. It was thought that the General Conference should decentralize geographically into three or four constituent sections of equal standing. Thus the committee's key recommendation—a replacement for Olsen—was held hostage by the ongoing debate on decentralization right up until the final two days of the long session. Even then, accepting the nominating committee's recommendation caused "many hours of warm discussion."[12]

Ellen White's anticipation that Prescott would be appointed the new General Conference president went unfulfilled. He ended up being sent to England instead. Was she losing her influence? Had she not written to the right people and made herself very clear?

This was one occasion when Ellen White's considerable influence and people skills were insufficient to achieve the outcome she thought desirable. Admittedly, she was not present in person at the conference, a fact that undoubtedly diminished her strength in this area to some degree. Perhaps if she had been available "on the ground" to counsel with the nominating committee when it met, things might have turned out differently. Absence obviously complicated matters. While thoughtful consideration of possible candidates prior to a session was appropriate, direct lobbying was not, and thus this option was not available to her.

On this occasion, Prescott's own significant skills as a leader were also not enough to persuade delegates that he was the best person for the role of president. This is not to suggest, of course, that he actively campaigned for the position. Given the circumstances, it was not a role he even thought he could carry. Nevertheless, delegates and the nominating committee members would have been gathering their impressions as Prescott engaged in the to and fro of discussion as well from his preaching and the general attitudes he demonstrated while interacting with his colleagues. Those impressions were not the kind to persuade that particular nominating committee. What had gone wrong? Much indeed, if the account of the proceedings Prescott gave to Ellen White is to be believed.

Reflections of a failed candidate

It was not until August, five months after the session, that Prescott re-established his correspondence with Ellen White. Previously, he had written to her regularly and in return had received frequent valued letters and copies of articles from her pen. But in the months immediately following the conference, he had experienced "a broken up and busy time" in moving to his new field of labor and had not been able to write. By mid-1897, he was hoping "to make the connection again." At the same time, he asked once again to "be put on the list of those to whom you send such matter." If only he could see her in person, he said, he could talk "a long time about the experiences at the General Conference and of things which have happened since." But he was sure W. C. White would have kept her informed of the developments.

In fact, Willie White had not been able to return to Australia quite as quickly as anticipated and did not arrive home until November. Thus it was months later that Ellen

White got the full picture. Prescott had gone to England with what he saw as the "most signal evidence" of God's guidance in the matter. He was happy in the conviction that Britain was where the Lord wanted him to be for now. Battle Creek still had far too many problems.[13]

A month later, Mrs. White replied to Prescott's request to be put back on her mailing list and sent him a number of manuscripts. She expressed "surprise" that the General Conference session had sent Olsen to Africa, that "Irwin had been chosen as President of the General Conference," and that Prescott had ended up in Britain. It was not what she had expected or apparently thought was a good idea.[14] While she did not reflect on the episode in her writing, a number of questions do suggest themselves. Had she not made her counsels widely enough known? Had she not been forceful enough in making them? What else might she have done to achieve the outcome desired?

In the absence of an opportunity to have a personal discussion with Ellen White, Prescott ventured to write out his assessment and an account of "his own experience in this matter," although he said that he had not spoken of it much to others. Of course, he noted, this was his own reflection. He could not "speak for the others."

Prescott began his explanation by acknowledging that, following W. C. White's comments to him in late 1896, he "thought it might possibly be expected" that he "should be elected to take Eld. Olsen's place." But he did not feel "prepared to accept such a responsibility," which was why he had asked for Ellen White's counsel prior to the conference. He had taken at face value her assurance that he would "know what was duty, when the time came." The time, in fact, didn't come. Instead, he found himself feeling quite "peculiar" and uncomfortable.[15] Prescott thought he knew why.

The professor had gone to the conference charged by Ellen White to do what he could to help change things, but such a thing was easier said than done. He found out it was much easier to talk about change than to accomplish it. Right from the "opening of the conference," Prescott explained, "I could not feel in harmony with the way that things were going and protested earnestly against it." He tried to get delegates to understand that the longstanding practice of granting the incumbent chair of the executive committee the power to name all the standing committees that would serve during the session, including the nominating committee, represented a serious conflict of interest and actually prevented progress in making the kinds of transformation that Mrs. White was asking for.[16] Prescott felt it was better to have the session delegates themselves nominate the members of the plans and recommendations committee, the nominating committee, and other standing committees. Furthermore, he argued, the General Conference executive committee should cease functioning while the session itself was in progress, rather than following the current practice of continuing to exercise executive power even during the session.

Some interpreted Prescott's protest against the practice as an attack on Olsen himself and as a concealed pitch for office. "In some way there seemed to grow out of this a feeling that I was seeking Eld. Olsen's place and trying to crush him, while at the same time I dreaded more and more the possibility of being selected for such a place," Prescott explained. Delegates reacted negatively. As a result, Prescott's future work ended up being "very freely discussed." It seems that the liabilities he carried because of his support and advocacy of Ellen White's reforms had lost him much influence. Although the committee initially publicly nominated Prescott to head up the newly created European General Conference, delegates saw his lack of fluency in German, French, or Italian as a major handicap. The professor's expertise in Latin, Greek, and Hebrew would not suffice. The bilingual O. A. Olsen therefore became the preferred choice for this role. Returning him to the presidency of Battle Creek College was not thought desirable, he confided, "on account of the feeling against me by several of the teachers." And the presidency of Union College was not thought wise because "I did not have strong enough hold upon the people to arouse their interest and secure their hearty support." His advocacy of Ellen White's educational reforms had severely damaged him among the faculty at both places. Other supporters of her reforms sensed this and rallied to his aid on the floor of the session, but to no avail.

Prescott indicated to his colleagues that he was "willing to go anywhere and to do any work" that the Lord wanted him to do. All he asked was that the Lord "should guide in the matter." As things turned out, on the last tense, tumultuous day of the conference in an out-of-order nomination by E. J. Waggoner directly from the floor of the session, Prescott was "requested to labor in England." The resolution of the deadlock in this manner provided a mighty release to the pent-up tensions at the session and led the delegates to break out spontaneously in singing the doxology. Prescott took the unusual manner of his appointment "by direct action of the full conference" as a sign of the "special guidance of the Spirit of the Lord," because, he noted with some irony, the suggestion had not come from any of the "boards and committees" that Ellen White had so sharply criticized and condemned. "It would have been an encouragement" to both him and his wife, Sarah, he said, if Mrs. White "had expressed herself as seeing light in this move."[17] But she was far away in Australia. All he felt he could do was to move forward in faith.

It took some time for Ellen White to come to terms with the electoral outcomes of the 1897 session. She didn't think they had really changed anything or solved any problems. Nor, apparently, was she confident in her heart of hearts that George Irwin was really the man for the job. In mid-1898, almost a year and a half later, she still expressed the opinion that the General Conference was no longer the "voice of God." She was thus inclined to take things into her own hands and bypass its processes altogether, as for example, in pressing an invitation on Ellet Waggoner to work with her in Australia. In a letter to the charismatic editor, she reported that both she and W. C. White viewed his monthly *Present Truth* as "the best paper published by our people." She was clearly hinting that she had much more confidence in the London-based periodical than in the official *Review and Herald* in Battle Creek. "I hope that something will take place that will give me stronger faith than I now have in Battle Creek" she wrote, acknowledging again her disappointment that Prescott had not remained there in 1897 as General Conference president. She hoped that it was the "providence of God" that he was now in London. "I do hope and pray that the Lord will adjust the work so that 'proper ones' will take hold of it in Battle Creek," she lamented. In addition, she reported that she still needed to send "reproving messages for them [the leaders at church headquarters]."[18] While Ellen White was careful not to mention names, was she intimating that she did not think Irwin a "proper" president?

A day after her letter to Waggoner, Ellen White wrote to Prescott himself with an invitation for him also to come to Avondale for an academic term as president. In her letter, she reflected further on the recent developments in church polity. While the delegates to the 1897 General Conference Session evidently thought they were carrying out her counsel in bringing about a spring cleaning in the leadership, she understood things differently. The record clearly shows that church leaders had certainly tried hard to understand what she was asking and had prayerfully studied her counsels at length. And they had prayed for the leading of the Lord. But she expressed her conviction to Prescott that somehow the evil one had "snared things up." It was Satan who had worked with "deceptive, intriguing power to entangle everything in America," and thus "the work that you and others could and should have done has been made impossible." Time was short, and "the work which is essential" needed to be "done quickly." The evil one knew this and disrupted things. Furthermore, more recent actions taken at headquarters indicated to her that those serving in Battle Creek had "not yet learned their lesson." She was worried because "striplings, who have had but limited experience," had come to the front. This might be all right, she conceded, "if they have learned the meekness and lowliness of Christ." But, clearly, she was not sure. "I want you to know," she wrote to the exiled professor, "that we sympathize with you and with Brother Waggoner."[19] Prescott's opportunity to contribute at the highest levels of leadership at the General Conference would not occur until four years later.

Did Ellen White have any regrets about her decision not to return to America to attend the 1897 session? If she did, she did not confide them in her diary. In any case, financial circumstances had ruled out the option. What more could have been done? She was not inclined to say. But perhaps if she had attended, Prescott would have had a better chance of being elected and progress toward reorganization may have happened at a quicker pace. Perhaps the denomination could have established a renewed structure that more adequately embraced the medical program and thus pre-empted the later troubles with Kellogg. But maybe not.

George A. Irwin: Not a "proper" president?

If George Irwin was one of the "striplings" that Ellen White saw coming to the fore in 1897, at least he was a more mature sample at fifty-three years of age. But that didn't make his introduction to the life and duties of the General Conference president any easier. His initiation was something like a baptism of fire. Immediately following the session, a series of upheavals occurred in the numerous boards of the allied church agencies for which he was now responsible. For example, an intense political struggle broke out into the open for the control of the Battle Creek College board. This institution, like others, had been structured as an association, owned and controlled under Michigan state law by stockholders—church members and leaders who actually owned shares in the organization. The stockholders appointed the board of trustees. A group of anti-reform faculty members unsuccessfully tried to use the proxy voting system, practiced in stockholder meetings at the time, to accumulate sufficient shareholder votes to secure the appointment of their own representatives. Likewise, the election of managers and officers for the Review and Herald publishing company also became a highly politicized process at the shareholders meetings for that association. In the case of elections for the Review and Herald board, the appointment of a slate of members that included one or two new members was achieved only with great difficulty. The nominating committee had proposed both a minority and a majority report, and counting votes became very complicated. In addition, the formal inquiry into working conditions and general affairs at the Battle Creek publishing house that Ellen White had requested Olsen to undertake still waited to be done.[20] Meanwhile, the financial situation at headquarters continued to deteriorate rapidly until the situation became "quite distressing." The new president reported to Prescott three months into his first term that the church was living "from hand to mouth, so to speak." Some days, he noted, "we have not a dollar in the treasury." But Prescott knew this already. His own budget allocation for Britain, for example, had been savagely slashed from an annual $20,000 to $3,000.[21]

Irwin's economic anxieties were also heightened by a legal claim for $50,000 in damages that Archibald R. Henry had filed against the church two months after the 1897 session. The former church official claimed he had been libeled, that the statements about him in Ellen White's letters and manuscripts were harsh and untrue. But more problematic was his allegation that the public circulation of these matters—the public reading of her letters and the naming of him at the General Conference session and in other places—constituted nothing less than defamation.[22] Harmon Lindsay was also planning to initiate a lawsuit for damages against the sanitarium. Battle Creek, it seemed, was in complete turmoil. It was definitely not a place for administrators who were "striplings" or for those who were not "proper persons" to serve as leaders of the church. How would Ellen White adjust to this new set of circumstances? How would she now seek to exert her influence?

We find no indication that she or any of her associates sent a telegram of congratulations or a personal message of affirmation, assurance of prayers or support, or good wishes upon Irwin's election to office. But that may not have been unusual. People were extremely busy. At any rate, it was apparently not the practice. Irwin was at least half acquainted with Ellen White. He had met her briefly for the first time during the General Conference session in Battle Creek in 1891, six years earlier, just before she went to Australia. As the president of the Ohio Conference, he had also received a series of three short letters from her around the same time. A fresh, new church leader, he had been eager to meet Ellen White in person, according to Alta Robinson, and had "walked straight up and introduced himself" to her at the Battle Creek Tabernacle and then became so engaged in conversation with her that he walked with her to her home.[23] Evidently, the encounter did not stand out in Ellen White's memory. Following the brief exchange of letters in 1891, she had had no direct personal communication with Irwin for more than five years. His correspondence with her, which eventually resulted in his receiving thirty or more personal letters during his term of office, got off to a slow start.

In 1897, in his new role as president, he had to introduce himself to her again. Three months after his appointment to office he wrote diffidently to her: "I presume of course that you are aware ere this that I was chosen at the last General Conference as President of the General Conference in America."[24] His first letter was formal and rather stiff in tone as we might expect for an introductory letter. Later ones reflected more familiarity and personal warmth, particularly after he met her in person again during his visit to Australia in 1899.

In his first letter to Ellen White, Irwin indicated that he felt "very seriously" the burden of responsibility, that he desired "to move with caution," and that he was eager to receive advice and counsel from her. "I shall be glad to be a constant recipient of any light that the Lord may give you that you feel that I should have." He did not desire to place his own "mold upon the work of the Lord." Nor did he want "to pursue a headstrong course." Indicating an awareness of his limited experience and in deference to hers, he wrote, "I beg an interest in your prayers, that I may ever receive the advice and admonitions that your long experience in the work of the Lord makes you so fully competent to give."[25]

Irwin took the opportunity to update Ellen White on developments at the General Conference and, in particular, the problems arising from A. R. Henry's libel suit. He noted that the new leaders who had assumed responsibility at the Review and Herald office had now become sufficiently aware of Henry's past management practices there to feel sure that "everything that the Testimonies had said in regard to his manner of doing business" was substantiated. Henry's involvement in Union College finances was still a dilemma for them, because he was refusing to give up some of the accounting record books of the college "so that it is very difficult to know just the exact situation of things there." This was "something unusual in the experience of the body," Irwin observed.

Henry's allegations of the libelous use of the testimonies in the church clearly concerned both W. C. White and the church leadership. A small ad-hoc group, including W. C. White, was assigned to work through the problem. It seems that the committee was prepared to concede at least some legitimacy to Henry's complaint. The whole Henry lawsuit problem posed an ethical dilemma about the exercise of Ellen White's influence and authority.

Her influence, to be effective, surely needed to operate in an ethical manner. How could the church avoid the risk of problems re-occurring—problems such as reading names in public or circulating copies of letters without the knowledge of the person concerned? The committee discussed the matter of "the way the Testimonies should be handled hereafter." Some felt a better system was needed. Irwin reported to Ellen White that in the discussions "it seemed to be the unanimous opinion of the brethren that you be provided with the necessary help there in Australia to copy, put in proper shape and address testimonies to whoever in your judgment they might be sent." The committee thought that if this could be done, "it would avoid the possibility of any one individual to whom they might be sent, making a wrong use of them by withholding parts of them, or sending them indiscriminately." This "might avoid the possibility" of further suits being brought "as in the case of Bro Henry." Irwin reported to her that the General Conference committee was proposing to assign W. C. White to a full-time position with her for that purpose, and they would also ensure her other adequate clerical help.[26]

Naming individuals for their wrong decisions or attitudes in general circular letters sent to multiple recipients or in letters read publicly in churches or conference sessions, effectively focused the spotlight of attention on problems that Ellen White believed needed to be addressed. It was a practice that in the past had helped create strong motivation, if not an imperative, for making changes. Yet it could be an uncomfortable process both for the individuals concerned and for their colleagues. Sometimes the strategy led to a change in assignment for the person rebuked. At other times, the individual responded to the counsel and changed sufficiently to avoid further attention. But whether the transformation had been sufficient or whether the individual needed further remedial attention or the organization required further initiatives was not always clear, and in this matter the denomination could run into trouble. At the outset of the 1897 General Conference Session, for example, the delegates had devoted one hour each day to the public reading of Ellen White's letters and manuscripts. Although spiritually helpful, the process also posed an ethical problem that leaders were aware of and wrestled with—as A. T. Jones, who did most of the reading, noted at the beginning of the these hour-long meetings. Jones said that if a person had changed in response to a letter when it was first written or received, that individual need not feel bothered or threatened by Ellen White's counsel to him or her being read in public. But did everyone hearing the later public reading know that the person had altered course?[27] Often during his time in office, Irwin found himself wrestling with the problem of how to handle confidential letters from Ellen White about others.

In Ellen White's reply to Irwin—her first letter to him after his election—she made no reference at all to his new position or to the new challenges he faced. It was a cool businesslike letter. She simply acknowledged that she had received his June 6 letter on July 20 and then went on to talk about her work arrangements and to lament the quality of graduates that Battle Creek College was producing.[28] She stated that she appreciated Irwin's consideration in allowing W. C. White to connect with her fulltime in the "preparation of writings and book-making." But while she was "pleased" if it could be so, she was "not at all confident that this plan will be carried out." Drawing her son away from conference administrative duties might actually be difficult in practice, she thought. Thus she wrote that she "had another proposition to make"—bring Sarah Peck over from South Africa to assist in her editorial responsibilities. "I must have a lady worker," she stressed. A male helper spending time alone with her would not have been appropriate. She needed someone to sit with her who could read her letters aloud to her before sending them out to make sure that they said things correctly.[29] It was a problem that Ellen White increasingly worried about as the century drew to a close. As we will note later, her correspondence with Mrs. S. M. I. Henry at this time gave her the opportunity to reflect on the difficulties she faced.

In his next letter to Ellen White, written three months later, Irwin reported that he had been able to fulfill her explicit instructions directed earlier to Olsen about the need to conduct a thorough investigation of the working conditions in the Battle Creek publishing plant. Olsen had not been able to implement it earlier because of time constraints, although some may have thought that the delay had been related more to a general resistance to following through on Mrs. White's counsel. But that would be an unfair assessment. The matter had achieved greater urgency, and it was important for the new president to fulfill the request if he wanted to maintain good relationships with Cooranbong.

The Review and Herald publishing house was clearly under stress as it struggled to cope with the financial recession. It had ample work, however, and the pressrooms often ran twenty-four hours a day. However, as noted in management's report to the recent General Conference session delegates, the institution had very little financial surplus. Operating margins were exceedingly thin. Foreign language books published on behalf of and by order of the church had small circulations and therefore ran at a considerable loss. In fact, more than half of the material manufactured by the plant went to the church's branch publishing houses or to the General Conference itself, and by agreement, no margins were to be charged against such work. The publishing house was to supply these at cost. Operating the plant in a financially viable way was thus evidently a major challenge. But that was no reason for poor management of employees. The task of investigating working conditions at the plant took the panel almost three full weeks. Irwin, who was a panel member, reported that they had "found very many things that were not right" nor "in harmony with the principles of justice and equity." Nearly all of these situations, he noted, had occurred under the previous administration of A. R. Henry. The new General Conference president was convinced, however, that the present management was "endeavoring to do what is right," although there were still "things yet that need to be corrected" in order "to meet the mind of the Spirit of God as revealed through the testimony." But at least "quite a good work has begun."[30]

In the balance of his letter Irwin shared items of general news. Clearly, he intended to keep in touch with Ellen White. He reported that her suggestion of a call for Sarah Peck had been approved, and he noted that he had written to O. A. Olsen in South Africa about the matter. Also he commented that A. F. Ballenger and A. T. Jones had recently been preaching in the Battle Creek Tabernacle with good effect and that the Battle Creek congregation had responded well to a recent testimony from Cooranbong. After mentioning that A. T. Jones had been appointed as the new editor of the *Review,* Irwin then (almost as if thinking out aloud) mused about what other points of interest he could mention. The new General Conference president seemed determined to strengthen his relationship with Ellen White.

By now Irwin felt confident enough to correct her on one issue in which she had been critical of the Review and Herald staff in what he felt was an unjustified way. The episode illustrates in a simple way that the interaction between the gift exercised by Ellen White and the gift of administration exercised by Irwin was not one-directional, flowing only toward Irwin. The issue concerned the handling of aspects of Stephen N. Haskell's financial affairs that Ellen White seems to have elevated to an issue of properly respecting the pioneers. "I noticed in your letter which you wrote to the Review and Herald," Irwin said, "that you spoke about the matter of Brother Haskell's audit and settlement of account, and rather felt to censure the young men here in Battle Creek who had dealt with his account in the way that they had, expressing yourself that you thought we should honor these old veterans." Irwin noted that he certainly appreciated the point and believed that "we should and have always been careful to do so." But he felt the clerks in the office had been unfairly blamed and needed to be defended. "I would like to say that the young men who have come into the office are not at all to blame for Elder Haskell's account." He explained that W. H. Edwards, the former publishing house treasurer and now the General Conference treasurer, seemed to have taken it on himself to make arrangements for Haskell's account, or allowance, without consulting anyone else. "Upon inquiry," Irwin went on, "I find that the incoming treasurer, Brother Adams, or the secretary, or anyone of them had not anything to do with it." Then with a touch of delicate irony, he noted, "We find upon enquiry that your son Willie took Brother Haskell's account, saying that he would see to it." Respectfully and diplomatically he concluded, "So I just simply write this to you to disabuse your mind on any intention on the part of anyone here to in any way distress Brother Haskell, or to show him disrespect, because I feel sure that all of these younger men who have come into the work, have the greatest reverence for the pioneers."[31] "Striplings" they might be, but they, too, needed care and nurture.

Irwin threw much of his energy and skill into implementing the significant organizational changes introduced with such high hopes at the 1897 session. He spent considerable time visiting the five United States district conference session meetings, advising and counseling, but they nevertheless continued to be preoccupied with theological and pastoral concerns such as evangelistic training for pastors and church members. Events proved that Irwin was no more successful than Olsen had been in moving the district organization structures into genuinely autonomous administrative sub-divisions. Only overseas in Europe and in Australasia did the union conference concept begin to take effective shape.[32] Furthermore, the relocation of the Mission Board to the east coast, as Prescott had earlier warned during the discussion of the matter at the General Conference session, added only confusion rather than efficiency to its work. And overall, in spite of the fact that the central administrative leadership had been divided up so that Irwin, as president, was no longer responsible for chairing the Publishing Association, the Tract Society, or the Foreign Mission Board, he still needed to be involved and informed and thus seemed to be as busy and as pressured as ever Olsen had been. The church was probably worse off, rather than better off, as a result of the 1897 changes. The continuing problems indicated that the system of church organization itself was as much at fault as the people who had to run it.

Irwin's difficult experience at the annual spring meetings in Battle Creek during his second year in office confirmed this for him. He reported to Prescott at the close of the council that intense politicking had again disturbed the annual stockholders meeting of the Review and Herald board. The session had spent much time considering the settlement recommended by the arbitrators for the A. R. Henry lawsuit, and there had been "strong influence brought to bear" in an attempt to unseat W. C. Sisley as chair of the board. Sisley, an architect and builder who had been of great value to the church in designing and supervising the construction of many denominational buildings, had been appointed to replace A. R. Henry in 1896 as manager of the Review and Herald publishing house in response to Ellen White's pressure for change. Apparently misunderstanding her complaints about the publishing house leaders and thinking that she had Sisley in mind, people now thought that he was not a "proper" person for such leadership, either.

Even greater trouble arose in the meeting of the Battle Creek College stockholders, with a more intense repetition of the previous year's efforts by the faculty group opposing reform. This time the rebel faculty successfully managed to secure control of the board through use of the proxy voting system. They removed Sutherland, the college president, from the board along with J. H. Kellogg, the other reform-minded board member. The problem was righted shortly afterward, Irwin reported, and the opposition enjoyed only "temporary success." But he certainly realized the depth of the problem. Subsequently he had convened several meetings of his colleagues to discuss further plans for reorganization. It was the money-based voting power prevailing at stockholder meetings that created the perpetual contention, he argued. During the next twelve months he devised a new system for the election of leadership at stockholder meetings that he hoped would see "the last of this cumulative voting and a few men thwarting the will and desire of the majority."[33]

In a revealing aside to Prescott, Irwin indicated he was not overly enjoying his experience at church headquarters. "Battle Creek is a very trying place in which to live and be connected with the work in a general way," he wrote. "I certainly do not blame anyone for getting away from it if they do so without seeming to run away from duty." He could give "but little idea" in his correspondence but "after having passed through these meetings and seen the spirit of opposition" he "felt to dread the thought" of having the next General Conference session meet in Battle Creek and commented that a camp-meeting type format in some rural location would be much more preferable. Perhaps, he suggested, it could be held at a site on the Potomac near Washington, D.C. To convene it elsewhere would, at least, enable the church to get free of "the disturbing element that we would be more likely to meet in Battle Creek." Things were so bad, Irwin feared, that if "the spirit increases and intensifies from this until another General Conference as it has from the last to this spring council, a General Conference held in Battle Creek would be a disgrace to the cause."[34] Irwin was clearly frustrated. But as it turned out, the 1899 General Conference Session did not take place at a camp meeting site. It did, however, meet away from Battle Creek, at South Lancaster Academy in Massachusetts.

In the meantime, Irwin himself had had an opportunity to get away from Battle Creek for a while, making a visit to Germany to participate in the European Union Council held in Hamburg, July 8–14, and taking time to visit Prescott and denominational projects in England. This was Irwin's first visit overseas, and it helped to broaden his perspective as he met with Olsen, Prescott, and other European leaders. Working with ten different language groups at the Hamburg conference and coping with their need for simultaneous language translation during council proceedings also exposed him to the enormous challenges of the task of mission beyond Battle Creek.[35]

I. H. Evans, the president of the General Conference Association, concurred with Irwin in his assessment of the organization's systemic problems. The experiment with decentralization and the breaking up of supervision functions was not working at all well. "The facts are, that no one can ever know the sad condition that things are in here on this side," he observed to Ellen White in early 1899. "Even we, who pretend to be in the light, cannot agree on many things among ourselves, letting alone those who are disaffecting and sowing discord. What we need at the present time is unity in our midst. There is a prevailing feeling that every man should do as he pleases."[36]

From Ellen White's perspective, general church affairs continued to deteriorate in spite of the substantive personnel changes in boards and committees and in church structure that occurred in 1897. The need for an organization that was genuinely in touch with, and able to respond quickly to, the needs of distant areas such as Australia, South Africa, England, and Europe was imperative. "The General Conference—what is it?" she challenged in utter frustration in an 1898 manuscript. "What does it comprehend? Is it a General Conference, or is it something wrapped up and called by that name?" Struggling desperately to establish the school at Avondale and coping all the while with agonizing financial and personnel restraints, she questioned why everything had to be controlled at the center. Why was it that the leaders wanted to "bind about the conscience of another"? Recalling what had happened to Prescott and Waggoner, she observed that "in the present condition of things, if one stands fast to his integrity, he is by some scorned, scouted, criticized, and dropped out if it can be brought about."

The current administrators were no more qualified to lead "than are the children to guide the steamships over the broad ocean."[37] Such criticisms no doubt stung Irwin, but there was little he could do except to work with the system already in place and try to perfect it.

Toward the end of 1898, sensing the seriousness of the situation and the continuing deterioration in the organizational culture in the church, Irwin strongly requested Ellen White to attend the 1899 General Conference Session. As the year progressed, it is clear that the relationship between them grew warmer at the personal level. The correspondence involved more exchange of items of personal or family news, sharing of feelings about things, and warmer salutary greetings. She signed one letter "Your sister in the blessed hope" and another "In love to you and yours."[38] Later in the year, she sought Irwin's help in recovering some of her money that had become caught up in a complicated misunderstanding and dispute involving the sale of a church property in Chicago. The money was meant to have been transferred to her through C. H. Jones in California, but others had laid claim to it en route.

In December 1898, Ellen White replied to Irwin's invitation to come to the United States with a firm *No.* Just a few days previously, she had turned seventy-one, she said, and was no longer young. But that was not the reason she would use for not returning. The real difficulty was that she was right in the middle of the struggle to get the Avondale school firmly established, scratching desperately to find appropriate faculty and enough money to complete the buildings in the face of a doubting membership and a reluctant local church leadership. "Unbelief, and 'you can't do it,' and 'It is impossible,' have met us at every step" in the development of Avondale, she said, "and still we advance." She could see no alternative but to remain at Cooranbong "until the work is placed on a solid foundation."[39]

Another factor behind her refusal to come back to the United States was that she now had assembled an excellent team of editorial assistants and was loathe to have that broken up. But it was the lack of finances in particular that prevented her from returning in 1899, she pointed out, and the church in America was to blame. "Could we have had the means that has been used up in different ways in America, we could have advanced the work, and have it placed where we could have responded to your call. But not now."[40] She particularly explained that she personally was too heavily in debt to "feel at liberty to leave" and make the journey at that point. She had personal loans amounting to about $25,000 that she had assumed in order to finance projects in Australia. The amount was not small. To pay it back using her total annual salary would have taken thirty-one years. She was not sure how the debts would eventually be repaid, but she was sure that in God's providence "every one [would] be settled" in time.[41]

Aware that Ellen White had criticized his own leadership and that he was up for re-election, Irwin sought her prayers on behalf of the General Conference session "that the Lord may overrule every evil influence, and that the right persons may be chosen to lead out in the work of the coming 2 years." The church's election processes and the appointment of the right personnel had become a very difficult issue.

Finding the right balance in the organizational structure between efficient, centralized coordination and effective delegation of administrative responsibility was also proving exceptionally difficult. Ellen White's strong emphasis on decentralization had begun encouraging important institutions such as John Harvey Kellogg's sanitarium to conclude that she favored more autonomy and independence—something that, of course, appealed to Kellogg's own ambitions. But this created headaches for Irwin and his colleagues. As the year 1898 neared its end, Irwin began to fear that the church would fracture into completely separate and autonomous entities. Kellogg, for example, had begun to keep the institutional tithe from sanitarium activities and was using it exclusively for sanitarium programs. He was also proposing to have a parallel but totally separate institutional constituency meeting at a different time from the General Conference session. His Medical Missionary Board would meet in Chicago, and its members would not need to go to the General Conference session at all. Irwin felt that such a practice "would work harm," and he counseled Kellogg against it.[42] Nor did Mrs. White see it as a good way to proceed. But others thought it was in harmony with her strong criticisms of centralized control.

Prescott arrived in Battle Creek prior to the 1899 General Conference Session and joined A. T. Jones in conducting revival meetings at the sanitarium. Irwin feared that Prescott and Jones were both running to extremes in the area of decentralization; for a time he even thought they might throw their influence behind Kellogg's drive for autonomy. In an interview he had with Prescott at this time, Irwin took the opportunity to read him a recently received confidential warning from Ellen White about Kellogg's growing independent streak. Prescott indicated that he would try to modify his teaching and shape his preaching "to impress a unifying of the work in all its branches."[43]

"We as a people are so liable to go to extremes on, well, almost everything," Irwin continued in his complaint to Ellen White. "When the testimonies came two or three years ago, speaking about arbitrary authority," he reflected, "and these testimonies were given quite a publicity [*sic*] at the last General Conference, then it seems that the opposite turn came in." Since then, he noted, "there has been more or less of a spirit of independence on the part of institutions and conferences, that, it seems to me, will work harm." Irwin was clearly struggling to keep things unified. His great burden, he said as the session approached, was for "union in the work." This could not be achieved by legislation or anything of that kind, he believed, but it must be upon "the great underlying principles of the truth." He saw the need for a more moderate position.

"The medium ground between the two extremes, it seems to me, is where the truth lies. The Lord wants organization and systems in his work: but he does not want that organization to be arbitrary, and dictatorial, and binding; neither, on the other hand, does he want our work to break up into little independent integers, and thus give the devil an opportunity to come in and separate and divide."[44]

Ellen White did not let up, however, in her criticism of centralized leadership. In a letter that crossed Irwin's in the mail and was addressed to the church leadership in general, she was quite specific about the upcoming elections and the outcomes she expected. She reiterated her previous counsel that the Lord did not design "that one man shall carry all the responsibility." In the past, she alleged, "Satan had commenced his work in Battle Creek through men who occupied important positions in God's work for they had no correct sense of its sacredness." Even though she herself had been a delegate at the sessions she was referring to, nevertheless she went on to state that "careless work" had been done "in the selection of men for certain positions in the church." As a consequence, she advocated a further replacement of problem personnel. "The leaven of fraud and injustice brought in because of their course of action has not yet been purged from the work." Testimonies had been given, but "notwithstanding this, men have been retained in office who were not worthy."[45] She did not name anyone explicitly, although she clearly had in mind specific individuals.

If mentioning names had previously led to the charge of libel, not doing so now led to confusion and appears to be the background to the renewed attempt by some to have W. C. Sisley removed from the Review and Herald board in early 1900. A. T. Jones, who led the move against Sisley, thought he was carrying out Ellen White's intent. Sisley thus got voted off the board and out of office. Later, Ellen White had to explain to Irwin that Sisley was not one of the leaders she had had in mind. Since he was now free, however, he should at least be available to help with the building of the sanitarium in Australia.

Sisley himself was rather confused and hurt by the process and, according to Irwin, was apparently not prepared to move anywhere until Ellen White had re-endorsed him.[46] Again, the cumbersome electoral processes and the statutory requirements regarding the governance of the various organizations (which in some circumstances set specific legal criteria for membership on the boards involved) made Mrs. White's recommendations difficult to implement, even if it was clear to senior leadership to whom she might be obliquely referring as unsuitable.

As already noted, at other times Ellen White could be quite specific and outspoken in naming an individual. And she could be extremely frank both in her assessment of a person's fitness for a presidential appointment and in her denunciation of the individual. For example, she thought that the appointment of H. E. Robinson to lead the denomination in England in 1896 was almost insane. "I thought I could not have heard aright," she remarked to Olsen, "and then when his work was laid before me, with you to strengthen it, I thought indeed your eyes must have been put out." Her objection to Robinson's appointment related not only to his own ineffectiveness but also to his wife's lack of spirituality. "His wife is unconverted, unsanctified in tongue and in heart and is a channel of darkness. Her influence is bad and only bad continually." She had made these observations to the Robinsons publicly in New York, she reported, while in a meeting "in a hall full of people." At that time, she recalled, the power of God had come upon her "in a marked manner," and she had given her testimony. As things presently were, she was not prepared to call Robinson's wife "a sister even, because her spirit and works forbid I should do this."[47] Whether Ellen White later changed her assessment of the couple is not clear, but they served in effective pastoral work for many years afterward.

The 1899 session

In his presidential report at the 1899 General Conference Session, which convened February 10 and ran until March 1, Irwin reported on the difficulties he had experienced in implementing the reforms voted at the previous session. He had not, for example, been able to establish formal "union" administrative structures. Apparently, the primary difficulty standing in the way of such reform was a lack of agreement over how to divide the spoils. "The carrying out of this recommendation," he reported, "with its consequent division of territory and separation of funds that had formerly been operated under one management, consumed time and entailed many perplexities that were unseen and unprovided for by the conference." He acknowledged that some ill-feeling had arisen and that although there had been "no serious friction thus far" there were "questions that needed the careful and prayerful consideration of the delegates." Simply decreeing or demanding change did not actually achieve it. It was all much more complicated than it seemed.[48]

Irwin had done his homework carefully and had gone to the session with a number of items on his agenda of difficulties. These included the question of how to provide for the immense indebtedness that existed in the General Conference Association and also the need to define more clearly the relationship between the various boards, associations, organizations, and institutions. The whole structure needed a revamp.

He had a clear grasp of the problems, but what were the solutions? Which model of governance would be best and also be theologically appropriate? On that he was not so sure. Other items that he listed for the conference to address included: funding the development of the church in the southern states, the translation of Ellen White's books into foreign languages, the expansion of the door-to-door literature sales system, the lack of good candidates for ministerial training, how to achieve better foreign mission support, and the idea of lengthening the term between General Conference sessions from two years to four years. The latter item, though discussed at some length, went nowhere. Structurally the church was in too much difficulty to afford a four-year term before the problems could be fixed. But at least Irwin was intentional and clear about the problems and the challenges ahead.

The 1899 General Conference Session achieved at least a small step toward preserving unity and diminishing the political infighting involved in the elections for the institutional boards in Battle Creek. Irwin's new plan involved having the General Conference in session appoint twenty or thirty electors who would then, in turn, select the various boards of trustees. But the 1899 meetings accomplished little else in the way of structural reform. As Richard Schwarz observes, delegates were not yet ready for a major overhaul of the machinery. They had no clear consensus on what the future structure should look like. But they were certainly ready to point out mistakes in the existing one.[49] And that was probably to be expected.

According to classic change theory, a first important step in unfreezing the status quo in an organization is for everyone involved to understand and agree on the problems and the inadequacies of the present arrangement. In hindsight, it seems clear that the 1899 session became focused on this stage of change management—although there was actually not much management of the process involved. Prescott and Jones were particularly vocal throughout the session in identifying structural problems and advocating the need for overhaul, but the delegates often perceived their ideas as a threat and as having the effect of "tearing down" rather than "building up."

Irwin, on the other hand, feeling keenly the pressure coming from Kellogg with his intention to make his medical institutions and health programs independent of the church, reacted in the opposite direction by emphasizing the need to hold the present lines as firmly as possible. In a series of talks he gave at the session on the topic of organization, Irwin stated that he had studied the church's formal constitution documents in preparation for the conference and that he was pleased to find that only five words had been changed between the present constitution and the one first approved in the 1860s. "I believe the Lord was in the framing of that constitution," he remarked, "and that we would better let that constitution go on to the end, rather than begin to tinker with it and abolish some portions of it." J. N. Loughborough, the oldest of the pioneers at the session, affirmed Irwin's position. He and Uriah Smith had been members of the committee that drafted the document after "more than half a day of solemn prayer to God," he remembered. "God was in it, and if God was guiding then, I do not see why we should tinker with it now."[50] Citing strong statements from Ellen White about not moving pins from the platform, Irwin gave the impression that the organization was not to be tampered with. It seemed almost a reactionary stance.

On the other hand, Prescott—along with Jones—seems to have led the charge for reform, although his ideas were often cryptically expressed and rather idealistic and theoretical. They were not easily understood or grasped. Furthermore, he caused considerable embarrassment among some delegates early in the conference when he asked probing questions directed at bringing out into the open a major case of financial mismanagement. Problems needed to be understood, he argued, in order to find the right kind of solutions. He argued that this financial mismanagement situation was the very kind of ethical problem that was badly hurting the church. In this case, church members had apparently made private donations to Ellen White for her projects in Australia, and church treasury officials, when they heard of it, had taken the opportunity to subtract an equivalent amount from the official church funds assigned for her work. The shortfall contributed to the exacerbating of her financial distress. For Prescott, this was an example of "officialism" and of the organization coming between God and His people. It may have occurred only once, but he feared that it could be a problem that had not totally vanished from the church.

The raising of the financial mismanagement issue led to much discomfort and an extended discussion about church and mission financing. It highlighted many of the inadequacies in policy and practice. In succeeding meetings A. T. Jones read an August 1898 letter from Ellen White making an extremely serious criticism about the General Conference. The presentation, one he was reluctant to undertake but which the delegates had urged upon him, brought into the open a statement that Mrs. White had frequently made—that for several years she had not regarded the General Conference in session to be "the voice of God."[51] No one previously, it seems, had felt brave enough to discuss such a strong criticism in a public forum. Following the reading and a lengthy exhortation, Jones called on Irwin by name along with treasurer, L. A. Hoopes, and Foreign Mission Board president, A. E. Moon, and the whole of the executive committee to come forward in public repentance of such actions and attitudes. The extended meeting became a prayer session with prominent administrators offering twelve lengthy prayers of confession.

Irwin, using the language of corporate prayer, confessed wrong attitudes and his shame and shortsightedness. "Could we do so we feel like running away," he admitted. Not only was he "willing to be separated from" the work if necessary, he was also willing "that anything should come" if only the cause of God could prosper.[52] Then he publicly apologized to the delegates because he had not "shown the right spirit" when his colleagues had not done "just as I thought they ought to do in different things." He had been "cowardly about taking hold" of some of the difficult things that needed confronting and "called by the right name." Furthermore, he acknowledged that "when I saw some of these things and the influences that surrounded them, I have shunned duty." But he did not mention any specific details.[53]

The prayer meeting did not immediately solve the organizational problems, but it did help to create a closer fellowship among the administrators. On March 2, the session re-elected Irwin for a further term as president when the delegates voted on the nominating committee report just before the end of the session. Delegates could sense that light was slowly breaking in, but major reform was still a long way off.

Much of the discussion and misunderstanding at the 1899 session concerned not only a lack of clarity about what should be done to refine and renew organizational structure, but first, how to actually unfreeze the status quo. That had now partially been achieved. But how, then, should the church make the transition to a new structure? How could it even get to the point that delegates could be free to envision a new structure and begin to construct it? After all, Ellen White had not cited any particular model of organization, and many of her comments primarily concerned individuals and their weaknesses and the consequences of the current inadequate arrangements, rather than concrete suggestions of specific alternatives.

Prescott was convinced that the General Conference president's power to name standing committees for the session and the practice of the president and his executive committee continuing their executive functions even during the meetings of the session prejudiced things against change and tended strongly to preserve the status quo. It was a procedure that prevented innovation and renewal.

The executive committee should begin to function only after the session had disbanded, he argued, and was to carry out the will of the session. He agitated this question on numerous occasions, urging that the church adopt an approach that would enable the session itself to elect its own committees at the beginning of the session, achieve a wider representation of input, and thus be able to explore fresh ways of operating. Prescott could see no other way to unfreeze the status quo and jolt the organization forward out of its state of virtual paralysis. Toward the end of the conference, it appears his agitation on this issue led to an emerging consensus that perhaps his ideas should be tried. S. H. Lane, for example, noted that the issue had come up at the three previous General Conference sessions and was now being urged with increasing persistence. He argued that "if the Conference can be run with the committee at the end instead of at the beginning, why not try it." Why not try such a plan at the next session?

Two years later, A. G. Daniells, fresh from the antipodes and having counseled at length with Prescott en route to Battle Creek, implemented that very strategy. The ice melted, and the fresh waters of reform flooded the church with long awaited renewal. At that time, George Irwin was washed to one side in its wake and then swept out to be marooned in Australia. In the intervening two years, however, he found himself engaged in a continuing struggle to contain the increasing threat of Kellogg's medical juggernaut overtaking the church.

CHAPTER 6

A SECOND TERM for GEORGE IRWIN (1899–1901)

He carries with him "a little notebook in which he has noted down perplexing questions which he brings before me," Ellen White recalled as she reported her visit with George Irwin in Cooranbong in mid-1899. Then "if I have any light upon these points, I write it out for the benefit of our people not only in America but in this country."[1] It had been eight years since she had first met Irwin in person, although she had corresponded with him several times in the past two years. She seems to have shown no anxiety about his re-election to a second term of office in early 1899. In fact, she made no reaction or reference to the event at all. But increasingly worried at what he felt was a downward drift of events in the church, Irwin was eager to visit with the matriarch who, in spite of her years, was still robust enough to cope with the rigors of pioneering in Australia. And she was still vitally engaged in church affairs at the center, writing copious impassioned and troubling letters to church leaders. Irwin felt the need to talk with her in person.

Therefore, three months after his re-election at the General Conference session in South Lancaster, Massachusetts, he had set off on a three-week-long voyage across the Pacific to attend the fourth annual Australian Union Conference session in Cooranbong, to visit with Ellen White, and to become more familiar with the needs of the rapidly developing young church in Australia. En route he also took the opportunity during a port stop to examine the recently opened work of the church in Suva, Fiji. This chapter will explore the impact on the relationship between prophet and president that Irwin's lengthy personal visit had and how the relationship changed and developed during his second term in office. It will also illustrate further dimensions of the interaction between Ellen White's charisma and the administrative function in the church. These dimensions become particularly evident in the way she sought to work more closely with the president, seeing him as a means of being able to exercise an influence on J. H. Kellogg, who, as the century came to an end, moved further away from her.

Unfortunately, a communication breakdown about the arrival details of Irwin's visit to Australia found him making his own way to Cooranbong. While he was alighting from the train at the station, seventy-five miles north of Sydney, Ellen White and her son, W. C. White, together with A. G. Daniells and other visitors, waited at the port in Sydney to greet him. The Whites hurriedly retraced their steps to Cooranbong and caught up with the lost president the next morning. In the meantime, feeling quite at home with the countryside, Irwin introduced himself to the wagon driver from the new college, who happened to be collecting goods from the Dora Creek station. After arranging a ride for his luggage on the cart, Irwin himself walked the four miles out to the school property, where he obtained a bed for the night. The next morning, Ellen White's carriage picked him up and took him to her own home, "Sunnyside," where he would spend the rest of his visit.[2]

What Irwin saw at Cooranbong impressed him. The abundance of fresh garden vegetables meant a pleasing variety served for lunch each day. And the way the whole Avondale property was being developed met with his hearty approval. Meeting Ellen White again in person had elements of both the familiar and the new. In her "thank-you speech" after the union session and near the end of Irwin's time in Australia, she spoke as if getting acquainted with Irwin at Cooranbong had been like encountering him in person for the first time. "I am very thankful to meet Brother Irwin," she stated. "It has seemed like having a little piece of America here, and here we can speak and pray together."[3] Although she had been sick for a week early in his visit and therefore could not get out, she still had plenty of time to discuss things with him.

The arrival of the General Conference president provoked some serious heart-searching on the part of Ellen White about the whole question of how to manage the exercise of her influence in church affairs. She confided to her friend Sarepta Henry, with whom she was corresponding at this time, that there were many things she would have preferred to have kept to herself rather than being obliged to discuss them. "But Brother Irwin has conversed with me," she reported, "and asked for light which I have been instructed to give him." At the time, Ellen White was feeling discouraged about the ineffectiveness of her writing. Wrestling with Irwin's many questions reinforced her feelings of inadequacy. Why did people misunderstand her so easily? she asked herself. She would "much prefer to meet the people in America face to face," she said, "than to send written communications." Why? Because, she explained, "there are many who interpret that which I write in the light of their own opinions." "You know what that means," she wrote to Mrs. Henry. "A division in understanding, and diverse opinions is the sure result."[4] Her appraisal of the effectiveness of her writings was quite the reverse of her stance just three years previously. Then, when Olsen had asked her to attend the 1897 General Conference Session, she had refused to return to America, stating that she felt she could accomplish tenfold more in influencing the church by her pen in Australia than through being physically present at meetings and in committees in America. At that time, she preferred to stay in her haven in "the far-off country."[5] Now she was feeling quite the opposite.

During this period, she gave considerable thought to the matter of how to exercise her influence more effectively. Choosing whom to send her letters to, when to send them, and whom to include on the copy list drained her. And then there was the matter of her inability, at times, to express herself clearly in her writing, which hampered her ability to influence leaders. Creating confusion was not what she wanted to do. It made her less effective at guiding the church in the direction that she felt it should go based on the insights that she said the Lord was revealing to her in her role as His spokesperson.

During a week when she was confined to bed with a respiratory infection, she pondered the questions Irwin had raised—and became rather discouraged. But the opportunity to write of these things in her correspondence with Mrs. Henry was a helpful way of working through her self-doubt. Mrs. Henry (no relation to Archibald Henry) was a noted American temperance reformer and women's advocate who had recently converted to Adventism. She had participated extensively in the 1899 General Conference Session, and Mrs. White found herself readily identifying with her.

"How to write in a way to be understood by those to whom I address important matters, is a problem I cannot solve," she confided in one letter. It bothered her that even those who knew her best could so seriously misinterpret her. "When I see that I am not understood by my brethren who know me best, I am convinced that I must take more time to express my thoughts." She received insights from the Lord, she said, and she dared not do otherwise than communicate them. The burden weighed heavily on her. But how to present it effectively was a challenge. "When I am misunderstood and my words misinterpreted I am afraid. I fear that I have been premature, or have not expressed myself as I ought." It was true. The passion and strong language of her letters during this period frequently caused confusion and conflict. She was aware, too, that sometimes her intensity caused only "sorrow of heart, but not reform," a reality that made her "sick and sad and depressed." As a result she was often not able to sleep. Her insomnia had become almost chronic and apparently contributed to a vicious cycle of stress, anxiety and discouragement—and further sleep deprivation. More common in people sixty years of age and older, an inability to sleep contributes to mood swings and irritability.[6] Lying awake at night, with her mind constantly running and not finding rest, she found that the problems she wrestled with tended to take on a much darker hue and a larger and more sinister perspective. Eventually she decided that perhaps it was best that she "write fewer personal letters" and confine herself to her "Bible subjects," thus avoiding controversial matters. "I will endeavor to write much less," she concluded.[7]

Although Ellen White might fear that she was losing her influence—particularly with Kellogg—that definitely was not the case with Irwin. With his notebook in hand, he valued the opportunity to get a clearer understanding of some of the perplexing things she had recently written. It is clear that the extended visit enabled his relationship with Ellen White to develop at a deeper level to a cordial friendship. Later correspondence, following the visit, evidences a warmer intimacy of communication.

Irwin's visit to Cooranbong occurred not long after the most anguishing incident that union president A. G. Daniells and Ellen White ever endured in their pioneering work at Avondale. According to Daniells, it had been his absolutely worst experience ever, anywhere in the work. They had found themselves totally destitute of funds and under serious obligations to a wide range of creditors. Mrs. White, as did Daniells, lost many nights of sleep distressed about the matter. Things were so bad financially that she had not been able to pay her half dozen or so household and editorial staff their regular salaries for more than a year. The accrued back pay which she owed her workers just kept mounting up. She could give them only a small living allowance to provide for bare essentials. On top of this, she had run up a worryingly large six-month bill at the grocer's shop in Newcastle. Neither had the school organizers been able to pay the contracted workmen on the school site for many months. They, too, were able to give only a small living allowance as the arrears piled up. They were seriously in debt with no security other than Ellen White's faith. Daniells was not convinced that they should have gone ahead and was inclined to fear that they had been reckless and presumptuous. Their reputations and credibility were suffering. Finally, Daniells found himself obliged to tour the churches in Melbourne and Adelaide in search of funds of any kind, whether loans or donations. And he contacted numerous banks, seeking a sympathetic manager willing to make a loan. Denominational leadership had previously accepted sizeable loans from church members, with the church functioning as a kind of assured and safe bank for the trusting depositors. When a church member in Adelaide called for the repayment of her loan earlier than expected, it exposed the lack of collateral and reserves and brought the whole system near to collapse. The anguish drove Daniells to spend a sleepless night in the bush in agonizing prayer for deliverance, and it seared the horror of debt into his memory forever.

The embarrassment and humiliation associated with the plight of Daniells and Ellen White reached right back to events that had occurred in Battle Creek. It was an episode they did not like to recall. Appeals had been made at the General Conference session to help raise funds for the completion of the "College Hall" building at Avondale, and Ellen White had hoped that there would also be sufficient funds to begin construction on the sanitarium building in Sydney, the next major Australian project. During the session, in the midst of the fund-raising appeal, a certain Captain Henry Norman stood and made a substantial pledge. Frank H. Westphal, a missionary to South America, had met the man on his way to the session from South America and had brought him along. Norman, posing as a wealthy ship owner, had promised large donations to other branches of the work and a total of $15,000 to the Avondale project and other needs in Australia. This unexpected intervention in the fund-raising had consequently diminished the flow of small donations from church members. What did their contributions mean alongside such largesse? They anticipated that the "wealth of the gentiles" would soon flow toward the church to help with its development. Ellen White and her helpers also looked forward keenly to the May deadline when Norman's pledge would be fulfilled and their financial distress relieved. But just before Irwin left Battle Creek for Australia, it was learned that "Captain" Norman had absconded from Battle Creek along with a young woman's affections and her savings. It later became apparent that he was a complete sham and fraud.

This roller-coaster experience of the promise of funding, the dashing of hope, and the embarrassment of being deceived was a difficult experience for Ellen White, the other pioneers at Avondale, and for the church at large. The full reports about the scam artist arrived during Irwin's visit.[8] He thus experienced firsthand what it meant to "pioneer" in Australia and came to a better understanding of the privations and high levels of stress Ellen White and her associates experienced in establishing the denomination in the antipodes. Avondale was not a "big bang" creation like Union College or Battle Creek College had been. It was built at the cost of great personal anxiety and stress.

The union session meetings convened in the new two-story College Hall completed and opened April 13, 1899, just two months before the session. Landscaping had not yet been finished. The session preempted the school program. The 150 students "sandwiched themselves together" into rooms on the upper floors of their respective residence areas to allow the approximately one hundred delegates attending the session to use their bedrooms in the main residence hall areas. "Self-sacrifice and thoughtfulness of others are among the best lessons our students can learn," the faculty reasoned. Classes were also interrupted as students attended the session meetings lasting almost three weeks. "As a matter of education," the privilege of participating in the event "would be of more value to them than the regular routine school work," was the logic. The teachers felt that "in these respects" their hopes "were more than realized." Instructors in twenty-first century "Hospitality and Tourism" courses would have been impressed with this example of hands-on work experience.

The union session took place during the southern hemisphere winter (July 4–23). Irwin found the session to be rather unusual in that it scheduled no business meetings in the afternoons. Instead, delegates were expected to join forces with the students and to spend two or three hours a day felling the immense eucalyptus trees and clearing the top of the knoll in front of the school buildings. Several days of rain with the subsequent oceans of mud did not interrupt the task.[9] Irwin's farming background would have stood him in good stead.

Several times Irwin preached at the session and gave several talks on "Healthful Living" based on Ellen White's recently published compilation of that name. The delegates also called upon him to interpret and explain the decisions of the 1897 General Conference Session and the circumstances and implications for his own altered role as president. When they commented that they did not understand what the changes meant, Irwin read the paragraph from Ellen White that had been so crucial in triggering the modifications—that it was "not wise to choose one man as president of the General Conference." Either the responsibility or the field should be divided "or some other plan" should be devised, she had said. He then described in detail the union conference concept as a regional grouping of conferences. It is clear from his explanation that the "union" idea was a work in progress. The implications were still being thought through. For example, administration had yet to consider how to determine representative union delegations to General Conference sessions. The Australian delegates felt they should be more adequately represented at the next General Conference session. Irwin stressed the organic unity that should exist in the General Conference and that none of the branches represented by the various extra parachurch organizations—such as the medical missionary or publishing entities—"can be independent of this body."[10]

Problems with the publishing program

A significant cause of distress for Ellen White during the 1890s arose from complications and disappointments due to her involvement in the publishing interests of the church. Difficulties in the publishing program also caused significant tension at times between Irwin as president and Ellen White as prophet. Sorting out the problems consumed large amounts of his time. The issues were complicated, perplexing, and often highly sensitive, because they involved income that various church employees had come to rely on to meet living expenses. It is helpful to explore the publishing difficulties in some detail, for they feature significantly in the search for balance between the gift of administration and the gift of prophetic guidance exercised through Ellen White.

As a result of his visit, Irwin better understood the critical importance to Ellen White of the income from royalty payments on her books produced by the denominational publishing houses. He was also able to grasp why the vexed issue of royalties caused her to feel so strongly and to vent her frustration when she addressed the matter. The perceived injustices that occurred from non-payment of royalties, reductions in royalty rates, or the non-promotion of her publications rankled deep in her soul. For example, she had composed a strongly worded criticism of her colleagues, asking that it be read at the 1899 General Conference Session. In the document, she had criticized Olsen for relying so heavily and trustingly on his flawed financial associates such as A. R. Henry and Harmon Lindsay. Further, she also wrote in pointed terms of the alleged malpractice in the publishing program, again criticizing the lack of support for the promotion of *The Great Controversy* during the early 1890s and alleging "false, dishonest work" on the part of publishing leaders. She lamented that Olsen had "worked away" from the light he had been given and alleged that C. H. Jones and his colleagues at Pacific Press® had also intentionally "sought to spoil the work of God and to betray the Lord into the hands of sinners" by following "in the tread" of the administrators in Battle Creek. The latter were men "who had been warring against the purposes of God," calling "evil good and good evil." As a result, she saw their work as the long shadow of the Old Testament rebellion of Korah, Dathan, and Abiram. Session delegates should take time to study this particular biblical episode recorded in Numbers 16.[11]

In good faith, Irwin had previously attempted to sort out the royalty payment mess that had developed during the mid-1890s in the publishing branch of the church by setting up an investigative committee at Battle Creek during the first months 1899. Respected pioneer John Loughborough served as the chair. In Ellen White's view, however, the committee only made matters worse. The results of its inquiry and the recommendations it offered apparently circulated as a pamphlet— or at least, that was the intention. The committee's findings did not impress Ellen White at all. Therefore, she had written to Irwin and the publishing leaders strongly worded follow-up letters. Irwin would have received the correspondence just a few weeks prior to his departure for Australia. In these letters, she stated that she could not sleep for worrying about the injustices over royalties and what she considered to be an ill-proposed and unworkable solution.[12]

In an attempt to make restitution, particularly to Edson White concerning the mishandled financial arrangements for his book *Gospel Primer,* the committee had approved a payment of $1,000 to cover the "damage" caused to its circulation and the consequent estimated arrears on royalties for the book.[13] Edson White had originally produced the little book and another, *Christ Our Saviour,* as literary adaptations of selected portions of his mother's writings. The volumes were designed to help with his program in the southern states and as a fund-raising venture to financially support his mission to the South.

In its attempt to respond to Ellen White's earlier criticism of the alleged "robbery" practiced by the previous publishing administration and to deal equitably with all authors, the committee recommended to restore unpaid royalties to all disadvantaged authors and invited authors to submit their claims. It appears that the committee wanted to avoid dealing with only Edson White and Frank Belden so as not to create the impression that it was giving special treatment to these two men because they were close relatives of Ellen White. The attempt to be ethically consistent was laudable, but perhaps idealistic. Ellen White protested that if the denomination implemented such a broad approach, the publishing house would quickly be bankrupt. Any remedial plan still had to make financial sense. If all the various authors should "put in their plea," where would the money come from to pay them? Was not the recent case of the publishing house in

Norway (it was facing bankruptcy with an indebtedness of more than $25,000)[14] a clear enough example of poor financial management?

Furthermore, to treat the works of all authors in the same way was "not wisdom." The committee needed to adopt a flexible approach that dealt with the real world, not just ideals. Some books were much more valuable than others in the field. To do as the committee proposed "would make a worse error than has been made." As for herself, Ellen White recalled, "no one can have been hurt financially more than I was hurt." But even though she felt she had been wronged in being obliged to accept a reduction in royalties from 15 percent to 10 percent, and even though her unjust treatment over the publication of *The Great Controversy* still caused her bitter chills each time she thought about it, she nevertheless had "a heart to forgive all the debts that have been incurred against me by the publishing institution from first to last." And she called on her fellow authors to "stand with me in this matter." As for the committee, she pleaded, "Come now to your senses." Don't make matters worse.[15]

There was also the suggestion that once the total amount of arrears in royalties had been calculated, then perhaps the authors could be invited—or would feel inclined—to allow the amount to be written off. This idea caused further unhappiness, however, when the administrators themselves took the lead in "sponging out" the amounts. Ellen White's intention had been that the authors themselves should take such an initiative. It was a further misunderstanding of her counsel.

The committee's preliminary proposal, though financially unwise, seems to have been motivated by the intensity of Ellen White's earlier complaints and her emphatic statements that universal principles of ethics and justice were involved. Now, some on the committee wondered if they could ever do anything right. Did her pattern of response tend to intimidate leadership?

On the matter of copyright, Ellen White took a strong author's perspective and was firmly of the view that authors should not sign over their copyrights to publishers. "I cannot see that they [authors] have any liberty to either give away or sell their rights to books they have written." Her stance certainly made things difficult for publishers.

As for the publication of books such as Edson's *Gospel Primer* and *Glorious Appearing* by the Review and Herald, "not a penny should have been charged" for their production. They should have been published free as a charitable endeavor in support of the southern field.[16] Such detailed intrusion into the day-to-day management practices of the publishing house and the disbursement of their surpluses evidently caused some discomfort for managers struggling to satisfy competing demands and still achieve a balanced bottom line. Overall, it seems, they recognized that the counsel was for the general good of the cause, and they endeavored to comply as best they could. They probably did not fully understand the context which generated the strength and sharpness of the criticism. In Australia, Ellen White had been able to pay her own editorial staff "only a part of their wages" for more than a year. "Patiently they have waited, understanding the situation." But how long could they wait?

It was not easy to be a publishing house administrator in the 1890s, constantly struggling with financial pressures and competing demands on resources. Conflicts abounded on every hand over financial policies, copyright and marketing and distribution practices, claims on territories, and other issues. And mistakes occurred on many sides. The stresses and quarrels, it seems, were endemic—a natural result in some ways of the rapid growth of the program. Irwin, who did not have a publishing background like either W. C. White or W. W. Prescott, found himself urged to become more actively involved in helping develop a better framework for international relations in the publishing program.[17] But while Ellen White protested against publishing house managers in Battle Creek, others expressed their frustration about the attitudes and practices followed by the publishing house in Australia. Could W. C. White, as a manager, be as problematic as those in Battle Creek? Some thought so. At times, even some loyal colleagues perceived Willie to be as heavy-handed, dictatorial, and prone to adopt sharp business practices in his promotion of the Australian publishing house as were his counterparts in Battle Creek.[18] A heated conflict, for example, erupted for several months between Willie White and the publishing house Prescott was responsible for in London. The episode was another illustration of the fact that many problems arose from the inadequacies of the organizational structures as much as they did from the people charged with running them. A demanding, dictatorial letter from W. C. White in August 1899 set out how the Australian publishing house planned to control certain marketing territories and book products. The letter stunned Prescott. He was able to reply only after he had read White's letter several times and after he had laid it aside for a while to give himself time to reflect more soberly on its meaning and its tone and how he might respond. Then, in very carefully chosen words and perceptive expressions, Prescott penned a powerful and highly indignant response, scolding White for wanting to control everything and dictate unfair terms to other institutions and denominational employees. To Prescott, White's practices seemed no different than the harsh, calculating "officialism" of those in America.[19] Was the evil business spirit that was so problematic in Battle Creek also infecting the Australian publishing enterprise?[20]

After his visit to Australia in mid-1899, Irwin returned to America feeling that he understood at least some of the perplexing publishing house issues more clearly. He certainly had a better grasp of the financial stresses that darkened and disrupted so many of Ellen White's nights. But simply having a greater appreciation of the impact in Australia of the problems at Battle Creek did not make them any easier to fix. And some of the advice from Australia on what to do was still not always easy to comprehend. A stinging letter from Mrs. White, for example, four months after Irwin returned to America, alleged that he was failing in his duty as president just as had his predecessor. That certainly gained Irwin's attention. He did not want to be perceived as another Olsen, scolded regularly for not doing what was needed.

But why had the publishing problems suddenly flared up anew just as soon as he returned home? History was catching up with the church. Ellen White had apparently read a letter and an accompanying pamphlet sent by her nephew Frank Belden. The materials contained a litany of complaints about the commercial practices of the Review and Herald. Reading about the continuing problems distressed her greatly. Hypersensitive as she was at this time to stress and anxiety, the troublesome reports from Belden actually induced a period of physical illness. About this same time, she had also received inquiries from the committee commissioned to investigate the issue of royalties. The group had sought more clarification from her regarding what they should do, because they now felt uncertain and somewhat intimidated that they might do the wrong thing.

In language that was as strong as any she had ever used, Mrs. White responded bluntly and in a tone of almost utter frustration. She addressed the letter to A. J. Breed, perhaps as chair of the committee, with copies addressed to several other committee members. "I cannot give you any clearer definition of your duty," she exclaimed (implying, "Isn't my previous counsel clear enough?"). When the committee eventually found its way out of its confusion, it would not be "because you have greater light and more definite particulars." Then, alluding to a different, but related, problem and telescoping them together, she asserted that those who did not respond to being called "robbers" would "never have any clearer understanding." The related problem concerned the issue of sending money raised "by the most earnest appeals" for one field to meet the needs of another. Such a practice was simply unethical. It had happened to her in Australia, and now it was affecting others, including her son Edson. Any action that kept back means from "the destitute southern field" simply could not be vindicated in God's sight. She could say no more. Her exasperated tone is unmistakable. "I have no words with which I can make matters plain to you." It was not more evidence that leaders needed, nor more light. Their attitude was the problem. "There is no way whereby you may be made to comprehend." The real issue was a spiritual one. "Your councils are not pure and clean and sound before Him." The tone of the letter is one of strong judgment. The denunciations of Jesus in Matthew 11:21–24, she alleged, surely applied to Battle Creek. In fact, she thought "a species of madness had come upon them."[21]

As for Irwin, Ellen White told him frankly that she felt there was no use "in my continually writing to the brethren in responsible positions in Battle Creek." The diverting of funds from the American South, even though they had been used, not for selfish enrichment, but in some other needy place to advance the work of the church, was as bad as what Achan had done in misappropriating the loot from Jericho. It was "an evidence of the perverted principles brought into the work."[22] Then Ellen White became more pointed and laid the burden of responsibility directly on Irwin. He was in danger of becoming another Olsen, she said, because he "should long ago have set things in order." If he had done so, she asserted, "there are those who would have worked with you."

"And you do not act in this matter," she continued, "considering all the light given as the position you occupy demands you should act. You are, I fear, in danger [of] acting as [did] Elder Olsen. There is not a semblance of justification of the course pursued by men in office before you came in to bear the great responsibilities required of you as President of the General Conference."[23] She warned that God would not remove His censure from the General Conference "until clean work is made and everything has been done that can be done to make full restitution."[24] Did Irwin understand this as an allusion to the fact that he might also need to resign? Did he worry that he might be inadvertently falling into the same trap that Olsen had slipped into? Would he also be moved out of office?

What particularly upset Ellen White in this episode was what she considered to be the trifling amount that had been awarded her son and her nephew Frank Belden. She did not understand the mathematics involved in arriving at the decision of the committee to give $1,000 to the two men to divide equally between them in recognition of unpaid royalties, but she was "surprised beyond measure" when she heard of the decision. She felt a "holy indignation stirring her soul." Restitution should at least be made of both "principle and interest," in her calculation. But she would not give a figure. In fact, she would rather have heard that nothing at all was being done, "than the trifling representation to redeem the past by the restitution made by the people who have been instructed."[25]

As the sense of indignation washed over her, she again urged that there needed to be people removed from authority in Battle Creek, and she quoted a telling scripture from the story of Achan: "Neither will I be with you any more until the accursed thing is put away from among you." But she would "not specify names."[26] It was unclear to Irwin, at least, which of his associates she had in mind. Was it I. H. Evans, W. H. Edwards, or W. C. Sisley? Or was it all three who were guilty and needed to be dropped? Henry and Lindsay had already been engineered out, and Eldridge and Belden had left, so who else was there? Irwin wasn't sure.

The following month, Ellen White wrote to A. T. Jones as the editor of the *Review* and also as a member of the committee, and again expressed her view that the $1,000 fell "far short of correcting the wrong." From her prophetic perspective, she saw the unfortunate episode, as it were, brushed out onto a much broader canvas. There the picture seemed to have more profound, cosmic implications. She was distressed that it appeared to some "that the transaction in regard to the *Gospel Primer* was a little matter." The fruit in Eden, she argued, "was a little matter." The loss of income for the southern field was not just a loss of income. There was also "time lost that could never be recovered."[27] The tone of the letter echoes that of the oracles of Amos and Joel.

But at the same time there comes through the letters the desperation of a mother eager to help ensure the success and welfare of her son and his work. Her letter to Irwin at the end of August 1899 illustrates this. After assuring him of her remembrance of him in her daily prayers, she pleads with him to take care of Edson and his projects. She would no longer press her son to come to Australia where he could be near her. "But brethren," she asked, "what are you going to do? Are you going to cooperate with him, and help him?"[28]

Ellen White wrote to both the Review and Herald board and to the General Conference committee on various issues. Speaking to the board in a more moderate tone, she pointed out its lack of understanding of its duty to undertake charitable work. Some books, such as *Gospel Primer* and *The Coming King,* needed to be printed at cost. Instead of the publishing house laboring to take all it could get from its employees in order to add to its profits, the board could have given the profits to help the poverty-stricken mission in the South. In doing so, the publishing house "would have been abundantly blessed." The difficulty for the board was that the publishing house was not making much at all by way of profits. According to Irwin, it was struggling with "great indebtedness."[29]

To the General Conference committee Mrs. White was more blunt. Again, she stated forthrightly that a new board of directors needed to be appointed for the Review and Herald publishing house. "A change must be made." Individuals selected for the board should be those "who seek the Lord with their whole heart." They were not to be young, inexperienced individuals but "experienced, God fearing, proved men who will bear the message of reproof sent by God." But still she did not specify names. And although she wrote to the General Conference committee with her instructions, it was actually the publishing house stockholders meeting that would appoint the board. Even the nominating process for the board was being changed, but it was not a simple or easy thing to effect. Board members needed to be drawn from the existing list of stockholders. Furthermore, by law, candidates for board membership needed to have been a stockholder in the company for at least twelve months prior to their election.[30]

Irwin addressed the problem by calling a joint meeting of the General Conference committee and the Review and Herald board. It was a difficult session because, on the basis of the critical language in the testimonies, *Review* editor A. T. Jones made some extreme statements of his own and stirred up angry feelings. Editorial staff pitted against management was not going to help matters. Some already could see such a situation as one of the pot calling the kettle black. It might be appropriate for one with the spiritual gift to offer criticism and still be effective in exercising a positive influence. But for Jones to echo the sentiments and say that "justice was a thing not known in the office" or that the publishing house "needed some Christians as directors and managers" created only hostility. At least, Irwin reported, it certainly made the work of the nominating committee embarrassing. It all became murky indeed.

The episode illustrates how difficult it was for Ellen White to exert her influence in an effective way to achieve the leadership outcomes she thought desirable. The meeting did lead to the appointment of some new members to the Review and Herald board; however, it had not been an easy or simple thing to do, as Irwin later told her. "While this [new board] could not be said to be a new board in the fullest construction of the term," he explained defensively, "yet you can see that three of the most positive, leading spirits; namely brethren Sisley, Gibson and McCoy were left off the Board."[31] It wasn't a large board, and now it dropped J. I. Gibson, whom Olsen had added two or three years previously in an attempt to fulfill Ellen White's earlier counsel. Apparently Gibson was not considered to be effective.

Similarly, there arose a problem with W. A. Sisley's appointment to the board as noted in the previous chapter, although in a different context. On the basis of Ellen White's direct testimonies addressed to him, Jones thought that she clearly wanted to have Sisley removed from the board, and so he had argued strongly against Sisley's nomination. Apparently, he felt that Sisley was too sharp in business practice and perhaps had been too close to Henry. Therefore, Sisley, too, was removed, much to Irwin's chagrin. But neither was Ellen White happy with this step. "I am so sorry that A. T. Jones appears to have been the one who has managed to get Brother Sisley off the Board, saying it was through a Testimony," she wrote. She explained that she had copies "of all my testimonies, and there is nothing in them that prompts to any such action."[32] She must have wondered to herself again why people got it wrong so often. But how was Irwin to know? The only good thing that she could see in the development was that Sisley would now be left at liberty to go to Australia, "for we need him here in Sanitarium building."

But finding replacements for the Review management was not that simple. And as it turned out, the publishing house still needed Sisley to serve for a while as plant superintendent. Irwin had kept him on and had thus found himself having to defend doing so to Ellen White and to others. And even though Sisley had sold his personal effects and was physically ready to go to Australia, Irwin reported to Mrs. White later in July that Sisley would not now leave until she had straightened things out with him.[33] Working in Battle Creek was like walking through a field of landmines.

Did Irwin read the January letter from Ellen White comparing him with Olsen as a veiled threat? He was doing his very best and was not unaware of his predecessor's difficulties. The letter certainly succeeded in pushing the problems of the publishing program higher up on Irwin's crowded agenda. He reported in April, after the spring committee meetings, that the aim of the Review board, of which he was now himself an elected member, would be "to as rapidly as possible change the policy of the institution, and have it run more in the interest of present truth." Because of the institution's great indebtedness and its expanded facilities (which had created a large capacity for doing commercial work), the board did "not deem it wise to make a sudden change." But its policy "first, last, and all the time," would be to increase the sale and demand for church literature until it would "gradually crowd out the other." Furthermore, longtime employee George Amadon had been appointed as a "spiritual father" to look after the young men and women at the plant. He would not be confined to regular hours as other men were, but could pursue his chaplaincy duties at anytime as needed.

Irwin also reported to Ellen White that because of the extreme financial pressures facing the church, the auditing committee of the General Conference had voted a reduction to the monthly salary for all church employees. The rate had been reduced to fifteen dollars per week. Irwin stated that as for himself, he was happy to take an even further reduction of three dollars per week. But although twelve dollars per week might have been fine for him, his colleagues had urged him not to pressure others too heavily with his example. Besides, Irwin evidently had private means on which to draw. Fifteen dollars per week was little enough as it was.[34]

In spite of Irwin's best intentions and focused efforts for the publishing program, he too found that change was hard to achieve. Organizational and personnel problems were more systemic and deeply entrenched than they at first appeared. Even the matter of resolving the disputed royalties problem on the *Gospel Primer* and other publications was complicated. The *Gospel Primer,* for example, involved other contractual parties and had become tangled in awkward financial arrangements because of Edson White. It thus took quite a long time for the matter to be finally settled.[35]

But publishing complaints were not the only issues creating stress between the charismatic authority of the prophet and the gift of administration represented in the president and his colleagues. Tension arose in other areas as well. In particular, stresses developed within the church leadership as how best to control and administer the broadening scope of the church. These tensions would lead eventually to a sharply focused struggle between the medical program and the ministerial and evangelistic programs of the church. The charisma of Ellen White became a central issue in this conflict, and she found herself sometimes being uncomfortably triangulated between two opposing forces within the church system.

PROBLEMS WITH DR. KELLOGG AND THE MEDICAL BRANCH

The problems facing Irwin were large and complicated in the publishing program, and the dealings he had to work through with the publishing house managers were tangled and complex, but they would soon be dwarfed by the complications and problems presented by John Harvey Kellogg and his drive to increase the independence of his medical system. The church's relationship to its medical branch became highly politicized during Irwin's second term of office, making things exceedingly difficult to manage. The challenge from Kellogg not only stretched Irwin's administrative abilities, but also significantly challenged Ellen White's ability to exercise her influence. Thus she found herself working much more closely with Irwin on this issue, and she had to plan and study the various moves that she should make to employ her influence more effectively. She may not have thought of this process as political or used the language of governance, but the issues, nevertheless, very much involved ideology, control and allocation of assets both physical and financial, and lines of responsibility for the management of personnel.

Much of the correspondence between Ellen White and Irwin during the remaining eighteen months of his presidency had to do with how to handle the Kellogg problem. Ultimately, it was the rise of Kellogg's threat and the complexity of the organizational implications it had for the church that brought about the replacement of Irwin as General Conference president. Some consideration of the background to the rise of Dr. John Harvey Kellogg helps to provide a context for the relationship between Irwin and Ellen White. It also helps clarify the developments that led to the 1901 General Conference Session. The record of Kellogg's growing dominance during the first years of the Irwin presidency also reveals the role that conflict and competition over diminished financial and personnel resources played in fostering polarization within the church.

During 1898, Mrs. White had become increasingly concerned about Kellogg's work and his personal spiritual welfare. Altogether that year, she penned seventeen letters to the doctor, many of which contained messages of caution. She was particularly troubled about his critical attitude toward his ministerial colleagues and his push to expand the medical program in a way that began to compete with, and overshadow, the evangelistic focus of the church. In addition, she also appealed to the General Conference president to seek to unify the increasingly divergent branches of the denomination and the personnel involved. Irwin responded positively and endeavored to implement her request, but he found it impossible to do so, because, as he reported, "the Doctor will not permit it."[36] During 1899, Ellen White composed another twenty-six letters to Kellogg, although not all were sent at the time they were written. As she began to realize that her letters were not always accomplishing what she desired, she gave much thought to how she could better exercise her influence to prevent Kellogg from getting into further difficulty.

Through the years, her letters had developed in the consciousness of her community an aura of authority in their own right, even though a particular letter might not say a word about God's leading her to write it nor mention a particular visionary experience. Both Ellen White who wrote and a president who read were aware, often only at a subconscious level, of the weighty assumptions that were implied, but that undergirded such an authority and relationship. To realize that her letters, in this new situation, were not being taken seriously or were not being as effective as she had hoped put her at a loss. Some of the other persuasive approaches described in chapter 2, therefore, became more significant.

The medical program and the challenges that Kellogg presented were among the matters that she and Irwin discussed at length during his stay at her Cooranbong home at the time of the Australian Union Conference session in July 1899. Denominational leadership had begun to perceive Dr. Kellogg's medical projects as posing a threat to the unity of the church. The situation had quickly grown quite sensitive, and it became apparent that Irwin needed help in coping with this particular challenge as well as with his other duties. During the Australian session, it was decided that S. N. Haskell and his wife should return to America with Irwin, an unexpected turn of events that caught the local members by surprise and led to significant disappointment on the part of the Australian denominational leadership. "We had built our hopes very largely upon having Elder Haskell's labors and counsel with us for a time," Eugene Farnsworth, a newly arrived missionary leader, complained.[37] The General Conference president himself had to step in to complete a series of talks that Haskell had been scheduled to present at the session in order to allow Haskell to pack and prepare for the trip to America. Irwin expressed his appreciation to the Australian delegates for acceding "so readily to the request for Brother Haskell's return" and for being willing to forgo their local needs for the benefit of the "great field at large." Ellen White said she was sorry that "we cannot have the labors of Brother Haskell here and have them in America, but we cannot have both." The *Union Record* editor, for his part, noted that "it was to help Brother Irwin in his arduous labors that it was thought expedient for Brother Haskell to go to America."[38] It was probably the first step in building a coalition against Kellogg.

Just prior to the 1899 General Conference Session, Irwin had alerted Ellen White to Kellogg's desire to have his constituency meetings in Chicago separate from the General Conference session. As a result, it seems that a considerable part of the correspondence that she sent to be read to delegates at the session involved cautions about the directions being taken in the medical missionary program. They addressed some of the theological and philosophical concepts that Kellogg and others had adopted to underpin the medical emphasis. Furthermore, they also spoke to the relationship that the medical missionary program should have to the main evangelistic thrust of the church. About this time, Ellen White also began to send to Irwin copies of the personal letters that she had addressed to Kellogg. In these letters, Irwin reported later, he found statements that "positively startled" him. Her letters confirmed conclusions about the situation that he and some of his close administrative associates had already been developing for some time and "thought they could see." At the time, Irwin and J. H. Morrison, the superintendent of District 2, were the only representatives of the General Conference committee who served on Kellogg's Medical Missionary and Benevolent Association board, and they felt a little outnumbered. Irwin was glad for the letters from Ellen White, for they helped him "to be sure of his bearings." But he trembled at the responsibility they laid on him. She requested him not to divulge the contents of the letters except to such close colleagues as he thought might be helpful. Mrs. White was beginning to sense the need to build a broader resistance against the Kellogg juggernaut.

In the months that followed the Australian Union session, events and plans taking shape in Australia soon became fatefully and inextricably linked with those developing in America and elsewhere. The interplay of organizational crises, the competition for resources, and the movement of personnel occurred quite beyond the conscious awareness of the individual players at the time. It would have been hard to have predicted or determined a particular outcome. Ellen White couldn't, although some thought she had tried. To an observer today, with the benefit of hindsight, the intersecting developments appear intriguing to say the least. Their linkage would eventually cause Irwin considerable grief. The story of what happened is a little-known episode in Adventist history that illustrates the extent of the intrigue associated with the reorganization of the church in 1901. It also depicts the challenge Ellen White faced in legitimately exercising her influence as she fostered the development of the work where she lived, but at the same time needing to be seen as standing outside and above the politics of the process.

As Irwin sailed back to San Francisco on the steamship *Alameda* in August following his visit to Australia, Ellen White was confiding in her diary that she had just written three more letters to Kellogg. But she noted that she had not sent them. She was still wrestling with the challenge of how best to maintain her influence with him. "I am so afraid of being misunderstood that I dare not send them. I feel so intensely, and want to help his mind in many things, but how can I do it?" she pondered. "My words are misapplied and misunderstood by humans [so] that they do more harm than good. This has been the case with Dr Kellogg."[39] If her testimonies to him were doing more harm than good, what else was she to do? Was there some other way of getting through, some other way of reaching him?

During the weeks that followed, she took the opportunity to inspect a number of properties in Sydney for the location of a new sanitarium. A major undertaking, the project would require significant investment, but she had no idea where the funds would come from. Ellen White knew without a doubt, however, that Australia needed a major sanitarium and that it must be built. Furthermore, she would need Kellogg's help as well as that of many others to get it going. She must keep him engaged and on her side.

Several months earlier she had invited John Wessels, of the wealthy Adventist family from South Africa that had found diamonds on its farm, to join her in the endeavor. He arrived in early 1899, and before the end of the midyear union session he had accepted the role of chairman of the Sydney Sanitarium board with the responsibility of making the project happen. Soon afterward he transferred his wife and children to Australia and settled in Sydney. All were hopeful that somehow the Wessels family would underwrite the project financially.

The union session at Cooranbong had given much discussion to the Sydney Sanitarium project while Irwin and Wessels were present. On July 21, the last Friday afternoon of the session, the Australasian Medical Missionary and Benevolent Association organized itself and then moved directly to voting approval for the construction of a medical and surgical sanitarium in the vicinity of Sydney. The vote followed a lengthy but moving address on the need for such an institution from Ellen White. Immediately following the vote, a memorable half-hour meeting had raised more than £900 from a total of seventy donors. It was an extraordinary meeting indeed. Most of the donors were ordinary church employees.

The project would require much more money, of course, but at least a start had been made, and a deposit was now in hand to secure a suitable piece of property when found. The union conference had wrestled with the problem of whether to proceed without adequate funding. Some felt that they needed to advance in faith. Others, more cautious and still feeling the pain of the extreme financial stresses involved in starting up the Avondale school, felt that to undertake further major debt would be disastrous. The "venture of faith" party pushed for an early start, resulting in Ellen White's inspection of various properties in August. By November, the church had located an attractive property in Wahroonga, and after due consideration J. J. Wessels negotiated the terms and put down the deposit to secure the site. Having Kellogg contribute to, and help establish, the institution was going to be important on several levels.

Meanwhile, in the United States during the months of August, September, and October, Irwin, together with S. N. Haskell and his wife, Hetty, was making his way around a circle of late summer camp meetings. The group's travels took them through the Midwest and back to Battle Creek. In his assigned meetings, Irwin occupied himself in reading extensively from the recent testimonies that had come from Ellen White. Some of them addressed the need for more financial support from church members for the task of mission. Others protested the clamor for higher wages and the necessity for wage restraint and sacrifice. Yet others warned of the organizational dangers ahead and of the need for unity. According to Hetty Haskell, the letters impressed the campers; some issues, such as the wage reduction question, "were talked about all over the ground." S. N. Haskell's task was to seek opportunities to raise money and support for the Sydney Sanitarium and the other desperate needs in Australia. I. H. Evans, of the Foreign Mission Board, was also traveling with the group, and his specific responsibility was to encourage support for missions in general, especially given the alarming crisis in the lack of funding that had descended upon the church. The competition for scarce resources could not have been clearer. Haskell, in fact, found it difficult to compete with Evans or even to raise much interest in Australia, because the needs seemed so desperate elsewhere.[40] He reported that his wife chided him that perhaps he carried too great a burden for Australia.

When they arrived back in Battle Creek in November, the Haskells made themselves available to conduct revival meetings for the benefit of the nurses at the sanitarium, and they continued to seek donations for the sanitarium in Australia. Haskell reported to Ellen White that the spiritual condition of the sanitarium staff was good but that the going was hard on the fund-raising front, and he suggested that Ellen White not proceed so quickly on the Australian sanitarium project. It was better not to go into further heavy debt.[41]

At the same time, Haskell was able to report to her on the state of the tensions between the church and Kellogg's medical institutions, as well as to keep her informed of the many quirky theological ideas now springing up. The blind pastor, W. H. Littlejohn, for example, had strange ideas about the Sabbath and an odd dateline for the Advent. Others espoused the idea that angels were really the Holy Spirit, and still others emphasized the sanctity of all life to such an extent that they considered killing even bugs and insects as immoral. "There is queer soil in Battle Creek," Haskell reported to W. C. White. Furthermore, it was "not a very desirable place" for fund-raising. "It is more difficult to move the people."[42]

Haskell didn't think that Battle Creek was a place to which Ellen White should return should she be inclined to come to help with fund-raising. "Should you be here," he wrote, "I fear you would be carried down to the graveyard before you ever got through the mist of darkness here." There was "money enough," he reported, "that could be invested in the institutions in Australia if the people only felt it." But as for Mrs. White joining them, Haskell's opinion was that she would not be able to "stand it." One part of him wished that she was in Battle Creek, but the other part of him thought better of it. "I shall never ask you to come to this country." Furthermore, added the elderly pastor, "You must not in any way let things trouble you as though you had neglected some things you ought to have done in any way of that kind. Do not think your mind is weakened in any way." Evidently Haskell had picked up that Ellen White was still wrestling with the challenge of how to make herself more clearly understood and how better to express herself. Had he visited with Mrs. Henry? As far as he was concerned, there was no problem at all. "Your testimonies never had in them greater power than now," he asserted.[43]

The response that Haskell gave to an inquirer about what it would take to induce Ellen White to return to the United States illustrates the vital importance of the fund-raising program for the church in Australia. "I told some, the most powerful argument I could think of would be to send you the means so there could be accomplished in that field what the Lord has shown you it was his will to accomplish." But even then, he reported to her, "I did not know as you would come. It would depend on what the Lord told you to do."

The conflict over scarce resources and the tendency of the Whites to give priority to their particular need was depicted by W. C. White's leaning on Irwin at this time to send teachers to Australia for the coming school year. E. J. Waggoner had finally declined Ellen White's thrice-repeated invitation to transfer to Avondale. It greatly disappointed Willie and his mother, because it had been partly on the understanding that Waggoner would be available that they were willing to release Haskell to help Irwin. Rather presumptuously, Waggoner's assignments had already been announced in the Australian church paper. With Waggoner now backing out, W. C. White felt his situation becoming "perilous" and begged Irwin to "send someone suited to the work." Without the help of Irwin and Haskell to find staff for Avondale, he feared that the institution would come up to the new school year "in confusion about teachers." It would be "a demoralization of our plans if we fail." And surely it was easier for Helderburg College in South Africa to find teacher replacements than it was for Australia, Willie suggested.[44]

To Prescott, on the other side of the Atlantic and also desperately struggling to find suitable personnel for his own field in England with its membership of only eight hundred in a population of forty million, White used a very telling point to make his plea. Coming close to pulling rank, he asserted that the Australian church employees would find themselves in dire straits "unless some of the parties interested are willing to make large sacrifices in behalf of the Australasian work, which because of Mother's connection with it is of more than ordinary importance in its relation to other branches of the work."[45]

The difficulty was that some in the denomination felt that more was already being done for Australia in the allocation of personnel and financial resources than was fair and reasonable. This viewpoint came to figure quite largely in the tensions between Kellogg and the General Conference. It was an opinion that John Wessels had apparently formed during his short tenure in Australia, and he began to feel that his own homeland, South Africa, was being overlooked. Irwin also picked up similar sentiment, apparently, as he traveled around the membership. Kellogg shared the same attitude, and besides was highly focused on pouring resources into his new medical college in Chicago, the development of a sanitarium in Mexico, and the expansion of his "gospel wagon" project, a social outreach program in some of the working class suburbs of Chicago and among the poorest citizens on its streets.

The Chicago Medical Mission project spawned many subsidiary activities as it gained momentum and soon began to consume large amounts of resources, to the distress of Ellen White. She fretted that it was a low priority getting out of hand. While Kellogg's mission in Chicago had merit and she initially supported it, she realized that it could easily mushroom and end up becoming an all-consuming program, soaking up valuable financial resources that would consequently hamper the church in its evangelical outreach in other places. Evangelistic outreach with its emphasis on seeking Christian commitment through conversion and baptism, with a subsequent personal involvement of people in "the cause," would be much more productive for the church. In the long run it would also bring better returns to the denomination in terms of church growth, generating further resources and potential for witnessing. Thus she cautioned Kellogg not to run too far nor too fast with the social welfare program. Certainly, she exclaimed, there should not be anyone visiting congregations to siphon off money for it through fund-raising campaigns. Money for his project should come "from those not of our faith."[46]

The conflict over allocation of resources and Kellogg's surreptitious, subversive planning for independence came to a head in early 1900. By then, the stakes involved began to become much clearer to Ellen White. A simple request she made to Kellogg for a donation precipitated the confrontation.

Back in late 1898, she had written Kellogg asking him for a donation of $5,000 from the Battle Creek Sanitarium toward the building of the Sydney Sanitarium. As one of the founders of the Battle Creek institution, she felt that she had some right to exercise a measure of stewardship in the disbursement of its profits. After all, the sanitarium "had been established at first with the funds of our people," she pointed out. Kellogg had responded to her request by saying that he was unable to make the donation from the sanitarium itself, because under the organization's revised legal charter, adopted in 1897, none of the profits of the institution could go for anything outside the state of Michigan. Kellogg himself, however, would make a personal donation. News of this state of affairs shocked Ellen White.

In February 1899, she replied to Kellogg's offer by declaring that she would not accept a donation either from his personal funds or from his own fund-raising efforts. There was a principle at stake. She believed that the Lord had instructed her that she "had a right, as his steward, to call for means from the Battle Creek Sanitarium to establish a sanitarium in Australia." Although she did not challenge the legal issue, she somehow conflated it with her general concern that the use of church money for the projects in Chicago "was not a right disposition of the money."[47]

It was becoming clear to her where Kellogg was going and the danger he was getting into. Her letter reflected the sharper lines of divergence between them. "You think I am no longer your friend," she wrote, "but all my sympathy and influence are with you when you are working in harmony with God." The Chicago program was absorbing money that should support other mission fields. "Whatever opinion you have of me, I cannot sustain you in the wrong." She assured him that "Sister White has not changed." But she made it clear that he was "working on wrong lines."[48] More than any other issue, it was Kellogg's inability to legally send her money from the Battle Creek Sanitarium that appeared to trigger her decision to return to America. The incident set off alarm bells all around the denomination. Kellogg's drifting sanitarium was going to need her physical presence, not just her letters, to keep it properly moored to the church.[49]

As the warm summer weather began to adopt its most humid garb at Cooranbong, Ellen White felt the oppressiveness of the conflict with Kellogg and his medical system pressing in closer and closer by the day. Sometime during this period, a copy of an article published three or four years earlier in the New York *Observer* came into her hands. The article reported on developments at the Battle Creek Sanitarium, how financial embarrassment had struck the institution, and how Kellogg at the time it was granted a new charter in 1897 had designated it to be a non-denominational institution. Church leaders were familiar with Kellogg's terminology "non-denominational" and "non-sectarian" and knew that he used these terms to indicate that his work was for anyone who was sick regardless of their religious tradition. Toward the end of the century, however, Kellogg began to give a wider, but plainer, meaning to the terms. It became clear that he did not want the sanitarium to be directly denominational or evangelical in any way.[50] When Ellen White read the report in the *Observer,* it was as if scales suddenly fell from her eyes. She sent copies of the article to Haskell and alerted Irwin to its significance and urged him to read it. Also, she felt it important to send copies of her letters and the article to Prescott in England. "The reason I write," she explained, was that "others who know not what they are about may come to their senses." She did not need to go into the particulars. "I know you will understand these things," she confided. Mrs. White was seeking to keep her allies informed.[51]

At a meeting of leaders in Cooranbong later in February 1900, those in attendance soon realized that in light of the new insights about Kellogg they might need to act quickly to safeguard the medical work and the newly established health food manufacturing program in Australia to keep them from falling into the doctor's clutches. The entire Australian medical and health enterprise must come under the ownership of the church itself through the union conference, rather than that of a parachurch entity such as Kellogg's Benevolent Association with its legally independent stockholders. Such a conviction had been growing for a number of months "on the part of a goodly number of our people," reported the church's paper. It was clear that the specter of Kellogg loomed large. Finally, the local leadership decided to call an urgent special meeting of the Australian Medical Missionary and Benevolent Association branch to deal with the issue. The old Association would be legally dissolved, and the union conference would absorb its operations, properties, and financial obligations under the umbrella of "a department."

The special meeting convened in Geelong on the western side of Melbourne on March 16, and the union conference committee followed up immediately by formally organizing the Medical Missionary Department.[52] At this same time, denominational leadership apparently began to worry about the status of the South African sanitarium and the medical missionary projects there and elsewhere in light of the threat that Kellogg now posed. Much was at stake. Ellen White struggled with the question of whether Kellogg could be trusted. For his part, on the other hand, Kellogg wondered how it could be that Irwin should be "poisoning" her mind against him.[53]

By this time, Ellen White obtained some relief from her anxiety by writing out her thoughts in letters even if she did not intend to mail them or was not sure she should, or could, send them to the addressee. This diary style of writing helped her clarify her thinking, express her emotions, and consider the best ways of dealing with the situation. It was like thinking aloud. In March 1900, she often wrestled with the Kellogg issues in this way, because she could not sleep. "I write this not knowing that I shall feel free to send the letter to you after it is written," she stated in one midnight entry. "I feel the condition of things keenly as it is from time to time presented before me. I shall trace upon paper the things that the Lord represents and then it may be best as I have done before to lay them aside until the case may be worked out and developed." Still she noted that she did "not have the courage or hope" that Kellogg would "change his plans." Despite that, she trusted that the Lord would ultimately "bring about his purposes in some other way." But, "lest I shall be called away suddenly, as was Sister Henry," she noted to herself as much as to anyone else, "I shall leave my testimony behind written in my diary at different times." Then, as if talking to Kellogg, but again, really to herself, she wrote, "I shall be very cautious what I send to you."[54] The impact of the stress on Ellen White was so severe that at times it made her physically ill. Such situations, she feared, could quite literally "worry her to death."

The new awareness concerning Kellogg's subversive designs persuaded her that however much she had learned to enjoy Australia, she must return to America in spite of the fact that she still had important projects yet to complete where she was. She wrestled with the problem following the February meetings at Cooranbong and wrote to Kellogg of her thoughts. She would try to get to the next General Conference session if she could "see her way clear" to do it. Her letter was a strong protest about the fact that Kellogg had committed himself to working "undenominationally" in a program that had taken money "from a people who are decidedly a denominational people." She told him that "God says you are not right." It worried her that "your influence no one dares to dispute but myself."[55] As a result, she would need to confront him in person.

The reluctant return to America

All the way from Sydney to Melbourne on the train, Ellen White's mind had chased the problem around and around in circles as she weighed alternatives and options and revisited the options time after time. Sleep eluded her "the entire night." In fact, for three nights she continued sleepless until finally the conviction began to settle that she must return to the United States. She had not yet fully settled the matter by mid-March, but she was becoming increasingly sure that she must go, and she explained her reasoning in a letter to her longtime friend and confidant, C. H. Jones in California. In addition, she needed to inquire of him about the state of her account with Pacific Press.

After mentioning that she had still not received any royalties for *The Desire of Ages,* she explained she was concerned that she was unable to settle the large amount of back pay she owed her staff. She then mentioned her thoughts about returning stateside. "I have been much drawn toward America of late," she confided. Perhaps A. G. Daniells and his family and at least Sarah McEnterfer and she might go. For how long she didn't know, "maybe not at all." The decision was still in the balance. But if she went, her reason was clear: "We see that some things must be investigated, who is having control of institutions and of Sanitariums, who is feeling authorized to use the means coming into that Sanitarium at Battle Creek to be submerged by hundreds and thousands of dollars in that work in Chicago." The cities of Melbourne and Sydney and desperate mission fields elsewhere were just as needy if not more so. How could "large donations have been swallowed up, from every source possible"? It was "consuming and not producing." She had begun to think that her "letters were not sufficient" any more to get the point across to Kellogg, but that her spoken words "might be of real benefit more than pen communications." However, she would actually like to stay in Australia "because the climate suits me so well." At that stage, her plan was to return to Australia after twelve months—if she went at all.[56]

After she arrived in Geelong for the special meeting on March 16, called to ensure that the Australian medical program came under the control of the church, she had become even more settled in her conviction that she must go to the United States. So much so that she informed her son Edson and her daughter-in-law that they should abandon the idea of joining her in Australia. Why? "Before many months" she might actually be with them in America. There were "many considerations that weigh and balance me in the direction of America," she wrote. By the end of March, things were clear enough for her to inform Irwin of her plans. "I have had upon my mind a great burden, but the matter is now settled. If the Lord spares my life, I shall leave this country." She would visit America for a short period of time and then return "after my period of stay seems to be ended." Her initial plans were still vague; she thought it would probably be four months before she could leave. However, we see the sudden seriousness with which Ellen White now viewed the situation in her statement to Irwin that "if there is an immediate necessity, we could wrench ourselves away." Again, she indicated clearly, that it was "more in regard to the Sanitarium than any other enterprise that we should come."[57] Irwin agreed. It was to secure the future of the Sydney Sanitarium and the whole Australian enterprise that she must travel to the States. Mrs. White could do "much more for the work there by being here," he would argue from the battlefield in Battle Creek.

In early April, she informed her friend Haskell of her decision. "I hope to meet you in America for we shall need all the help we can possibly obtain," she wrote. Clearly, she was gathering a coalition for the coming struggle. Although she dreaded the thought of going, she confided that she could not feel free to say she would not go. "I expect to go, just how soon, I know not."[58] As soon as Prescott received the news he applauded her decision and sent her an urgent invitation to visit England en route. Everyone, it seems, was aware that her presence in Battle Creek would be critical. "Your presence and counsel" there is "almost a necessity in order to save the cause from very great trouble," declared the professor. Prescott mentioned that he was exhausted by dealings over the publishing business with its never-ending conflicts about marketing, sale territories, book rights, and royalties, and he looked forward to the opportunity for her counsel on those specific issues as well.[59]

When Irwin received her letter, he expressed his disappointment that she could not leave for another four months, a response that indicated the sudden urgency he saw in the looming conflict. But he was glad that Daniells had also decided to come. "I think it is very important for him to attend also. I feel that our next GC will be a very important gathering." Irwin assured Ellen White that he "stood ready to cooperate" with her "to the fullest extent, so as to make your visit both pleasant and profitable." Things as he saw them, however, had become extremely serious, and he found himself becoming more and more discouraged. He was not sure just how much he should tell her about the perplexing details of the problems in Battle Creek. "You will soon begin to think that my letters are rather 'blue.' "[60] He need not have worried. She herself was growing extremely distressed.

From Dr. Edgar R. Caro, a New Zealander who was one of Kellogg's recent graduates and now a leading doctor at the Sydney Sanitarium, she heard that Kellogg was declaring that he was "going to give up and separate" from the church. He would pitch his tent elsewhere, he had stated in a letter to Caro. The prospect shocked Ellen White to the core. The fact that such statements were becoming public indicated the depth of frustration on the Kellogg side. "This is a terrible crisis we have to meet," she wrote to Irwin. She had recently learned that Kellogg was in financial difficulty; it was she who had helped close the doors of fund-raising in the church against him. Kellogg obviously felt cornered. He was financially embarrassed, and she felt "deep pity for him" in his dilemma, knowing from personal experience what such financial pressure felt like. Mrs. White wanted Irwin to do his best to "save him if possible." In his use of the copies of the letters she had sent him, the president should feel free to read them "to such ones as you choose" if he thought they would help. "But do not I entreat you, give him [Kellogg] occasion to think I am his enemy."[61] Managing the flow of information, building a coalition in defense, but at the same time struggling to keep Kellogg inside the denominational tent was a challenge such as she had never encountered before. It required much careful thought. Her spiritual leadership was about to require a sharper focus.

The looming showdown was clearly developing into a power struggle with strong political dimensions. Ellen White intuitively saw the need to influence Kellogg to do what was best for the unity of the cause, while also seeking to isolate him and to protect the church from him should the desired outcome of unity not be achieved. Irwin was going to be a key ally, and she would need to work closely with him.

Again she wrote to Irwin and enclosed copies of her continuing letters to Kellogg. Mrs. White did not inform the doctor that she was making copies of her letters available to others, although he probably assumed that such was the case since it was her common practice. She sent Irwin one letter addressed to Kellogg with the instruction that he read it to him. "You can judge by the state of his mind," she suggested, "how to use it." With another Kellogg letter that she sent Irwin, she enclosed the instruction: "please keep still about it and see what the Doctor will say or do in regard to the matter." The General Conference president would thereby "be armed if he [Kellogg] misstates" because Irwin could see what had been written "and can make the thing straight." It would call the doctor's bluff if he should misrepresent things and was also a way of protecting herself should she be misquoted.

Another approach she adopted was to try to isolate Kellogg by appealing to the denominational loyalty of his employees and associates. She requested that Irwin find an opportunity to talk to Kellogg's medical staff, seeking their support. At the same time she was aware that "they have not been true to Dr Kellogg," saying one thing to his face and something else to others. "God is not pleased with middle men." Such double dealing brought only confusion. Obviously, it would be much better if the medical staff would help Kellogg to see the dangers of his course and indicate that they were with the church. The conflict was already beginning to take on the aspects of a civil war, with families and loyalties being tested and divided.

After Irwin had the opportunity for further discussions with the doctor, he reported to Ellen White that Kellogg had developed a negative view of her role. He "still holds to his opinion that you are influenced by others, and in what you hear and read." In fact, Kellogg later expressed the view that it was Irwin who was probably the source of the negative information Ellen White was receiving about him. Had he not "poisoned Ellen White's mind against him"? As for Irwin himself, knowing that she was returning made him feel of "better heart and courage" than he had experienced for some time, even though calamities seemed to be happening all around.[62] Even as Irwin dictated this particular letter he recounted that the Kellogg's nut food factory "Sanitas" had burned to the ground. Kellogg had started this manufacturing plant privately for the purpose of commercializing his health food products. The sanitarium board had refused to become involved in the commercial development of the products, wanting to focus instead on preparing food simply for patients and guests of the sanitarium. Therefore, Kellogg had struck out on his own in partnership with his brother Will. Irwin could not estimate the amount of loss on the building, but guessed that it would be substantial and that the machinery would be quite difficult to reproduce. Would the calamity further harden Kellogg's resolve?

Ellen White, at this time, was concerned to keep informed about the rapidly developing situation in Battle Creek so that she could get a correct reading on where people stood in the conflict enveloping the church. "I want you to speak freely your minds and tell me how it appears to you," she wrote to both Irwin and Haskell in late April. What was the "present state of things?" She lamented that the difficulties with the Review and Herald board had been exacerbated by some leaders once more seeming to misunderstand her counsel concerning the need to change the membership of the board.[63] But what else had she meant by what she wrote? It was confusing for Irwin and others. Haskell stated that he planned to spend the most part of 1900 in Battle Creek trying to serve as a bridge between the parties. Irwin was stuck there whether he liked it or not.

As the winter rains settled in again around Cooranbong, the chill winds of the controversy with Kellogg grew more biting. In late May, Ellen White received a letter from Mexico, where the doctor was trying to establish a branch sanitarium. "I see by your letters that you still have the same spirit of accusation against your brethren in the ministry," she replied. With the empty coffers for the building of the Sydney Sanitarium confronting her, she again accused Kellogg of having "misappropriated God's money in doing a work you were not supposed to do, while missionary fields white to the harvest have been left without facilities." His refusal, she said, "to work in harmony with your brethren" was a rejection of the light that the Lord had given. He might feel that "Sister White has turned away," but in reality it was Kellogg who had changed and that "decidedly."[64]

By June, when Irwin learned that Ellen White's return to the United States might be delayed or perhaps not happen at all, he reported that his "heart sank." Then he pressed her hard. Having experienced the confusion that had arisen over the various interpretations and understandings given to her statements at the previous General Conference and in board meetings in which he had been the chair, he did not wish to experience it again. Her statements, he was suggesting, were not always that clear. "Nothing short of your personal presence can adjust satisfactorily to all parties," he stressed. She must come. "I would dread very much to enter into another General Conference unless you were present, or within very close reach, for matters are very sure to come up at that time that no one but yourself could settle to the satisfaction of all."[65] He was clearly intimating that she needed to be on hand to interpret herself when it came to a dispute about what she had in mind. Irwin had called the session to meet in Battle Creek, but if this did not meet her mind, could she reply by return mail? Lengthy notice would be required to change the location. It was essential that she attend, because some issues on which she had given instruction were difficult to support, and Irwin did want to see them accomplished. Events that had occurred just a few weeks previously in February had reinforced his conviction on this matter.

At the annual meetings in Nebraska early in 1900, further conflict had broken out at Union College over the vexed question of intellectual property rights. The college had set up a bakery and associated equipment for the production of Will Kellogg's granola health food. The plant generated income for the college and much needed employment for students. But with Kellogg's sanitarium board unable to become involved in the development of the food industries, and with John Harvey having to take the risk of the venture, the doctor had claimed patent rights on the health foods and demanded license fees and, it seems, a share of the profits. Union College was unwilling or unable to pay. Without a satisfactory resolution of the licensing dispute, the industries at Union had to close down for a time at considerable loss. The fact that the Nebraska Sanitarium under Kellogg's supervision and the college were located on the same property and used many of the same facilities jointly made for a frequently conflicted relationship.

News of the new conflict caused a great deal of stress for Ellen White and induced a collapse. "It made me feel as if the pangs of death had come upon me," she recalled several weeks later. "I was as cold as marble and no clothing could warm me. For a while I lay terribly ill." When the news reached her, she had been away from Cooranbong and had to return home because of the sudden illness it brought about. Consequently, she "could not attend meetings for 3 or 4 weeks." "Astonished" and bewildered as she wrote about the situation to Kellogg, she stated that she could not understand "that men who claimed to be Christian should work as you did, to cripple and limit the resources of an institution." He should "put things back as they were before."[66] If only it could be that simple. From Kellogg's perspective, such a thing would be completely unjust.

Reacting to the ethical issues that had come up in this specific conflict, Irwin expressed his view that the health food inventions were really for the whole church and not just for Kellogg's personal benefit. Had the doctor not invented the products while employed at the Sanitarium? he asked. And had not Kellogg used hospital staff and their skills in the development of the foods? added Ellen White. The doctor, for his part could not see that patents on inventions were any different from copyrights on books, and if Ellen White thought authors should receive royalties, even though those authors were employed by the church as editors, then surely inventors should receive patent fees. And besides, the church had not been willing to put up any venture capital to start the business. Kellogg himself had to undertake the risk of investment. In the absence of any clear intellectual property agreement, it was perhaps a moot point. But the larger question for both Irwin and Ellen White was: What principles should apply in determining a resolution of the conflict? In Ellen White's view the welfare and mission of the whole church should be the deciding principle. She tended to adopt a pragmatic approach to gray or complicated ethical issues. There was a need to be flexible. The larger good was the good of the cause. But Kellogg's view was that her approach was simply another example of inconsistency.[67]

In other situations where difficulties occurred over competing interests, the acceptance of Ellen White's charismatic role as an "umpire" and a willingness to let her operate in this role for the good of the whole community usually enabled the church to keep moving beyond the particular issue involved. The players on the field might have different views of the details or even of the accuracy of the umpire's call, but the willing commitment to accept the decision enabled play to proceed. Sports fans understand such an approach intuitively. It is necessary for the good of the game. And usually the principle worked in a spiritual way within the church. But on this occasion it was much more difficult for Kellogg to accept gracefully, given the enormous financial pressures he was facing.

Irwin reported shortly afterward that he had spent five hours in discussion with the doctor, but that "it was very unsatisfactory." Kellogg was "more persistent than ever in his opposition" and made stronger statements that day "than I have yet heard." Still evidently quite angry about the Union College bakery issue, Kellogg spoke openly to Irwin about Ellen White being his enemy. He vowed that if she had it "in for him," he would fight like the "Kilkenny cats."[68]

As Irwin saw it, he thought that the doctor's younger brother, Will K. Kellogg, was the "power behind the throne" at the sanitarium. Will was not an attending member of the church or even a Christian, Irwin thought. He belonged to "secret societies downtown" and was "the silent partner" in what Irwin labeled "that whole sanitarium affair." Irwin was of the view that Will Kellogg "manipulates almost everything that is done," and he worried that A. T. Jones was also becoming affected and was being drawn to the doctor's position.[69]

For Irwin, the "whole sanitarium affair" had become a nightmare that had robbed him of many nights' sleep, short though the nights might be anyhow during that Battle Creek summer. Very quickly it was becoming a highly charged situation, and Irwin clearly recognized the impact the ongoing saga could possibly have on his own tenure as president. Irwin also seems to be referring to the surprise visit to Battle Creek of John Wessels from South Africa. Irwin had met the man in Australia. Wessels had brought with him to Battle Creek quite credible rumors of developments that clearly unnerved the president. The rumors concerned a proposed change in the presidency, and they purportedly originated in Australia with Ellen White's blessing. They had found their way to Battle Creek via South Africa. The story behind the rumors, to be considered in the following chapter, illustrates the significant implications of the looming Kellogg crisis. It also highlights the inherent tensions encountered in the interaction between the administrative and charismatic function in the church as well as the dire need for extensive organizational reform. Would Irwin be able to carry through the necessary reforms?

CHAPTER 7

RUMORS and TRANSITIONS: G. A. IRWIN to A. G. DANIELLS (1900–1901)

As the final months of 1899 ticked away, political tensions between church administrators and John Harvey Kellogg heightened rapidly. Kellogg, feeling cornered in Battle Creek, was breathing threats of a giant catfight. Also, the outbreak of war on the other side of the planet raised political tensions in numerous capitals around the world and had an unexpected impact on church development in Battle Creek. The interwoven connections between these two developments at this important juncture in the story of the Adventist church are not insignificant. In both the church and the world at large, they reveal high levels of concern among leaders hidden behind a public façade of apparent peace and prosperity. Not all was as well as might appear on the surface—in either the church or the world.

On October 11, 1899, the Second Boer War in South Africa broke out with the Boer invasion in the north of the Cape Colony and the famous siege of the town of Mafeking. Between October and December, the Boers (Dutch farmers) quickly gained the upper hand, and the strategically valuable Kimberly diamond fields came under threat. The British military response, beginning in January 1900, was highly determined. The army's relief of the siege of Mafeking in May essentially ended the Cape rebellion, although it did not stop the guerilla fighting that continued for another two years in the northern territories. But the war had exacted a huge cost in both lives and property on both sides of the conflict, and it generated lingering bitterness. Tensions between the Dutch and English spread throughout the colony and infected the Adventist community there.

Among the Adventists at Battle Creek, the strains between the central church organization, on the one hand, and John Harvey Kellogg and his medical program on the other, also threatened to become open warfare. Church leaders genuinely feared a major schism. Skirmishes had already occurred in various places over a number of issues. Different views both of the methods of mission and of the form of organization best suited to support such mission clashed openly in the highest governing bodies of the church. Coalitions of supporters assembled on either side of the divide. Kellogg and his loyalists had quietly and secretly employed policies that suddenly left valuable properties under serious threat—properties the church thought it owned or considered that it should own. In significant ways the 1901 General Conference Session was shaping up to be a major battleground. Informed leaders greatly worried about the outcome. Meanwhile, rumors about a takeover of the presidency excited the leadership in the Kellogg camp.

As it happened, the Boer War had a more direct impact on the church than just as a "sign of the times" for Adventist preachers of the day. The outbreak of the war started A. G. Daniells, president of the Australian Union Conference, on an around-the-world journey to eventual leadership of the church in Battle Creek. The occasion of the war also provided the crucible for a fascinating conspiracy theory alleging that Daniells and W. C. White were plotting a takeover of church administration. The rumor circulated among various factions in the church and rumbled along the corridors of the General Conference in Battle Creek.

Just three months after war on the southern continent had erupted, an urgent petition reached Ellen White, requesting that she and her son visit South Africa to attend and counsel with the upcoming South African Union Conference. The immediate question, in light of the political and social divisions rending the country, was the sensitive one of whether the Dutch and the English church members should work separately or together. At Cooranbong in February 1900, John Wessels and the Australian church leaders had discussed the implications and the problems that the war posed for the unity of the South African church, its approach to the task of mission, and consequently the role and ownership of its various institutions. W. C. White did not feel it was advisable to accept the invitation to attend the South African Union Conference, and neither did his mother. Besides, they had pressing editorial work to complete, and the needs of the Sydney Sanitarium project were high on their agenda. Initially, some thought that neither would it be useful for Wessels to return to South Africa "at a time when so little can be accomplished, as Ellen White wrote."[1] Perhaps it would be best to go later. But, as Daniells explained to his Australian church membership in April, "after further communication with the South African brethren, and further counsel among ourselves, the conviction became general that I should go without delay." The two-year-old, four-story, rather grandiose Claremont Sanitarium in Cape Town was in trouble. After a quick rearrangement of schedules and appointments, Daniells sailed from Melbourne for South Africa with John Wessels on March 28, having just concluded the reorganization of the Australasian medical program under union administration.

At the time of Daniells's rather hasty departure he reported that he could not speak more definitely of his future plans. His colleagues, he said, had advised him to plan to attend the upcoming session of the General Conference tentatively scheduled for early 1901. But whether he should return to Australia before doing so or proceed directly to America by way of England, he was not sure. The General Conference session was still ten months away. But then, Daniells had been serving outside of his homeland for almost ten years without a furlough. Perhaps it was the time to fit one in—or at least its equivalent, for the denomination had not yet devised a furlough policy. Daniells's Australian associates simply suggested to him that he "be guided by the providence of God" in making the decision about his movements.[2]

Daniells and Wessels arrived in Cape Town on April 25, too late to be of any help in conducting meetings at the conference session, for it had concluded shortly before their arrival. But because there was important business still to be addressed regarding the sanitarium in Cape Town, members of the conference committee had stayed on until Wessels and Daniells arrived. The Claremont Sanitarium operated under J. H. Kellogg's International Medical Missionary and Benevolent Association in Battle Creek and was reputedly the best-equipped medical facility in the southern hemisphere at the time. The Wessels family had contributed largely to its construction, and it had attracted a large patronage. But at the height of the Anglo-Boer War in early 1900, the British imperial government had requisitioned half of the building for the treatment and convalescence of wounded officers returning from the front. As a result, the Christian standards of the institution rapidly broke down, particularly after the military set up a bar in its section of the building. But there was little that could be done. It was wartime, and the military prevailed.[3]

Daniells quickly became absorbed in a heavy preaching schedule in South Africa. He became well known among the leaders and members. He reported that in the forty-seven days that he stayed in the colony he preached at least fifty times, besides attending innumerable boards and committee meetings and visiting with church staff. The country was under military rule at the time, and the authorities restricted travel to Natal province and other northern regions, but Daniells was able to get a good grasp of conditions in the country through discussions with book salespeople and teachers who had returned from the troubled northern regions. He also came to a sympathetic understanding of the unique challenges of mission that made work more difficult in South Africa than in the Australian colonies. And he took time to explore the impact of the war, checking out "the soldier's camp," taking a look "at Cronje's prisoners and guns," and visiting a military hospital with its 6,000 sick and wounded soldiers. "I can tell you that war is a terrible thing," he reported to his correspondent back in Australia. Up to seventy-five military transport vessels at a time were moored in Table Bay, unloading soldiers, mules, fodder, food, and ammunition. Daniells could only gape at the immense cost of the war effort—£200,000 per day.[4]

Because of the travel restrictions applying in South Africa, Daniells soon concluded that it would be better for him to proceed directly to London early in June and spend two months in England and on the continent before going on to New York later in the year. W. W. Prescott, seeing Daniells's earlier notice in the Australian church paper, had written an invitation to his old friend to come help with work among the British churches in the month of July and then to assist with the summer camp meeting-cum-conference and evangelistic program planned for Birmingham in early August. If possible, could Daniells also fit in attendance at a scheduled conference in Denmark in early July?

Daniells embarked for England on June 11 on the *Bavarian* and arrived in Southampton twenty-one days later on American Independence Day. Special arrangements had allowed him to take passage to England on a largely empty military troop carrier returning to Britain. The budget-conscious traveler was glad that his ticket cost only a third of the normal price. Although happy to be safe in England, Daniells found himself whisked away by Prescott the very next day to the first camp meeting ever held in Germany. Five hundred people attended, and Daniells was a featured speaker, although barely a dozen people on the campground understood a word of his English. L. R. Conradi translated for him. The Daniells name was getting known in many places. He struggled to cope with the German believers' appetite for long meetings. "I think the Germans can endure more meetings than any other people I ever met." Camp "was almost a continuous meeting from six o'clock in the morning till nine o'clock at night, and everyone was as loyal as could be in attending." But Daniells valued the opportunity to learn of the work in the immense German field with its membership of just under 2,000 in a population of 116 million inhabitants. (At the time, it embraced Austria, Hungary, the Netherlands, Romania, and Bulgaria as well as Serbia.) The potential for church growth was huge. Daniells was storing away his impressions just as Adventists around the world were gathering their own views of the forty-two-year-old leader.

Back in Birmingham, the carefully planned camp meeting was a washout. Rain and strong winds spoiled the event and brought home to Daniells the difficulties of tent evangelism in England. Only a small number of interested people responded. It was a valuable lesson.

Time was also available for Daniells for his own professional development and the broadening of his horizons. He attended a large international Christian convention in London and visited the usual tourist sites, particularly enjoying London's places of historic importance. Later, at the invitation of L. R. Conradi, he also took the opportunity to spend substantial time visiting other Adventist centers and meeting Adventist workers in Europe. He enjoyed the educational experience of visiting famous historic Reformation sites in Europe in the company of Conradi. Not only did he find the Reformation tour inspiring, but the first-hand introduction to the challenges of Adventist mission in the European context was highly educational. It was all very good grooming for a General Conference president in the making.[5]

It would be hard to imagine that the problems of the church in Battle Creek and the difficulty of how to bring about the much needed organizational change at the denominational center were not repeated topics of discussion between Daniells and his hosts. How to achieve a closer relationship with Kellogg's programs would also have been a frequent topic of conversation. Prescott and Daniells shared many perspectives in common, and their travel time together would have provided an ideal opportunity to prospect for solutions even if the process turned up useable nuggets only occasionally. They probably raised and explored many "what if" scenarios. Unfortunately, and problematically, one of these "what if" scenarios took flight to Battle Creek and arrived well before its time while Daniells occupied himself with his European travels. Daniells had tried to alert Irwin in advance about some serious trouble brewing in South Africa. Sometime in June he had reported to the General Conference president that he had heard that John Wessels was "likely to go to Battle Creek to counsel with Dr Kellogg." He was oblivious, however, to the story that Wessels would carry with him.

Apparently, Wessels had left South Africa about the same time as Daniells and had also gone to England, although we have no record of the two men having traveled together on this leg of the journey. Daniells had learned somehow that Wessels and his brothers wanted to make "a fund for running the medical work in Africa on independent lines, the same as Dr Kellogg has decided to do in America." For this purpose, they had requested back from the General Conference the large sum of money that they had earlier placed on loan with the church. "It is one of the most scandalous things I have seen amongst any of our business affairs," Daniells reported to the General Conference president.[6] But it seems that Irwin may not have received Daniells's letter in time to be prepared for the forthcoming request. He later reported great surprise at seeing John Wessels alighting from the train at the Battle Creek railway station in the company of Kellogg. The pair had traveled from Chicago on the same train as Irwin, but without either party being aware of it.

The General Conference was seriously embarrassed at Wessels' request for the withdrawal of funds. It simply was not in a position to repay just at that time. The demand was so troubling that it prompted Irwin to venture a rare criticism of the work of his predecessor. He felt that the church was about to reap the whirlwind from some of Olsen's decisions. "We are right face to face with the extravagant policy pursued by Elder Olsen's administration, and with the effects of A. R. Henry's and H. Lindsay's influence as they have gone from place to place sowing doubt in regard to the testimonies of God's spirit," he complained to Ellen White.[7]

CONSPIRACY FEVER BREAKS LOOSE

It was with "utter surprise and astonishment," Irwin recalled, that he set eyes on John Wessels, "about the first man after we got off the train at Battle Creek." Irwin was returning from a trip to California. The president recovered quickly enough, however, to greet Wessels and Kellogg with composure and pleasant surprise and immediately invited Wessels to his home for the evening. Wessels visited for about an hour and chatted about his trip to South Africa, England, and then on to the United States. He briefed Irwin on some new information about the Sydney Sanitarium and problems with Edgar Caro and concluded by stating that "first thing the next morning" before daylight he was going back to New York and Philadelphia in preparation to return to England, where he needed to appear in person to pick up some important documents.

However, the following evening, to Irwin's further surprise, he found John Wessels sitting on the platform of the Battle Creek Tabernacle next to Will Kellogg, participating in the graduation exercises for the second class of students from the new medical school. J. H. Kellogg had given the graduation talk and had spoken effusively about the Wessels gift that had made the Adventist medical school possible. In the past, the Wessels family had donated almost $40,000 for Kellogg's program in Chicago. In his speech, the doctor had talked about future possibilities in the development of the medical school and alluded to the fact that one of the Wessels brothers was with them that night. It was excellent public relations. But behind the hoopla was something sinister and cynical. Wessels had been duplicitous with Irwin. Why? Irwin found out the following night when he attended the Sanitarium board meeting. The General Conference president related the sequence of events in detail to Ellen White.

Some time earlier, she had asked him to keep her informed about things in Battle Creek. Now he felt the time had arrived when he should respond to that request. "I feel it my duty now to tell you plainly just how things stand here, viewing them from my standpoint," he wrote. She had said in her previous letter that he should feel free "to write fully of the situation of Battle Creek," he noted. Then he proceeded to relate the details of the sorry, but alarming, story.[8]

During his visit to Battle Creek, Wessels had a long meeting with A. R. Henry and, according to Irwin, had reported to the disaffected Henry that "while they [the Whites] condemned the Doctor [Kellogg] for expending money so extravagantly, that was just what they were doing in Australia." It was after his visit with Henry that Wessels had gone to the General Conference treasurer's office and demanded that the denomination pay back the money it had borrowed from his mother. The money was needed, he said, "within six months." The sum involved was huge. According to Irwin, it would "necessitate us raising about sixty thousand dollars." In a further interview with Wessels, Irwin tried to establish "why the haste." Wessels' response was simply that his mother was the guardian of the money, that it was now due, and that the church would need to produce it. Irwin noted to Ellen White that it seemed clear that the family was pressuring Mrs. Wessels. And it was clear to Irwin that John Wessels was now antagonistic toward the church leadership.[9]

Percy Magan, head of the Bible department at Battle Creek College, had also provided further background information for Irwin. Magan reported that since seeing the work Kellogg had been doing in Chicago, Wessels had entirely changed his mind about its merits. Irwin quoted Magan as saying that Wessels now believed "that Sister White 'had it in for the Doctor' as they say." Many knew that Ellen White had written to the Wessels brothers stating that they should not have given their large financial gift to the medical school. But, according to Magan, the Wessels family had concluded that they had "done the right thing and were glad they gave it."[10] Such determined opposition alarmed the president. But he was yet to hear more.

The evening following the medical school graduation, Kellogg had called a meeting of the board of the Benevolent Association. It was one that Irwin would never forget. At the meeting Kellogg reported that he had received letters from Ellen White dealing with the Union College "Bakery Business" and talked quite outspokenly about her having been wrongly informed. The doctor informed his board that he did not propose "to be on his feet one day, and on his head the next," but that he would "act upon his own convictions." Apparently, he cited numerous examples of Mrs. White's inconsistencies and had spoken boldly and openly of his troubles with her. The doctor was clearly struggling with episodes that he believed were invalidating Ellen White's charisma. And now he was endeavoring to invalidate her gift among his colleagues. Irwin felt that perhaps Kellogg had gone on "quite at length," seeing that he had an opportunity "to address himself to me." But what really worried the president was that the doctor appeared not to be reacting emotionally to some particular disappointment or perplexity that would allow Irwin to understand him as simply venting his feelings. Quite to the contrary, Kellogg "was not excited in the course of his talk." Nor did he talk "in a disrespectful way to me," Irwin recalled. "But he spoke with a calmness of a man who had firmly and determinately made up his mind what he was going to do."[11]

The bombshell of the night for Irwin, however, was the story that Kellogg related openly to his board, one that he presented without the slightest concern that Irwin was in the room—or more probably, precisely because he was there. Kellogg's narrative concerned plans to push the General Conference president out of office. Irwin sat with mouth agape as he heard the details.

As Irwin later recounted the incident to Ellen White, John Wessels had reported to Kellogg that there was "a scheme on foot in Australia, implying that it was hatched up by WCW, with the sanction of yourself [Ellen White], that Elder Daniells was to be elected President of the General Conference at the next session, and that WCW was to be President or Secretary of the Foreign Mission Board: that this scheme was gotten up by WCW because he could twist Daniells around as he pleased, and get him to sanction his schemes."

The claim took Irwin's breath away, and he could hardly believe what he was hearing. According to Kellogg, Wessels had quoted Daniells as saying publicly that "when he got to America and into that position, he would sell out some of the big institutions that the Medical Board had created, and send the money over to Australia to help in the work there."

While Irwin felt the account was not quite entirely believable, "the fact that Brother Daniells' having gone to Africa, and is coming around by England to the United States," gave "a little coloring to the statement," meaning that Irwin didn't think it was entirely void of credibility either. Wessels had clearly said to Kellogg that Daniells's travels and getting acquainted with the worldwide field was "part of the program." The story just might have something to it, and for many in Battle Creek, it certainly seemed to have a strong veneer of truth. Had not Wessels been closely associated with Daniells? Had they not traveled together? Clearly, Irwin was shaken, but he was not taken in completely. He confided to Ellen White, "I believe that Brother Daniells is a man of too good sense to make a public statement to that effect regarding a thing that is so uncertain." But where would such a tale originate? It would be entirely natural for Irwin to try to imagine how such a story could come about. Sea voyages can be long. Perhaps Daniells and Wessels had shared some vague "what if" scenarios on the journey to the Cape. That could at least have given a basis for some elements of the story.

The rumor did not take long to get around Battle Creek. In fact, it spread like wildfire. The very next day "several different ones" dropped into the president's office, "and all seemed to know of what had been said, because they began at once telling me and even bringing out further light along this line," Irwin reported soberly. Will Kellogg called the coup d'état planned to replace Irwin an "open secret," and he spoke about it freely. The whole drift of the effort, the General Conference president thought, was to get the official leadership "enlisted on the doctor's side."

It had been a challenge at first for Irwin to sit in the small circle of men at the board meeting and listen to the details of the alleged plot. But as he recounted later, as Kellogg drew his account to a close with its salacious details, it had "flashed" upon his mind "in an instant" that the story "was a trick of the enemy to get me stirred up, and to get my sympathies on their side of the question." Thus Irwin found himself able to answer the doctor "very quickly." He responded that "if he [Kellogg] had told that to me in the hope that I would become stirred by it he was mistaken." In fact, he asserted in reply, "I should be only too glad to be relieved of the burdens and responsibilities of the General Conference; and was I to make a choice of my successor, I would not know of a better man than Brother Daniells." "But," he said, pausing for effect, "however that may be, there is one thing that I want distinctly understood, and that is, that not only so long as I occupy this position, but I trust, until the Lord comes, I shall remain loyal and true to the third angel's message and the testimonies of the Spirit of God."

However, the fact that John Wessels had "thoroughly turned over to the other side, and was in sympathy with the Doctor and his movements" greatly troubled Irwin. And he was also deeply disturbed by Wessels's negative assessment of the situation in Australia. The report Wessels was giving was that when he went to Australia he "found out what had been done for Australia." He "thought that the General Conference had been very liberal to that field." Such a report would cause serious damage.

After the board meeting, the president recalled that he "slept little that night," because, he said, "it revealed to me at that time, the situation of affairs in the Doctor's condition." As he tossed and turned, he "reviewed the matter over and over" in his mind. Would this interminable conflict in the church and the unending competition over the use of resources ever find resolution? What was he to do? And how much credence should he really give to the conspiracy? How much should he report to Ellen White? And how soon would Kellogg make his moves? The whole episode nagged at him.

As soon as he had the chance to report to Mrs. White, he stressed urgently that she needed to return to America. "I will again urge . . . that you come to this country at the earliest possible moment after you receive this letter." The game was getting more than serious—it was becoming dangerous. It was clear, Irwin said, that "unless this wrong influence is checkmated in some way," he feared that "Australia will be boycotted." Irwin expressed the view that he hoped she would "fully appreciate the fact that we here are in a measure powerless to turn the tide without your personal presence." "The work there [in Australia] will be assisted by your presence here," he declared. In the meantime he would "endeavor to keep up courage" and "do the very best" he could "to hold things in even lines." But this was a task that was becoming increasingly difficult.[12]

Two and a half weeks later, Irwin updated Ellen White again on the Kellogg front. "It seems to me," he reported from the Battle Creek trenches, "that he [Kellogg] is trying to form a strong combination on his side of the question and get as many of the brethren confused over the Testimonies as possible."[13] The president realized that he would need to reverse the Union College "bakery business thing" but feared that if he did so Kellogg would use it "as an excuse for him to cut away entirely." The minefield that Battle Creek had become was proving perplexing beyond measure. Irwin felt that he had to walk on eggshells everywhere he went and to watch his back continuously. He concluded his report on the matter with a resolution to say nothing more about it "because it pains me to write it, as it seems so much like tattling and accusing." Yet Irwin knew that Ellen White was "anxious to know just how things are here."

Another sensitive issue that complicated the president's life at this time was the tensions within the White family itself. As these became known publicly, they tended to diminish the effectiveness of Ellen White's influence yet further, and Irwin, from the perspective of exercising his administrative gift, felt he had a duty to help protect against that. The incident also highlights the importance that he placed on the value of Ellen White's ability to continue to exercise her influence in the church.

W. C. White's interference in the sales campaign for his mother's book, *Christ's Object Lessons,* had created a number of problems. Ellen White had donated the book and its royalties to an effort to raise money to pay off the large burdens of debt on the church's colleges and schools. A committee at the General Conference had been set up to coordinate the campaign, and by midsummer of 1900 about 9,000 copies of the book had already been sold. The committee's task had been complicated, however, because it had to deal with "unnecessary perplexities" occasioned by Willie White's contrary communications with C. H. Jones of the Pacific Press®. Jealousies and competition in the publishing program lay at the core of the problem. White alleged that the committee was discriminating against the Pacific Press, but its members disagreed. The "general mind" of the committee members was that if they really had responsibility for the project, "they ought to be left free to make their arrangements and not have them broken into and changed by what Brother White may write, as he has done in the past," reported the president. In the view of Edson White, who was a member of the committee, if his brother "was going to mix in and mingle with it and confuse matters, then the committee might as well stop their efforts."

Irwin wanted Ellen White to understand that he wrote as he did on the sensitive matter because the committee had specifically requested it of him, "having passed a motion" to that effect. But then from his own perspective as president he added some advice. "In view of the strained condition of things in this country at the present time with regard to the Testimonies, I think myself" that "it would be well if WCW would not write so much in regard to things in general and be more careful in what he does write to be sure that it is in perfect accord with your mind and the mind of the Lord."[14] With Kellogg waiting to catch at any inconsistency, it was important for there to be a unity of voice. Again, Irwin reiterated that because of the condition of things in the United States, Mrs.

White could help Australia more by her presence in America than she could by remaining in Australia.

His repeated concern clearly suggests that even during her lifetime, when the exercise of her spiritual gift was able to operate in the dynamic of interpersonal give-and-take interaction with individuals through correspondence, there were still limitations to the effectiveness and clarity of such communications. Her written word was effective, but nevertheless, confusion still frequently occurred, particularly when the church faced rapid development and numerous complex problems during the late 1890s. Irwin felt that it was much more effective to have the prophetic gift "in person" to clarify her message for committees and for individuals. Hearing the tone and the inflection and the passion of her voice and having the opportunity to ask for something to be repeated, clarified, or further elaborated following feedback and discussion was important. For the Adventist community today, living with only the writings themselves and with the living "gift" no longer available, the problem of interpretation and understanding can become even more difficult. Of course, as the later history of Kellogg illustrates, even the presence of the living "gift" was not always effective.

As for Irwin, he was starting to weary of the incessant conflict and concluded that he was reaching the point of discouragement. He was beginning to worry that he was going to face the same end as Olsen. "It seems as though all my efforts have been a failure."[15]

Ellen White denies the conspiracy

By the time Ellen White received Irwin's panicky letter asking her to return immediately to the States, she had already booked her passage to leave Sydney on August 29. Irwin did not need to worry that she would not come. But two weeks before she left she wrote an eleven-page letter of encouragement to the despondent president and denied any knowledge of a conspiracy to replace him, calling it a "fabrication." It was one of the warmest letters he had received from her thus far.

"I am so sorry for the fabrication that it is our secret purpose to depose Brother Irwin for Elder Daniells, and that W. C. White is to figure as president of the Mission Board," she began. She certainly knew that the part about W. C. White's role was not true. If her son wanted that kind of work, there was plenty of it that he could do in Australia, she noted. But in fact, it was "to be free of such responsibilities" that Willie was interested in returning to America with his mother. He had already resolved not to live anywhere near a school, hospital, or publishing house so that he could avoid administrative entanglements and focus his energies on helping his mother with her literary projects. Any place less than at least ten miles away from an Adventist institution would be too close. Irwin could "take this for granted," and she hoped he would not let the "enemy" have any power over his mind. "I wish to say that I hope you thank the Lord that you have been enabled to stand firm."[16]

In denying the rumor she could, of course, speak only for herself and what she knew of her plans for her son. Her letter carefully avoided speaking directly on behalf of Daniells. He had already left the country. But for her part, as far as she knew, the reports were simply not true. She was distressed that Wessels would circulate such a thing. "I feel more than sad over the case of John Wessels," she observed and then gave an illustration intimating why his judgment on things was not sound. If South Africa had not followed the pattern of Battle Creek, the sanitarium there would not now be in such serious debt. It was simply the desire for an ostentatious "appearance" that had caused the South African project to absorb so much money. Wessels might say "in Cooranbong as in Battle Creek," but Irwin should know the truth. After all, she reminded him, he had been on the ground and "could speak intelligently in regard to this." He had seen for himself that they had not built expensively in Cooranbong.

Irwin should "take no notice of how men credit the words of men against God's servants." There were always those who "swallow false statements greedily," she observed, "without waiting to know whether they are true." She urged him not to give in to discouragement. "I will see you soon," she assured him.

"My brother," she concluded, "do not become depressed. Do not believe the reports that you hear . . . stand in the power of the Lord." But, at the same time, she indicated that she had half expected something like this. "The things have happened that I feared in regard to Dr Kellogg. I am so sorry."[17]

In her letter to Irwin, she enclosed a copy of one that she had written to Haskell about the same problem. Why she wrote just to Haskell and not to A. T. Jones as the *Review* editor, to get out a correction in the paper, as she sometimes did, or why she did not write to the Sanitarium board where the rumor had been reported, she does not say. The range of possibilities available to her for exercising her influence in a sensitive situation like this had to be thought through carefully. Would Haskell be tempted to believe the report himself and thus be more guarded and unsure and thereby diminish his support for Irwin? Or had it occurred to her that Haskell (and/or his wife) would perhaps be the best ones to get the word out to others? Clearly, it would be helpful and important to make the denial known to someone else in addition to Irwin. It would then avoid the situation of the General Conference president having to defend himself. It would also give the denial greater credence. In some ways Haskell was her agent behind the lines in Battle Creek, and she needed to keep him abreast of things, anyway.

In her letter to Haskell, she related the details of the report as Irwin had communicated them to her. Supposedly "WCW and A. G. Daniells had plans all devised." She then compared the conspiracy theory with the one circulated by William Healy of California just prior to the 1888 General Conference Session. In fact, "it seems to be Minneapolis acting over again in Battle Creek," she observed. "There is not one thread of truth in these statements. Such a plan has never been so much as thought of."[18]

In support of the denial, she again reiterated that when she and her son arrived in America, "under no circumstances" did they want to locate in Battle Creek or anywhere "east of the Rockies." They wanted to focus on "bookmaking," and thus W. C. White planned to "have no connection with any duties or offices that would demand our attention." Furthermore, she added, they were not planning to stay in America anyway. "Please be assured that we do not leave this field willingly," she wrote. "We intend to return as soon as it seems that God wills it."

Then in plain but carefully chosen language she stated her position about Irwin in a positive manner rather than negatively by way of denial. It seems that through Haskell she knew she was now addressing a wider audience. Clearly, she also seemed to be stating her position on the upcoming election just six months away. Whether she used the plural "we" to indicate that she was also speaking on behalf of W. C. White or just to give her statement more authority is not clear. "Now in regard to the work in America: we have the fullest confidence in Brother Irwin as the proper man for the place he occupies. We see no reason why he should be exchanged for another man." If in 1897 Ellen White had not been sure that Irwin was the "proper" person for appointment to the presidency, she had become convinced in the interim. She reiterated her denial of knowing of any plan for change. "The reports in regard to Elder Daniells taking his [Irwin's] place are without the slightest foundation as far as my knowledge is concerned. But they are just as true as were the reports that were sent over from Healdsburg to Battle Creek, to Elder Butler in regard to plans that were to be worked up and presented in Minneapolis." In conclusion, she declared, "We do not worry. The cause is the Lord's." Then she added the same line of argument as in her letter to Irwin. "Remember my brother, as you read this letter [to Haskell], that there is just as much truth in the statement made by John

Wessels as in the report that Brother Healy sent to Elder Butler before the Minneapolis meeting."[19]

It seems clear that even if Daniells had engaged in some indiscreet conjecturing about the upcoming General Conference session, he knew perfectly well how the church election system worked. He had not made any plans to uproot permanently from Australia. In October, shortly after his arrival in New York, he had written of his planned movements to Farnsworth, who was acting in his place in Australia. Daniells told him that he would be "unable to return to Australia before May or June" the following year, still another eight months away. His absence was certainly turning into a very long furlough! Still receiving full salary from the General Conference payroll, he had fallen into the role of revivalist and counselor at large and was beginning to "begrudge the time" that he would need to spend in America.

But the conspiracy rumor did not die. A month after Ellen White arrived in America and after having had the opportunity to consult with Irwin and others and after receiving a disturbing letter from Dr. Daniel Kress alerting her to the depths of the struggle emerging at Battle Creek, she realized that the situation was serious and the rumor had proved damaging. She needed to clear up the situation. "Here I am retired from the strife of tongues," she commented wistfully but with sharp irony and clearly with some annoyance at having to address the issue. This time she wrote more generally to the whole officer group at the General Conference. Were they possibly envisaging a wider purge associated with the rumored coup d'état? And were they doubting the disclaimers she had issued? This time she was more emphatic. But, again, it was the role of W. C. White that she focused on. Judging from Irwin's mid-July letter to her suggesting that her son do less writing of letters and less interfering, it seems that many perceived the possibility of W. C. White's involvement in church administrative affairs as a much greater threat and problem than that of Daniells. In either case, such a scheme was not only distasteful but dangerous.

"For the sake of the cause of God it is my duty to say that the reports made to you by [Wessels] that Eld. Daniells was to be the president of the next General Conference in the place of Elder Irwin . . . are most surprising falsehoods. Such a thought never entered our minds and we have never said anything to cause such a report to be circulated. All my workers and W. C. White himself understand that in leaving Australia WCW laid off every official duty that he might help me in my book work. I employ him as my general helper in the work."[20]

At the 1888 General Conference Session, though there had not been any real conspiracy prior to the meetings, nevertheless, events at the session turned out fairly close to what the alleged conspiracy had projected. It was to be the same in this situation. Irwin would not find this out, however, for another six months. As events unfolded and the predicted change in his role took place in early 1901, he was deeply hurt. He wondered what he had done wrong and puzzled over what mistakes he might have made. But if he harbored any suspicion that there might actually have been elements of truth in the presession rumors—elements that Ellen White was not herself aware of—he kept such thoughts to himself. Believing that the cause was bigger than just one person, he gave his full support to his replacement. But all that was for post-session rumination. For now, in August 1900, he had more urgent things to deal with.

Where to live and where to meet

The final few weeks before Ellen White left for America were frantic ones of packing and preparation for her staff, who worked through numerous long nights in order to be ready. A hastily called union conference council met at Cooranbong during the last two weeks of August, as well, just to ensure that all the details related to the transfer of responsibilities were properly cared for and loose ends were tied up. And on top of this, Mrs. White was still writing important materials and needed them typed and copied for publication right up to the very night before she left. By the time her party boarded the ship in Sydney on August 29, her helpers, if not she herself, were at the point of total exhaustion. Two days out from port, Sarah McEnterfer had still not gotten out of bed "except to have it made more comfortable." If Mrs. White was planning to return to Australia, she had packed and prepared as if she had left forever. The family's houses had been sold, complete with furniture and other appurtenances such as horses and carriages, and almost everything else had been disposed of. Personal effects and all her manuscript files and writing materials went with her. At her age, now almost seventy-three, she had to plan for all contingencies.

It was a difficult departure, as she recounted to Edson just before embarking. She did not want to leave Australia. "We feel this is our home." And the timing was not good, especially just when the Sydney Sanitarium was about to be built. But "things have not been moving in right lines," and it was imperative that she make the trip for the good of the cause.[21] By the time her traveling party arrived in San Francisco by way of Auckland and Samoa and had anchored in the bay, it was Thursday night, September 20. But they then had to "go through the mill at the quarantine station" which took all the next day so that they were not able to disembark until after sunset on Friday evening. Colleagues, friends, and well-wishers were on hand to greet them, including General Conference president Irwin, who had traveled three days across the country just for that purpose.

The very next morning they attended church in the city. Irwin did the preaching, and in the afternoon Ellen White held sway. The families were staying temporarily at a rural health retreat at St. Helena while they looked for a more permanent residence. By the following Sunday, the last in September and only a week after Ellen White had arrived back in the States, she participated in an all-day consultation with her two sons and three other church leaders, sorting out problems and misunderstandings in the publishing program and in regard to the work in the South. Difficulties were still occurring over the financial transactions between Edson and the publishers and the Southern Missionary Society. Edson never found it easy to keep his financial affairs in order, and it caused his mother considerable stress and worry.

In the meantime, Irwin had been able to brief Ellen White on the ongoing developments at Battle Creek and to discuss the timing and location of the next General Conference session. It was urgent that the arrangements be confirmed. Although the date and place had already been announced for the meeting, some uncertainty still lingered. The day-long meeting at St. Helena the following Sunday provided opportunity for wider input. Leadership had to give careful consideration to the implications of each decision. Relationships were so sensitive and every action open for interpretation or misinterpretation by one side or the other that a wrong decision could easily exacerbate the threatening schism. Both Irwin and Ellen White realized they needed to move with great care. As a result, the matter seesawed for several weeks, and Irwin became not a little embarrassed because of it. The episode illustrates the high level of tension in the church over Ellen White's perceived influence and the way that she had to carefully consider her role at this time. Knowing just how to exercise her influence for the overall good of the church had never been so difficult. The episode also illustrates the level of diplomatic understanding church administration had sometimes to exercise in relating to the gift of the charismatic leader.

In addition, Ellen White had to weigh personal considerations. She was advanced in years, and her health was not really robust. Being in Battle Creek during midwinter with all that meant in terms of extreme cold outdoors, heated, stuffy meeting rooms, chilly bedrooms, and the risk of infection, did not seem at all wise to her. Had not her new friend Mrs. Henry not long ago put herself similarly at risk by overexertion during the winter months and sacrificed her life to pneumonia? The loss of her labor was tragic. "I feel this keenly," Mrs. White stated. The prospect of it happening to her was frightening. That would be far too high a price to pay. But had she not endured the enormous upheaval of coming back to America "especially" to be at the session at Battle Creek?[22] Still, convening the conference in Oakland, California, was perhaps another option. After all, one had to take into account certain political and spiritual considerations. Would a better spiritual atmosphere be more easily achieved away from Battle Creek? Irwin had argued that case for the previous 1899 session. But would bypassing Battle Creek leave the field of influence among the large groups of general institutional employees there open to Dr. Kellogg and his criticisms of Ellen White and her role? Would it suggest that there was an intent to isolate and abandon him? Would it confirm suspicions of the alleged conspiracy to change leadership? Such considerations were not easy to balance against each other. But at the end of the informal consultation on the question in late September (informal, because it was not really the role of this small group of five to decide the issue), convening the session in Oakland, California, close to Ellen White's residence, seemed the better option. Irwin left to return to Battle Creek prepared to argue the case and recommend to his committee that the meeting site be shifted to Oakland. The Annual Council that began October 10 confirmed Oakland as the session location, but it was not, according to Dr. Kress, a unanimous decision. Some had abstained from voting. Neither Ellen White nor W. C. White had been able to go to the Autumn Council because they were busy doing what they could to find a new home before cold weather set in.[23]

Eventually, after Mrs. White had done considerable searching, a property in the Napa Valley in northern California came to her attention, and it was available for early occupancy. The property complied nicely with the earlier criteria that W. C. White had spelled out about distances from denominational institutions and the need of a location to avoid unnecessary interruptions. By early October, Ellen White was ready to move in. The home soon became known as Elmshaven and provided a delightful retirement setting for her family. The locality was "most agreeable and healthful." She hoped that her longtime friends, the Haskells, could also settle close by. "This is what he and I, old way-worn pilgrims need," she sighed.[24] But the arrival of a letter from Dr. Daniel Kress just a few days later shattered her dream of a quiet retirement. About to leave for Australia after attending the union conference session in Battle Creek, Kress felt strongly that the decision to convene the General Conference session in Oakland was a mistake and described the political impact such a decision would have on the meetings.

Kress reported that given the looming crisis in the church, the majority of those at the council believed that Battle Creek would be the much better location. But, he candidly pointed out, "they were afraid to go against her wishes." Had the heated language of her previous communications intimidated them? Were they afraid of receiving criticism? Kress thought they had begun to stop thinking for themselves. He went on to explain his conviction that meeting away from Battle Creek would only reinforce Dr. Kellogg's perception that "every hand is against him." And Kress believed that the doctor's view was not altogether without reason, "for some of our brethren have used the testimonies which were given to correct him and save him, as a club to destroy him and his influence." Thus, Kress reported, "the doctor thinks you also are trying to crush him." He had already heard a rumor that Kellogg was planning to leave the denomination.[25] While this was not news to Ellen White, the reminder was no less troubling. Furthermore, Kress hoped that she could somehow find the opportunity to have a good heart-to-heart talk with Kellogg.

The letter disturbed Mrs. White. It was all becoming too difficult. After all, she did not want to be "in the midst of scenes of contention and strife." Nor did she think the Lord was calling her to place herself "where I will be subject to unsanctified speeches," another reason she did not want to go to Battle Creek. The whole climate of resistance was distasteful. She did not want to be in the situation of having to watch her every word and to be careful to whom she should speak. Why was everything so difficult? "What I might say in private conversations would be repeated as to make it mean exactly the opposite to what it would have meant had the hearers been sanctified in mind and spirit." Unfortunately, this was not a new experience. "I am afraid to speak even to my friends; for afterwards I hear, Sister White said this, or Sister White said that." By now she was coming to the conclusion "that the Lord desires me to keep out of large assemblies and refuse private interviews."[26]

What annoyed her about the new picture emerging after she had read Kress's letter was the idea that, in the mind of the church, blame for the late change of the meeting location rested on her. "He said that the reason given why it was proposed to have it in Oakland was that it was Sister White's preference." That was true. But she did "not like to have the matter stand in this way." If church leaders really thought that it was "best" to have the General Conference session in Battle Creek, she would not "stand in the way." She did not have to be there. "The meeting can be held all the same," she argued. In fact, her presence wasn't necessary even if the session were to be held in Oakland.

Did she really mean what she seemed to be saying—that she had come all the way back to America from Australia and yet might not attend the General Conference session after all? Would she really just not show up, even if rescheduling the event to be convened in Oakland was going to add somewhere between five thousand and eight thousand dollars to its cost?

To some degree Ellen White was expressing her frustrations in all this. As Arthur White notes, her correspondence during this period "reveals the struggle in her heart."[27] She did not have any clear light as to whether to make the journey to Battle Creek in midwinter, and she was fearful. After all, she was now seventy-two years old.

In late November, Kellogg himself decided to make a surprise trip to California to visit with his longtime spiritual mentor, whom he thought had now become his nemesis. Somehow the ice needed to be broken. It was an awkward meeting at first, with each wary of the other, but as the interview progressed the relationship soon warmed again. A sense of relief seems to fill her words as she reported the meeting to her colleagues in Australia. "Well, I have seen Dr. Kellogg, and have had an interview with him. I think there is now a much better understanding, and that the Lord will work out the whole matter." She sensed from him a new willingness and hoped that the ministry and the medical branch could indeed be solidly united. "Health reform is the helping hand of the ministry," she remarked, reflecting upon the interview and on the fact that both Dr. Kress and J. A. Burden were almost on their way to Australia to help get the Sydney Sanitarium on its feet. Also she had actually begun to feel better physically already, and in the days that followed, her opposition to going to Battle Creek began to weaken. "I must meet the people at Battle Creek sometime," she began to reason with herself, and perhaps, after all, "the sooner the better."[28]

Among the topics she and Kellogg discussed was the problem of holding the session in Battle Creek. In response to her anxieties about the Michigan winter weather, Kellogg asked if it would make a difference if the date for the meetings could be postponed a few weeks. Then he suggested that perhaps she would benefit from treatments at the sanitarium and possibly should come several weeks prior to the session to receive them. Kellogg was trying to be helpful. And besides, as Ellen White thought about it more, she did not at all like the idea that in the future some would claim that the session had met in Oakland just to accommodate her and thus the impression linger in minds that "Sister

White said the Conference must be held in Oakland, and all must do as she said."[29] Again, she was reflecting on how she might best exercise her influence and enhance her effectiveness in achieving her desired outcomes. She realized that such a state of affairs would actually demean and belittle her influence and make her exercise of it even more difficult.

Thus, several days after Kellogg's visit, she wrote to Irwin indicating that if the meeting could be postponed until after February or March, she probably could attend even if it were held in Battle Creek.[30] However, ever since Kellogg's return, Irwin had heard second hand the "flying rumors of a change of the time and place." Before he received Ellen White's letter, he had talked with the doctor, trying to understand the situation. They discussed the options, but Irwin did not think it was possible that the time could be shifted. It was just too late. The meetings were only ten weeks away. The denomination had already contracted for transportation, and people from overseas had booked berths on ships. It was too complicated. Besides, back in 1899 Irwin had tried to persuade administration to have the session later in the spring and to have it outdoors. The state conference presidents had voted down his suggestion unanimously. Although he doubtless did not mention this to Kellogg, the General Conference president had also understood that Ellen White had been rather fearful that the doctor might try to influence her unduly regarding the venue of the session. Irwin later learned that Kellogg had said nothing to Ellen White that could be construed in this way. But it is clear that both the timing and the location of the session had now become something of a political football. It was in Kellogg's interests to have the session in Battle Creek, and it now seemed to be in Irwin's interests to have it elsewhere.

Irwin received Ellen White's letter on December 10, six days after she had written it. From it, he understood that she would "assume responsibility for the change" of location for the session back to Battle Creek. That made things easier. All that was left for the committee to do, then, was to "set the time." Immediately he called together the available members of his officer group and did his best to confer with all the absent ones. They approved the change and set the new date for April 2. Although uncomfortable about the whole affair and feeling somehow that he had been wrong-footed and was now embarrassed at having to reverse himself on the matter, still Irwin was willing to go along with it. "The only thing that commends itself to me," he wrote to Ellen White after the vote, "is that you have been impressed with the responsibility of a duty . . . to meet the situation as it now exists and bear your testimony, and that it should be at the heart of the work." Every day that passed, he said, only confirmed in him more "the conviction that we are on the eve of the greatest crisis that has ever come to the work," and that it would "take all the moral force of those that are loyal and true . . . to stem the tide of skepticism and personal ambition that is rising up amongst us." Therefore he was willing "to forego any personal feelings or convictions in the matter" in order that the session "be held in a time and place that will be conducive to the best interests of the Lord's cause."[31]

Ellen White's uncertainty and ultimate reversal certainly caused problems for Irwin and his officers as they scrambled to implement all the resulting changes. Travel arrangements were one thing that must be dealt with. Prescott, for example, had already booked passage and would therefore end up being kept out of his field for a "very much longer time." Others probably found themselves in similar situations. Irwin himself had a major personal problem. He had been leasing his house in Battle Creek on a month-by-month basis and had not made plans past April. This was probably wise, even apart from the conspiracy rumors of a leadership change. As he explained to Ellen White, "I supposed by that time I would know definitely whether I should want the house longer or not as that would be after the session of the General Conference." Now, however, the session had been postponed, and meanwhile the landlord had put the house on the market and would not extend the lease any further. The owner did not want to miss the "selling month" of April. Thus Irwin faced the prospect not only of being thrown out of office but out of his house as well. No wonder he did not feel comfortable.

No less difficult was the challenge of explaining things diplomatically to the state conference presidents and others. Irwin told Mrs. White that he thought it would be necessary "to send to the presidents a copy of the communication" that she had addressed to the General Conference committee "that gives the reason for the change." He did not think that it would perhaps "be prudent to publish that in full in the 'Review'" and was sure that the shift in time and place would "evidently please some and disappoint others."[32] Also, he acknowledged that it would "bring some individuals into trying places to explain to the satisfaction of others why the change was made, without their knowing the real reason." Obviously, there were things that could not be fully disclosed. The General Conference president felt trapped, knowing that he would be criticized whichever way the decision went. Being an administrator, he must have thought to himself, was sometimes exceedingly difficult.

For her part, Ellen White had agonized over the matter, trying to come to terms with the prospect of having to face the difficulty that Battle Creek posed for her. She had been extremely reticent to commit herself. The additional expense of the Oakland location had worried her, but the weather issue made her most fearful. For a week, she reported, she had lost many nights' sleep before fully resolving the matter in her mind. Earlier, when she thought she had mustered the courage to deal with the discomfort and the tension of Battle Creek, she had actually written a letter to Irwin agreeing to go, but then did not feel comfortable enough to actually mail it and held it back. Finally, she felt that she had no choice but to attend. "I dare not do otherwise," she wrote a fortnight later.

As it turned out, it was important for her to be at the session. Her role as a catalyst for change was crucial. The session of 1901 managed to implement radical shifts in the structure of the organization that enabled it to cope much better with the rapid growth the denomination now experienced. It also provided an opportunity to defuse, at least for a time, the tensions that had been developing between the medical and the ministerial segments of the church.

Engineering change: The 1901 General Conference Session

In the period just prior to the 1901 session, Ellen White's general letters continued to reflect an intense tone, and issues assumed a large cosmic dimension as she addressed the continuing problems at the General Conference. "A change must come," she wrote at the end of December. "Men who do not feel any special reverence in officiating in the various lines of the work should be dismissed much more decidedly than a man who does bungling work in a temporal business." The point she was trying to make was that the work of the church should be done "with sanctified judgment and clear discernment."[33] The immediate episode giving rise to her comments was a situation in which denominational auditors were using cheap or coarse and harsh words as they reviewed accounts. But surely she did not mean that due process should not be followed or that warnings should not first be given before such individuals were dismissed. Was she really advocating summary dismissal as practiced by arbitrary and authoritarian bosses in the business world? No doubt, she would have agreed that such a step needed to be done with justice. But at the same time, she was clearly speaking in an overarching, prophetic tone, emphasizing the ideal that such behavior needed to be put right immediately and in a take-charge way.

Her letters immediately before the session also reveal the depth of the complexities in Battle Creek that made even fairly simple decisions complicated. Consider just the issue of where she should stay during the session. Having at last decided to go to Battle Creek, Ellen White faced yet another perplexity in choosing her lodgings. Political considerations forced her to approach every option with great care lest she give offence to someone, be misunderstood by others, or present a wrong or misleading impression to yet others. Of course, she had many friends with whom she could stay, but that complicated things too. She had an invitation from the General Conference president's wife. By February, it seems, Irwin had solved his housing problem. In addition, she could stay with friends or at the sanitarium. Or she could join Dr. Kellogg himself at his home, for he had pressed an invitation upon her. Was his invitation a gesture of conciliation or did it have political motivations behind it? What if she had to decline it even for practical reasons? On the other hand, if she accepted, would some think that by associating with him in this way she had come to side with Kellogg or perhaps was endorsing his course? The simple act of residing somewhere had suddenly assumed great significance. It was a further indication of the political dimensions of the conflict and of the fact that Ellen White thought carefully about such things and the impact her actions would have on the exercise of her influence. Everybody was watching. What was the proper thing to do? Ellen White recognized the implications of her choice. Eventually, she decided that the advantages of accepting the doctor's invitation outweighed the disadvantages, and she stayed at his home. But she needed to explain herself.

In the early months of 1901, leading up to the session in Battle Creek, Ellen White also found that she needed to monitor her interviews, choose carefully the people she met and talked to, and not give the wrong impression by being seen with the wrong people. Even in social, more relaxed situations, she deliberately had to avoid certain topics of conversation. During such situations, even apparently innocent and casual things are read carefully for their possible meanings. Diplomacy becomes much more important, and every move becomes vested with significance. For example, when a group of denominational officials including Daniells, Irwin, Haskell, and others visited her at Elmshaven just weeks prior to the session, a recreational drive through the countryside surrounding Elmshaven was arranged. Careful thought had to be given as to who should ride with whom and in which carriage. And certain topics of conversation were astutely sidestepped.

Surprising outcomes

When the 1901 General Conference finally convened on April 2 in Battle Creek, apprehensions of doom and disaster gripped many delegates, particularly those closest to the struggle going on at the core of the organization. But chaos and disarray did not engulf the proceedings as many thought might happen. A desire still existed among the two major branches in the church to keep working together, and they found mechanisms that enabled a much better integration of the church's overall endeavors. The denomination was still not out of the woods concerning the powerful divisive forces within it, but at least it had discovered a possible path through the thickets of gloom and foreboding.

At the session's end three weeks later, Ellen White expressed utter surprise at the outcome. "I was never more astonished in my life than at the turn things have taken," she marveled.[34] The session had adopted major structural changes that held promise for coping with the rapid growth of the church and for the sharing of resources. The establishment of union conferences had been authorized with real power to manage the work in their territories, a delegation of authority that would ease the congestion of decision making at headquarters. The auxiliary organizations had been absorbed into the conference structures, and the General Conference executive committee was much more representative. These were substantial changes. But the cast of new leaders who had been appointed generated as much amazement as the structural changes.

As already noted, Ellen White had expected that Irwin would be reappointed as president and in fact had felt it necessary to declare herself and say so publicly to the executive committee several months before the session to counter the dangerous rumor of a conspiracy to change leadership. As it turned out, however, the session elected A. G. Daniells. Ellen White's favored candidate at the earlier 1897 session, W. W. Prescott, was appointed to serve as his deputy, heading the Foreign Mission Board. The conjectures of the pre-session conspiracy theory—that Daniells was to be General Conference president and W. C. White head of the Foreign Mission Board— had turned out to be at least half right. Even Prescott could hardly believe what had transpired. A year later he was still amazed, particularly when he heard that just prior to the session the planning committee had formally voted that neither he nor Waggoner should have any speaking part at all in the 1901 session. If his claim is correct, it probably indicates how counterproductive Irwin and/or his district conference president associates thought Prescott's confrontational reform tactics had been in 1899.[35]

In fact, it was Daniells who effectively became the change agent at the 1901 session as he exerted leadership, directed the agenda, and achieved what some may even have seen as an organizational coup d'état. At a pre-session meeting the day before the session was to begin, Ellen White received an invitation to share her thoughts with a representative group of the delegates. Even though Irwin was present, Daniells served as the meeting's chair. The group met in the Battle Creek College library. Mrs. White spoke for an hour, issuing a stirring call to arms. She repeated a common theme that there should be no "kings" in the administration, that the evangelistic and medical programs should be blended, and that delegates needed to breach the defenses of the old order right from the outset in order to make the needed changes. The denomination must not continue the same "manipulating" and other negative procedures as in the past. To do so would be a calamity. She did not know how the change should happen, she said, but happen it must. It was the preaching of revolution.[36]

The next morning at 9.00 A.M. when the session formally began, following the traditional roll call of delegates and the admitting of new conferences into the system, Irwin gave his report reviewing the previous two years. He then declared the session open for business, and in the familiar idiom, asked the pleasure of the delegates. Ellen White took this as an invitation to speak and immediately made her way to the podium to address the assembly. She spoke for almost an hour, reiterating many of the same themes she had referred to the previous day. "Do not wait until the Conference is over and then gather up the forces to see what can be done," she declared.[37] Again, the trumpet called for a revolution. Was the message coded? It almost seemed so. At least the sequence seemed planned. Irwin responded to her address and acknowledged that the previous pattern of conducting business at General Conference sessions had been restrictive and that it was time to make a new start. Again he asked, "What is the pleasure of the Conference at this time?"[38]

Daniells immediately picked up on the cue, stood, asked for the floor, and strode directly to the podium where he briefly recounted the meeting of the previous day. Then reading from a carefully prepared statement, he moved that "the usual rules and precedents for arranging and transacting the business of the conference be suspended." He suggested that a large "committee on counsel," the membership of which he clearly detailed by office or by name, be appointed by the session to steer the overall business and think through the necessary reorganization. It was a revolutionary step, replacing the pattern of having the usual standing committees appointed by the incumbent president. The proposal evoked significant apprehension, prompting vigorous and extensive discussion. Ellen White had to speak again to calm some fears before Irwin, who was chairing the meeting, was asked to put the proposal to the vote. It secured solid approval. The session then immediately adjourned to give the committee a chance to meet and organize itself.

Had Daniells lobbied with others to ensure the success of this approach, one that Prescott had fruitlessly advocated at the previous two sessions? In essence, Daniells succeeded in shattering the forces of inertia and outflanked the defenders of the status quo. The initiative gave the opportunity for the church, at the organizational center of its operations, to implement a structure that Daniells and W. C. White had successfully run as a kind of pilot study in Australia during the previous four years.

When it came time for the nominating committee to present its recommendations for the leadership of the newly restructured organization, the delegates approved a much larger and more representative executive committee with the power to appoint its own chairman. For the initial term it chose none other than Daniells himself, who was thereby effectively "president," although not in name. He was now responsible for leading the denomination and implementing the radical changes that the session had authorized. Again, Ellen White's previously stated personal preference for the person to fill the leadership role was bypassed. This time, however, it was not just the electoral process that left the previous president on the sidelines; it was also the result of a new system of choosing the leader. But in spite of her sympathy for Irwin, Ellen White clearly saw Daniells as ideally suited to the role.

The change in personnel, unexpected but not without some foreshadowing, was nevertheless a deeply traumatic experience for George Irwin. Did the outcome suggest failure on his part? Was it an expression of no confidence? Had he failed Ellen White's standard? Daniells described it as "the greatest crisis" of Irwin's life. At Irwin's funeral service a dozen years later, Daniells recalled that he had "stood by his [Irwin's] side personally and physically in that hour." He "remembered well the morning" it happened. He recalled that as he locked arms with the displaced leader he had said, "Well, Brother Irwin, how does all this look to you?" Irwin said in reply: "Brother Daniells, it is all clear and straight and true. It is right, and I bow to it."[39] Evidently, Daniells himself felt sympathetic and uncomfortable, although not apologetic nor guilty.

O. A. Olsen, who also knew what it felt like to have to vacate the office—although in less traumatic circumstances, because he had more time to think about it in advance and control the process of his exit—also commented that the 1901 event was "a severe day" in Irwin's life. "He and I went down to his [Irwin's] office and locked the door, and there we shook hands that we would stand by the work of God whatever experience it might lead us to pass through."[40] Irwin appreciated the moral support. As with Olsen before him, Irwin's particular pain was associated with the idea that many in the church would interpret his removal as the result of a personal failure or because of mistakes that he had made, and furthermore that it must have been at Ellen White's behest. Had she not been almost constantly calling for new blood in the leadership and heavily criticizing in non-specific terms the moral faults of those in leadership? Since Irwin had served only two terms, would not most consider that his removal had been because of her loss of confidence in him due to some hidden failure or weakness?

If Prescott had had his way, as he understood the thrust of the testimonies prior to the session, none of the previous leaders at all would have continued in office. He thought Ellen White was very clearly calling for the breaking up of the entire "old ring" of former administrators, and that included individuals such as G. A. Irwin and I. H. Evans. Several months earlier he had despaired of any change and lamented to W. C. White, "I suppose the next General Conference will solemnly elect the same men with possible slight change of office position to continue the same sort of policy for another two years and so the blight will continue."[41] It was only after a good deal of persuasion by his colleagues in 1901 that Prescott was prepared to concede that these men might still have a useful, but lesser, role to play in spite of the thrust of Ellen White's counsel. Prescott had evidently not seen her July 1900 letter to Haskell about Irwin being an appropriate or "proper" person for president and that she did not anticipate any need for change, at least in his role. Whether the large Committee on Council had called Ellen White in for advice on the leadership issue or whether they had consulted with her in other ways at the 1901 session is not known. We have no record that any such conversation took place, although it may have been expected. But perhaps, having written and spoken as she had, she now determined that she would step back from the process. It seems, however, that she was involved in some kind of later discussions about where Irwin should serve and that she consented to the plans for him.

Leadership failure or simply the process of democracy?

Before the session drew to a close, Irwin received an invitation to move to Australia to fill Daniells's shoes as president of the Australasian Union. It was a task with significant challenge, and bowing to the system, Irwin had expressed his willingness to serve wherever needed. At least he was already somewhat acquainted with the territory. But it was with a heavy heart that he vacated office and house and transferred a few weeks later to Australia. The Australian church paper reported that the passengers arriving in a wintry Sydney harbor on the *Mariposa* had experienced a very rough voyage south.[42] The stormy seas and huge swells mirrored Irwin's feelings rather accurately. Although he was resigned to accepting things as they were, the pain of rejection was real, and the awareness of living with a damaged reputation stung. But Irwin was resolved to make a success in his role as a union conference leader. He settled at Cooranbong initially, and his first union conference session convened July 11–29. Later he took up residence near the new sanitarium at Wahroonga.

Settling in to the Australian colonies, however, did not come easy. Irwin and his wife, Sarah, and the sizeable group of other recently arrived Americans found themselves struggling with culture shock. How Sarah Irwin felt about the whole episode is not known. How she helped to "pick up the pieces" for her husband would enrich our insights into the human cost of the turmoil to their family life. Colonial attitudes, anti-American sentiment, and a totally new environment proved difficult to cope with at first. Irwin, in spite of his best intentions, found himself brooding over matters. It bothered him to recall the events, conversations, and conflicts of the previous year, and as he revisited decisions, he pondered how he might have done it all better. Could he really have done anything differently? What mistakes had he made that made him so un-re-electable? And if Ellen White had meant what she said prior to the meetings, why had she not spoken out in his favor during the session when it might have been appropriate? Why had her prior word on the issue had no effect? There were no answers, and the very fact that he was even asking the questions discouraged him.

Back in California, as the upheaval subsided and as Ellen White settled back into the routine at Elmshaven, she thought about Australia and the work she had left. Apparently, she also thought about what had happened to Irwin and worried about its impact on the discarded leader and his wife. Evidently, she felt uncomfortable with the way things had turned out, particularly in light of the strong statements she had made to the executive committee just a few months prior to the session. In the struggles in which she and Irwin had participated together regarding Kellogg, there had developed a deepening trust and a much closer personal bonding of spirit. Had she misled Irwin?

A year later, she reflected on the change in his role that had occurred in 1901. "My brother," she wrote, to emphasize the personal connection, "I hope that you never entertained the idea that you were sent from America because you were not wanted here. I do not want you to think this; because it is not the case at all. I felt sorry to have you and the rest go. We needed all the strong, experienced workers, and we miss you."

The affirmation was reassuring. "Understand, my dear brother and sister, that you are very dear to me," she confided. They had her "heart and soul," and she desired "to cooperate with him most heartily."[43]

In whatever forum the 1901 discussion about Irwin's future role had occurred, Ellen White had apparently kept her silence. She recalled that it had been Irwin who had actually "proposed to go, and to take others with you, and we did not dare say one word against it, fearing that one might interfere with the Lord's plans for Australia." In fact, she felt that it might be "selfish" of her "to hinder" him in going, but felt glad that he did, because he "would be a special help to the believers in Australia." With Irwin present, she thought, the Australian church "would not feel our leaving so much." It had been her intention at first to be gone for only two years. But now she was approaching seventy-five years of age, and she had a strong hunch that "I may never see Australia again." In this light she mentioned that she was particularly grateful for the work that both Irwin and Haskell had undertaken in late 1899 and 1900 in raising funds for the church in Australia. "That enabled us," she recalled, "to place the work [in Australia] where we could leave Australia to come to America at a time when my testimony was needed. The Lord has been very good."[44] She evidently felt deeply about the painful experience. "The intensity I have felt as I have written these things can never be expressed," she concluded.[45]

Four months later, Ellen White still worried about the pain inflicted upon Irwin. "I wish to tell you of a dream I once had," she wrote in a friendly letter sent in October. "You were sitting in a room. I came in, and you looked up with sad face, and said, 'Sister White, please tell me what my mistakes have been, that you could not trust me any longer in America?' I said, 'My Brother, you are entirely mistaken, in viewing the matter that way. It was a great trial for me to give consent for you to go to Australia.' " Evidently, in spite of her confidence in God's leading and the conviction of an overriding providence, the sequence of events still haunted her at a subconscious level. "I knew that you had been passing through a trying experience and I thought that it might perhaps be a relief to you to go to Australia." Ellen White recalled that it had been Haskell who had reported to her that Irwin "felt drawn to Australia and that you had decided to go there. I dared not say anything to disturb your mind; for Brother Haskell told me that your preparations were made."

"In my dream," Ellen White went on, "it seemed to me that when I had given you these particulars, you were relieved. So I wrote to you as I did." She apparently had in mind her earlier letter written four months previously. But she wanted to be clear with Irwin that, in her view at least, it was not for failure that he had been replaced. "Be assured, my brother, that you did not do or say anything in your work here that made me glad to have you leave."[46]

Irwin found the explanation helpful and indicated that she had read him correctly. "You will never know," he replied, referring to her June letter, "how much good it did me, and I wondered why you wrote as you did, whether the Lord had revealed to you the struggle through which I had passed." He acknowledged that he had been "tempted time and again" to think that his assignment to Australia was more or less a consolation prize, so to speak. Many times he had felt that "I was simply permitted to go to Australia for a time to make that matter as easy for me as possible." Her letter had "removed every doubt," and he felt he could "now go forward with more hope and courage than ever before."[47]

In the months and years to come, as the struggle with Kellogg worked its way to a climax, Ellen White continued to correspond with Irwin and confide in him about the developments taking place. But it was Daniells who had the task of implementing the necessary reforms and of trying to bring the doctor further into the organizational fold. It would not be an easy task. How would Ellen White relate to the new president? Fortunately, she had already worked closely with him and knew him intimately. She felt he was the man suited for the position if ever there was one. In 1901, Kellogg also concluded that "Daniells was certainly the man for the job." But he held that view only for a short while. Before long, Kellogg thought that the church president needed to be someone else. What would Ellen White's role be then? The struggle, in a sense, had only just begun. How would she now exercise her influence with these two strong leaders, who soon became locked in combat with each other? As Irwin wrote to his successor shortly after the traumatic 1901 session, "I know from past experience that it is very much easier to pass the action than it is to carry it into effect. . . . You certainly have my sympathy and prayers."[48]

CHAPTER 8

A. G. DANIELLS and the PROCESS of REFORM

(1901–1903)

"There is a very persistent report circulated on the hill here [the sanitarium in Battle Creek] that a Testimony has been sent, reproving us strongly." *Review* editor and General Conference vice president, W. W. Prescott, had heard the rumor and passed the information along to A. G. Daniells, who was out of town. It was late January 1903, and both men were feeling quite concerned. Had Ellen White really spoken on the issues? The rumor was vague. But the next day it had gained substance. "I heard in a very direct way to-day," Prescott reported to his president, that "they [Kellogg and his colleagues] were expecting on the strength of this Testimony that we should be put out of office at the next session of the General Conference."[1] With only six weeks to go before the session met in California, things were clearly getting serious. How had they deteriorated this far?

Another day later, Prescott again warned Daniells of the dangerous waters now swirling around them both in Battle Creek. "Every day brings some new development with reference to the medical work in its relation to the evangelical work," he said. Elder S. H. Lane, a General Conference executive committee member, had had a long interview with Dr. Kellogg the previous Sabbath. On the basis of the interview "we understand clearly," noted the vice president, "that every possible effort will be made to overthrow the present administration at the next General Conference." Kellogg had spoken about "a combining of all other interests" to make A. T. Jones the new president of the General Conference.[2] It sounded like serious plotting, much more than the usual pre-session office politics.

Daniells appreciated the updates from his colleague, but he did not really need Prescott to tell him he was in trouble. He already knew it. Since his election as General Conference leader in April 1901, a state of war had broken out. As he explained to Ellen White in mid-March, just a few days before the 1903 session was scheduled to begin, "Two years ago we started in to make a great effort to establish peace, harmony, and cooperation between the General Conference and the medical association, but we have signally failed."[3] At first, the sharp conflict had been only between himself and the doctor, but now "the trouble has enlarged. . . . It embraces the whole work, and involves hundreds of our workers." Facing the bleak prospect frankly, Daniells stated that he was "fully aware" of what his "stand in all these matters" might mean to him personally. "I may suffer an apparent defeat, and be banished from this country. I am in a measure prepared for that." In some respects, he thought that would be much the preferable way to resolve the problem. But he could not, and would not, change his position. "This is where I stand regardless of personal consequences. I may be turned out, and down, and be exiled in Africa. I leave all that in the hands of my God."[4]

Forty-two-year-old Arthur Daniells understood reasonably clearly the mandate for reform given him. Had he not been the one in the forefront of persuading his colleagues of both the importance and the value of the new way of organizing the church? Furthermore, had he not been the one who had experimented in Australia with the new structure? Daniells also had a reasonably clear view of the specific organizational reforms that needed to be implemented. What he did not fully comprehend, however, was just where the journey of change would take him and what it would cost him and just how rugged and painful it would be to travel it. Resistance from the medical branch had been enormous. Being a change agent, Daniells had discovered, exacted a huge personal cost. "The struggles through which we have passed during the last year, have almost wrecked us physically," he acknowledged at the end of 1903. "We are sick and tired of them. If we could be excused, we would gladly retire from the arena, and go wherever."[5]

As it happened, however, Daniells didn't have to go "wherever." Ellen White came to his rescue at the 1903 General Conference session held in Oakland, California. There had indeed been much at stake for both of them. Working together, they were able to outmaneuver the coup-makers. Subsequently, two years turned into almost twenty-two before Daniells finally left the General Conference presidency, the longest tenure of any of the leaders of the church. Daniells was nothing if not resilient.

This intriguing episode in the development of the church suggests a number of questions to engage a church historian's curiosity. Was it only Ellen White's support for Daniells that saved his presidency? Did he not genuinely carry sufficient confidence from his colleagues in ministry, independent of her support, to ensure his continuation in the role? Ellen White had not always been so apparently wholehearted in her support for him. Or if she was, Daniells did not know it, at least not until the 1903 session itself. And why did she not support the A. T. Jones candidacy? Had she not proposed Jones and then defended him as president of the California Conference in the period leading up to 1903? Did Ellen White's support for Daniells exacerbate the schism between the medical program and the ministerial work force of the church? Would a compromise candidate, such as A. T. Jones, have better enabled a rapprochement between the two branches?

This chapter will discuss the emerging crisis over leadership in the church during Daniells's first term of office and will attempt to understand the dilemmas facing both him and Ellen White and the difficulties such things posed for their relationship as they responded to the developing schism. Mrs. White clearly describes how during this period she experienced many occasions during the night when she knew that the Lord had given her help and insights and convictions of what needed to be written. She also reports that during many sleepless nights she reflected at length on the issues before the church and how she might best relate to the various parties involved in the conflict. On occasion she would abandon a particular approach when it appeared not to be effective and then adopt another.

It was during Daniells's presidency that John Harvey Kellogg finally broke from the denomination. His congregation voted to dismiss him in 1907. Departing with him over a period of time were a large number of other physicians, pastors, and church members, and in the process the denomination lost ownership and control of the Battle Creek Sanitarium. From one perspective, the inability of A. G. Daniells to keep the two branches of the church working harmoniously together could be seen as a failure of his leadership (and in the same sense also a failure of leadership on Ellen White's part). Of course, the decision not to respond to advice is the choice of the person choosing to ignore it. No blame should be assigned to Daniells or to Ellen White for Kellogg's choice. But would a different strategic approach to the collaboration between administrative leadership and the prophet have secured different results? Or was Kellogg so committed to his determined course that nothing they might have done would have changed his mind or his attitude? Second guessing history in a "what if" manner is hazardous and not always productive. But the questions, at least, serve to remind us that there usually exists more than one way to solve problems. It is possible to reflect on what might have happened even as we seek to discover what actually did happen.

The next two chapters will also illuminate how the Kellogg crisis affected Daniells's relationship with Ellen White. We will see that it had a significant impact on the formal relationship between her and the General Conference president. The study will also illustrate the kind of partnership or modus operandi that developed between the gift of prophecy and Daniells's evident gift of "apostleship" during these critical first years of the twentieth century.

Antecedents

Born in Iowa in 1858, Arthur Daniells lost his father to the Civil War when he was five years of age. Consequently, his childhood had been one of poverty and struggle, including time in an orphanage when, following his father's death, his mother had been unable to support her family. Her remarriage to an aged farmer by the name of Lippincott two years later at least provided a home, if it didn't offer love. The young Arthur clashed often with his stepfather, which did not make family affairs any happier. An active involvement with the local Adventist church, which his mother joined about the time of her second marriage, did somewhat compensate for the unhappiness at home. Arthur was ten when, as a spiritually sensitive youngster, he made his own commitment to God. Seven years later, that same spiritual commitment took him to Battle Creek College in spite of his financially difficult circumstances. Rigorous instruction under Goodloe Harper Bell and Sydney Brownsberger equipped Daniells and his childhood acquaintance, Mary Hoyt, as primary school teachers, although ill health forced Daniells to withdraw from college studies early. But at college he also had the opportunity to see Mary as more than just a good friend and, following his marriage to her at the age of nineteen, they both taught public school in his hometown of West Union, Iowa.[6]

What really fired the young Daniells's passion, however, was pastoral and evangelistic ministry, not school teaching. But conference administrators were not persuaded. A serious speech impediment seemed to bring into question the validity of such a sense of personal calling. But if Daniells could not be employed as a minister, why could he not, at least, be a volunteer? The couple therefore gave up their teaching after a year and joined evangelist R. M. Kilgore in Texas. Daniells would serve as a tent-master for a tent mission.

The decision to go to Texas was fortuitous. Ellen White and her family also moved there to link up for a short while with Kilgore and provide a period of rest for James, her husband. Thus began a close association between the Whites and Arthur and Mary Daniells. The Whites invited Arthur and Mary to board with them and requested Arthur to assist James as needed. It was a most pleasant association for the young couple. Daniells recalled years later that he had "not had a mother" since he had been a lad, "and it seemed the most like having a mother and sisters of any experience since I was small." It apparently also helped to model home life for him; "there was a hallowed sacred influence that did not pervade my home when a child."[7]

Daniells's two years of ministerial training under Kilgore apparently persuaded the Iowa leaders that he really was preacher material, and they employed him as a pastor. Two years later, George I. Butler ordained Daniells at the age of twenty-four. Four years of successful evangelistic and parish ministry ably demonstrated his pastoral leadership gifts and led in turn to an invitation in 1886 for him to go as a pioneering evangelist to New Zealand in the South Pacific. Evangelistic activities in Northland, Auckland, and Napier soon led to the establishment of new churches. Then, after three years, Daniells had his first brush with administrative responsibilities. Shortly after he had established New Zealand's third Adventist church at Napier, he organized a conference of churches and was promptly elected as its first president, although the role was little more than a formality and for the sake of order. Total membership at the time was only about 150. He carried the responsibility for only ten months before passing it on to the more experienced M. C. Israel, while Daniells again focused on evangelistic outreach.[8]

In 1891, plagued by persistent health problems, Daniells and his wife transferred to Australia. The change in climate and work circumstances helped improve things, but it was some time before the evangelist discovered that a long-term dental problem lay at the root of his ill health. With it corrected, he began to feel quite normal again. The same year that he went to Australia, Daniells was able to renew his acquaintance with Ellen White. He was part of the dockside welcoming party when she disembarked in Sydney in late 1891. This time it was the Daniellses' turn to provide the hospitality, and Mary and Arthur welcomed Ellen White and her traveling party into their Darlinghurst terrace house for several days before she traveled on to Melbourne.[9]

The arrival of Ellen White in Australia provided Daniells with his first real introduction to a role in church leadership, but it was not the most comfortable induction. Ellen White had been there barely a month when, at the end-of-year meetings that convened in Melbourne in December 1891, she took a direct and controversial role in suggesting who should be the president of the Australian Conference. Her involvement in the election process gave Daniells his first experience of church electoral politics. American pastor, George C. Tenney, the incumbent president, had literary skills, argued Ellen White. Such talents would be more valuable in the publishing house working on the *Bible Echo* and other pamphlets. The delegates to the conference were not easily persuaded and, according to W. C. White, they were "very loath [*sic*] to consider a change." But if Tenney had to be released, the Australian delegates thought, then surely S. N. Curtis was the obvious replacement. Willie White reported that the local delegates felt that Curtis and Tenney were the only Americans among the whole work force in Australia who really "understood and appreciated the Colonials." In keeping with their anti-establishment heritage, the Australians did not take kindly to being pushed around by anyone and certainly not by Americans—particularly by those who had barely arrived on the scene. Ellen White found herself facing considerable opposition to her recommendation in what seems to have become a lively discussion on the floor of the conference rather than behind closed doors in committee. Only a "few" others agreed with her, she reported to O. A. Olsen six months later, and emotions ran deep. "The selection of a president for the conference was by no means a small affair, in consideration of the feeling that existed," she said. But she was not to be deterred. In spite of the fact that Daniells was not the ideal candidate either, she was convinced that he was "the best choice that could be made." She did not see much other presidential material available. Daniells was certainly the one "standing in the best place spiritually of any of them," she argued. As she saw it, the role of president in this situation demanded pastoral skills as well as the ability to undertake effective personal labor among the churches. W. C. White supported his mother's position. Daniells "would be better fitted for the work than any other man in Australia," and she told the delegates just so. To quell the opposition, she had to call on her considerable diplomatic skills. "We moved guardedly in selecting the man," she explained. The Australians, for their part, thought the whole affair was very high-handed and that Daniells had been forced on them. It took some time for him to be able to win the confidence of the membership and his fellow team of church employees.

It did not help matters during his first year that Daniells wanted to get things done in a hurry. In his "stirring" about among the churches he found himself offending colonial sensitivities. W. C. White, who had picked up the undercurrent of dissatisfaction, had to caution the new president not to move with too much haste. "I find that there is in the minds of the brethren, quite generally two thoughts which are rather against us," he wrote to Daniells ten months after the thirty-four-year-old had taken up his new duties. "One is that we Americans cook up our plans quietly and then spring them suddenly upon the people, expecting them to be accepted because of their confidence in our greater experience. The other," he went on, "is that we do not understand and appreciate the colonial laborers and that we do not give them their proper place in the work. . . . We must take particular pains not to sin against anyone on these lines."[10] Daniells seems to have gradually developed his cross-cultural skills, and slowly confidence developed in his leadership. By the end of Daniells's first year, W. C. White was able to report that there was less local feeling about American ministers having a tendency "to manage shrewdly, to dictate, and to rule in an arbitrary fashion."[11]

AUSTRALIA A PROVING GROUND

The eight years that A. G. Daniells spent in church leadership in the Australian colonies, from 1892 to 1900, were not easy ones. The church was still very young, and much of the work it did was pioneering, church-planting projects. In the midst of this period, a severe economic depression wiped out many hopes and plans, making life exceptionally difficult just at the time when there was a need for the development of institutions. The economic situation led to a constant battle for adequate personnel and sufficient financial resources to implement the broad vision for the expansion of "the cause" espoused by Ellen White. But the experience, hard though it was, gave Daniells a broad introduction to the array of challenges that administration brings. He considered himself fortunate that he was able to work closely with Mrs. White and her son, although, as Milton Hook points out in a study of their relationship during this period, their association had its fragile periods.[12]

In his conference administration, Daniells worked hard at maintaining a focus on growing the church. He took an active part in evangelistic leadership through preaching and through planning innovative approaches to evangelistic camp meetings. The camp meetings at Ashfield in Sydney and at Brighton in Melbourne were notably successful. Camp meetings became a particularly successful strategy for growing the Australian church.

Daniells also expanded his skills in the development of institutions, commencing first with a school in Melbourne and then becoming involved in a major way in the development of the one at Cooranbong. His participation in the latter project was the source of much friction with Ellen White, because of his doubts about the location chosen and whether the project was more than the membership could afford at the time given their economic constraints. Financial issues involved him in a number of uncomfortably desperate fund-raising campaigns to meet huge debt obligations. The experience forever thereafter made him extremely cautious about developing any institution without first having the funds in hand. Although supportive of the Sydney Sanitarium project, which opened in 1903, he had returned to America before the detailed planning for that enterprise got under way.

His Australian experience also gave Daniells a valuable opportunity to develop an understanding of key management principles and organizational relationships. The 1893 General Conference Session, at W. C. White's urging, established the Australian colonies and New Zealand as District 7, with Willie appointed as the superintendent. Such an insubstantial organizational arrangement fell significantly short of what both Daniells and White felt was actually necessary, and White vigorously protested to the General Conference about the inadequacy of the "district" arrangement. In January 1894, Daniells and W. C. White worked together in establishing what they called an "inter-colonial" conference that had real delegated authority to serve as a "Union" of conferences, and the General Conference president, O. A. Olsen, joined them in launching the new entity. Daniells served as the chairperson of the group charged with drawing up the constitution documents for the new body and then having them approved by the delegates to the specially called district session.[13] The effectiveness of the new structure was soon obvious, but according to W. C. White, who was elected the first president, they soon discovered that the leader of the new organization had "a great deal more to do than was first anticipated."[14] Daniells was elected vice-president of the new union but also maintained his role as president of the Australian Conference.

With the relocation of Ellen White and her family from Melbourne, Victoria, to New South Wales in 1893, Daniells and W. C. White became aware of how increasingly unwieldy it was to administer the rapidly growing work of the entire Australian Conference from Melbourne. Willie argued that it was necessary to separate the state of New South Wales as a separate conference under the new Australian Union. The separation faced significant opposition from a number of churches who felt that establishing a new structure just at that time was economically unwise and premature. Daniells was concerned that the new entity would begin life saddled with debt. Furthermore, confusion developed about how best to accomplish the move, and again some felt that the American ministers were foisting their will on the local church. Appointed as president of the new conference, W. C. White soon found he had significant explaining to do about why it had been pushed along so rapidly. Some delegates questioned the legality of the move. Others felt they needed much more say in the appointment of officers. For Daniells, the exercise was a learning experience—probably as much about how *not* to attempt the establishment of a new conference as about how to actually achieve it.

The relationship between W. C. White as union president and A. G. Daniells as conference president was cordial but not always smooth. Particularly irksome to Daniells was the repeated crossing of wires and the breakdown in communication over the calling of personnel. On several occasions, as the local conference president, Daniells found that he was expected to provide a salary for someone whom White had employed in his role as union president and about which he had then simply forgotten to inform Daniells. It necessitated frequent apologies and adjustments. Such issues were probably inevitable as the leaders became familiar with the various inter-relationships between the new structural entities. But it was W. C. White's willingness to accumulate debt and his lack of a natural gift for administration that soon caused much more significant concerns. Willie began to lose the confidence of his fellow administrators, and his health deteriorated badly. General Conference executive committee member, W. W. Prescott, who was on a visit to Australia in mid-1895, received the delicate task of making an assessment of the problem aspects of W. C. White's management in the union conference. He reported to Olsen that "the difficulty" seemed to be "in Bro. White's lack of proper executive ability in managing the various interests of the district, both the financial and the spiritual." It was an exceedingly sensitive problem to address, and Prescott was most diplomatic and gentle with White. Willie acknowledged that he should be replaced, "although it would no doubt cause me some pain at first, to be separated from the work I have been trying to do." But he thought he could bear that. He acknowledged that he was "much better fitted to work as someone's assistant," than as a superintendent.[15] The General Conference session of 1897 approved his appointment to work alongside his mother assisting her in editorial projects. In his place as union president, the General Conference selected the thirty-nine-year-old A. G. Daniells.

There appears to be no record of any direct discussion with Ellen White about the replacement of her son by Daniells. However, she had been extensively involved in establishing both the position and the budgeting process for Willie's new role as her assistant. Both Olsen and Prescott talked with her about his future responsibilities. For some time she had been seriously worried by the state of her son's health. His "brain fever" and the work pressures he had been under alarmed her.[16] It seems unlikely, then, that she would not also have had a keen interest in who the new union president might be. And it seems just as unlikely that she would not have been consulted. Local leaders had suggested several names to the General Conference, including E. W. Farnsworth, R. C. Porter, and J. P Holser. W. C. White had hinted at the desirability of a Daniells appointment by mentioning that "God was raising up men in Australia" who might be suitable. Olsen was more specific. "There are but few members of our General Conference Committee," he observed, "that have as many good qualifications as Daniells has." General Conference president Olsen thought that Daniells was not only a good speaker, but "a careful manager" and had "order and neatness in his work."[17]

Another important development in Daniells's grooming as a future leader through his Australian experience concerned his exposure to other aspects of organizational reform. They involved the introduction of "departments" under a central conference administration. The new concept resolved the independence of the church's various "auxiliary" activities such as the Tract Society and the Sabbath School Society, and concentrated their activities under the conference executive committee. A committee chaired by W. W. Prescott at the 1889 General Conference Session had first proposed the idea, but it had been scotched and the discussion expunged from the records.[18] Having already experimented successfully with the idea in South Africa, Asa T. Robinson tried to introduce it when first appointed to the local Central Australian Conference presidency in 1897. Daniells, as union president, did not see any merit at all in the idea at first and called it "anarchy" and "confusion." His main concern was that he felt it went directly in opposition to Ellen White's counsel against centralization or "consolidation" in the church. She, herself, had opposed the idea for the same reason when Robinson first suggested it in South Africa. W. C. White felt much the same. But the lay delegates in the Central Australian Conference in 1897 apparently did not place the same weight on these apprehensions and insisted that leadership at least try the idea. It was only a small conference after all. Not long afterward, Daniells himself introduced the plan in the various new conferences he was organizing in the Australasian Union. Apparently, he recognized the efficiency in the new approach and was humble enough to admit he had been mistaken in his earlier opposition. Interestingly, when the "department" concept was advocated at the 1901 General Conference Session as a reform worth adopting, Daniells was happy to put a certain gloss on the development to make it seem as if it was a natural response to Mrs. White's counsel. "We understood from the light given, that we must simplify our organization so as to have as little machinery as possible." He traced the origin of the process to a reluctance in 1894 to add a Religious Liberty Association as "another cog-wheel in the machinery" in Australia. As a result, the Australians did not organize the Religious Liberty Association as yet another external parachurch entity. "This led us to consider the matter more closely, and finally we made up our minds" that the various activities could be "merged" into the conference.[19] Daniells's generalizing and his gloss is understandable in that he was speaking in advocacy mode. But evidently in regard to this matter at least, it was easier to see with hindsight what the Ellen White counsels seem to have been urging. Gaining a clear understanding of the meaning of her counsel and trying to find a way forward in the heat of discussion and in the midst of the fray was not nearly so easy.

Learning how to relate and respond to the various kinds of communications from Ellen White was an important part of the development of Daniells's leadership abilities in Australia. During this period, he received thirty-three known letters addressed to him from Mrs. White and wrote forty-eight to her. There were, however, innumerable times during the decade when he was able to meet with her directly in the ordinary course of his work or while attending meetings that provided opportunity for discussion and counsel.

Daniells valued her counsel and actively sought her advice on many occasions. At other times, when he received counsel that he found painful, he was not sure how to respond. For example, when he and Mary received a reprimand in 1894, Daniells struggled with the content of the letter and had to read it many times. Some things, he said, he understood; others he did not. On some things he felt as if he could make reply, but knew that to do so would not help matters and so he accepted it and tried his best to benefit from it.[20] It made for a fragile relationship for a while, however. On occasion he felt that further explanation to Ellen White would be helpful, as when he received a rebuke for the way he reportedly handled the irregular transfer of a colporteur by the name of Hickox. Mrs. White suggested that Daniells had dealt with the incident from first to last "in an evidently faithless manner" and instructed him to "take your hands off your brother. He is God's property." In his reply, Daniells explained what he had actually done and supplied a copy of the letter he had sent to Hickox. He indicated that he had not asked the leaders in New Zealand not to employ him. "I did not dare to speak anything like as pointedly as you had written," he noted with reference to what she had said about the responsibilities of colporteurs.[21]

Her counsel concerning the management of personnel he found especially helpful as when, despite the best of intentions, he lost the services of two longtime printers, W. H. B. Miller and J. H. Woods from the Bible Echo Publishing House. Attempting, again, to explain the situation in detail, he added, "I sincerely wish we had heard from you earlier." But there were things to learn from the mistakes. "I think it will teach me a lesson that I shall not soon forget. I thank you most heartily for the warning and admonition that you have sent to us, and to me especially."[22]

At times Mrs. White felt strongly that Daniells should have asked for advice and didn't. It particularly "aggrieved" her at not having been consulted about the appointment of H. Camden Lacey as principal of the new school at Avondale. "Not one reference [was] made to me or my judgment or my opinion," she wrote. Lacey was not the right person for the position. He was "a boy among boys." The appointment of the young Australian graduate of Battle Creek College had created tensions with S. N. Haskell, the senior spiritual leader on campus, and it appeared that Haskell might resign. "As sure as Elder Haskell leaves, I shall leave also," she told Daniells and the board of directors.[23] Lacey was replaced.

The development of the school of Avondale caused particular difficulty for Daniells in his relationship to Ellen White. It took a lengthy period for him to recognize that his apprehensions and fears about the Cooranbong school were not well grounded. In the meantime, his foot dragging had thrown heavier burdens on her. Eventually, he came to see that his attitude on the issue "had not been right in all respects." Feeling that he had injured Ellen White, he asked her forgiveness. But it took him two years to do so. In retrospect, Daniells was enormously grateful for her counsel and guidance. As he hurried to South Africa in early 1900 to help the South African church deal with the emergency arising from the Boer War, he had tried to persuade his fellow traveler John Wessels to accept an appointment back in Australia where the South African was needed to help build the new sanitarium. He recounted to Ellen White his conversation with Wessels.

"I reviewed my experience in Australia during the last nine years. I told him where I had promptly responded to the light and been blessed. I also told him when and where I had swerved, and how it had hurt me and the cause. I could honestly state that in all that time—nine years—the Spirit of Prophecy had never once led me into trouble but that I had got myself in trouble by failing to obey promptly."[24]

Of course, he did not mean that the counsel that came to him from Ellen White was infallible and without blemish. She did not claim that herself. And he knew from experience that he still needed to use his own mind, good common sense, and the good advice of other colleagues in resolving issues in the light of counsel that came from Ellen White. But clearly, he was glad for the special charisma that she exercised, and he had learned to trust in the important role it played in helping to forge church unity in Australia and, on a larger scale, a clear strategic direction for the church.

THE REFORM AGENDA AND CONSULTATIONS WITH ELLEN WHITE

Daniells's hurried departure from Australia with Wessels in April 1900, as already noted, eventually led to his election as General Conference president ten months later. The major restructuring of the denomination, implemented at the 1901 session, set the agenda for his first term. What the meetings had decided, he now needed to spread through the entire organization. The first several months following the historic session, therefore, found Daniells constantly on the move at meeting after meeting of delegates throughout the church, turning "districts" into legally constituted "union conferences," and creating new ones where there had been none before. He also had to explain and re-explain to each new set of delegates in each new location just how the system would work, resolve issues of irregular territories, and help facilitate the sensitive task of dividing and assigning assets and responsibilities. It was extremely taxing work, but the largely positive response to the initiatives that he met energized him. "The Spirit of reform has swept through the entire denomination and they are in for anything and everything that will bring about a better state of things," he reported to his vice-president, Prescott, three months into the process and after he had completed the organizing process for the Lake Union Conference.[25] By the end of his first term he had organized thirteen union conferences, three union missions, and reorganized twenty-three local conferences. As the reform drive took on the nature of a popular democratic movement, it temporarily swept aside the technical problem of who was, and who was not, a "delegate" and from which entity a delegate derived voting rights. Everyone who happened to be in attendance at a session was given the franchise. Daniells found it more effective to be flexible and to do away, for a time, with the very concept of delegate, allowing every member of a conference to be considered "a member of the conference in session for the transaction of all the business." Believing it better to have "all the people taking interest in the work,"[26] he suggested that Prescott follow the same pattern as he sent him off to Europe to implement the reform structure on the continent and in Britain.[27]

It was not until July 1901, three months after the session that elected him, that

Daniells eventually had the opportunity to read the transcript of the address given by Ellen White in the Battle Creek College library. It had been stenographically recorded and typed up by Maggie Hare and sent to Daniells by W. C. White. "I have read it with profound interest," Daniells replied. He saw it as "an epoch making address" that reinforced for him his conviction of the essential rightness of the reform program he had undertaken. It was a "revolutionary" speech in that it was "not merely a criticism of wrong methods, but a setting forth of right, corrective matters and measures." Daniells believed he could see more clearly every day "the divine source of instruction" W. C. White's mother had given that April day in the Battle Creek College library.[28]

Receiving a copy of the address also reinforced for Daniells the importance of maintaining clear channels of communication with W. C. White and his mother, although he really needed no reminder. The charismatic voice with its guidance and counsel for him, he knew, would be essential for his success. He also valued the counsel of W. C. White and kept up a stream of sometimes daily correspondence, asking for advice and informing the Whites of the progress of the reorganization. His correspondence from this period clearly shows the importance he placed on such communication. During the balance of 1901, following the General Conference session, Daniells received eleven letters from Ellen White and wrote eight to her. But to W. C. White he dispatched seventy-four in the space of about six months. The next year seven letters arrived from Ellen White, and he wrote four to her while sending twenty-seven to W. C. White. Again in 1903, he followed the same pattern: twenty-two letters from Ellen White and thirteen to her. But to her son he mailed fifty. The correspondence sought both to inform and to seek advice.

"Perhaps I ought to write this letter to you and your mother," he began a letter of July 1901 to Willie. Explaining that he needed advice on the proposed site for the relocation of Battle Creek College, he asked W. C. White to study the proposal in advance of the upcoming meetings that would decide the issue. It was proposed to locate the institution in Berrien Springs. Daniells also requested that Willie read the letter to his mother and tell her that "I earnestly solicit any counsel she may have to give." He wanted to hear from them just as soon as possible. Another question he sought advice on was the proposal that O. A. Olsen be assigned to South Africa to superintend denominational functions there. "What do you say to this?" he asked "Please write me." It was typical of the many letters that flowed between Daniells and W. C. White.[29]

Finding other associates and helpers whom he could trust and rely on and who shared and understood the reorganization vision was one of Daniells's first challenges.

He appreciated enormously the help of his trusted colleague, W. W. Prescott. Daniells realized the vital importance of effective communication not only with Prescott, but through him to the church through the pages of the *Review.* It was essential for Prescott to keep in touch with him. "Let us hear from you as often as possible," he had urged as Prescott left for Europe.

It was his casting about for trusted and competent clerical help that gave rise to one of Daniells's first exchanges of correspondence with Ellen White following the historic session. It illustrates the competition for scarce human resources within the denomination. Both Mrs. White and Daniells wanted the assistance of Clarence Crisler, who was an excellent stenographer. Although Daniells was prepared to release Crisler to help her, he felt he needed to delay the time of the transfer. Crisler had indicated an interest in connecting with Elmshaven, and Mrs. White was certain he must join her just as soon as possible. There should be no delay. "My work demands the very best workers, workers who will not cause me any anxiety," she wrote. Daniells could "get workers more easily" than she could, even though "they might not suit you quite as well as some you might choose." Crisler had previously worked for George Irwin, and the fact that Irwin had not offered Crisler to Mrs. White irked her. "Brother Irwin knew my perplexity and distress for want of help, but never mentioned the fact that the one working for him was the one I needed. I think this was wrong."[30] In this case, Daniells decided it was not worth pursuing his suggestion to delay Crisler's transfer.

The issue of laying claim to the title of "president" when he had been officially appointed only as "chairman" of the General Conference was, however, not so easy a matter to bypass. Did Ellen White have anything to say on the matter? She certainly had decided views on the kind of person who should occupy the position of leader of the church and had voiced her opinions loudly and clearly. But did she have a particular view of what term the denomination should use to describe the precise role and responsibility that individual should have? The issue was sensitive, because Daniells's appointment as "chair" had been assigned by the committee set up to function as an executive group during the long period when the General Conference was not actually in session. He did not want to antagonize his colleagues over the use of a title. The matter was also a delicate one, however, because a number of the key leaders who had been persuaded of the reform program understood that a Testimony she had written in 1897 proscribed the title of president.[31]

In actual day-to-day practice, however, the title of "chairman" of the General Conference was not adequate for business purposes. Contracts and business documents of the time required something with more legal substance. Thus the General Conference retained the title of "president" on official letterheads. Prescott, who had been a champion of the "chairman" title, found that the various adjustments in language needed to meet legal requirements was cumbersome and lacked clarity; he eventually conceded that the title "president" should be retained. Both men restudied the original 1897 document from Ellen White and agreed that it did not necessarily require the discarding of the title itself. Rather, it was "kingly autocratic power" that was anathema. They noted that the testimony retained the use of the term *president* even when asserting what kind of president the individual holding the position should not be. But who was to make the case publicly for the reversal of policy? Prescott suggested Daniells do it, since he was the one who had started using the title again. Daniells urged Prescott to do it since he had been instrumental in introducing the narrower interpretation. But neither wanted to risk being seen as opposing Ellen White on the matter if she understood things differently. Eventually, Daniells asked W. C. White if he would counsel with his mother and that they then write out whatever explanation they thought best. It would not trouble Daniells either way. "I care little about it," he asserted.[32] As became clear at the next General Conference session, however, many others did care a good deal, and the issue became highly contentious. At that time, W. C. White felt obliged to clarify for session delegates what his mother was referring to in her objection to "kingly power" and in her earlier counsel that it was "not wise to choose one man as the president of the General Conference." After recounting the successes already achieved in decentralizing denominational administration, W. C. White noted concerning the use of the word *president:* "I do not think that there is very much in a name." It is probably safe to assume that before making these remarks, he had discussed the matter with his mother as Daniells had requested.[33]

The need to replace the seventy-three-year-old Uriah Smith as editor at the *Review and Herald* within the first twelve months of Daniells assuming the General Conference leadership was a dangerous undertaking and also a harbinger of troubles to come. But Daniells felt he had little choice. In an editorial in the 1902 New Year's issue of the *Review,* Smith had clearly positioned himself against the need for the structural reforms that Daniells was trying to implement.[34] How, Smith challenged, could perceived problems with the publishing program that some labeled "an odium" be lifted simply by transferring the publishing house to another organization? It was clear that Smith was not going to lend his editorial voice in support of the reform agenda. But the matter was even more complicated than that. Daniells knew that old-time leaders Butler and Haskell were also skeptical of the new organizational structures and that they were in league with Smith. The looming trouble with Kellogg, the knowledge of Smith's leanings in that area, and thus the alarming possibility of a grand coalition in opposition to the reorganization persuaded the General Conference committee that it had no choice but to remove Smith. The only person they felt that could provide the leadership necessary was Prescott. The professor's name had surfaced from discussions within the board itself as it wrestled with the dilemma following the publishing of Smith's controversial editorial.[35]

Revolt in the medical branch

One of the most important planks in the 1901 reorganization concerned building bridges between the medical and health branches of the church and the regular evangelism and conference programs. Ellen White had strongly encouraged the restoration of these relationships, and both Daniells and Prescott worked hard at this. The "Forward Movement" devised by Prescott was a direct attempt to build an ideological bridge between the two camps, and Daniells actively nurtured better partnerships at the personal level and through stronger organizational linkages. It had been agreed at the 1901 conference that physicians, for example, employed by conferences in the new conference health departments, would be paid from tithe on the same basis as ministers—a significant symbolic action. Every effort, it seemed, was made to try to meld the two branches together. But the attempts bore little fruit. It was failure in this initiative, and the profound opposition to legal and organizational integration of the two aspects of the denomination, that brought on the extremely serious crisis that dominated the second half of Daniells's first term and almost caused him to be ousted from office.

As he recounted the episode two years later, Daniells recalled that the issue with the medical program surfaced quite early in his first term. He wrote, "Soon after I took office in this country a communication came to us [from Ellen White] condemning the plans of the medical association for tying physicians and nurses and institutions to the central association at Battle Creek." Of course, Daniells already knew of the underlying danger that the church faced in its effort to retain control of the medical program. The incorporation of the medical and health food programs within the union conference structure in Australia under his leadership at the turn of the century was a direct response to such a threat, as was Ellen White's decision to return to the United States so that she could be on hand to help address the issues. But these moves were anticipatory ones and occurred behind the scenes. People privy to the flow of correspondence among the leadership might be informed and grasp the issues playing out, but nothing was appearing in public discussions. Because many of the warnings and counsels that came to Daniells and others were in the form of letters and testimonies of a private nature, the General Conference president was actually open to being misunderstood in the actions he might take should he base them on the confidential information that came to him from time to time. In the case of the employment bonds being insisted on by Dr. Kellogg, for example, Daniells later wrote to W. C. White that "from the time I received that communication until this hour, [December 1903] I have felt that the light given in these communications ought to be given freely to the whole denomination." He believed that it would make his work more effective and help him to have more influence if people could have access to the same information that came to him. On the other hand, Ellen White, in carefully considering how to best exercise her influence, felt that to confront some issues in a public manner would risk escalating the conflict in such an unmanageable way that the struggle might well be lost. It was not long, however, before the basic conflict broke out into the open, anyway.

The tragic fire that destroyed a substantial part of the Battle Creek Sanitarium on the night of February 17–18, 1902, set in motion a series of events that clearly demonstrated that Dr. Kellogg and the church were traveling on two different sets of tracks. While the fire took one life—an eccentric patient re-entered the building to save his money—the impact of the loss of the hospital building on the church was profound. But it was the proposal for rebuilding that set the two factions in the church at furious war with each other. Daniells, who was in California when news of the fire first came through on the wires and whom Prescott kept up to date with more detailed news by daily correspondence, was convinced that the right way to rebuild was to do so modestly, not on a grand scale.[36] Furthermore, the budget should be limited to the cash resources on hand. The rebuilding was not to increase further the monumental level of debt the church already carried. Such was this indebtedness, that the failure to honor some obligations had already begun to threaten the denomination's good name and undermine the credibility of leadership. Kellogg, on the other hand, did not feel bound by any such restraints and preferred that a grander vision shape the future dimensions of the new hospital. He felt that if he could get the local community committed and involved, he could then realize his dream of putting Battle Creek near the center of the medical map of the United States. Money would not be a problem. Clearly, these were two different visions. The fact that the sanitarium operated under its own legal association, one structured to be at arm's length from the church, made it extremely difficult for the General Conference to hold the sanitarium managers to the General Conference agenda.

While willing to do all it could to help with the rebuilding project, the General Conference wanted to make sure that it happened on the denomination's own terms, a difference in basic orientation that would cause much sharper tensions in the early months of 1902. The difference of viewpoint lay behind the personal clash that occurred between Daniells and Kellogg in London in mid-1902. Kellogg wanted the General Conference president to undertake thirty thousand dollars' worth of additional debt for a medical institution in Britain and authorize the money immediately. While Daniells agreed that a sanitarium in Britain was an excellent idea, he was adamant that it should be built or purchased only when the money was in hand.

The doctor "brought very heavy pressure to bear on me," a disturbed president later informed his predecessor in office, George Irwin. "I was forced to inform him that he had no right to try and force my convictions," he recalled. "I also told him that I should absolutely decline to join him or anyone else in creating sanitarium debts to be thrown upon our people. We had a very plain, clear-cut, stiff argument over the question, with the result that the doctor entirely broke with me."[37] It was this "stiff argument" over a resolutely held management principle that, in Daniells's view, led to the increasingly public clashes and the widening rift between the two branches of the church's outreach. But was the principle really all that important? Was it really just an argument about how to fund expansion? If that is all it was, how, then, would Ellen White respond to this struggle with Dr. Kellogg or to the issue that had sparked it? Daniells was not sure.

THE UNCERTAINTIES OF PRAGMATICS

Shortly after the London quarrel, Daniells received a letter of advice from Mrs. White. It arrived just as he was leaving Battle Creek for meetings in California. "I am much worried about Dr. Kellogg," she wrote. Then, she continued, "My brother, I wish to write a few words to you confidentially in regard to the Doctor: Do not let him beguile you by his statements. Some may be true; some are not true. He may suppose that all his assertions are true; but you should neither think that they are, nor encourage him to believe that he is right. I know that he is not in harmony with the Lord. Do not sanction his effort to gather from every source all the means possible for his line of the work; for God does not favor so great an outlay of means on it now being made in Battle Creek; nor does He favor the way that the Doctor is managing the health food business."[38]

The letter let him know that he should be on his guard and that he should not become beholden to Kellogg. Perhaps she was thinking of the intractable problems that Olsen had let himself in for through his unavoidable links with Henry and Lindsay. But this was a confidential letter to Daniells personally. Just where Ellen White would stand in public and how she would respond to the numerous difficult decisions that he and Prescott were having to make as 1902 progressed was not clear.

In the discussions between the two men and others in their close circle, such as G. A. Irwin, C. W. Flaiz, and W. C. White, a recurring theme occurs: Where would Mrs. White stand? Initially, in these early stages of the conflict during 1902 and 1903, leaders did not know what her position on many issues would be, even though they sought guidance as and where they could. Sometimes, of course, they did not have time to seek her counsel, and leadership simply had to make decisions in light of their prayerful assessment of a matter. They would base their decision making in such circumstances on their own convictions, on the counsel they took together in light of what Ellen White might previously have said, and on the basis of the evidence or information before them. But "where Sister White would stand, and what she would say, none of us knew," recounted Daniells to North Pacific Union president C. W. Flaiz toward the end of 1903.[39] It is clear that their uncertainty regarding her response sometimes made them nervous about whether there would be later, critical correspondence from Elmshaven dealing with some of the decisions they felt they had to make. Thus Daniells had several very understandable reasons to feel uneasy about his lack of certainty of her position on particular issues.

Daniells was not sure, for example, how Mrs. White would feel about his stand against Kellogg on the matter of having the cash in hand before building for, in fact, she was sometimes flexible or pragmatic on his "no debt" approach to church and institutional development. With Daniells, the principle was very firm, and he felt that he had to be almost rigid in adhering to it, because he recognized the immensity of the mountain of debt that the church and its institutions struggled under. He knew that many church entities were facing bankruptcy, because they could not carry their load of debt.[40] As a result, he felt keenly that undertaking debts to get things established and then going cap in hand to the church membership after the fact was not right. The task of persuading church members to accept responsibility for debts others had undertaken for them was something he did not enjoy and did not believe was ethical. But would his rigidity on the policy actually hamper church growth and allow opportunities to be passed up?

Although assenting to the "no debt" policy and believing in it, Ellen White could also at times urge the assumption of a large debt in order to grasp what appeared to be providential opportunity. For example, as 1903 commenced she was advocating the purchase of a property for a sanitarium near San Diego on borrowed capital, even writing to Dr. Kellogg's brother, H. W. Kellogg, to urge him to lend money for the enterprise. She believed that the conference leadership was being too cautious on the matter, and it was clear to her that Providence was opening a unique opportunity. In a dream she had at the time, she heard herself saying to someone else that there would not be objection to the plan of two or three individuals uniting to buy it, if they were "picked" men, by which she meant persons who would not adopt a "rule or ruin" policy.[41] Whether she was alluding to Daniells or Kellogg is not clear. Both used the phrase to describe each other. The proposed new sanitarium should come under the control of the conference, she argued, even if financed by individuals. But it was this approach to development that was actually causing such a problem for Daniells in Battle Creek. At the same time, Ellen White was pushing hard for the establishment of sanitariums in New York, Washington, London, and in other California locations on a similar basis. She was not averse to borrowing capital if an opportunity arose to secure a good property. As she reflected on the frustration she felt, she confided to Henry Kellogg, "in Australia I had to push every step of the way in order to advance; and it seems as if I shall have to do so in California."[42]

Another example is suggested by her inclination to excuse the debt that had been accumulated on the Nashville publishing plant that worried Daniells so much. "It would have been best not to work on borrowed capital," she acknowledged, "and the brethren would not have needed to do this" if the believers had worked unitedly. The fact that there was a large debt gave the enemy an advantage. Nevertheless, she argued, every square foot of the building was needed. And furthermore, she felt that the "financial embarrassment had been magnified" by leadership. It had done so "in such a way as to make the work harder and to leave a wrong impression on minds." Clearly, Ellen White was prepared to live with debt if it meant the work would go forward.[43] This was also her policy with regard to her own affairs.

Daniells was aware at this time that she herself was heavily in debt and that she was normally able to live with the stress and worry of carrying large overdrafts in her personal finances in order to seize opportunities to advance the work. During this particular period, however, her debt load was very uncomfortable. "I cannot help the work in the Southern field financially," she wrote to Edson in the first days of 1903, because "I am thousands and thousands of dollars in debt, and I am obliged to keep borrowing continually in order to pay my running expenses." She was drawing only $50.00 per month (about half) from her General Conference salary, she explained, noting that during the previous year she had received "scarcely any royalties" which put her in "a very straight place" financially. "My trust is in God," she went on, "but I must begin to think where the money is coming from with which to pay my workers."

Barry Oliver notes that both O. A. Olsen and G. A. Irwin also struggled to relate to this approach to church growth, one that asserted that the work should be pushed forward without "waiting to see the funds in the treasury" before something began. "God forbid," Ellen White had written, that the work should be retarded by the statement that "our treasury is exhausted." Oliver notes that her sharp sense of the Second Coming created an urgency that overrode the fear of bankruptcy.[44]

As administrators, the General Conference officials, however, did not at all welcome the idea of leaders at the local level creating debts that they then had to carry. The balancing of the very real tension between exercising faith in moving with what appeared to be the openings of Providence and not being presumptuous in overstretching beyond what could be adequately managed in terms of funding and staffing was not an easy issue to resolve, and both Ellen White and Daniells approached achieving balance differently. But imposing debt on someone else's shoulders was not something Daniells felt good about. His nightmares about the financial crisis in Australia caused by the Avondale school still haunted him, as did the agonizing struggle he was currently facing to repay the large debts contracted by the General Conference during O. A. Olsen's administration. Thus he struggled in his mind and soul to reconcile and balance these competing patterns.[45]

Another reason for Daniells's uncertainty about Ellen White's stance regarding the decision making of his team stemmed from her reaction to the roll-out of the reform program at Nashville, Tennessee. Here he had encountered another particularly perplexing set of difficulties created by her pragmatic approach to applying the reform principles. On both of the twin thrusts of the new reorganization—the no-debt policy and church ownership of institutions—Edson White and his colleague, W. O. Palmer, posed a problem. They fiercely resisted both aspects. In this delicate area Daniells knew he had to tread with extreme caution, but in his mind the problems could not be sidestepped. Palmer and White operated the Nashville publishing house and an extensive network of schools and public health outreach programs for African Americans under the auspices of the Southern Missionary Society. W. C. White reported to his mother that the word had spread that when Daniells and his colleagues would go to the southern field they would be opposed on the basis of things that Ellen White had supposedly said, such as, "wicked efforts have been made to separate the two men [Edson and W. O. Palmer]" and "the word of the Lord has forbidden anyone to antagonize them in their work."[46] The Nashville publishing house was in difficulty because it had accumulated twenty-five thousand dollars in debt, which fact it had somewhat deceitfully hidden by a flurry of positive public relations statements. Furthermore, the enterprise was continuing to hemorrhage significant amounts of money each month in operational losses. It was the view from Battle Creek that poor management decisions and practices had led to the financial embarrassment. Edson wanted to retain the independence of his Southern Missionary Society and not have it brought under the direction of the new Southern Union Conference. He also wanted to maintain his own treasury department. According to Daniells, the union conference, on the other hand, did not appreciate Edson contracting debts for his southern projects and then sending in "the bills" for the union conference "to settle, in some way, from their treasury." The union view was that it should "have a right to say something about the debts that are contracted if they have to pay them."[47]

In mid-October 1902, just before Daniells returned to Battle Creek for the annual council meetings, he and W. C. White, along with local west coast church leaders, spent a morning at Elmshaven discussing these delicate issues with Ellen White and seeking counsel from her. Daniells felt the consultation with her had been profitable and that it had cleared the air on a number of issues. Mrs. White gave helpful advice on the scale of the rebuilding of the Battle Creek Sanitarium as well as on other medical program issues. She endorsed Daniells's position on not undertaking debt for the new sanitarium in Great Britain. Also, she understood the dilemma that denominational leaders faced in dealing with her independent-minded son in Nashville. Concerned for clarity on the approach they should adopt in resolving the impasse at Nashville, both W. C. White and Daniells were quite specific in the questions they asked. In response, Ellen White stated that Edson White was not to have his own treasury nor was he to maintain an independent work. The clarity of her answers encouraged Daniells. "This statement will do our brethren in the Southern Union Conference a world of good,—to know that this is your position," he explained. "This is my position exactly," she responded. She acknowledged with gratitude that Edson had done an immensely valuable work in the South when few others were ready to help, but that time, she noted, had now passed. "It is highly proper that the work of the Southern Missionary Society should be under the direction of the Southern Union Conference," she asserted. "I cannot give countenance to Edson's operating independently." W. C. White asked further if it was appropriate to make a change in the management of the Nashville publishing house in order to stem the alarming financial losses. "Has the time come for this action?" he asked specifically. Ellen White was just as forthright. "It has; and I say, Go ahead. God's cause must not be left to reproach, no matter who is made sore by arranging matters on a right basis." Furthermore, she urged the men to "act just as they would act if my son was not there."

What made this issue particularly perplexing for Mrs. White was that an intense animosity had developed between her two sons. Edson had not been "backward about showing dislike and lack of respect" for Willie. He had "exaggerated matters" and put "a wrong construction" on them. The fact that he cherished such feelings had an unfortunate consequence—unfavorably influencing Kellogg and his associates. On the other side, evidence of the tension between the two brothers had persuaded Daniells and his colleagues that Edson was most certainly in the wrong and the problem simply had to be fixed.[48]

A few days later, after Ellen White had experienced several sleepless nights of anguished reflection on the complexities of the situation at Nashville and the risks of making changes too quickly, she reported that she had been convicted by the Spirit that she had spoken too soon and on the basis of inadequate information. In a letter written several weeks later, she bravely reversed herself and retracted the advice she had given about Nashville.[49] Her reversal was understandable and based on good pastoral principles. The situation in the South was not simple. In fact, it was a very complex and delicate issue of managing human resources. Although Edson and W. O. Palmer had made serious mistakes, they were not to be precipitously re-assigned, she now counseled. They should be given more time to sort out the problems. Larger issues were at stake. Too many good people would be badly hurt, she thought, and they were people who had done their best. More time should be allowed so that things might adjust themselves, if possible.

Upon further reflection, Ellen White became convicted that not all the evidence was in regarding the problem and that even if her son and his colleagues had made mistakes, they had had good intentions.[50] As she thought and prayed about it, she had become absolutely sure that those who had been criticizing the situation from a straight management and efficiency point of view would not themselves have done one bit better if they had been in the same place at the same time faced with the same perplexities. It might be easy to judge a matter on the basis of "aftersight," but those who had to grapple with the complexities only on the basis of "foresight" should have more grace and understanding extended to them. Besides, as she struggled to explain, the nature and the context of what the denomination had to do in the South was different and much more complex than mission work elsewhere. Regular policies and practices would just not fit.[51] And she was absolutely right. That is what prophets do. They take the side of the minority and the marginalized and the downtrodden and stand over against the establishment and the status quo. Given unique insights with a more far-reaching viewpoint, they plead for justice and fairness. Ellen White's gift in these circumstances was simply being true to itself, and she was the vehicle for an important and valuable, though uncomfortable, perspective.

But, of course, Daniells was also right. It was the responsibility of leadership to ensure that a right and proper use is made of resources. Making sure that the long-term viability of a church enterprise is secure and that money is not wasted was a stewardship ethically and morally required of Daniells. And it was a sacred responsibility to protect the good name of the church and to appoint reliable and trustworthy management. What, then, was one to do when two good things—two right things—found themselves in contest with each other and it seemed that only one alternative was possible? What does one do when two duties conflict? Whether or not Daniells had thought through this not uncommon ethical dilemma that leaders face, he certainly knew from experience the tension that arises from it. In such situations he had learned to balance, and sometimes even suspend, his judgment and his sense of responsibility while in the presence of the charismatic gift of insight—and to value the counsel that Ellen White brought to his leadership even though it might cause considerable discomfort.

From a management point of view, the "flexibility" approach to implementing policy created quite a practical dilemma for Daniells. Clearly the intent of the 1901 reforms was that institutions would come under the ownership and supervision of the church's general administrative structure, a policy clarified and reiterated after much painful discussion at the 1903 session. It focused particularly on regaining control of the Battle Creek Sanitarium for the church. As we will discuss in greater detail in the next chapter, Ellen White firmly supported the general principle that all institutions established by the "people" of the denomination through their offerings and support should be owned and operated by the "people" through the church structure. But if a place such as the Nashville publishing house could remain independent, why could not the Battle Creek Sanitarium also? And the same could be said for the Madison School in Tennessee that Sutherland and Magan established in 1904 as a project independent of church administrative oversight. At that time, Mrs. White vigorously supported the project as an "independent work" and later advised the two men that they should steadfastly resist any attempt to bring it under the church's overall administrative supervision.[52] But from administrator Daniell's perspective, why should not Battle Creek Sanitarium receive the same treatment? How was he to be able to tell when policy should apply and when it should not? And in his determined stance against Kellogg, would he find himself standing on a hill, ready to die for what he thought was a principle, only to discover later that it wasn't and that he had been standing on the wrong hill? While the Madison School problem was a future one, the medical program in Battle Creek was a present crisis. And Daniells was already familiar with Ellen White's pragmatic approach to accomplishing the church's mission. How to live and work within this creative tension was the basis for some of his uncertainty as he approached the 1903 General Conference Session.

For his part, Vice President Prescott, who was further away from the action, could not understand the inconsistency in the approach to resolving the Nashville issue and had confided to Daniells earlier in the year when the issue first began to surface, "It is very difficult for me to understand these things, and I have about made up my mind that I must simply let them alone."[53] What he meant was that the approach seemed so wrong to him that he had to withdraw from any engagement with its resolution and resign himself to accept the decisions of others. When Ellen White later advised the appointment of a new manager at once for Nashville, Prescott could not help but wonder why she had not suggested that in the first place.[54] For her part, she also was sensitive to the framework in which Daniells had to operate. She warned Edson, "You and your brethren are in trouble" in what they were doing in the South. "I entreat you to be very careful of what you say in the meetings you attend."[55]

The experience with the Nashville publishing house and its managers had the effect of causing both Daniells and Prescott to be, if not less sure about their judgments on other related issues, at least to be apprehensive about the criticism they might receive. They also knew that the same complexities applied in considerable measure to the matter of how to relate to the issues surrounding the activities of John Harvey Kellogg. Daniells knew of the strong personal links between Kellogg and Ellen White and that the two leaders had a history, so to speak. At times, Kellogg had served as personal physician to her and her family. He had cared for her husband, James, through his times of critical ill health and regarded himself as Ellen White's son in an extended family relationship. The early struggles to get the health work established had knit their hearts together. Daniells knew that she would rightly do everything within her power to save the doctor and hold the church together. That was also Daniells's objective. But just how pragmatic and flexible she would be and how far she would bend in order to accommodate Kellogg he was not sure. And Daniells and Prescott were not alone. G. A. Irwin shared the same uncertainty. "As you may imagine," Irwin wrote to the General Conference president, "I have been very anxious to learn definitely how things were going in Battle Creek and how Sister White regarded the moves that were being made there." Irwin elaborated further: "It was more than simple curiosity on my part to know what stand Sister White has taken in this controversy." Rumors had been flying and attempts had been made to lobby her through acquaintances and close friends. Sarah McEnterfer, Ellen White's personal nurse and assistant, for example, was a graduate of Kellogg's nursing school and a close friend of Kellogg. Reports circulated that she was a conduit of information from or to Kellogg.[56] Irwin had heard such rumors. From his perspective, he "could not see how she [Ellen White] could take any other course consistent with the stand she has taken in the past." Nevertheless he wasn't sure and had written to find out.[57]

Yet another reason for Daniells's uncertainty about what position Ellen White might take stemmed from her tendency on occasion to refer to disagreements that arose between church leaders as "quarrels," phraseology that she had used to refer to the Kellogg-Daniells conflict. She spoke, for example, in her Sabbath morning sermon at the 1903 Session about the leaders in the church being like "quarrelling children" and stressed that they should quit doing so over minor matters.[58] The admonition in a Sabbath sermon was undoubtedly sound biblical exhortation, but in the context of a deep disagreement involving a highly significant fundamental principle of organization, such a way of describing the conflict could be misunderstood. In this case, both parties were convinced that their particular view of how the church should be organized was based on principles that she had herself enunciated. Alluding to the conflict as a "quarrel" about a minor matter may well have added pressure on Daniells and his associates, causing them to feel less certain about their convictions—if it did not also do the same for Kellogg.[59]

Prescott was expressing how Daniells felt when he wrote in October 1902 in a rather discouraged state of mind, "I hardly know yet whether to take courage or not concerning the outlook for the future of our work. So much depends, humanly speaking, upon the general attitude which WCW takes in regard to the whole situation." Both men were aware that W. C. White was also emotionally wrenched by the dilemma of having good friends on both sides of the divide. But it was not just in the American South where W. C. White's influence counted. As Prescott and Daniells saw it, the position he took would count "in the whole wide field." Clearly, the tensions arising from the conflict caused considerable ambivalence on matters. Political alignments were inevitable. "I shall wait for further information as to his [W. C. White's] decision before I settle down to anything definite," commented Prescott.[60] It is clear that a lack of assurance about what Ellen White's response would be made Daniells and Prescott quite nervous at this time regarding whether there would be a backlash from Elmshaven due to some of the decisions they felt they had to make.

Almost tipped from office

Daniells arrived back in Battle Creek on November 1, feeling apprehensive about what lay ahead. He was aware that after Kellogg had returned from England he had been actively trying to influence Daniells's friends and colleagues against him. As the vulnerable president saw it, the doctor's opposition had grown "more widespread and hostile every month." Therefore Daniells thought it best to call for as full a participation of the executive committee as possible for the year-end meetings and hoped to confine discussions within just its membership. Much to his chagrin, however, events quickly spun out of control. At Kellogg's insistence, and with the help of his supporters on the committee, meetings of the committee were "thrown open to the doctors, nurses, and medical students." It was a highly unusual maneuver. But it mirrored, in a sense, what Daniells had himself been allowing in the organizing sessions he had been conducting throughout the denomination. The result was that any Battle Creek church member who desired to attend the meetings was also let in. This led to stormy sessions and "an undesirable publicity," as Kellogg angrily laid his charges against Daniells and as the president then responded. On later reflection, Daniells felt that the publicity, although embarrassing, may not have been as detrimental as he feared, since it at least gave him a chance to state his own position clearly and publicly. According to him, Kellogg "had been representing matters according to his own views, and these differed very much from mine."[61]

The sessions were the worst that Daniells had ever had to endure. "I cannot begin to tell you what those meetings were like," he reported to George Irwin a month later. "They were intense. The strain was fearful. I do not wish to ever pass through another experience like it," he reflected, adding, "The minutes do not convey anything like a just view of the situation. They present the merest or dimmest outline of the controversy." Daniells stated that he was not alone in his assessment of the seriousness of the situation. "Those who have been attending the General Conference Committee meetings during the last fifteen or 20 years say that this was one of the most critical councils ever held." But he would rather suffer the experience again, if he had to, than "to enslave" his mind. "I can not consent to be bound to any man's chariot to be led according to his will," he declared with some defiance.[62] In fact, Daniells had been almost tipped out of office.

Kellogg had realized that the best way to overcome the opposition to his sanitarium expansion plans was to engineer the appointment of a new chairman of the General Conference executive committee—one more accommodating to his view of things. During their argument in London, Kellogg had reminded Daniells in a veiled threat that he "held office by his [Kellogg's] influence." The doctor was apparently alluding to the fact that almost 25 percent of the membership of the General Conference executive committee consisted of representatives of his medical association and that they were loyal to Kellogg. It had been the doctor who had nominated Daniells as chairman, and A. T. Jones had seconded the motion.[63] "I felt almost paralyzed when he told me this," Daniells recalled. It had "stuck" in his mind "like a poisoned arrow ever since."[64]

Under the 1901 constitution, Daniells was responsible to the executive committee that had elected him. The office had no stated term, and the committee could replace him at any of its meetings. Thus, at the October meetings, the Kellogg forces launched a full-scale drive to have Daniells replaced. But he was not so easily removed. According to Jones, Daniells had defended himself with the memorable line, presumably uttered outside the committee, that he was "not a football; to be kicked into the ring, and then kicked out again." But this was not just a friendly game of football. It was a serious situation with long-term consequences. As George Knight points out, an attempted coup d'état was in full swing, and the scary developments highlighted, to the ministerial portion of the General Conference at least, a serious weakness of the 1901 system. Knight believes that it also indicated to Jones that his own hope of achieving a significant role in denominational leadership would have to be realized by aligning himself with the Kellogg party.[65] As things turned out, the move to unseat Daniells failed, and he retained his role as chair of the executive committee.

From Kellogg's perspective, the council "very clearly" revealed "a disposition to rule or ruin" him. He lamented that F. M. Wilcox of the Boulder Sanitarium had not attended. Had Kellogg been counting on his vote? And the doctor identified Percy Magan, Edward Sutherland, and A. T. Jones as having "stood with the medical side." The rest, he noted, other than his own medical association representatives evidently, "were pretty much lined up against us."[66] In a sadly ironic way, Kellogg hoped that the Review and Herald fire, which had burned the publishing house to the ground on the night of December 30, "had cleared the atmosphere considerably." He was of the opinion that "some of the matters brought up at the Council will now be buried" and that the fire would somehow turn things in his favor. But he was misreading both Daniells and Ellen White.

Pre-session nerves

The fire that destroyed the church's leading publishing house in Battle Creek not only heightened tensions at the denominational headquarters, it increased the pressure on church leaders to find an alternative location for the Review and Herald's publishing activities. Ellen White's almost immediate response to the disaster was one of relief. She urged Daniells and his colleagues to reflect on the meaning of the event and advised that not a brick should be laid in Battle Creek to rebuild the institution. To emphasize the strength of her conviction on this point, she mentioned to her son Edson and others her resolve that if any attempt was made to rebuild in the city, she would take away her printing plates and have her books published elsewhere.[67] With Daniells traveling in the southern states at the time, Vice President Prescott had to provide pastoral care and leadership for the traumatized Battle Creek congregation as they grappled with the enormity of the disaster and its implications. Despite it being midwinter, Prescott convened a meeting of the full congregation "according to the Colonial custom," he noted with a wry twist, referring to the Australian custom "of not having the building heated." The steam for heating the church had been supplied from the Review and Herald plant and was now inoperable. In the frigid sanctuary he read the letters from Ellen White to the sobered and shivering congregation.[68] Because of the severe cold it was a short meeting, and members made their way home for Sabbath lunch pondering the impact of the disaster on their employment, local real estate values, and its meaning for the mission of the church.

As January marched relentlessly on with its increasing complexities, life for A. G. Daniells became no easier. During the next three months in the run-up to the General Conference session scheduled for March, the implications of the disaster and the lack of harmony among the leaders made for an uncertainty that became almost unbearable.

Both sides to the dispute became increasingly nervous about possible outcomes and were concerned to have their perspectives understood. As might be expected, and as would have been entirely natural in such a sharp conflict over a substantive principle with so much at stake on the outcome, both sides jockeyed for advantage and sought to shore up support for their positions. Persistent reports circulated around Battle Creek that Ellen White had issued a testimony strongly reproving Daniells and Prescott for the course they took in the November council. The story went that the sanitarium people were expecting, on the strength of this testimony, that both Daniells and Prescott would be put out of office at the next session of the General Conference. Apparently, neither man got to see the letter, and it unsettled them to hear that sanitarium management was prejudicing their staff "against the General Conference workers" on the basis of the alleged testimony. But there was nothing they could do, reported Prescott, except "to go forward in a straightforward manner with our work."[69]

The letter that may have sparked the rumors in Battle Creek was one that Mrs. White had sent to a Battle Creek attorney, Judge Jesse Arthur, lamenting the outcome of the previous General Conference session. Although at the time she had reported that the breakthrough and the turn things had taken in 1901 had surprised and delighted her, what had happened since that date had discouraged her. "The result of the last General Conference has been the greatest, the most terrible sorrow of my life," she said, because "no change was made." Leaders had continued to exhibit throughout the church "the wrong principles that had been prevailing in the work at Battle Creek." The spirit that should have spread through the whole church as the result of that meeting had not been brought in "because men did not receive the testimonies of the Spirit of God."[70] The letter probably referred to the attitude adopted by Kellogg and his associates, but the medical forces may have considered it as an attack on Daniells and his administration.

During the first week of January, Ellen White wrote to E. R. Palmer and Daniells, stating that she had been "disappointed and grieved over the course" that both of them had followed in the South. Their actions, she said, tended to discourage those at Nashville. In a further defense of her son and his colleague, and pleading the need for patience, she pointed out that Daniells needed to remember that he was "not dealing with ideal men, but with real men of God's appointment." They were persons of "like ambitions and infirmities" who "fall into the same errors that we do." She suggested that Daniells's interference in Edson's work was not right. In a letter that an administrator in any conference today would require some discernment to understand aright, she argued that "to no man has been assigned the work of interfering with the work of one of his fellow laborers." Daniells had not been "appointed the work of being an overseer of his fellow men. Every man is to bear his own burden."[71] Knowing just how to implement the 1901 mandate when it got to Nashville was particularly difficult.

By late January, she again stated bluntly to Daniells that she did not think he was right in his approach to the way her son and others had done things in the South. "I have not admired your wisdom nor the wisdom of those who have so little burden to take up the work that the Lord has for years been keeping before us—the Southern States." She also mentioned the needs of cities such as New York. In a shift of emphasis from that of her earlier Australian years, she protested Daniells's overemphasis on overseas mission outreach. "All the means that can be gathered up is not to be sent from America to distant lands while there exists in the home field a dearth of means and of laborers." The delicate art of appropriately balancing the distribution of resources was now becoming a very complicated issue for the General Conference leader. With Ellen White settling back into the United States, local concerns there began to take on new urgency. And the complexities of denominational expansion in the South and the attitudes of northern people to it exasperated her. Her own financial circumstances and her inability to help the South reinforced her sense of frustration. "I have been and I am still carrying very heavy burdens" for the church in the South, she reported, "and I want no more. My soul is sick and discouraged at the outlook. I will say no more," she concluded.[72] She also noted that she would have little to say whether the forthcoming session should be held in Healdsburg or at Oakland, because it was a serious question with her "whether I shall attend at all." (Eventually, it was decided to hold it in Oakland.) The letter helped with guidance in resolving the southern dilemmas, but it also undoubtedly increased Daniells's own anxiety levels about what should be the way ahead. Tangling both with Edson White and with Kellogg was opening too many fronts at once. But what else could he do?

Yet another Ellen White letter, written a little later, if it had come to the notice of Daniells, would also have given him great anxiety about the length of his tenure as president. One could have easily interpreted her letter to Californian church leadership in a way to fuel the rumors in Battle Creek. It discussed the possibility of shifting the forthcoming General Conference session to the Healdsburg church. The local congregation had offered to do the catering free, and the location would make it much more convenient for her to attend the meetings. She confided to her California church leader colleagues that her courage at that moment was "not the best." In spite of having tried to let go of the burden for the southern work, she continued to worry about, and to be discouraged over, the troubles at Nashville and the ongoing tension between her sons. A week or so earlier she had grappled a little more with the thorny issue, advising Edson that it was best for him not to work so closely with W. O. Palmer. Each of them should labor where they could have "elbow room" that would allow for their individual capabilities.[73] "I have carried the burden of the Southern Field in direct opposition to the plans of leading brethren," she complained and commented further, "I have lost confidence in some of these men as being taught and directed of God. If they are thus taught and directed, I am not teaching the way of the Lord. Therefore I am convinced that my place is at home. . . . I care not to face such matters any longer; for it seems useless. I long for retirement."[74] She was not at all inclined to attend the upcoming General Conference session. A. T. Jones, who was now quite clearly claimed by Kellogg as a supporter of his cause, would undoubtedly have seen Daniells, Prescott, and E. R. Palmer as the targets of her comments. And it may well have strengthened his hopes that he might be Daniells's replacement at the upcoming session.

At the time Mrs. White sent this letter, both Daniells and W. C. White were involved in trying to sort out the problems in Nashville. Back in Battle Creek, Prescott was waiting interestedly to hear "whether you really made any change in the management at Nashville." He was also glad that Daniells was traveling onward with W. C. White to Mexico City, because it would give them "a good opportunity to consider the whole situation." Then he noted, "I do hope that Brother White will carry with him to California a clear view of our general situation, and of the issue through which we are now passing."[75]

As he approached the 1903 session, Daniells was plagued with anxiety. While he protested that he would not mind being put out of office and sent to Africa, in reality he did not relish the prospect. Nor did he look forward to what he knew would be a head-on clash. He was aware that Kellogg was writing long letters to Ellen White setting out the doctor's side of the story. And he heard that Jones had visited Elmshaven to discuss with her and W. C. White "the way the work should be conducted."[76] How could he have his own position adequately understood by Ellen White?

Her ill health in the lead-up to the session complicated matters for the administrators and for herself, since her feelings fluctuated from day to day. In early January, she was "fully decided" that she would not attend the session "unless clear light comes to me." Stressful sessions unfitted her for writing.[77] But by the end of January, with health improving, she informed Edson that she had now decided to go "because of impressions made on my mind last night." She did not think, however, that her son needed to attend at all. Four days later she had thought again about Edson's situation and wrote that he should indeed plan on being at the meetings.[78] By the end of February her health was indifferent again, and stress complicated by severe hypertension caused her much discomfort. Again, she had to lay aside her work. For example, she informed Haskell that although she had received long letters from Dr. Kellogg and her disaffected nephew, Frank Belden, she "dare not read them lest in them there might be some things that would sadden my heart. Anything that causes me to feel sad is a great injury to me physically," she explained, reporting the symptoms of her hypertension. "My head becomes hot, as if it were a heated furnace, and my nose bleeds. Then for a time all work has to cease." She could not write much even to Haskell, for her head was hurting. But, she concluded, "We expect you to attend the General Conference."[79] He didn't. Duties detained him in New York. But the next day she again struggled with whether she should go or not. "I am not sure that it will be wisdom for me to attend," she commiserated to her close friend, Lucinda Hall. For the moment, she had lost confidence that her influence would be effective in changing anything anymore. In a very down mood, she noted ironically, "If I went, I could not give any further evidence in anywise, than I gave at the last General Conference." All the leaders had to do was simply "read the Bulletin of the last Conference," she added. She certainly did not think it her "duty" to go through "the same amount of labor" that she went through at the previous session.[80] By now she was beginning to fear that the whole complicated issue of "organization" would have to be thrashed out once more at the upcoming session, and it wearied her to think of it.[81]

During late February and into March, nose bleeds and hypertension continued, and Ellen White had to halt her writing entirely. By March 6, however, her symptoms began to subside. She reported that the previous day, with W. C. White back home, "for the first time Willie ventured to read to me some letters from Elder Daniells and Brother E. R. Palmer and to tell me something of his experience while in the South."[82] Maybe attending the 1903 session would be possible after all.

When George Irwin arrived from Australia in early March, he was able to spend time with both her and W. C. White. He found "quite a strained condition of affairs" in the church, he wrote to his colleagues back in Australia. But, at least, Ellen White was now stronger in health and able to give more of "her usual attention" to the matters that came before her. On the basis of his lengthy discussions with her, Irwin reported that Mrs.

White felt "the time has come to lay down the thing straight and clear in regard to Dr Kellogg's course, and the way he has been trying to manipulate things." She would not be surprised if a schism were to occur. In the course of her remarks about her experience since the previous General Conference session, "she made some things clear and plain to me that had been a little mysterious." In Irwin's assessment, "her confidence seems to have been almost entirely shaken in his [Kellogg's] integrity." Mrs. White had heard the rumors that the doctor was expecting to come "in full force and capture the session and make A. T. Jones president." Irwin, however, for his part thought it more likely that Kellogg would not attend the conference at all. (He guessed wrong.) Irwin certainly felt impressed, however, that they were all "on the eve of something" but what that "something" was, "the good Lord only knows." At the same time, he was concerned that E. W. Farnsworth, back in Australia, not misuse what he was sharing with him.[83] As for Daniells, who had survived one coup d'état, the question was: Could he outlast another? Only the weeks ahead would tell.

CHAPTER 9

A. G. DANIELLS SURVIVES the 1903 GENERAL CONFERENCE SESSION

Just how worried and vulnerable Daniells felt as he came up to the 1903 session is indicated by the letter he wrote to Ellen White just two weeks before the session opened. He reported to his spiritual mentor and advisor that in recent weeks he had been in such perplexity and trouble with Dr. Kellogg that he had "not known what to do regarding many things." As a result he had taken some time to step back and get his bearings. After having done some personal stocktaking, he now wanted to make sure that Ellen White was aware of his positions on the issues. He might not know what she thought about all this trouble, but he wrote, "I have made up my mind to write you plainly some things that I know and where I stand."[1]

In his long letter, he outlined what he saw as the root cause of the conflict and traced how it had become so public and intense. He reported that he had "many times reviewed every step" that had led up to present situation and acknowledged that with hindsight "he might have done better in some of the details of the conflict." But with regard to the main issues, he asserted, he did not know how he "could have taken any other position than I have." Daniells felt very bad that he had "signally failed" in establishing peace, harmony, and cooperation with the medical branch despite making a great effort. From his perspective, however, the basic problem was that Kellogg was simply "out of harmony" with Seventh-day Adventism. The doctor's commitment to the doctrinal essence of the church no longer held. Furthermore, he had tried to undermine Daniells's own confidence in Ellen White's work and was determined to have his own way.

Of particular interest in Daniells's letter is his recounting of some unique personal spiritual experiences that he saw as "tokens of assurance" from the Lord and that, in his mind, vindicated his course. It was as if he were saying to Ellen White that whatever counsel she might have for him and whatever assessment she might make of his efforts, he was sure on a self-authenticating, spiritual, and kind of charismatic basis that the Lord had been endorsing his efforts. He was not arrogant or pompous in this, but he was clearly saying that the Lord was with him too. One experience had involved a physical seizure and a dreamlike premonition that startled him during the night prior to the 1902 year-end council. This experience had led him to call his council members to a special day-long Sabbath of united prayer before the meetings began. The other experiences had involved the timely receipt of letters of affirmation and encouragement from unknown church members or pastors who had been praying for him. "I can not throw all these to the winds, stultify my judgment, and violate my conscience in order to keep in harmony with the Doctor," he wrote. "As much as I want peace, I cannot purchase it at such a price." In a very direct way, Daniells staked out his ground. "I am fully aware of what my stand in all these matters may mean to me personally. I may suffer an apparent defeat, and be banished from this country. I am in a measure prepared for that." But he was now "reigned up day by day with the burning conviction that I am not to swerve an inch from the right to gain Dr Kellogg's favor." "Regardless of personal consequences," this is where he would stand. "I have passed through a fearful experience, and feel very deeply. I would have been driven into despair and ruin if I had not known how to go to the Lord and get help. Pray for me," he concluded.[2] At this point, Daniells did not feel that he necessarily required advice. Rather, he needed courage and support.

Daniells was still "in terrible perplexity and anxiety" as to what he should do when he arrived in California for the session. "I set apart the first Sabbath that I was in Oakland for fasting and prayer that I might know my duty at that time," he later confided to W. C. White. "I was sorely tempted to leave the work in the United States, and go to Great Britain, and give the remainder of my life to the work on that side of the Atlantic. I did not want to be rash, nor do anything that was wrong; so I set apart the day for prayer that I might get special light from the Lord with reference to my personal duty." After long, intense pleading, he reported that he sensed that the Lord came graciously near to him, and gave him "a most profound impression." Every doubt had been removed from his mind. "I was deeply impressed that I must not run away from the work in this country; that I must stop all questioning about that, and stand at my post of duty with my brethren." At the same time he felt "very deeply impressed that I must be as true to the spirit of prophecy as the needle to the pole, that I must do the part of a man in standing by the Lord's servant, upholding her hands, and leading this denomination to recognize and appreciate this great gift."[3]

The intensity of Daniells's personal turmoil and struggle pushed him to the very extremities of anxiety and helplessness. "I was [so] completely overwhelmed with this thought that my strength departed from me," he recalled as he relived the events of the agonizing experience. "Filled with a terrible sense of the responsibilities resting upon me, I promised the Lord with all my heart that I would be true to this cause, and do all in my power to prevent anything from arising in this denomination to dim the glory of this gift, and of the Lord's servant who had exercised this gift so many years."

On the hospital compound in Battle Creek, J. H. Kellogg was also extremely stressed as he approached the Oakland session. He also had written a strongly stated assessment of the situation to Ellen White from his perspective. In his seventy-nine-page letter, Kellogg had related the whole sad background to the conflict in London and had detailed a long catalogue of organizational sins that Daniells had committed. He complained that the General Conference president had been persecuting him and was not interested in supporting the medical aspect of the church's outreach. After he had written the letter, the doctor had second thoughts about whether he should mail it and decided not to. But the letter arrived at Elmshaven anyway. It had been sent by Judge Arthur, the church's attorney and legal counsel, who also represented the sanitarium and worked closely with Kellogg. In an explanatory note a few days later, Kellogg noted that the rebuilding of the sanitarium was rapidly approaching completion, that businessmen outside the denomination had advanced loans for the project, and that there would be no financial burden to the denomination.[4] But later, Kellogg wrote a more aggressive letter to W. C. White, in which he stated that he had read his seventy-nine-page letter with its catalogue of complaints to his college faculty and his sanitarium board of managers as well as placing it in the hands of Edward Sutherland and Percy Magan, college administrators at Berrien Springs. The letter "was unanimously endorsed by all these persons," Kellogg noted. Therefore, he did not want Elmshaven to regard the document as simply from himself but "as a letter from all the persons" named.[5] This was serious pressure. The heavy artillery had been rolled out.

Just a week before the session opened in Oakland, Dr. Kellogg once more corresponded with W. C. White, expressing his absolute frustration with Daniells and his team. "I have no hope for the future of this work unless the Daniells-Evans-Prescott ring can be broken up," he expostulated. "If this ring undertakes to go on the next two years as it has been doing in the last six months," he fumed, he was absolutely sure "they will receive no recognition from a large contingency," of the church.[6] Kellogg's message was unmistakable. It was clearly calling for a change in leadership.

On the day of the opening session, Kellogg again wrote to Ellen White, warning her that the church was facing the real prospect of schism. "The schemes of Daniells and Prescott to become rulers over Israel are in direct opposition to the whole plan of reorganization which the Lord gave us through you at the last General Conference," he asserted. "If they are allowed to triumph in this thing, it will drive out of the work and into a separate movement, all self-respecting doctors and nurses and many ministers as well." Daniells and his party had "determined to have war," he said, but he, for one, would "stand on the platform which you have laid down." With both parties claiming to be allied with Ellen White, what was she to do? Kellogg was sure that she did not see him as a "traitor" or "an apostate," and he wanted to assure her of his "great respect" for her and "his confidence" in her.[7] According to Prescott, the doctor had been arguing this position to his own sanitarium staff for some time, with the purpose of holding medical branch employees "loyal to their management."[8]

Ellen White did not attend the Oakland session as a delegate, so officially she had no voting rights. This appears to be the first session she attended in which she was not formally listed as a delegate.[9] But she was a welcomed guest speaker for the meetings and was scheduled for numerous sermons and addresses. It appears, however, that she did not sit in on all the business session discussions or participate in many of the major debates. If she did, she did not speak to any of the live issues as had been her custom at previous sessions in the 1870s and 1880s. Only in the closing meetings do the stenographer's transcripts record comments made by her, other than what she presented in her scheduled sermons or addresses.[10] Clearly, she sought to remain above the fray. Although her health had recently improved, she was not strong enough to be able to walk to the meetings. Her helpers rented a second-hand wheelchair for the duration of the meetings, and each day they wheeled her to the church.[11] Well aware of the enormous issues at stake, her goal throughout the session was to re-establish harmony between the two branches of the denominational outreach. She knew that not only would this involve bringing about a totally different attitude on the part of John Harvey Kellogg, but also the challenge of keeping the church moving forward together on its reform agenda. As the events of the historic conference unfolded, Ellen White had to draw on a whole range of methods to exercise her influence on the leadership of the church. Some of these methods worked, and some didn't. Whether she went to the session with the conviction that Daniells should remain as the General Conference president and was committed to keeping him in office is not known. She gives no hint of what she regarded as the desired outcome. But from the way she exercised her influence, it can probably be safely assumed that despite whatever failings Daniells might have, she preferred that he continue in office. Certainly, she felt this way later as the crisis unfolded.

"A man for the place"

Fifteen months after the session, in May 1904, after renewed bitter clashes at the Lake Union Conference session at Berrien Springs, Ellen White would confidently declare that Daniells had "shown himself to be the man for the place." Her comments were carefully nuanced, however, if not stated somewhat unusually. She asserted that "the Lord has declared that he will harmonize with Elder Daniells and Elder Prescott," and she pleaded with Sutherland and Magan to do the same. Sutherland and Magan were in the process of resigning from the leadership of the college at Berrien Springs to move south and start up their own educational institution. Ellen White pleaded with them to make peace with their fellow administrators. Daniells was not without his weaknesses, she acknowledged, but "my brethren" she wrote, beseeching the two men, "let us do our best, not to discover wrong in Elder Daniells, but to help him." She could speak with confidence, she said, "because these things have been presented to me." Also, of course, she had worked very closely with the General Conference president. "You catch at straws concerning Elder Daniells," she elaborated, but much worse than this, neither of them had "discerned the true condition" of Kellogg and his associates in the medical program, nor had they "placed a correct estimate upon their actions." Daniells, on the other hand, she pointed out, had "shown himself to be the man for the place." Furthermore, "at this time there are needed men who dare to differ with those who are counter-working the plans of the Lord for his people."[12] If her defense of Daniells was not an unqualified ringing endorsement of him, at least it was a clear declaration that she supported his presidency. She had not been as outspoken about Daniells in public back in March of the previous year in the midst of the attempted coup d'état. But she had known at that time that she had to move very carefully with respect to what she said publicly and with respect to Dr. Kellogg simply to avoid being compromised. She had to consider carefully whatever she did.

Right at the outset of the 1903 session, Ellen White felt she had been instructed to adopt the basic strategy of having no personal interviews at all with Kellogg. By contrast, during the 1901 session she had stayed in his house. This time she did not want to be in a position where he could tell her falsehoods or misquote her. This strategy effectively isolated the doctor, and he certainly sensed the exclusion keenly and probably felt humiliated. Even a chance meeting on the street during the session resulted in an awkward situation. "I passed you somewhat hurriedly this morning, only because I did not wish to embarrass you," he wrote Mrs. White on April 8 in a sad, dejected letter right after the incident. "I did not know that you cared to see me, and I did not wish to take advantage of an accidental meeting on the street." They did not speak to each other as they passed, but clearly the doctor was hurting. He said that he was praying that the Lord would "make my dish more palatable to the brethren," if that could now be at all possible. The sanitarium was now built, although it had "cost an effort such as God only knows." With nothing more to occupy him at the session, Kellogg left before it ended. Not sure now that anything he wrote would find its way into her hands if he sent it in the usual way, Kellogg gave the letter to Edson to read to his mother if he "should have a good chance."[13]

In stark contrast, Daniells reports that right at the outset of the 1903 meeting Ellen White greeted him warmly when he visited her rented house and assured him of her support. As he went to greet her on her arrival in Oakland on Tuesday, March 24, she apparently saw him coming down the hallway and welcomed him with a firm handshake followed by the quiet admonition, "Don't you waver a particle in this crisis." The words were like music. Daniells felt that they "were the most precious words" he had ever heard.[14] He reported also that on numerous occasions during the conference she requested both himself and Prescott to meet with her and W. C. White to counsel together on how to resolve issues and prevent a wholesale takeover by the medical forces. "We were in great trouble at the Oakland General Conference," Daniells recounted to W. C. White three decades later, "and you will remember how often your mother called Brother Prescott and me to her room to counsel with us about the crisis we were in." For Daniells, it was the "most serious and perilous crisis this cause has ever had."[15]

Isolated from Ellen White, Kellogg resorted to several strategies to attempt to communicate with her. For example, he would send a handwritten note through Edson or a note along with a small gift or some favor that he did for her. He had ordered some "specially prepared" potato meal that he sent over with the hope that it would "please" her. "I wish you would call on me for any other little service," he offered.[16] Occasionally, she referred to him and to his sanitarium work in her public addresses, but she never spoke to him personally. Several times during the conference she felt convicted that she needed to be direct and confrontational in public with respect to his attitudes. Frequently, she spent a large part of the night rehearsing the kind of speech that she would give and the things she felt the Lord was indicating that she must present. But on each occasion, when in the pulpit, she shied away from the confrontation for fear that Kellogg was not ready to receive it and that such an approach at that time would only make things worse. On one occasion she reported that she changed her topic even as she was standing in the pulpit.

In the days immediately following the session, she adopted another approach. She wrote a number of letters to Kellogg and sent them to A. T. Jones for him to read to the doctor when he went back to Battle Creek. Even though it appears that Ellen White knew of Jones's identification with the Kellogg faction, she saw him as one who could bridge the divide to reach Kellogg in an effort to keep him within the religious community. The primary letter that she sent to Jones for Kellogg, with a request that he pray with the doctor before reading it, was a kind, pastoral, and personal appeal pleading with Kellogg to seek a new spiritual experience. Other manuscripts mailed to Jones actually addressed the delegates who were then attending session meetings of Kellogg's Medical and Benevolent Association in Battle Creek. The doctor had convened a large conference/convention to coincide with the official opening ceremony of the new sanitarium building. Ellen White apparently intended that Jones read the attached manuscripts at some of the convention meetings. She gave him significant pastoral latitude in choosing the time and the occasion for approaching Kellogg. This is a good illustration of her carefully thought out plans to make her influence effective. "I am sending to you a copy of a letter that I have written to Dr Kellogg," she explained to Jones. It contained "very many plain admonitions," some of which it could be "difficult for the doctor to understand." The letter had not yet gone to Kellogg himself, nor would she send it at present. Her wish was that Jones should watch for an opportune time to "talk and pray" with the doctor "and then read my letter to him." Greatly desiring that Kellogg would "see his danger, and turn to the Lord,"[17] she explained that she was resorting to this approach, because she had been unable in the session meetings at Oakland to speak safely about his dangers. She feared that others would misunderstand and make unwise use of what she needed to say.

A session of animated debates

It is helpful to review the arguments and debates that swirled around the floor at the 1903 Oakland General Conference Session. They give an understanding of the high tension and the maneuvering that took place around the re-election of Daniells as president. The session was not all sunshine and light. Ellen White had been heard to lament that it seemed the session would have to re-work the whole re-organization discussion that should have been a settled matter two years earlier.

Although the session proper commenced on Friday afternoon, March 27, Mrs. White arrived in Oakland on Monday, March 23, so that she could be present for some of the pre-session committee planning meetings. She apparently met with the group for its morning worship periods and gave advice as needed.[18] The session opened with the acceptance of the new union and local conferences. The list indicates just how busy Daniells had been during the previous two years. Twelve new union conferences had been organized along with three union missions and twenty-three new or re-configured local conferences.[19] The first weekend of the session provided a heavy menu of preaching (morning, afternoon, and evening), with the recurring theme being a call to remain true to the prophetic distinctives of the Advent movement.[20]

For her Sabbath morning sermon, Ellen White chose to preach on lessons from the Old Testament story of the twelve spies who were sent into Canaan. It was a general hortatory sermon on the dangers of unbelief, the need for courage, and a lament on lost opportunities to finish the gospel. But during her talk she made two short passing references to the highly charged issues of the rebuilding of the sanitarium. God "wants no more mammoth buildings erected; for they are a snare," she commented. It was a brief aside. Then later in the sermon she stated that "centralizing in Battle Creek, putting up so many buildings there, has robbed other places of light." Means had been employed there, she said, "that should have been used in proclaiming the truth in other cities."[21] Though these were quite brief statements in the context of the entire sermon, they stung Kellogg sharply. On Monday morning, she did not appear for her scheduled address at eight o'clock, and those in charge made alternate arrangements. The delegates were formally seated and recorded, and then Daniells gave his presidential report. It was not until midafternoon that Ellen White was wheeled into the session to deliver her second address. On this occasion, she spoke passionately for about ninety minutes on the theme of the Old Testament boy-king Josiah and his program of reform. The emphasis was heavy on the lack of progress made by the church since 1901. The sermon was a free-flowing exposition on the experience of Josiah, but the punch line challenged the congregation to "find out" what God means "when he sweeps away our sanitarium and our publishing house." The overall impact, whether intended or not, cast a heavy pall of judgment over the congregation. The immediate response of Irwin, who had the responsibility as platform chairman for that part of the program, caught the mood in the church. He needed to transition the congregation into a "social meeting" and a season of prayer. On rising to his feet, his first comment was "Brethren and Sisters, we all stand condemned." Although the editors of the official session *Bulletin* deleted this response, the stenographers did record it. Irwin's further comments reflected some theological confusion about law and gospel, but it seems clear that delegates heard more of the application of law and judgment than gospel and hope in the address. Nevertheless, a spirited testimony meeting followed, again not reported in the *Bulletin* but recorded by the stenographers. The *Bulletin* editors simply summarized the proceedings by noting that it was a good social meeting with numerous acknowledgements of repentance and confession. This was true, but the meeting was also quite spirited in other ways.[22]

A fiery reaction

Two loosely phrased sentences in Ellen White's address on Josiah provoked a fiery reaction from Kellogg that led to his speaking at some length in the Social Meeting and then being granted what was, in effect, a right of reply at later sessions. He occupied two extended sessions that day and the next to set forth his position. Later, Mrs. White needed to clarify and explain what she had meant to say. Whether intended or not, her Monday afternoon address certainly set the fuse alight for the fireworks that lay stored up in the dry straw of brittle emotions that Kellogg and other delegates brought to the session.

In her Monday address, Mrs. White, in commenting on the Battle Creek fires, had stated that she was "so thankful" the college had moved from Battle Creek to Berrien Springs and then added that "a wrong policy has been followed in centering so much in Battle Creek." She followed up this sentence, several moments later, by saying: "In the place of erecting large sanitariums, we should establish smaller sanitariums in many places." During the extended testimony meeting that immediately followed her address, Kellogg spoke for about twenty minutes. The first part of what he said was basically a rebuttal to her comments on Battle Creek. Kellogg pointed out that James White himself had told him of his wife's dream after an earlier sanitarium fire when she had seen that "this institution which is now so small would develop into a great institution which would be known all over the world." He recounted how the dream had supposedly shown that the institution would grow until buildings would cover the entire city block. Furthermore, he explained that he had been to Ellen White on every occasion whenever the question of expansion had come up. Thirteen or fourteen years previously, in a General Conference session, she had endorsed the adding of the hospital. When he had asked about the chapel, she had said "we should have built it years before." Recently, she had urged the hospital to purchase the college buildings across the street. Thus his work had "not all been confined to Battle Creek," but he had been doing "what we thought was the Lord's will." Then he explained that the 1902 fire had not burned all the hospital, only "about a third of our buildings"—two out of twenty. "It seemed impossible to move away." And while the new building was larger in dimension, in fact they had planned smaller. The previous structure had 341 rooms for patients, while the new contained only 296. But the standards expected for patient care had risen, and rooms therefore had to be more commodious. The new building was thus both smaller and larger.

The doctor was speaking in public relations mode again and being a little less than straightforward. The board had authorized the erection of only one building not to exceed five stories and not more than 450 feet in length. Kellogg had overseen the construction of an elaborately equipped building. True, it was only five stories high, but it was an extra 100 feet longer than the board restriction allowed, and it had an extra combined 500 feet of extensions abutting each side. Furthermore, it had been ornamented with marble and mosaic work supervised by the master craftsman who had worked on the Library of Congress in Washington, D.C. It was a very presentable building—some might even say ostentatious. Daniells and his colleagues viewed the development as being carried out in patent disregard of their counsel.

But having defended the development, Kellogg then took Ellen White's statements about moving out of Battle Creek at face value and directly challenged the delegates. If he had made a mistake in erecting the new building, it could be corrected. It would be possible to find a buyer for the entire institution. They could then easily transfer from Battle Creek to another location. He could guarantee that the enterprise could be sold quickly, and the corporation would be in a better state than if they had simply abandoned the enterprise as it was after the fire. The doctor hoped that the session would advise him clearly "what ought to be done under the circumstances." He disingenuously denied that he had "any personal quarrel with anybody" and that there were "not any conspiracies." Furthermore, he did not know whether any "two men have put their heads together and said let us work for this, let us stand up for one another." As a testimony suitable for a "social meeting," this one was long on defense and short on confession. Kellogg acknowledged in one fairly brief statement at the beginning of his talk that he felt "his work has been very imperfect . . . full of mistakes" and that he had not been "what the Lord wanted me to be all these years," but the rest of the testimony was a vigorous defense of his course of action.[23]

In subsequent meetings, Ellen White found herself having to clarify her counsel, and she was obliged to concede that it seemed that the church had no choice but to support the sanitarium. Again, she was pragmatic in addressing the issue of mission. She rejected the idea that her expressions had indicated that the sanitarium should be sold and allowed to go into the hands of others. "Let me say," she explained in her Wednesday morning talk in a significant concession, "that God does not design that the sanitarium that has been erected in Battle Creek shall be in vain. . . . Now that the building has been put up, He wants this institution to be placed on vantage ground. He does not want His people to be looked upon by the enemy as a people that is going out of sight."[24]

For the rest of the first week of the session, delegates wrestled with the problem of whether to bring ownership of the various Adventist institutions under the General Conference and its subsidiary union conference entities. They appointed a committee on "Institutions" to review their status and suggest a general plan for their reorganization in line with the new church structure adopted in 1901. In its report, the committee recommended that "all institutions be owned directly by the people, either General Conference, Union Conference, State Conference, or organized mission field." The constituents for each institution would be the church membership of the local or regional area denominational body. The conference would elect controlling boards representing the people, and the bodies would be limited in their power. They could not sell property without the approval of the constituent body. While the recommendation addressed all institutions—publishing houses, colleges, and sanitariums—the elephant in the room, of course, was the Battle Creek Sanitarium. Kellogg's vigorous defense of its independence indicated clearly that everyone knew what issues were being addressed.

In the heated, and often personal, debate that engulfed the session on this issue, Kellogg made his position abundantly clear. He believed that the resolution represented simple tyranny. "I want to say to you that I raise my protest here, and I wish to be put on record, because you will find me stout and strong as I can possibly make myself in opposition to the principles laid down here in this resolution, on every possible occasion and in every possible place."[25]

The focus of the debate on Kellogg and his institution made the discussion extremely painful for some, because of its frankness. The possibility that the doctor might leave the church and take the sanitarium with him openly emerged several times on the floor. After five days of on-again, off-again wrangling, Waggoner observed that as far as he was concerned, "a great deal" of the discussion had been "rather painful, . . . and unprofitable." In comments not reported in the *Bulletin,* he asserted that the mention of Kellogg's possible apostasy struck him "more painfully than it ever had before," because he felt that the General Conference had become preoccupied only with saving the denomination's property, not the doctor's soul.[26] Kellogg defiantly declared during the debate that even if the session voted to approve the recommendation, as he suspected they would, he had determined "that he did not need to be bound by it." His stance clearly did not endear him to either Ellen White or the administration and probably explains why he was not elected to the General Conference executive committee or any other church position following the conference.[27] Kellogg had declared his intention to be insubordinate. He had chosen the hill on which he would stand and fight, and he would defend it with his life.

The delegates finally passed the resolution on institutional ownership right near the end of the session, along with a formal action to investigate the status of the sanitarium and a recommendation to the institution's stockholders to reorganize the board so that the sanitarium was clearly and "indisputably" an Adventist institution owned by the church.[28] Ellen White firmly endorsed these actions in her letters. But Kellogg had planted his flag for independence, and the next four years comprised a series of acrimonious skirmishes and legal battles that eventually ended with Kellogg being disfellowshiped from the church, but with the sanitarium still under his control.[29]

By the end of the first week, the 1903 session had resolved the issue of institutional ownership, but the matter of the process for electing a leader and revising the General Conference constitution still remained to be addressed. For some reason, the Committee on the Constitution was not able to bring its report to the floor of the session until two days before business was meant to wind up—and even then with a highly unusual twist. Along with the committee's majority report, a minority group within the committee presented its own dissenting report. Both reports were tabled and held over to be considered the next day. Not until after "a very protracted" testimony meeting lasting three hours the next morning, were the delegates able to consider the reports. The testimony meeting had heard pleas from Ellen White for unity and confessions from her son, Edson, and others. But in spite of it all, unity somehow eluded the delegates. The contents of the reports launched a massive and heated debate. The committee had found itself deeply divided on one particular point: a proposed revision to the constitution that the president be selected by nomination of a session-appointed nominating committee and a vote by the full delegation in session. This proposal would take the place of the arrangement voted at the 1901 session giving the General Conference Executive Committee the power to choose a leader designated as the "chairman." In this 1901 scenario, currently in place, the delegates in session elected only the executive committee itself.

A high-profile minority of three members of the Committee on the Constitution, led by Ellet Waggoner and including Percy Magan and Dr. David Paulson, respectfully but vociferously argued that the majority proposal was "subversive of the principles of organization" given by Ellen White since 1897. They saw it as a move that "reverses the reformatory steps that were taken and the principles which were given" in the previous two sessions. To approve it would be to fly directly in the face of her counsel at that time. The level of emotion in the minority response is clearly indicated by its choice of language. The new constitutional proposal was so subversive that the three dissenters "could not possibly subscribe to it." They therefore counter-recommended that "the Constitution of 1901 be given a fair trial before it be annihilated."[30]

Confusion reigned for a time as delegates argued their way through a series of points of order and appeals to the rulings of the chairman, trying to sort out whether they should deal first with the minority report or the majority report—or even whether to discuss the minority report at all. Waggoner, fearing he had lost the opportunity to speak to the report when ruled out of order, found himself appealing for permission to address it. Some interpreted the confusion as an attempt to hold off discussion. Emotions ran deep on the issue. Waggoner offered a longwinded and complicated explanation of the reason the minority group submitted a separate report, taking the opportunity while he was at it to elaborate on his view of the biblical principles of organization. After that, some delegates attempted to limit speeches to five minutes. Waggoner had spoken for more than thirty.[31] Acknowledging that although the matter was complicated and complex and that time was short, nevertheless, A. T. Jones argued that "every delegate has inalienable rights to be heard." How long that would take was anybody's guess. But any "complexity," he felt was the fault of the conference managers who had brought the matter to the floor too late in the session. "If you adopt this Constitution without the discussion that belongs to it," warned Jones in a thinly veiled threat, "you will get a good deal more complexity than you are now in, in more ways than one."[32] Openness prevailed as the debate extended into the afternoon, evening, and on into the next day. Eventually, the delegates agreed that speeches could be made without time constraints and that discussion would be appropriate on the minority report if confined to the overarching principles of the proposed new constitution.

It had not been planned to happen this way, but there seemed no way out. Intense and impassioned debate consumed the final days of the session. Each of the three minority report supporters had opportunity to speak, and A. T. Jones vigorously supported them. Waggoner's chief arguments were that the proposed new constitution was creedal and against biblical principles, and that to adopt it would go against what Ellen White had earlier very clearly counseled. Other delegates objected strongly to this interpretation. New York Conference president G. B. Thompson protested the attempt "to clothe this old constitution with inspiration." He did not believe that the old constitution was inspired simply because "God called for reorganization two years ago." He objected to the idea that had "crept into a good many speeches" that "unless you vote for the old constitution you are going back on Inspiration."

Ellen White did not participate in the discussion as the delegates wrangled over what she may have or may not have meant by her various statements. Her consistent position was that it was best left to the leadership to figure out how the constitution should be framed. Eventually, however, as the debate went around in circles, W. C. White, who had "hoped to avoid any part in the discussion regarding this constitution," felt he needed to try to clarify what he thought his mother might have meant in her statements about "kingly power." He urged delegates to take a broader view and look at the wider context of her articles. In keeping with her approach to issues such as these, he argued that the delegates needed to look at actual conditions. "We have to face conditions, and not theories. We have to deal with what is before us, and not altogether an ideal condition or ideal situation." Flexibility and a pragmatic approach to mission and organization should determine the way forward. If that meant re-instituting an elected president, such a thing surely could be done without returning to the exercise of "kingly power." Others noted that the old constitution was not being "annihilated" anyway. It was merely being revised in just two areas that had to do with the appointment of the church leader and the powers of the committee.

After several hours of debate, exhausted delegates decided to take a meal break and then reconvene in the evening to attempt to bring the matter to resolution. The evening debate lasted long into the night until some concessions were made through a series of amendments dealing, for example, with the matter of the size and function of the committee quorum. Eventually, the chair called a vote. The atmosphere was tense, and a season of prayer was requested before delegates stood in exercise of their ballot. Of the 108 delegates present, 85 favored the revised constitution, and twenty stood for the old. Daniells silently breathed a huge sigh of relief but did not gloat. While it was comforting that the opposition had not been able to muster enough support to defeat the constitutional revisions, it was, nevertheless, a most sobering realization that a substantial and highly influential body of opinion had now been alienated.

The debate on the constitution, as recorded in the proceedings of the session, clearly shows Daniells's ability as a statesman. He speaks in measured language with a stance of respect for the critics despite their hostility. His speeches are not defensive, and they reveal him speaking with confidence and clarity of thought. Furthermore, he is able to defuse tension by building bridges to his critics, as in the discussion of the emotionally charged term *annihilation* used by the minority group in describing his approach to the previous constitution. Calmly and with forbearance under evident pressure, Daniells tried to avoid boxing in his opponents as he simply insisted that there had been a misunderstanding and he now sought to correct it. He had matured in his two years of leadership.[33] And winning over alienated colleagues was going to require significant leadership skill.

The next morning, when a number of his colleagues playfully but pointedly asked A.T. Jones if he had slept well in spite of losing his campaign, he evidently was sensitive to the jesting. At the start of the day's proceedings, he immediately took the floor to relate the taunting conversations and to assure delegates that now that the session had voted, he was not "wedded" to the old constitution. "The constitution that has been adopted is my constitution now," he affirmed. "There will be no more loyal man to the constitution than I am." Furthermore, he added, "whoever shall be elected as president will have no more loyal standby or co-operator than myself, because we are all brethren." But in a subtle statement indicating his continuing unchanged conviction, he said that he took comfort knowing that though ancient Israel had started back to Egypt several times, "they never got there, you know."[34] Unfortunately, he didn't find it easy to carry out his protestations of loyalty. As George Knight observes, in spite of Jones's conciliatory words, he never reconciled himself to the reinstitution of the General Conference presidency. Increasingly, he identified with Kellogg, and by 1906 he had thrown in his lot completely with the medical faction and launched scathing attacks on Ellen White and the General Conference.

With the method of electing the president finally settled on Thursday night, the nominating committee could at last do its work. Yet another extended report and debate lasting all day consumed Friday's session. This time, the topic was education and the implications of the new initiative at Berrien Springs. The nominating committee was not able to present a report on Friday. Instead, a special Saturday-night session convened to help process the large backlog of business. It ran until well after 11:00 P.M., with the very last action being approval of the nominating report. These had been extraordinary times indeed. The election of a president at a special late-night session did not match well with the idea of good, safe practice. But there seemed no other choice. Time was simply running out. Daniells was elected president; L. R. Conradi and W. W. Prescott as vice presidents; W. A. Spicer as secretary; and I. H. Evans as treasurer. It was the Daniells's team again for another two years. The voting numbers were not recorded, so it is not known whether the opposition to electing Daniells was the same as it had been for the constitutional amendment. Conspicuous by his absence from any listed committee was J. H. Kellogg. But both A. T. Jones and David Paulson had been elected to the executive committee.[35] Kellogg's interests still had representatives on the committee, although both men would soon feel the uncomfortable tension of divided loyalties.

Sunday the delegates spent refining and approving the recommendations designed to bring the Battle Creek Sanitarium under the General Conference, and eventually the session wound up with routine housekeeping requirements on Monday morning. It had been a long and highly stressful three weeks. Ellen White was very nearly burned out and returned home extremely weary. Daniells was relieved, but left not wanting to ever have another experience like it. The cost on his health was too high.

A medical director in revolt

Although his re-election meant that Daniells did not need to plan on an immediate transfer to Africa or some other mission field, it still allowed no time for relaxation. The problem of a medical director in revolt was a serious issue that still had to be dealt with. Immediately after the Oakland session, Daniells and other delegates returned to Battle Creek, where for legal reasons they re-convened in session. Some General Conference constituency meetings had to be conducted in the legal jurisdiction of the state of Michigan, among them the sanitarium constituency meeting. For this constituency session, Kellogg had organized a major convention event as well as the legally required meetings. It was also a good opportunity, he thought, to introduce his constituency to the recently completed sanitarium facilities. The convention, with its special guest speakers and banquets, brought together the largest attendance of Adventist medical and health personnel up to that time. The political implications were significant.

The first letter Daniells received from Ellen White after his 1903 re-election was written probably less than twenty-four hours after the delegates voted him into office. She had barely reached Elmshaven when she put pen to paper to remind him of the challenges that lay immediately ahead—particularly in the meetings to be held in Battle Creek that very same week. The letter conveyed to Daniells the need for an important new strategic approach to Kellogg. Back in her own room, she had felt "a great sadness" come upon her. She was still bothered by some of the personnel problems at Nashville. But more particularly, she was "much perplexed" at Kellogg's attitude. She recounted that she had gone to the meeting on Sunday morning prepared to say some very direct things to him, persuaded that he had to be confronted.[36] But even as she went, she had been convicted that it would be better not to "say anything that would arouse resentment." The previous Sabbath she had felt under severe pressure and had thought it important to warn the session that they should not be taken advantage of in the matter of sanitarium finances and other issues. But she reported that she felt "forbidden to say the things" that she thought that she "must say." Another topic came to her mind, and she spoke on that instead, trying to "lead the minds of the people away from the difficulties and perplexities around them." Above all, she must avoid "anything that would stir up confusion and strife in the Conference." Mrs. White urged Daniells and Prescott to join her in saying "nothing that will drive Dr. Kellogg to desperation." Above all, she did not want him to feel that he had been "driven into a corner."

Illustrative of Ellen White's self-awareness and of the fact that her feelings unavoidably helped shape the letters that she prepared, she indicated to Daniells that he should remember that some things she had said to Kellogg she had written when she was emotionally stressed over the issues. "Do not use the words that I have spoken under great perplexity and distress, to hasten a crisis," she pleaded with the president. Dr. Kellogg was clearly a danger to the church and had the potential to cause enormous damage, but Ellen White was sure that "God's hand" was "on the wheel" and that "much must be left with Him, to work out as He will." This would seem to be a softer, more nuanced approach to dealing with a problematic leader than that which she had used toward A. R. Henry or Harmon Lindsay several years previously. The "referee" function that Ellen White exercised in conflicts like this she had to employ with great care, and when she, as the referee, blew her whistle to order a free kick or a time out, both sides needed to comply with the ruling. On this occasion, one side was not acknowledging the whistle. This time she was evidently aware that the stakes were much higher and that the church had significantly more to lose. Now was a time to reveal a "conciliatory spirit," to "step softly and wear the gospel shoes." Daniells should not give the doctor any "occasion to wrench himself from the faith." She hoped that it was not too late to save Kellogg from himself.[37]

A few days later, she again wrote to both the parties in the conflict—the General Conference leadership and the members of the Medical Missionary Association. This time, she pushed hard on the unity theme. The two branches were to "act in concert." Yes, the 1901 policy of creating union conferences had been correct, she asserted. And yes, the sanitarium must come under the authority of the General Conference just as the publishing program had done. No, large numbers of people should not be brought to Battle Creek, and no, the issuing of sanitarium bonds was not the way to fund sanitarium capital developments. She also felt that the church needed to find a better way to help support the medical program, that it was a risky time for church members to be putting confidence in medical projects under Kellogg's Benevolent Association. The membership needed to be protected. The committee appointed should examine carefully "the standing of the Battle Creek Sanitarium, to see whether the God of heaven can take control of it." Evidently, she understood the sanitarium to be in other hands at this time. Clearly, Ellen White understood the seriousness of the issues.

It was with some initial delight, therefore, that she received a telegram jointly signed by Kellogg and Daniells following the Battle Creek meetings of April and May. The telegram promised peace and reconciliation. She had been waiting for this response. But her rejoicing was short-lived. Ellen White had had a premonition that it wouldn't last. Caution prevented her from recording in her diary that peace had fully broken out, as she realized that the accord was nothing more than a statement of good intent. Neither party had been able or willing to change its basic principles, which all but ensured that the conflict would erupt again. It was not long before it did.

In August 1903, Kellogg announced the re-opening of Battle Creek College. From

Kellogg's perspective, there were reasonable academic and accreditation issues underlying the necessity of the initiative, but both Daniells and Prescott saw the action as flagrant opposition to the "move out of Battle Creek" program and interpreted it as undermining Ellen White's counsel. They also perceived it as an opportunistic measure to attract and control the medical education program of the church. Both men saw Kellogg's move as a danger to the church, and Prescott vigorously denounced the initiative in the pages of the *Review*. Both were eager to see what W. C. White or his mother would do. No one knew. But, because of time pressures and publishing deadlines, Daniells and Prescott had to act on the basis of the best information they had after taking counsel with whichever loyal colleagues were available at the time.

A publicity war quickly broke out, with circulars and letters going to health leaders and conference leadership throughout the church in the United States and overseas as both sides explained the rationale they had for the actions they had taken.[38] Then, piling quickly on top of this episode was the issue of whether the church could, or should, endorse Kellogg's book, *The Living Temple,* as a fund-raising venture for the new sanitarium. Both Prescott and W. A. Spicer felt that the volume contained many problematic statements, and a reading committee had earlier recommended that it not be published. According to General Conference administration, since that time Kellogg had not made enough of a change in the theology and philosophical underpinnings of the book to warrant a shift in policy.

In spite of her hopes of harmony and her desperate desire for peace, Ellen White had been convicted in a dream in early August that the medical program under Kellogg and the ministerial branch were like two vessels only loosely roped together, and that tied together like this they were not going to weather the storm. The apparent prosperity that Kellogg was boasting about in his circulars and the surge in patient load was not necessarily an evidence of God's leading, she pointed out. The fire less than eighteen months earlier must certainly be seen as a judgment.[39] Employing a dramatic metaphor, Ellen White finally declared herself during the first week of August and issued a clarion call to medical personnel in the church to "cut loose, cut loose" from Kellogg. Each sanitarium, she declared, was to stand on its own feet—they were not to link up any more with Kellogg's Medical Missionary and Benevolent Association in Michigan. Although she saw the rough shape of the huge financial loss looming ahead, she could now see no alternative. She affirmed that the reform moves taken by Daniells had been the right ones. Just as if she were standing on the deck of a foundering ship, she issued the order: "be calm" and "fixed" and "make not one concession."[40]

Suddenly, allies became vital, as did the perceived ability to have influence with Ellen White. In late August, A. T. Jones secured an interview with her at Elmshaven and reported the news to Kellogg. He had done his best, he said, to explain to her the academic necessity for re-opening the college in Battle Creek, and Kellogg deeply appreciated that he had taken the bold step. Jones was wanting to join Kellogg in Battle Creek, but as the doctor saw things he was fearful that if Jones were to move just at that time from California to the Battle Creek Sanitarium, then the influence of W. C. White on his mother would be unstoppable, and that would not be a good thing. The doctor also reported that Sutherland and Magan claimed that a letter addressed to himself had been circulated, that a copy had gone to Mrs. Druillard at Berrien Springs, but that Kellogg himself had not seen it yet. He was, however, expecting a rebuke from Ellen White over the college issue.[41]

During October and November, Mrs. White worked diligently to build and reinforce a coalition in support of the General Conference. Her letter to David Paulson in mid-October pleaded with him to distance himself from Kellogg, to cease supporting him with his writing activities, and to throw his influence behind the General Conference.[42] In November, she wrote to Stephen Haskell and George Butler, urging them to become actively involved in leadership again and to stand loyally behind the General Conference. She wanted Haskell to work in the South once more to help secure institutional loyalty for the General Conference. Also she worried about the association between Sutherland, Magan, Edson White, and Kellogg.[43]

Daniells also had to study carefully any alliances he had set up. He had been utterly stunned in late March of 1903 to suddenly find Waggoner directly opposing him on the issue of reorganization. "You can imagine my utter amazement when the Doctor [Waggoner] came to the Oakland Conference apparently entirely opposed to the plans of the General Conference Committee," Daniells commented to a colleague some months later. It wasn't just the revision of the constitution, however, that Waggoner objected to, but the reconfiguration of institutional ownership as well. "He took his position squarely against our plans, and is now entirely out of harmony with us." What astounded Daniells was that Waggoner had not offered one word of protest to the process of reorganization as he had traveled with Daniells around Europe and the United Kingdom while the General Conference president introduced the new denominational structure following 1901. At the Oakland session, however, Waggoner argued that Daniells was establishing "a Seventh-day Adventist papacy" through the revisions to the constitution. In his view, constitutions were like creeds and were not needed at all. The "consideration of constitutions" was so "utterly foreign to the line of study he had followed," he said, that having to sit through discussions about them was just "painful" and "really a bit of torture." He preferred to find freedom in reading his Bible during such discussions. By the end of 1903, however, Daniells had had to stake out a stand against Waggoner's negativity, and he refused to endorse him for a teaching role at Emmanuel Missionary College. It had been a difficult thing for Daniells to do, but Irwin, who also felt very deeply over the matter, was convinced that had he been in Daniells's shoes, he would have done exactly the same thing.[44]

A. T. Jones, for his part, clearly identified Daniells as the problem in 1903, not Kellogg. In Jones's view, the General Conference president himself was the subject of Ellen White's lament that no progress had been made in reform since 1901. "If that constitution [1901] had been followed strictly in the spirit as it was intended," and as the Bible principles had called for, he asserted to the delegates at Oakland, "we would have been far more than two years ahead of where we are today." Reintroducing the idea of a presidency in the denomination was the primary mistake. "Thank the Lord that we got rid of it in the General Conference affairs," he said, "[and] let us hold that advantage and not go back to Egypt."[45]

The fact that Jones himself served as president of the California conference in the run-up to the 1903 election did not seem to him as being hypocritical or inconsistent. He anticipated, rather, that even his own office would be done away with within a short time. Perhaps he had also become aware that he may not have had the "executive ability" needed in order to be a good conference president. In fact, he had been reinstated in the California conference by the bare skin of his teeth at the end of 1902 in session meetings that caused Ellen White some embarrassment.

In reality, Jones would not have been re-elected president on the conference floor at the 1902 Fresno annual meeting of the California conference had it not been for Ellen White's very direct intervention. She had to plead his case strongly. His union president, W. T. Knox, saw only chaos developing throughout the conference under Jones's leadership, and by the end of the second year he was pleading with the General Conference administration to find something else for Jones to do so that they could get some order back into local conference affairs again. Daniells did not want to tangle with that problem. His hands were full elsewhere. Increasingly, Jones became a loose cannon.

By the end of 1903, the conflict with Kellogg was again in full tilt even though the doctor had made some statements about his errors. Any common ground, it seems, had disappeared beneath the swirling waters of the rising flood of hostility. George Irwin's affirmative letter to Daniells encouraged the embattled president as 1903 drew to a close. "You have my hearty support in the attitude you are taking in the controversy that is now going on in the States," Irwin declared. He encouraged Daniells to hold firm and not allow himself to be sidetracked by Kellogg's "so-called confessions." In Irwin's view, the doctor had adopted the "confession dodge until he can get his wind and have time to hatch up some new scheme to carry his point." All trust between the two leaders, it seems, had broken down completely. According to Irwin, the question could "never be settled until it is settled right." That would happen only when Kellogg "saw the iniquity of his course."[46]

As 1903 began to wind down to its close and Daniells reflected on the events and agonizing stresses of the past ten months, he was certainly more hopeful and of stronger courage than at the year's start. "What wonderful progress we have made in one short year," he wrote to C. W. Flaiz, a union president on the West Coast. "It was just a year ago that the storm broke on us in our council meeting at Battle Creek. How terrific it was! How unprepared we were for it." Daniells recalled that at that time only three or four individuals in the council understood him, and he felt keenly his sense of isolation. Even the majority of the members of the General Conference committee, he thought, "did not understand the issue." He recalled that he felt pretty sure of where Prescott, Spicer, Evans, Cottrell, and Flaiz would stand. But aside from them, he "did not know what the other men would do." And "where Sister White would stand, and what she would say, none of us knew."[47]

By the end of the year, however, it seemed to Daniells that all had changed, and he breathed a huge sigh of relief. "Sister White has spoken in unmistakable language. The destiny of 'The Living Temple' is settled. The paramountcy of the General Conference over all branches and departments is established. And last of all, the backbone of a strong, determined revolutionary movement has been broken."[48]

Daniells was hopeful that if the church made the same progress during the coming year, "this cause will emerge from the darkest period it has ever known and escape the greatest danger that has ever threatened it. I most earnestly pray that this shall be done." Unfortunately, another four years would pass before the denomination finally resolved its conflict with Kellogg with the removal of his name from church rolls. And the cost was high.

His experience in administration during 1903 had taught Daniells two things about the importance of his relationship with the charisma exercised by Ellen White. As he reflected on the matter to W. C. White, he expressed his gratitude for the assistance she had given. In one sense, it had not made his work any easier. He still had to grapple with uncertainties and to make judgments based on the best information available. And he still had to seek the counsel of his colleagues. But he was certain that the counsel he had received from Ellen White had ensured that his work would be successful. This had two important implications for him.

"In the first place," he wrote, "I have felt that I must personally square my life and all my doings with the administrative work of this denomination, with the counsels of the spirit of prophecy." Then, "in the next place," he observed, "I have felt that the value of this gift must be made plainer and clearer to our people." He strongly believed that the communications that he and his colleagues had received should be available to the whole denomination.[49]

Daniells's affirmation and confidence in Ellen White's partnership did not mean an idealized or unrealistic view of her distinctive gift. His experiences during the Kellogg crisis had demonstrated that the communication was not simply all one way, and, furthermore, that it was mediated through a woman who worried, became anxious, lost sleep over matters, got upset, felt excited, and who wrote letters reflecting how she felt at that moment. But he knew also that she was a woman who dearly loved her Lord and who wrote letters because she saw things with deep insight and broad perspective. Because she perceived things beyond the present horizons, he knew that she felt compelled to write, because she knew that she was being impressed by the Spirit who placed the charisma within her. Many times the impulse gave her anguish and seemed like an enormous burden. At other times the impulse moved gently and with serenity. And Daniells knew her weaknesses as she did his. He realized that she worried about her inadequacies in writing, but that she had to do it anyway. Just as he did not always understand things well, neither did she. He had learned that the mystery of a charismatic gift could not always be understood or easily explained, but that it was, nevertheless, of exceedingly great value in the life of the church. Daniells, too, felt that the Lord had somehow, in some deeply personal way, placed a spiritual gift within him. This gift of leadership and administration he did not fully understand from a theoretical or academic perspective, but he simply exercised it in response to the needs of the church and his own spiritual sense of God's leading. In addition, he recognized that other church leaders also had that gift and exercised it through the medium of their own temperaments and personalities, for there was no other way possible. In earlier times the gift might have been identified as "apostleship," although Daniells would have been loath to claim that for himself. But others such as W. C. White recognized that this term was appropriate and helpful. For Daniells it was a genuine partnership between the gift of prophecy and the gift of administration. Both were gifts, and God had placed them in the church for the common good. He was simply delighted, but deeply humbled, to be the one the church felt it needed as a leader.

CHAPTER 10

ADMINISTRATION and CHARISMA in the POST-CRISIS YEARS (1903–1913)

As noted at the beginning of this study, the years between 1887 and 1903 were ones of extraordinary stress for the Adventist Church. Rapid growth and expansion created sharp tensions as leaders competed and quarreled over access to the limited available resources. The struggles exposed structural weaknesses and inadequate organizational arrangements and eventually led to radical reorganization initiatives. The management of resources was loosened and decentralized, while at the same time internal processes for maintaining unity and cohesion in belief and practice were maintained or even tightened. Entwined through the structural modifications were other stressful strands of change involving doctrinal realignment as the church developed theologically. Such changes led to adjustments in teaching and preaching as the community responded to the demands of an expanding vision of its mission. It was a turbulent period of radical and profound transformation for the Adventist Church. This period has been the primary focus of study in the preceding chapters.

Ellen White was deeply involved in the developments of this era of explosive growth, identifying leaders, helping ensure their effectiveness, and, when she thought necessary, influencing their removal from leadership. She also spoke frequently to the problems and inadequacies that became increasingly apparent. Thus she was an active agent of change and was directly involved in its processes. The story of this growth and development reinforces the long-held conviction central to Adventist self-understanding, that in a unique way the Holy Spirit was present and at work in the church through the role and influence of Ellen White. Adventists see in the distinctive charisma she exercised powerful evidence of the presence of the New Testament spiritual gift of prophecy. This gift, in turn, they understood as the fulfillment of the promise of Jesus to His followers, "I will not leave you as orphans; I will come to you" (John 14:18, NIV). The Spirit would be continually manifest in the midst of the believers. Through this spiritual presence, Jesus promised that He would guide the Christian community into a clearer understanding of truth and of the will of God. The Spirit would also equip believers for ministry and mission. Adventists recognized in the last book of Scripture references to the ongoing role of the spiritual gift of prophecy in the end-time community. The expression "the testimony of Jesus" (Revelation 12:17) took on particular relevance as a way of understanding the charisma of Ellen White.

The story unfolding in these pages reveals, through the interplay of human relationships and administrative decision making, how Adventists recognize and understand Jesus' promise in John 14 being fulfilled in the growth and development of their community of faith. In the process, the study provides valuable insights into the way in which the unique gift itself actually functioned. The charisma manifested itself through the realities of a frail, flawed, temperamental, but remarkably intuitive, passionate, and committed woman of dynamic faith. Our examination also helps to explain how, during the period under review, the gift related to those other valuable gifts of leadership and administration and apostleship that, according to the apostle Paul, the same Spirit would place in the church. Such gifts would also manifest themselves in the lives of flawed but gifted and equally committed men and women of faith.

The intriguing story of development, however, did not come to an end in 1903. Neither Ellen White nor A. G. Daniells concluded their ministries in that year when the more intense agonies of re-organization were largely settled—at least for a time. Both leaders would serve their church for many more years. This chapter provides an overview of the highlights of the final decade of Ellen White's involvement with General Conference elections and business sessions up until 1913, as it seeks to explore her continuing interaction with the leader who was reelected at each of the three sessions before her death. It becomes clear that the same patterns and dynamics evident prior to 1903 continued in these subsequent years. In her declining years, Mrs. White continued to guide and counsel with Daniells, and their relationship continued to have both its easy and its difficult stages. Still, these remaining years were less turbulent, characterized as they were by less critical issues. They were thus not so marked by the stresses of change and of radical organizational development and upheaval. Nevertheless, numerous episodes of tension did appear. Tension and conflict are an inevitable part of the life and growth of a community of faith. A community impassioned by a conviction of the nearness of the impending end-time, motivated by a strong sense of urgency, and shaped by a clear sense of identity and mission, could hardly avoid conflict.

A presidency extended

The re-election of Arthur Daniells to the General Conference presidency in 1903 was not his last unnerving experience of wondering what his job or place of work might be in the next few months. It was but the first of a further five journeys through the nomination/election process at General Conference Sessions. None of the five, however, were fraught with quite as much anguish as was the first in 1903—that is, until the last time Daniells's name came up for consideration in 1922. On that occasion, he did not return to office. The 1922 election was a highly politicized affair with a deeply divided delegation that had been subjected to a substantial anti-Daniells campaign prior to the session. Opponents had initiated a whispering campaign nurtured by a poisonous mix of slanderous, almost libelous, anti-Daniells pamphlets. The object was to try to prevent another Daniells reelection at all costs. As a result, the appointment of a president at the 1922 session, as in 1903, was not able to be resolved until just two days before the session concluded. It was impossible to get a clear consensus on any name prior to then. The sixty-four-year-old veteran was eventually appointed as General Conference secretary, instead of president, at that meeting, but he was deeply hurt in the process as he tried to defend his reputation. What stung him and his colleagues so sharply was not the fact that there were those who did not want him to continue. They had been expecting that. Rather, it was the political process used to prevent his reelection and the vicious attacks on his theology and against his character that brought his colleagues to his defense. Ellen White was not present in person at that landmark conference. She had died seven years earlier in 1915. Nevertheless, even in her absence, she was a dominating presence at the session.

In 1922, the primary charges raised by a group of vocal fundamentalist pastors alleged that Daniells not only personally disregarded Ellen White's counsel, but that he manifested a general attitude of criticism and disloyalty to the testimonies. These pastors came from a rapidly growing fundamentalist core group in the denomination. Furthermore, they argued, Daniells had been involved in a highly contentious Bible Conference held three years earlier in Washington, D.C. In his critics' eyes, this conference had been nothing but a "council of darkness." His alleged attitudes of doubt and disrespect toward Ellen White, they said, were in danger of spreading widely among the pastors and teachers of the denomination. What had gone wrong? This certainly did not appear to be the Daniells of 1903. Had he not been able to keep his resolution of confidence in the ministry of Ellen White he so gratefully made to W. C. White back in the midst of those dark days? Indeed he had.

The General Conference president, in fact, had not changed in his attitude toward Ellen White nor to the things she had written. A large part of the church, however, had developed a highly inadequate understanding of the nature of her gift and of the role that she played in the denomination. They had adopted an artificial and highly idealized, or romanticized, view of her and of the way she had gone about her work. Daniells knew, however, from first-hand experience through his extended personal relationship with her that her leadership in the church was a much more dynamic, interactive process between leadership and charisma than the static, one-way pipeline kind of process envisaged by his critics. As this study has noted, he had formed an effective working partnership with Ellen White during his early administrative years in Australia. That partnership developed and matured and grew when he moved on to the much wider stage of world leadership of the church in 1901. Surviving a coup d'état and being reelected as president of the General Conference in 1903 and seeing the church protected from morphing into an organization that would have been little more than a social welfare mission had a profound impact on Daniells. Such things had profoundly strengthened his confidence in the unique gift of charismatic leadership that Ellen White had been given to exercise in the community and in the valued partnership between it and the gift of authorized, institutional leadership exercised by presidents and other leaders. The years from 1903 until Ellen White's death in 1915 had enriched and strengthened that association.

Daniells also knew, however, the kind of minefield that her relationship to establishment leadership could be. The nature and the extent of her authority and the balancing of her gift with that of administration was not always easy to get right. Sometimes people were badly hurt by those who did not understand the nature of the balance or who thought that the relationship had slipped out of balance. Thus Daniells had pleaded with those attending the 1919 conference who felt uncomfortable with what they were learning about the way Ellen White worked and some of these complexities that had no easy answers, to take care with other people's reputations. "I know it is reported around that some of us men here at Washington, in charge of its general administrative work, are very shaky and unbelieving," he commented to the delegates. "But I want to tell you that I know better. I know that my associates have confidence right down on the solid platform of this whole question." His own experience with Ellen White's charisma had not answered all his questions, nor had it been without discomfort, but it had given him an unshakeable confidence. He was convinced that if the 1919 conference delegates "had gone at this thing and experienced what we have, you would have passed through an experience that would have given you solid ground." "Do not be careless," he urged, "in reporting or representing men's views. I have had this thing to deal with for years and years."[1] The criticism was distressing. But his confidence in the authenticity of Ellen White's gift was deeply rooted. It grew out of, and was shaped by, his experience.

Timed just right

One of the most conviction-shaping experiences of Daniells's entire ministry occurred at the very first October council meeting following his reelection in 1903. He had been planning for the council to give focused attention to the need to develop city evangelism programs and to the challenge of overseas mission. Ten colleagues of Kellogg's, however, including the doctor himself, surprised Daniells and appeared unexpectedly at the meeting in Washington, D.C. Such a large group was able to force onto the agenda an extended discussion of Kellogg's book *The Living Temple.* Dr. David Paulson, a member of the executive committee and supervisor of the medical missionary work in Chicago, had carefully studied the manuscript and attempted to show that it said nothing much more than what Ellen White herself had written elsewhere in various articles in recent years.[2] Daniells recalled that Paulson, supported by Magan and Sutherland and others, was extremely persuasive. The outmaneuvered president feared that the group had succeeded in convincing the council that it should endorse the book. "We knew not how it would turn out," he reported later, but deep down he had despondently concluded that the council would support Kellogg. The thought left him distressed beyond measure. But then, in what proved to be an astounding turn of events, two letters from Ellen White arrived at his office at what proved to be just exactly the right time. The following day, on the basis of these letters, the president was able to convince his colleagues that they should, in fact, not endorse the book and that it would be too dangerous to do so.

Daniells accepted this development not just as a remarkable coincidence but as a providential conjunction of events. Even though Ellen White had possessed a copy of *The Living Temple* for several months, she had not gotten around to looking at it until September 23. In recounting the sequence of events and comparing notes later, she mentioned that she had also recently read an account of a ship colliding with an iceberg somewhere on the high seas. The story, as these kinds of things were often inclined to do, troubled her with a series of sleepless nights. But then, finally, she had a dream in which the shipping disaster became a metaphor for what was happening in the church. That prompted her to get up and write urgently. Her editorial staff quickly found themselves engaged in a flurry of typing documents and rushing them to the mail. The letters, according to Daniells, arrived at just "exactly the right time" on the East Coast and helped turn the tide against Kellogg and his ideas. As Daniells related it later to her, "Your clear, clean-cut and beautiful message came and settled the controversy." It did this by giving "those who stood on the right side, strength to stand and hold their ground."[3]

Such experiences provided Daniells solid ground on which to stand. They did not, however, solve all the dilemmas he still found himself dealing with. Nor did every letter arrive just in time. His colleague, *Review* editor, W. W. Prescott, received two important letters from Ellen White in 1910—two years after they had been written—the contents of which, in the meantime, had been shared with others. Prescott felt that if the letters had been sent to him earlier, they would have been much more useful in accomplishing their purpose and he might have retained his job as editor.[4] Daniells still had to reconcile himself to the simple reality that the gift was exercised through Ellen White as a human being, with her own distinctive personality, intellectual ability, quirks of temperament, and life circumstances. The gift of prophecy could, in fact, function in no other way. It was simply the nature of the case. As would be expected, some aspects of temperament and personality became, perhaps, more noticeable during her sunset years, but such things did not invalidate her gift. Unavoidably, however, Daniells found himself more aware of these matters and more conscious of the need to find ways of relating to the perplexities and issues they might cause.

Although Ellen White took a decided stand against Kellogg's theological drift before the end of 1903, she still felt strongly that Daniells's team should make an effort to reconcile with the doctor. It was important to seek to avoid the threatening schism. How much she and W. C. White might be able to compromise in order to achieve this, Daniells wasn't sure, but it made him nervous. Willie White's willingness to approve the denominational circulation of Kellogg's book, for example, after the doctor agreed to remove a few pages of offending material, even after the Autumn Council decision not to endorse it, was just one step too far in Daniells's view. On the basis of Willie White's compromise, Kellogg could then claim that Ellen White now had no objections to the book. The General Conference view, on the other hand, was that inappropriate expressions still thoroughly riddled the book. Given all else that the Washington, D.C., people knew about Kellogg's strategy and his stubborn refusal to work with the General Conference except on his terms, the equivocation at Elmshaven conveyed a worrying sense of a lack of solidarity on the conflict. Daniells feared that it would undo all his efforts at achieving a working, committed coalition and that things would unravel quickly. The prospect made his associate, W. W. Prescott, quite angry. Both men felt betrayed. If W. C. White was going to support the circulation of *The Living Temple,* he was no more "excusable" than the doctor himself, the *Review* editor fumed. Prescott spoke for Daniells as well when he wrote, "You can perhaps imagine how we feel over this matter. I hardly need to put it in words." How could W. C. White be so naïve, was the insinuation. As a result, White found himself quickly called to Washington to be briefed on current developments and to help establish a common approach as the conflict with Kellogg became ever more hostile and political. Prescott reported with some relief after the briefings, "I feel quite certain that a view of the situation as it now is has been presented to his Mother."[5]

A major attempt at reconciliation of the feuding parties occurred at the May 1904 Lake Union Council meetings at Berrien Springs, Michigan. The meetings were held as an early summer camp meeting. Instead of achieving peace, however, charges and counter-charges, sharp personal attacks, miscommunication, and factional politicking exploded at the meetings, ensuring that the conflict escalated and that relationships became more hostile than ever.[6] The theological issue loomed larger, not smaller. Ellen White pronounced the camp meeting a failure.

A little later in the year, the legal transfer of a number of sanitarium properties to the conferences escalated the battle over property. Just how flexible Mrs. White would, and could, be apparently still unnerved Daniells even during this period. It is probably against this background that we must understand his observation to J. S. Washburn about her indecision. Washburn, an evangelist in Washington at the time, was later a leading activist in the fundamentalist attacks on Daniells. He recalled that Daniells had said, "We had all we could do to keep Sister White from going with Dr. Kellogg when the conflict was on."[7] The statement, even if authentic, would seem to be hyperbole. But it illustrates the kind of uncertainty and apprehension church leaders felt about what Ellen White might do or say or advise next. Daniells was still learning to live with this reality, and it doubtless contributed to no little discomfort on his part. In later years, W. C. White reported that some in the church entertained the view that "Sister White's movements, her testimonies, and her attitude" to Kellogg and his colleagues, were "largely" influenced by Daniells and Prescott. Although he denied the rumor, it is important to note that he was addressing a perception that such influencing of his mother may have happened "largely."[8] W. C. White responded by declaring that the two men were much more influenced by Ellen White than she was by them. On the basis of Prescott's comment above, it would seem, however, that to some degree at least, the president and the editor of the *Review* did help to shape Ellen White's movements and positioning vis–à-vis Kellogg. W. C. White rejected the idea that such influence "largely" explained her stance, and of course he was right. But we should not ignore the fact that there was a two-way flow of advice, counsel, and information. As is so often the case with many things, both perspectives are true and important and need to be retained to form a more complete picture of what happened. That is the nature of theological tension.

By late 1904, it seemed that both parties had almost exhausted themselves, creating a lull in the battle. Kellogg remained recalcitrant, however, and the denomination found it safer to deal with him only through its lawyers. With the task of getting the General Conference offices and the Review and Herald publishing program firmly relocated in Washington, D.C., as well as coping with the developing split with Kellogg, Daniells found himself stretched almost beyond his capacity. But he was determined to keep the church focused on mission and therefore planned to designate the 1905 General Conference session as a "World Missions" session meeting. He understood the importance of keeping the focus of the church away from internal problems and on outreach.

Focusing the church on mission and the big cities

The 1905 General Conference Session convened in May as a camp meeting on the grounds of the unfinished Foreign Missionary Seminary in Takoma Park, Maryland. It was an experiment. Administration had acquired a large tent for the session meetings and hoped that the weather would remain hospitable. For the main part the weather cooperated, something the delegates were grateful for. Many things were still in a state of transition. The Review and Herald publishing house still operated out of quarters in a building on North Capitol Street near the center of Washington, D.C., while the General Conference administration was temporarily located in a large house in Takoma Park, Maryland. As a last-minute initiative, with leadership realizing just how difficult the challenge of moving to Washington was proving to be, delegates from around the world brought with them financial contributions to help ease the strain and to get "the Washington Project" firmly established. The aim was to raise $100,000. Planning for new facilities was rapidly taking shape. During the session, Prescott submitted for approval the plans for the new publishing house to be erected on the Takoma Park site. He came under heavy pressure to take it on as a personal project, making sure that it would have a distinctive Christian culture. The session persuaded him to relinquish his position as General Conference vice president (which he held in addition to his duties as editor of the *Review*) in order to have time for the publishing house and still edit the *Review*. Daniells was struggling with the constant demands of his responsibilities, coping with establishing a new work environment, trying to ensure that church finances adequately matched the expansion program, and keeping a legal eye on the escalating property disputes in Battle Creek as well as in Mexico with the sanitarium there. Not only were there now hospitals at serious risk, there was the prospect that the church might lose the famous Battle Creek Tabernacle to the medical dissidents as well.

Daniells's re-election at the 1905 session seemed almost straightforward. Matters were in such a state of flux that continuity in leadership and the achievement of some stability had become an extremely high priority. The nominating committee presented his name to the delegates at the fourteenth meeting of the session on May 18, just a week after the session commenced. No objection came from the floor, not even any discussion, it seems. The major discomfort of delegates in regard to the elections related to whether it was right to bring back G. A. Irwin from Australia to serve as Daniells's vice president now that Prescott had been forced into taking on the reestablishment of the publishing enterprise. Would such a change damage things in Australia? Was it really being fair to that field? A lengthy explanation by the chair of the nominating committee eventually persuaded the delegates that given Daniells's great need for strong, experienced help in light of the continuing difficulties with Battle Creek, it was indeed the best thing to do. For Irwin, no doubt feeling a little awkward since being bypassed as church leader in 1901, it was the "most difficult" matter he had to decide in all his association with "this message." The suggestion had come as "a great surprise."[9]

Another surprise at the 1905 session was that Daniells did not insist on the hard-won organizing principle that in 1901 had enabled General Conference sessions eventually to break free from the parochial, reactionary procedures of the past. The 1901 session had removed the power of the incumbent administration to appoint the nominating committee and other standing committees that would work through the session's business. The conflict of interest inherent in this practice had always tended to favor maintaining the status quo. Instead, the delegates themselves, at their first meeting, would appoint their own nominating committee (the Committee on Counsel) to propose the names for the all-important session working committees. However, the 1905 General Conference Session reverted to the practice of having the outgoing executive committee submit names for the nominating committee and the other working committees.[10] It is true that the session delegates themselves suggested the procedure, but it seems that they adopted it primarily as a time-saving measure. No one protested that the measure represented the abandonment of an important reform principle designed to minimize conflicts of interest and make a session more genuinely representative. The political issues of 1901 and 1903 had now subsided considerably, and the danger of the medical forces taking over the church had been averted. And the use of the "Committee on Counsel" approach to appointing the session working committees had its own risks, a reality indicated in 1903 by the restrictions on the committee adopted by the session that "no member" of the Committee on Counsel could "nominate more than one candidate" to the nominating committee.[11] Probably, many also realized that the 1905 executive committee was a different creature from its predecessors. Instead of being a small group, it now consisted of twenty-nine representatives from around the globe, making it close to the size and nature envisioned for the "Committee on Counsel" anyway. The sheer logistical difficulty of working with larger numbers of delegates was probably also a factor that prompted the return to a more expedient approach on this occasion. As it turned out, incumbents inevitably played a larger role in the working committees, and inevitably the process also made it easier for Daniells to be re-elected.[12]

Ellen White attended and spoke at the meetings, but official records do not list her as a delegate. Whether the delegates consulted her about the election of the president is not indicated. It seems likely that her advice would have been sought on how Australia would best be served. After Irwin had been drawn back to Washington, the delegates sent Olsen to lead the denomination in Australia. The major issues confronting delegates at this session included establishing a medical department within the General Conference and seeking more adequate professional representation from the physicians in the work of the department at all levels of the church. Issues were still very complex, and the financial difficulties of the medical program in Battle Creek as well as the loss to the church of the sanitarium at Guadalajara, Mexico, were sore blows. If Daniells was tired before the session, he was near total exhaustion at its end. According to Prescott, on more than one occasion the General Conference president had become so weak that he would fall asleep during a committee and would have to withdraw while Prescott concluded the business listed on the agenda. The session had been held in the midst of the busy building program. An important reflection of confidence in Daniells's leadership, however, was embedded in an action taken earlier in the session. Delegates voted to extend the time period between General Conference sessions from two years to four years. They were happy for Daniells to continue in office until the time of the next session, now scheduled for 1909. But as Daniells was to find out, four years could be a long time.

Daniells struggled to make it through until 1909. Midway through his third term he was ready to quit. The pressures on him over the equitable allocation of scarce resources for the rapidly expanding mission of the church, tensions arising from denominational growth in the American South, and misunderstandings over the Madison School became almost unbearable. Particularly distressing was a letter he received from Ellen White that seemed to make impossible demands on him. He felt that the letter's veiled criticism of his integrity as a leader was unfair and simply made his work more difficult. The letter would have created complications for anyone in leadership because of its open support for independent work outside the organization and its idea that such projects should receive denominational appropriations. The incident is worth noting in some detail, because how Daniells responded to the pressure from Ellen White provides an interesting and helpful illustration of the robust interaction between the two individual leaders. It also reveals the inherent tension that arises between essentially competing sources of authority and how the tension was dealt with from an organizational perspective.

In October 1907, Ellen White wrote to him and his treasurer, I. H. Evans, with some explicit instruction that Daniells genuinely did not know how to carry out. The letter particularly troubled Daniells, because he realized that when it was circulated more widely, readers would think that he and his colleagues at the General Conference were being dishonest, or at least devious, in their manipulation of donated funds. Her letter quoted Calvin Bollman, who, at the time, was the secretary of the Southern Missionary Society which focused on projects for African Americans in the southern states. According to Mrs. White, Bollman had reported that "the work for the colored people" was "frequently deprived of means" and that it did not "receive all the donations intended for it." Had she taken Bollman's report to mean that the General Conference was diverting funds? Is that why she wrote to reprove Daniells and Evans? The letter was not exactly clear about who was actually at fault. But the rebuke was clear. "Not one penny of the means that comes in from different sources for the work in the Southern field should be diverted to the work elsewhere," she declared. It should not truthfully be able to be said, she urged, "that any portion of the means given was withheld from the field for which it was intended." Daniells and Evans should "be very careful" in how they handled the donations. "Not one dollar is to be turned aside to any other field. I entreat of you to be very careful." To an ordinary reader it would seem that the two men were the ones at fault.[13]

The second part of the troublesome letter went on to urge that the General Conference should financially support the Madison School in spite of the fact that it was an independent operation. She went on to explain that she had actively encouraged the Madison administration to remain separate from conference organization. Daniells bristled at this section, hardly believing what he was reading about Sutherland and Magan and their school in Tennessee. He read the section repeatedly and carefully, for Madison was a huge organizational conundrum to him. He acknowledged that he was "more perplexed and troubled over this matter [the Madison school] than any other one problem in this cause." To administration it constituted a huge organizational and management dilemma.[14] But Ellen White was clearly not on the side of leadership on this one. Independence, in this case, was a virtue, she argued, although she also thought that the "matter need not be blazed abroad." The implication was that too many independent entities would clearly not be a good thing. She believed that "a great mistake has been made in the exercise of human authority in God's work." It wielded too much control. Church members ought to feel free to move independently in establishing work wherever it was needed. The field was wide, and church members should "follow the directions of the Holy Spirit, and go [to any field of service to which they might feel called] whether the conference will pay your expenses or not." Furthermore, Mrs. White, challenged, while foreign missions were important, "there is missionary work to be done in this country, as verily as in any heathen land." In her Australian days, she had argued for more money to be spent overseas. Did she now mean that things had gone too far in that direction? She urged that the denomination should not neglect the United States. Was this a classic case of the swinging pendulum? Getting the balance right was not easy.

As he read the letter, Daniells could see it playing directly into the hands of "the opposing, disorganizing elements among us," and he felt his job getting harder by the day. It was the kind of letter that clearly challenged the status quo. Daniells read it as giving license to all those whose policy was to be against the church government whoever that government might be. Such a letter made the task of a conference administrator much more complicated than it already was.

First of all, Daniells was offended at the slight to his integrity implied in the first section of the letter. But several other difficulties with the document merited an urgent reply as well. He dictated one the very next day, evidently after consulting with Evans.

The president was respectful, but very forthright and firmly assertive in his carefully worded response. At the outset he re-affirmed his commitment to accepting and learning from her counsel, but he qualified this commitment by clearly indicating that he could not do the impossible. "It is my purpose always to heed the counsel that comes through the spirit of prophecy as far as I can understand that counsel, and know how to carry it out." Then he affirmed strongly his acceptance of the counsel about not diverting funds from the South "in its fullest and broadest meaning." This was a principle he heartily endorsed. Almost in the same breath, however, he strongly defended his integrity. Stating that, in fact, he applied this principle "to all other fields as well," he avowed strongly that it had been his fixed purpose, ever since he had come into office, "to never divert one dollar from the field . . . for which it was intended by the donor." If such a thing had ever happened, it had been a mistake by a careless bookkeeper. A very few cases had come to his attention during the past seven years, he reported, and he had them corrected as soon as detected.[15]

Daniells could hardly believe that Bollman would report such a serious charge to Ellen White, for he "knows that we have cheerfully cooperated with him in correcting any mistakes that have been detected." If Bollman knew of a "single instance" of "any kind of manipulation" why did he not come "straight to us with it?" Daniells questioned. The annoyance and indignation in his reply is unmistakable. Then he quoted Bollman directly back to Ellen White. He had just a few days previously received an effusive letter from the Southern Missionary Society secretary stating that not only he, but all the leadership in the South, felt "that the brethren in Washington have treated this field not only justly but generously." If there was any "dissatisfaction" in the South "toward the General Conference" Bollman did not "know where it exists." Daniells could not understand the inconsistency. Was Bollman being two-faced? Was he referring to church officials other than those at the General Conference who were diverting funds? If so, why would Ellen White write to himself [Daniells] and Evans?

The General Conference president was particularly chagrined, he explained to Ellen White, "because what you have written to Elder Evans and me will now be taken by some parties and used all over the country to convince the people that it is not safe to send money through the General Conference because we divert it." He knew that he would now have to "meet this everywhere I go." Was he implying that she had overstepped the mark? He had read the letter carefully and wanted her to know just how he would need to interpret it in his public responses. From his understanding of the situation, he said, he would have to take the position, "first, that your message does not say that Brother Bollman charged the General Conference with having done this; second, that your message does not say that the General Conference has done this; third, that the General Conference has not knowingly done this; and fourth, that we accept this message as a re-statement of what has many times been made to our men entrusted with the funds of our people." In an oblique appeal to her for more care in her writing, Daniells explained that he was "in a very trying place" just at that time, and "if ever we needed to be careful of what we say and do, it is at this time." Again he asserted that he did "not object to reproof," but he wanted "to be clear as to just what was meant." And from his certain knowledge, the General Conference clearly was not in the wrong on this matter. He then asked Ellen White, "If I am wrong in this [his interpretation that her letter was not pointing the finger at the General Conference] will you kindly correct me?" In a clear defense of his colleagues, he pointed out that the General Conference's books and correspondence belonged to the denomination and were at the disposal of the members of the General Conference committee for any investigation. What he was suggesting was that Bollman could check if he had a particular problem. The General Conference did not manipulate funding.

The president's response to the second part of Ellen White's letter about funding for the Madison school illustrates the sharp conflict he experienced in trying to meet two competing expectations. As the leader of an organization, he had to be responsible for the careful stewardship of funds, which inevitably meant accountability. Also, he had to ensure their equitable distribution to meet the many competing demands. He explained that he had earlier sent some money to Madison following a visit to its campus by his education secretary, Professor Frederick Griggs. Daniells had asked Griggs to check out the situation. It was a classic organizational difficulty. The General Conference president and Griggs had no way of knowing the real plans and needs of the Madison school. Furthermore, none of the men who had visited the campus in a show of denominational support (he cited W. C. White, G. I. Butler, and G. A. Irwin) "has ever [been] given any definite information regarding their plans for investment, nor their true financial situation." The school had its own board of directors and private account books. Without any financial reports, how could the General Conference have confidence that the money it might provide was actually needed? The school was "soliciting and receiving contributions from our people in all parts of the States, but no one but themselves [Madison school officials] knows how much is received or how it is spent." As a result, Daniells explained to Ellen White that realistically "we have no basis on which to make appropriations."

Again, Daniells quoted Magan back to her in his defense. In a letter to the General Conference president acknowledging the first donation sent to the school, Magan stated that independent institutions designed to train "self-supporting missionaries" would of necessity "pass through some pretty hard times," and Madison was no exception. They were, however, "not in need of 'the necessities of existence.' " In sympathy for Daniells's position, Magan stated that he felt that the General Conference committee already had "everything that it legitimately ought to be asked to carry." The tone of Daniells's reply to Ellen White at this point clearly expressed his frustration. "Now Sister White," he wrote in a teacherly voice, "I want to do all that I should in this matter, but so far no one seems able to outline anything definite regarding what is required."

Becoming even more specific, Daniells asked her what he should let go of in order to help Madison. The General Conference had "tremendous demands from all parts of the world," and with "our slender resources we must move understandingly in their distribution." Consider Elder Anderson and his family, for example, in the heart of Africa, because he had "a profound conviction that God had called him there," and they were living in a thatched mud brick hut with only a dirt floor. The rain washed parts of the walls away every so often, and "he or his family will die with malaria from exposure." They needed a brick house with a board floor. The General Conference had no funds for him, but they borrowed some so that he could have a suitable house. Daniells enclosed a photograph of the mud-brick house in his letter to illustrate his point.

Then there was the J. N. Anderson family in Canton, China. A fish market that opened at 4:00 A.M. every morning surrounded their house. The fish from the river were "slaughtered, washed, etc, all around their doors and windows," and by the time the sun was out the air was "reeking with the unsavory smell." The Lord had been blessing the missionaries' work wonderfully, Daniells reported, but it was too expensive for the family to rent a home elsewhere. To build one for them in a better, more healthful place was going to cost several thousand dollars. Prescott had returned from staying with this family in the midst of the fish market and had strenuously argued that they needed help urgently, for their health's sake. Should Daniells now not send money to China in order to send it to Madison? There were many other similar problems.

The conflicting demands exasperated him. Again adopting an almost lecturing tone, he expressed his frustration. "Now Sister White, these things almost distract me." He felt sometimes as if he just had to stop his ears "and run into the woods away from everything." That very day, he stated, "our treasury is ten thousand dollars overdrawn." The demands seemed impossible. "I know not what to do. I do not know what we ought to do in response to what you have written about helping the Madison school." Were there really hardships at Madison? "None of us in this country, not even Brethren Sutherland and Magan, have tasted hardships yet compared with some of these silent yet hardworking and successful men in foreign lands," he concluded. Should he stop sending out missionaries? Should he "call in a part of our force already there?" But then the membership gain in North America was less than 2 percent during the previous year, while mission field gain was 14 percent, and that was with a budget only a quarter the size of what had been spent in the United States.[16] Giving money to Madison was not a simple matter, and it all seemed just too difficult for Daniells who, "greatly perplexed" and "well nigh disheartened," was ready to throw in the towel. His exasperation is palpable.

"I have about made up my mind that it is time for me to clear out," he wrote to Ellen White. It was time for new blood—time for someone else to "take this place who will be able to get more means and plan better." The president was in good health and perfectly willing to go overseas himself. He had not fallen into unbelief. His "confidence in the cause" was good and he longed "to see it consummated." But he had tried to do his best, and it was clearly "too great for me." Daniells would ask his fellow administrators "to let me off to other lands." In the meantime, he was expecting to visit Elmshaven in the near future and sincerely hoped that he and Mrs. White would have time to talk matters over. Above all, he wanted to "get more light as to just what to do."[17] His letter is a remarkably frank dialogue between the two sources of influence and authority in the church. It does not show a compliant, unthinking administrator uncritically accepting a message from the bearer of the charismatic authority in the church. Instead, we find real spiritual wrestling involved in implementing the counsel received. And as it turned out, Daniells's fellow leaders did not see fit to release him for other lands. When it came time for the next session, they believed that he was still needed in the presidency.

Turmoil and controversy

Daniells third re-election experience in 1909 may not have been as stressful as his struggle to survive in 1903, but it was still not what one could call comfortable. Turmoil and conflict again intruded themselves into a General Conference session. Four years further along in its development, theological controversy again cluttered the church's agenda and set delegates against one another. This time it was not teachers in the colleges or editors from distant publishing houses or doctors in hospitals who were pushing the boundaries and disturbing the status quo as had been the case in 1888 or 1903. Instead, the advocates of the new ideas resided right at headquarters in Washington, D.C. This particular controversy worried Ellen White, because she didn't understand the details of the arguments involved nor did she grasp the theological significance of the new position being taken. That was probably to be expected. She was now edging past eighty-two years of age. What troubled her, though, about the new debate stirring the church was that it upset her aging pioneer colleagues. The gray-beard preachers thought that the new ideas not only risked undermining the authority of her prophetic gift, but that they actually did so. Such elder statesmen as Stephen N. Haskell, J. N. Loughborough, and G. B. Starr became so agitated and threatened by the new ideas that they lobbied Ellen White and her son, W. C. White, for several months before the 1909 session to have Daniells and his colleagues removed from office.

The argument that bothered the elderly leaders so much concerned the correct way to interpret the Hebrew word *tamid,* translated as "the daily" in Daniel 8:11–13. Hence, the whole dispute became known as "the daily." Haskell, following Uriah Smith, William Miller, and others, thought the term must refer to Roman paganism, which had been supposedly "taken away" when England converted to Christianity in A.D. 508. For Haskell and his friends, therefore, the issue involved what they took to be an important prophetic date. Furthermore, and more important to the situation, Haskell understood Ellen White as having clearly endorsed this particular interpretation in her book *Early Writings.*[18] The editor of the *Review,* W. W. Prescott, on the other hand, interpreted the expression in Daniel to refer to the high priestly ministry of Jesus that Roman

Catholicism had obscured from view or "taken away" by its teaching on the meaning of the eucharist and its perspective on salvation, one which Protestants regarded as being salvation by works. The expression, after all, was used of the daily sacrifice in the Mosaic tabernacle, Prescott argued, and the context of the passage clearly pointed to the significance and meaning of the sacrificial ministry and priestly mediation of Jesus. This was a much more Christocentric interpretation, and it arose from further study stimulated by the theological paradigm shift that had occurred in the church following 1888. Neither Daniells nor Prescott understood the *Early Writings* reference to be the determining voice in establishing the meaning of the scriptural expression. They saw Ellen White's comments as relating to a much broader and more significant issue—the problem of time setting. Her statement, therefore, was not a problem for them.

The occasion causing the debate to break out into the open, as happens so often with theological controversy, was linked to the need for the church to make clearer statements about its beliefs. It was an issue of apologetics. What was the best way to reply to current misunderstandings of the church's teachings and to set out clearly to the public what the church was really trying to say? In October 1907, two former Adventist editors published what many perceived to be a damaging critique of Adventism's interpretation of Daniel 8. Church leaders had asked Prescott, as the denomination's resident theologian, to prepare a reply. The professor felt that he could effectively do so, however, only by referring to the new understanding of *tamid.* In fact, Prescott had become convinced of the helpfulness and the validity of the new interpretation for several years, as had numerous others, but they had not made the matter public for fear of overloading the church's agenda and its ability to cope with change. Furthermore, the new interpretation had also appeared in Louis Conradi's German-language book on the prophecies of Daniel and Revelation and had been there for some time. A General Conference committee had even approved the book for distribution in the United States in either German or Scandinavian-language translations.[19] But the aging pioneer leaders in California did not read German, and what European Adventists were learning or what Scandinavian Adventists in America might read did not seem to bother them as much as what American Adventists might be taught in English. At any rate, they certainly did not make Conradi their target. Rather, they perceived Prescott and Daniells as much more of a threat.

After having waited more than five years to discuss the idea publicly in the church, Prescott gained permission from the General Conference executive committee to introduce it through a series of Bible study articles on the book of Daniel. The professor planned to begin the series in the *Review* in March of 1908 for the English-speaking church, and to deal with the idea of "the daily" in an unobtrusive, non-confrontational way. In the interim, representatives from each side of what now had become an overblown and threatening conflict met together at Elmshaven to discuss the matter with W. C. White and his staff and with Ellen White. Unfortunately, the discussions did not persuade the older men, at least, to consider the new view as a legitimate alternative. Nor did the meetings succeed in taking the heat out of the dispute. Shortly afterward, Haskell launched a sharp personal attack on both Daniells and Prescott, accusing them of disloyalty to Ellen White and the gift of prophecy. He misrepresented their position and committed himself valiantly to the defense of Mrs. White and her teachings against the perceived apostasy of the General Conference. Haskell's stance embarrassed W. C. White, who was not quite sure how to handle the older man. His mother was not in robust health at the time, and he knew this kind of problem stressed her greatly. But he clearly recognized that the aging pioneers were the unreasonable aggressors in the conflict and that in their personal attacks and character assassination they were not doing the right thing. Besmirching the reputations of their opponents was entirely inappropriate, and White pleaded with them for a better approach. But he seemed powerless to stop them, as was Daniells.

Reflecting on the controversy three years after it broke into the open, W. C. White felt that the church might have been better able to handle such conflicts if the denomination's college teachers could have better training so that they could "be considered the highest authorities" in deciding such things. This would, he suggested, open the way "to transfer the important responsibilities of trying out doctrinal controversies from the group of editors and book-writers in our publishing houses to Bible teachers in our schools." Perhaps "a select group" of Bible teachers, evangelists, and editors would be even better, he concluded.[20] But the church was a long way yet from developing such expertise. Experience would also teach it that even with better educated Bible teachers, the process would not be free of trauma and pain for those involved. In the meantime and in the absence of such expertise, the assertions and threats of the older men seemed to alarm and confuse Ellen White, whose friendship with, and confidence in, her older colleagues was longstanding. On the other hand, she also valued and trusted the younger leaders. It was not an easy conflict to resolve. Furthermore, if one does not really understand the issues, but knows that old trusted friends feel very strongly indeed about them, in which way might one be inclined to lean? Ellen White was in a dilemma. But so was Daniells. And so was the church.[21]

Ellen White's greatest fear about the whole "daily" debate was that it would distract the church from focusing on the more important task of mission. And she was right. But who was doing the agitating? Not the leaders in Washington, D.C. The "cause" would be in trouble, S. N. Haskell warned Ellen White, unless changes were made at the top.[22] Thus when Haskell and his colleagues began to agitate for the replacement of both Daniells and Prescott, she knew that things were somehow getting out of balance.

As Ellen White made her way across the continent to attend the 1909 General Conference session in Washington, she had other concerns that weighed on her mind as well. They also involved her son, W. C. White. Worrying tensions had developed between Elmshaven and the General Conference office. It seemed to the General Conference administration that the Californians were moving too rashly in developing many new health institutions. Denominational leaders in Washington, D.C., feared that the Whites were nurturing and encouraging projects out west without adequate financial resources and that, once again, the church was accumulating a large debt. General Conference officials were extremely worried. W. C. White's expansive publishing plans also disturbed them. For their part, the Californians were feeling increasingly uncomfortable with what they perceived as Washington trying to have too much control and insisting that everything go through the "regular channels." A year before the conference, W. C. White had shared with Daniells his mother's vague worries about the influence on the president of his associates, especially I. H. Evans, E. R. Palmer, and Prescott. Willie had written confidentially to Daniells that he should be careful of the weaknesses of the men who had been appointed to help him. Daniells felt trapped. Everyone that he knew had weaknesses, yet every leader had to rely on others. His reply to W. C. White was a carefully crafted, statesmanlike, diplomatic, but loyal defense of his colleagues. He appreciated the unique strengths of his colleagues, he said, and he was aware of their weaknesses. Furthermore, he reflected on the fact that a great many other leaders in the church thought that W. C. White himself had more influence over Daniells than was right and good for the church, and that Willie himself had weaknesses, as did Daniells, of course. Yes, the president would be more aware of weaknesses and seek ways among the leadership team in which its members could compensate for each other. But he was also glad for the unique giftedness of the people who worked with him.[23] It was only later in the year that Daniells realized that Haskell's agitation in the West and in the South was having more impact than he realized.

Almost 350 delegates convened in Washington, D.C., for the three-week long 1909 General Conference Session held later in the season than usual. The meetings took place in late spring in order to avoid the cold, untidy weather of March and April. Again, delegates assembled in a large canvas pavilion pitched on the headquarters property. Numbers swelled to 1,300 for Sabbath meetings, and the session was notable for the rapidly increasing size of delegations from the foreign missions. A sense of optimism and joyfulness emerged as report after report described exciting growth and the challenge of expanding horizons. Nevertheless, although the Kellogg conflict had died away two years earlier, both Daniells and Ellen White were disturbed by the strength of the new tensions roiling the church over the issue of the "daily." Some delegates brought their agitation with them as they made their way to the meetings at Takoma Park. The level of the personal attacks and the animosity that manifested themselves because of the unauthorized circulation of a pamphlet by O. A. Johnson at the session particularly distressed Daniells. The pamphlet accused the General Conference leaders of undermining the prophetic role of Ellen White in the church. S. N. Haskell, in his evening talk midway through the session, spoke on the importance of retaining confidence in the gift of prophecy. While he addressed the general congregation, it was clearly a particular president and a particular editor that were the target of his remarks.

Whether the nominating committee consulted with Ellen White on the names considered for president at this session is, again, not known. In all likelihood, given the fact that she had come across the continent for the conference and had been presenting a series of midmorning addresses, they probably did seek her counsel. Because Daniells had already served eight years, the nominating committee would also be aware that perhaps a change would be in order and might not be unexpected. O. A. Olsen, once more the chair of the nominating committee, reported that, indeed, his committee had approached the nomination of a president with particular care. "I have been a member of committees at different times, on various subjects," reported the respected Norwegian in introducing his report, but "I think that I never was a member of a committee that went so carefully into its work as the present Committee on Nominations. We have not," he emphasized, "taken things for granted." Instead, he explained, "we have carefully scrutinized and investigated and looked over every name that we report." It seems that he was aware of the low rumbling of discontent among the older delegates.

In an unusual move, reflecting the unusual circumstances, Daniells took the opportunity to make a speech after the reading of his name and before the delegates voted. It was, he said, the first time he had ever done this. While he was not even sure if it was appropriate to do so, he somehow felt that he needed to say something and talk frankly about how he felt concerning the matter. "I have given this matter a great deal of serious thought, not only since the Conference has been in session, but for many weeks and months before we came here," he reflected. Recalling the political turmoil and troubles six years previously, he commented, "At the Oakland General Conference, in 1903, I felt quite free as to being reelected, because I felt that the work we had started out to do in 1901 had not been completed. We had not carried the work of reorganization through as was necessary." At that time he was convinced that "two years was not enough time to inaugurate such great changes." But even more to the point, he declared, "a fearful controversy had arisen in our midst. We were then in the very heart of a great crisis, and there was a determination to get rid of men who, it was thought, were responsible for the trouble that was on hand; and somehow I did not feel very much like being gotten rid of in that way, and for that purpose." Thus he had "said nothing" at the time, but had "felt somewhat relieved to continue." Having been given another two years, he confided, he had then quite "fully expected" that it would enable him to "complete that work" and then he would go on to some other field.

He stated that during the previous session in 1905 when the committee talked to him about continuing his leadership role, he again did not raise any great objection. He "did not know but what it was duty, and so said nothing when the report was brought in and action taken." But he was certain that "four years more would terminate my position in this part of the work." Following the session, therefore, he "took hold" with all his might to do all he could "to carry on the work of reorganization and to distribute responsibilities, to decentralize as far as possible, and separate this work out over many shoulders, so that I would have done the best I could in the matter."

Now, four years later in 1909, having again been asked to continue, he reported that he felt quite "perplexed" about the matter and had consented "quite reluctantly" to accept the office once more. He knew the danger of making mistakes or of serious failure and did not want to "mar" his record or his influence. And he felt embarrassed to even talk about it to the delegates. However, he had "been helped very much" by his associates. Their "hearty support, and their readiness to share all the burdens, have been so great that I have been relieved and helped in every possible way." In what appears to be an allusion to the lobbying against him by Haskell and others, he stated that for a full eight years there had been an atmosphere "of harmony and brotherly love in our General Conference Committee. We have had peace and harmony and confidence, we have had more than respect for one another." In all the eight years he could not recall "one serious disagreement" among them and yet "all [had] been free to express our convictions and assert our individuality as much as we should." Should the delegates be inclined to support the nomination, he was absolutely sure that this would be his last term "as far as any of us can reason."[24] Future sessions would demonstrate that in this regard, at least, Daniells was not a prophet.

The 1909 session delegates voted to return him to office for a fourth term. How many voted against him or simply abstained is not recorded. It seems there would certainly have been some. Some simply could not excuse or overlook the issue of the "daily" and Daniells's support of it. O. A. Johnson's pamphlet marred the conference. Two evening meetings had to be added to the schedule at short notice to discuss the disputed interpretation and to try to clear the air of the attacks on the two leaders. The exercise in openness, however, backfired. It simply gave a wider platform for the supporters of what they called "the old view" to intensify their ad hominem attacks on Daniells and Prescott. The tensions clearly needed defusing. But rather than suggesting that Daniells be removed, Ellen White, three days before the session ended, told Prescott that he should leave the *Review*. A week after the conference ended, she met with the General Conference executive committee and presented her solution directly in person. Daniells needed to be able to focus the church's attention on city evangelism. The church should release Prescott from the editorship of the *Review* to conduct evangelism in the megacities of the Eastern Seaboard.

She later acknowledged that it was not easy for administrators to accept her recommendation. Many on the committee perceived the measure to be an injustice to Prescott in view of the fact that he had given his all to getting the publishing program reestablished in Washington, D.C., and that he had been very circumspect and pastoral in discussing the disputed issue. It had been the defenders of the old view that had been the aggressors and had created the negative atmosphere. Some on the committee did not "take willingly to the idea of losing Elder Prescott," Ellen White reported to her son sometime later, and she had been obliged to speak "plainly" to them.[25] A range of motivations lay behind the recommendation to jettison Prescott, among them the need to help Daniells continue in office. It seems that removing Prescott had become a necessary compromise. But Prescott was deeply hurt. The alleged loss of her confidence in the professor, a rumor the older men spread among themselves and their friends, cut deeply and shattered the professor's wife.[26]

The realignment of duties did not, however, lessen the critics' attacks on either Daniells or Prescott. Less than twelve months after his 1909 re-election, the General Conference president found himself in serious trouble with Ellen White. A series of pointed letters criticized him heavily for not doing enough to nurture urban evangelism. One of the reasons for moving the General Conference to Washington, D.C., she pointed out, was to be able to foster such projects more effectively. Why was it not happening? She became more and more insistent as 1910 wore on. What troubled her was that she was hearing many reports about discussion of "the daily" at various union conference meetings, but nothing about evangelism. Then, in addition to all this, rumors had found their way to her suggesting that Daniells and Prescott wanted to revise her books.

It was true that work was under way during this period to improve some things in *The Great Controversy*. And some other denominational books such as Smith's *Thoughts on Daniel and Revelation* and the popular *Bible Readings for the Home Circle* were being updated. But it was W. C. White himself who had initiated *The Great Controversy* revisions, and while Prescott contributed a list of potential changes (at W. C. White's invitation and insistence), W. A. Spicer and others, such as W. A. Colcord, had also made suggestions. The matter was so sensitive, however, that W. C. White could not fully brief his mother—nor Haskell, for that matter—on all the matters that the reviewers had raised. The knowledge would have distressed her—and Haskell even more. It was not until the process was almost complete that information about the project could be shared more widely with the church. All this was most unsettling for Elmshaven, and what news did reach Ellen White further exacerbated her failing health.

Daniells was genuinely unsure what else he could do regarding the problem of big-city evangelism. He had already taken a number of significant measures to make it happen, including providing large additional budgets and resources, training churches, transferring and assigning gifted preachers specifically to the task, and convening a conference to encourage and equip others for this work. Unfortunately for Daniells, for a variety of good, valid reasons, Prescott had not been able to pick up the prominent role in city evangelism that Ellen White had envisaged for him. Ill health, the tragic loss of his wife to cancer in mid-1910, and eventually an extended nervous breakdown had put the professor out of action for more than twelve months.[27]

By early 1910, Mrs. White had become seriously disturbed at what she thought was a lack of progress in urban evangelism, and she wrote Daniells further letters of strong rebuke. Daniells had respectfully replied through W. C. White that he was doing all that he could, and he appealed to Willie himself to help him find additional personnel to assign to the task. Otherwise, he wrote, "we shall not be able to do but little more than we are doing now." A celebrated incident in early 1910 aggravated the situation. When Daniells was in California and traveled to Elmshaven seeking an interview with Ellen White to explain what measures he was taking to carry out her counsels (which he thought would encourage and delight her), she pointedly refused to see him. His response to the challenge, she thought, was simply insufficient. In a yet stronger rebuke about what she thought was a lack of urgency and progress, she wrote again, suggesting that the president needed to be re-converted.[28] Neither he nor Prescott, she said, were at that point "prepared to direct the work of the General Conference" any longer. The letters were so strong that Daniells understood that in her own way she was ordering him to resign as General Conference president.

Daniells turned to W. C. White and her literary assistant, C. C. Crisler, for advice on how he should respond. Did they know what she really meant and what he might do about it? The two men, also puzzled by the urgency and stridency of her letters, sought to converse further with Ellen White to see if they could ascertain what she might actually have in mind about what should be done.[29] They then wrote to Daniells, suggesting that perhaps he could help focus the denomination's attention on city evangelism more effectively by personally conducting some city meetings. "What is the president of the General Conference for, if he is not to lead?" Ellen White had responded to their questions, and she had alluded to how her husband "used to lead personally." If after conducting evangelistic meetings, Daniells would write to tell her what he was doing and arrange for others also to write to her what he had done and what was happening, then perhaps the cloud might lift.

At a midyear consultation with his colleagues at the General Conference, Daniells felt that it was his duty to report on the receipt of the letters, and he shared them with his colleagues. By doing so, he was giving them opportunity to terminate his presidency if they felt that circumstances warranted it. He was happy to take an assignment elsewhere if that was what Mrs. White meant. Daniells's colleagues were also puzzled by the letters, but resolved that city work should have first attention and took action releasing Daniells from his administrative duties for a full year in order to do urban evangelism. A month later, on August 5, Daniells reported to W. C. White what he was doing. In this confidential letter, that Daniells asked his wife (not his secretary) to type for him, he stated that he felt he was not ignoring Ellen White's counsel. "I am doing the very best I know how to follow the instruction in the Testimonies. . . . That is all I can say." He asked W. C. White to share the letter with his mother. Then he noted that there was a "world of work to be done in other lands that is very inviting to me." Clearly intending to step aside, but to do so with as much dignity as it might be possible to retain, he wrote: "All I ask is that I may be allowed to quietly arrange the changes that will be necessary when it is time for me to go." The note of bewilderment tinged with disappointment and humiliation is unmistakable.[30]

Daniells was aware that Ellen White's health was even more precarious and fragile than it usually was. In addition, he realized that she had become hypersensitive to stress and that periods of discouragement clouded some of her days. Her son had to be very diplomatic and responsive to her diminishing capacity to comprehend and cope with the various problems he might bring to her. Often Willie had to "pigeonhole" matters until a more suitable time. But Daniells also knew that her insights and her counsel still carried spiritual authority, and they needed to be understood and valued and used in shaping the work of the church.

W. C. White processed Daniells's August 5 letter promptly. He shared it with his mother and then replied to Daniells the same day. As Willie related it, his mother had dreamed at night that she had seen herself talking to Daniells and telling him "that it was not best for you now to resign your place as president of the Conference." Rather, he was to use all his "tact and experience and all the influence that your position gives you in helping, strengthening, and building up the evangelistic work." She believed that he was taking "just the right course" and that in involving himself "personally" in "the evangelistic work" there would be blessing. It was a stepping back from the brink. W. C. White seems to have been indicating that his mother was not to be understood as forcing Daniells's resignation.[31]

Following his evangelistic series in New York, Daniells wrote to W. C. White to tell him about it with the request that he share the letter with his mother. The Atlantic Union Conference president also enthusiastically shared with Ellen White the results of the new approach. The experience of personally conducting a campaign opened Daniells's eyes to the fact that the denomination was generally not well prepared to undertake city projects. Four years later, Ellen White commented in a communication to the delegates at the 1913 General Conference Session that Daniells's problem had been an inability to understand how to prosecute a task rather than a crisis of a failed relationship with God. Daniells's strategy also worked for Ellen White. The "burden" lifted off her not long after his New York campaign. He continued to serve out the remainder of his four-year term. Prescott, on the other hand, was obliged to retire for a time to his home state of Maine to recover his health after the deep trauma of his double-barreled loss of his job and his wife. In time, the issue of the "daily" itself began to fade from view.

A fifth term and organizational refinements

Ellen White did not attend the 1913 General Conference Session, although up until just a few weeks before the event she had hoped that she might. But it was not to be. She had become so frail that it would have been difficult for her to participate in any meaningful way. Furthermore, she felt that she should focus what little strength she retained on her book production. By this time, she had given up letter writing, being able only to complete, according to her son, two or three short notes each month. She attempted to write letters to longtime friends such as the Haskells but frequently did not succeed in completing them.[32]

As the 1913 session opened, W. C. White conveyed greetings from his mother. "Her last words to me with reference to the Conference," he reported to the delegates, were "tell the brethren to be of good cheer. Tell them to have faith in God and to expect great things, to undertake great things, and in his strength to go forward." It was important, however, for her to stay at home and reserve her strength, she had said, so that she could continue "to help in the work of bringing my writings into book form." She was now eighty-five years old and feeling the infirmities of her age, though "not suffering with sickness." Actually, she was "comfortably well," still enjoyed reading the *Review,* and her courage was good. In spite of the reassurances from W. C. White, however, a quiet sense of foreboding spread among the delegates. The fact that she was not strong enough to attend was significant in itself. W. C. White's report hinted that she did not expect to live long.[33]

Daniells and his colleagues found themselves managing a major enterprise as they prepared for the forty-third General Conference session scheduled to start on May 15, 1913, at Takoma Park on the grounds of the Foreign Missionary Seminary (now Washington Adventist University). Although it expected only an additional forty-four delegates above the previous session total four years earlier, the total number present at the meetings had more than doubled. The officers found themselves almost swamped by the size of the undertaking. It was no small affair. Many more planned to attend than just the 376 delegates entitled to vote, and the event was scheduled like a large camp meeting.

The 612 family tents pitched on the grounds accommodated about 2,100 campers. Those in charge had purchased three hundred new tents (in addition to all that they could borrow from the nearby conferences) as well as huge amounts of lumber to timber the floors. Fortunately, the lumber was cheap, having been used just two months before at the presidential inauguration ceremony for Woodrow Wilson. Another four hundred campers found accommodation in the dormitories and in off-campus rented locations. On Sabbaths, the crowd swelled to at least 3,100, more than filling the brand-new canvas pavilion shipped across the continent from the California Conference especially for the occasion. The large number of foreign missionaries attending, many of them bringing their families with them on furlough, gave the session a festive atmosphere.[34]

It was the extensive growth of the church overseas that provided the largest issues to be decided at the session. Again, for most of the three-and-a-half weeks that the session lasted, reorganization problems occupied the delegates' attention. This time, they needed to think through the creation of the new "Division" structure. Developing such entities in the rapidly expanding Asiatic region and in Europe was not so much a problem, but establishing one for North America, when the General Conference was already located there, was not easy. Untangling the finances and dividing up responsibility for the various departments, some local, some international, was complicated. Would the new division conferences function completely like unions, with their authority ascending from the constituencies whose delegates appointed their presidents and staff? Would not this approach risk the essential unity of the church? And what if division conference presidents were to serve as vice presidents of the General Conference as had been suggested? Would this need another voting action by the general body itself for them to be able to act in that capacity? Daniells had been uncertain about the wisdom of the division conference idea from the start, thinking that it would potentially lead to fragmentation of the church. But by the time of the session he had become persuaded that it might be workable. Creating the new constitutional documents certainly involved detailed analysis and clear thinking. As the three new division constituencies and their committees established themselves and began their meetings, even while the General Conference session was proceeding, it required high levels of parliamentary skill to keep matters where they belonged and the lines straight. But Daniells and his associates, particularly vice president L. R. Conradi and treasurer W. T. Knox, had grown with the church, and they oversaw the cumbersome, but delicate, process masterfully. Debating the changes occupied many days, and understanding the intricacies involved would have been quite beyond the aging Ellen White. The session had to write new constitutions and significantly modify the existing General Conference one. But if reorganization again occupied center stage at this session, it did not carry nearly the same level of angst as the sessions of 1901 and 1903. Even though it had not been planned to form a North American Division at this session—and Daniells advised against it—the North American union presidents were insistent. The General Conference president was not able to hold them back. Delegates, therefore, had to do much of the thinking about it "on their feet," as it were, but the debates were not quarrelsome. Significant disagreement did arise about how many delegates to allow—one per five hundred church members or one per two thousand or something in between. Ensuring adequate representation was a major issue, but the debate on it was not fractious. For those apprehensive about the wisdom of the North American initiative and the number of delegates, there was a willingness to experiment. Daniells urged the doubters at least to give the new approach a trial.[35] They could undo it if it did not work.

Undo it they did at the very next session in 1918. Mature reflection on the constitutional connections between division conferences and the General Conference and the events of World War I brought the conviction that the 1913 arrangement was too great a risk to church unity. An independently minded division conference president might develop enough strength to break from the main body. To some degree, the isolation of Europe during the war harmed the church. Following the report of a special study commission in 1917, delegates to the 1918 General Conference Session decided to rewire the connections so that the current of authority flowed from the General Conference out to the divisions instead of the reverse. They dispensed with the word *conference,* and divisions became administrative sections of the church rather than constituent parts of the general body.[36]

The unexpected birthing of the North American Division and complications involving constitutions delayed the election of leaders until quite late in the 1913 session, just as it had been delayed at the critical 1903 meetings. O. A. Olsen, who once more chaired the nominating committee, explained to delegates that it had been unavoidable, not because of any rivalries or political problems but simply because the constitutional issues had taken so long to sort out. The significant constitutional rearrangements had to be settled before the committee could even know what number and what kind of officers to nominate. Constitutions were established and voted for the European and North American Divisions and then, finally, for the Asiatic Division Mission. When all had at last been agreed, the nominating committee brought its first partial report of names—that of Daniells for president, along with Spicer as secretary, and Knox as treasurer. The three were reelected on the third Friday of the session, fully two weeks after it commenced. The election was almost a formality and happened, it seems, without any discussion on the floor. At least we have no record of any. Whether there had been any consultation with Ellen White is also unknown, but it is not likely, given the circumstances. Under the new arrangements, the new division conferences had to have their own meetings to elect their own presidents and other officers before the main nominating committee for the session could bring in its final report for the remainder of appointments. There was much more public explanation justifying the nomination of I. H. Evans as the North American Division president than there had been about the General Conference president. Evans was not someone in whom either Ellen White or W. C. White had full confidence.[37] According to Knox, however, it was the fact that Evans had also been sorely needed by the Asiatic Division that had been "perplexing the committee for several days past," thus necessitating the explanation from the nominating committee. Evans's track record with publishing house finances and in the treasury had been the source of the Whites' discomfort with him.[38] However, that wasn't what delayed his nomination. The agenda was so crowded that the nominating committee was not able to report the rest of the slate of officers until three session days later. The overlapping of jurisdictions under the new structure certainly complicated things.

It was the woeful state of institutional finances, however, that gave Daniells and his treasurer, W. T. Knox, their biggest headaches at the 1913 session. In spite of Daniells's insistence a decade earlier that when acquiring or developing new institutions, the church needed to proceed only "with funds in hand," some had not rigorously followed this stipulation, because of encouragement from California to do otherwise. As a specially commissioned group, tasked by the General Conference committee to get a handle on the badly troubled institutions, found out just prior to the session, the combined debt load the church was carrying was immense. The figures shocked the executive committee. Between 1906 and 1911, liabilities on sanitariums had doubled, and on educational institutions as a whole they had almost quadrupled. Profits from the sale of Ellen White's *Christ's Object Lessons,* meant to remove the previous indebtedness, simply had not kept pace with the voracious appetite of the church for institutional growth. "The lesson of the figures," treasurer Knox informed the committee four months before the session, "was that first of all the denomination must stop making new debts."[39] A special meeting of the General Conference committee, along with a wide group of additional church leaders, convened in California in January 1913 to try to sort out the mess. It appointed a financial task force to investigate every institution and propose some kind of solution.

Problems were particularly acute at Loma Linda Sanitarium and the medical school. The financial investigation squad reported three months later that Loma Linda was operating very inefficiently and needed to reduce staff and take other measures to function more economically. It would survive if it could do so.[40] Others institutions, however, would fail even if they took economy measures. "There are now in the United States so many colleges and union conference training schools attempting in whole or in part, to do collegiate work, which number we deem too large for our constituency," the committee noted. Some institutions would simply have to close. The church could not continue living beyond its means.

The dilemma for Loma Linda and for the church was the increasing pressure from state authorities for higher standards in professional medical training. Accreditation by state licensing boards had become a critical, but expensive, issue. The church concluded that it had no option but to meet the new accreditation requirements and felt more free to do so after receiving favorable advice on the dilemma from Ellen White in 1912. Then it discovered that meeting the new accreditation standards would require building a large new hospital to provide the clinical training.

The proposal to build a clinical training hospital in Los Angeles posed a serious problem both for denominational leadership and for Ellen White. She had previously repeatedly counseled against the idea. Loma Linda was a place where patients should come for treatment, an approach much more in line with her whole thrust in healthcare. Now she had to reconsider as the demands of mission changed circumstances. The accreditation authorities argued that only a hospital in a fairly densely populated area would provide the wide range of clinical experiences that doctors needed to have. W. C. White reported that Ellen White had been persuaded of the need and had withdrawn her opposition. Writing some months later to explain the shift, Willie tried to emphasize continuity in theme and minimize the starkness of the reversal. In carefully nuanced language, he explained that his mother advised "that we do in Loma Linda just as much of the work as could be acceptably done there and carry the remainder to Los Angeles."[41] In order to meet the large added expense, leadership advised Loma Linda to sell some of its property.

In the meantime, the panel on the institutional financing crisis devised a special financial relief plan that it would recommend to the upcoming General Conference session. It involved rigorous compliance with the "no further debt" policy on the part of administrators and closing some of the weakest institutions. Also, it called on church members to increase their weekly offerings from an average of fifteen cents per week to twenty cents per week. Twenty-five percent of the new levels of funding would go to pay down the vast institutional debt over a period of five years or so.[42] The financial crisis made Daniells extremely uncomfortable, and he may well have felt able to say, "I told you so," although it would not have fixed anything. But the problem, now having grown to very large dimensions, undoubtedly reminded him of the painful experiences and tensions he had earlier encountered with W. C. White and his mother over their different approaches to funding institutional development. The session voted the educational relief plan, and church members valiantly rose to the occasion in ensuing months. The desperate need for immediate funding for the hospital at Loma Linda in order to secure its accreditation and retain its students led to a special appeal for help from the delegates at the session. On the last Thursday night of the session, a hastily planned three-and-a-half-hour fundraising program raised between $17,000 and $18,000, primarily through donations, but also through auctioning personal items such as treasured leopard skins that missionaries had brought home as gifts. The institution was saved.

The prospects were not so sweet for the sanitarium at Nashville, Tennessee. Although energetically promoted by Ellen White, it just did not seem to be able to make headway. A report from the Institutional Finance Committee in January suggested some interim funding to keep it operating for a few months until leadership could make a final decision, but the resident business manager concluded that "the institution could not be self-sustaining even were it filled to its capacity." It should be closed, or sold to someone, perhaps some Adventist doctor, who could make a success of it. At the General Conference session some months later, Southern Union president S. E. Wight expressed regret at the closing of the sanitarium. But it had failed "from the very first to pay expenses, running behind from two to five thousand dollars each year." The union committee and the board were thus "obliged to discontinue operating the institution."[43] The failure of this sanitarium, so important to the work of the church in the South in Ellen White's view, illustrates well the accommodation that eventually had to be made between the vision and impulse for growth expressed through Ellen White's charisma and the pressures and responsibilities of having to manage affairs within available finances and management abilities that constrained church administration.

During the summer, before affairs at Nashville finally wound up, administrators considered a variety of options to save the institution—some suggested by Ellen White herself. According to W. C. White, the General Conference discouraged the option of allowing Sutherland and Magan of the Madison School to take over operations. They preferred to sell the sanitarium to some Adventist doctor who would agree not to continue to call on Adventist Church members to support it financially. Otherwise, it would be offered "to outsiders." W. C. White also reported that Ellen White was keenly interested in the destiny of the enterprise and rather distressed to hear that it might be sold. When she asked why the alternative suggestions for enabling it to continue had not worked out, her son had to explain simply that "our people largely did not favor it." His account of their conversation is revealing, because it would seem to convey something of the delicate balance achieved between the operation of the two spiritual gifts—charismatic and administrative—in the community. The episode also appears to reflect an important adjustment and transition taking place in Mrs. White's exercise of her gift. Did she find herself increasingly having to "let go" of matters and trust in the wisdom of the church administrators with their gifts of leadership and administration?

Having spoken with W. C. White about her "deep interest in the work in Nashville," his mother concluded by saying that "her mind was not changed" on the subject. Ellen White thought there was still "the possibility of making the work a success." On the other hand, she was prepared to acknowledge that "if the brethren did not see light in this, she would not urge it, and they might go forward upon the plan that seems to them to be best." She had "given her opinion." Then she noted, "Having offered to help, that is all I can do, and I now leave the matter with them."[44]

The partnership ends

The realities of Ellen White's diminishing abilities associated with her aging and her increasing dependence on W. C. White to manage her communication with Daniells and other church leaders and the various church entities was something that Willie White had thought about a good deal as he approached the 1913 General Conference Session. What would happen when his mother was no longer on the scene? "What would be the influence on our work if Sister White should die?" How well would the church handle the loss of one of its most influential voices?

"God lives!" answered one emphatic voice from the congregation when W. C. White posed the question to the delegates midway through the session. The problematic prospect was significant from his own personal perspective. How would his own role change? How would he, in the future, relate to the General Conference president? Clearly, others in the church were also pondering the same issues, because W. C. White reported that numerous church members already were claiming to be Ellen White's anointed successor. Some of them had found their way to Elmshaven to seek her endorsement. Mrs. White did not know, however, who would be her successor or if there would be one at all. That there should be such a claim and that it would be validated by the church somehow in the mysterious working of Providence, was not an entirely unreasonable possibility. What, then, would be the implications for W. C. White's own role?

At the 8:30 A.M. Bible study hour on Friday, May 30, two weeks into the session, W. C. White took opportunity to address the issue directly. It was the same day that Daniells was reelected to the presidency. His purpose, he said, was to "speak of some of the questions . . . which are in the minds of our people regarding our future work." He particularly wanted to speak to "that part of the work" with which he was "most intimately connected," that is, "the work of Sister White." Laying down some biblical principles about the value of counseling together as a church, he reviewed several Bible promises that God would provide guidance. He then read a number of statements from his mother about her confidence in his own appointment as her helper and counselor, in which she positively asserted that he had been given special skills of "wisdom" and "understanding to manage wisely."[45] His direction of the work at Elmshaven, with all its involvement in manuscripts and books, would need to continue. And the church would require his important skills even after she had gone.[46] The problem was that while White's fellow administrators appreciated and valued his wisdom and judgment as well as his long experience in the church and his mature counsel on church issues, they were also keenly aware that if the Lord had given this younger son skills and "understanding to manage wisely," unfortunately such skills did not extend to preaching or to sound financial discipline. "You know that I am not a successful preacher, nor a financier," White had himself at one time reported to O. A. Olsen. And his colleagues knew full well that he did not have the kind of "proper executive ability" that would enable him to succeed in conference leadership.[47] The fact that the General Conference committee had to loan W. C. White ten thousand dollars later that very same year (1913) in order to support operations at Elmshaven because "it seemed necessary," reinforced this understanding of W. C. White's abilities. The committee made the loan with considerable reluctance and with a claim against royalty income as security.[48]

Even as he addressed the topic in the session, White felt uncomfortable. He realized that it could possibly sound self-serving. It probably would have been better for someone else to have offered the statements on his behalf. "Please forgive me," he commented, "if in reading this, I am presenting some things that it might seem better for me not to present." But he did not know how else to get the matter before the delegates. But having launched into the delicate topic, he then continued in an attempt to educate delegates about the realities of the document processing and book-making procedures followed at Elmshaven. He described the range of valued editorial help employed in the task. It was new information to many of the delegates, different to what they thought was involved, and it apparently troubled not a few. The information shared in the Bible study hour apparently led to other meetings and vigorous discussion with other session participants not preserved in the written records. Discussion extended to consideration of some letters that, to certain delegates, didn't have the ring of authenticity. Or, at least, if they were authentic, they conveyed ideas from Ellen White and about her that were difficult to harmonize with the regular explanations given to her work.[49] Some loyal church leaders, such as S. E. Wight, the Southern Union president, felt that the best way to resolve the difficulties apparent in some documents was to regard them as not carrying the same authority as regular testimonies. W. C. White was of the view, however, that trying to classify the material in this way was something that he could not do. Neither would such a solution answer all the perplexities. And he was correct. Later in the year, in a letter reflecting on the meeting, White recounted that the reaction to his frank discussion of the problems had caused him a great deal of "distress and perplexity." He had received severe criticism from certain individuals, and he felt that much of it was targeted not just at him but at the testimonies themselves. Feeling that he needed friends to defend him, he pleaded with Daniells to do so.

"I know that you love me, and that you will do what you can to help me in this time of distress and perplexity," he wrote. He was trying to do the right thing, but if Daniells thought he was "moving unwisely" then, he added, "I beg of you to give me counsel." W. C. White now shared the same pain of being misunderstood that Prescott and Daniells had experienced several years previously. Yet he felt that the church needed to understand better how his mother worked, though at the same time he did not want to "leave the way open for a great flood of doubt regarding the agency that God has chosen for communication with His church."[50] Achieving the right balance was not easy, and both Prescott and Spicer felt that W. C. White had not, in fact, been frank enough nor had he gone far enough in trying to correct the idealized and oversimplified views of Ellen White held by many. A wide segment of church members entertained serious misconceptions about the way she worked and about how the church needed to relate to her advice and counsel.[51]

Although Mrs. White had not been able to attend the 1913 session and managed to write only two or three letters per month, she was still able to give counsel, at times, on dilemmas perplexing the rapidly expanding church. But such interactions were now limited to problems in her immediate environment in California. Her withdrawal from any extensive engagement with denominational issues prompted a rethinking of the balance between the leadership gifts that denominational leaders believed the Spirit had manifested in the church. In the past the church had given significant emphasis to the prophetic charisma, but now the "apostolic gift" perhaps should receive more attention and gain more confidence.

W. C. White reflected some of this discussion occurring among leadership when he observed to Daniells at the end of 1913 that he was "fully in harmony with it." He was referring to "the effort that should be made to emphasize in the minds of our people, the sacredness, the authority of the apostolic gifts." On several occasions he had advised his colleagues that a biblical understanding of "the spirit of prophecy" could not be properly achieved "without a better understanding of all the other gifts in the church." For a long time, he said, he had been "praying the Lord [to] take the burden that for years has rested upon Mother" and instead place it upon "the seventy elders." White assured Daniells that his colleagues could know that "wherever there is occasion to speak of it," leaders would have his "sympathy" and his prayers. It was important that they should give "their efforts to build up and strengthen the apostolic gifts, and all the other gifts in the church."[52] Of course, those gifts had been functioning in the church all along. It was more a matter of readjusting the balance to a more inclusive approach in the way that the church informed and educated its membership through its numerous communication media.

CLOSING WORDS

Determining that it was better for her not to attend the 1913 session in person, Ellen White decided to send three written messages to the delegates.[53] W. C. White read the first on the first Sabbath afternoon of the session. Daniells presented the second one later in the session. Both were read again, in substantial part, along with a third on the last Sabbath of the meetings. Daniells presented them during his Sabbath morning sermon time. The messages were notable for a number of reasons.

First, Ellen White adopted a softer, more general, series of expressions to describe the source of her messages. Her mind had been "impressed by the Holy Spirit with the thought . . . " and it "reverted" back to the experience of her fellow pioneers in the 1840s. "Often in the night season" she was "bidden" to urge church leaders to seek a deeper experience. She had been "deeply impressed" by scenes that passed before her in the night. The letters contained significant personal references to her travels and daily routines and reflections on the things she had been thinking about as well as general exhortations to a consistent Christian life. But for the hearers, the messages were not just friendly encouraging pastoral letters. They were still what they heard as "testimony" even when they came without the urgent call for change and reform right there and then. S. N. Haskell, for example, was encouraged by the testimonies and "that we have the Lord's voice among us still."[54] Loughborough heard the testimony say "courage in the Lord" and knew that "the Lord is talking to us yet." Butler reported that some had feared that as Ellen White grew old "her writing would be less powerful," but he thought that "her later writings are the best." Daniells and Olsen referred to the messages as "a communication," as did J. O. Corliss. But whether they were letters, communications, or testimony, all recognized their note of spiritual authority. But it was the distinctive positive tone of the messages that impressed many.

The General Conference president, who had heard many sharp and reproving letters read at previous sessions, commented on what he heard as a distinctive change in tone in her communications. People had observed the note of confidence right at the beginning of the conference in the greetings that W. C. White had brought from his mother. "Tell our brethren to be of good cheer," she had stressed. In her first written communication, Ellen White asserted at the outset that it was the "privilege" of the delegates attending the session "to cherish a spirit of hopefulness and courage," "to be glad in the Lord, and to rejoice in the knowledge of his sustaining grace." She called for a renewed spiritual awakening, but her tone was uplifting. Ellen White had seen the outlines of the end times. "I see a crisis before us," and there was a need for deeper consecration. True, there had been missed opportunities at the 1909 conference and a work "in the heart" could have been done there "that was not done." Referring to the slow start to evangelize the cities four years previously, she commented that the leaders who were "in positions of trust in the general work" after study and prayer had "ventured to undertake by faith the work called for, a work they could not fully understand." But they had received rich blessing from going forward in faith. While at times she still felt "the deepest anxiety" about some of the administrators, she nevertheless "had strong faith in the workers throughout the field." She had been impressed there would be a great work of revival that would go forward "in many places." Quoting the apostle Paul, she rejoiced, "I have confidence in you in all things." The message was a positive affirmation and, according to the *Bulletin* editors, "tears flowed freely as Sister White's expressions of confidence in her brethren and in God's leadership of his people were read."[55] Daniells must have felt particularly encouraged to hear the positive assessment of his efforts made in contrast to the chill in his relationship with her during 1910 and 1911.

Her second message, titled "Courage in the Lord," Daniells himself read on Tuesday morning, May 27. Again, the general tone was warm and positive. The letter had a personal touch, recounting some details of her daily home routines, but emphasized that she had "words of encouragement" for the delegates. The Lord was coming soon, and she was glad that the God of Israel was still guiding His people. Daniells felt "greatly encouraged by the note of cheer" that he heard. Because not many were present in the pavilion on Tuesday, Daniells received many requests to re-read the letters during his sermon on the final Sabbath of the session.

On this latter occasion, as he read the high points of the three letters, he noted particularly the positive, encouraging theme that ran through them all. "These messages have breathed courage and good cheer and hopefulness all the way through," he observed. They were not at all difficult to read. Church members were to work together "intelligently," "reach a higher standard of spirituality," and labor "unitedly." Christians could "take God at his word." Daniells paused to relate to the congregation how, even after years as a pastor, this simple truth of taking God at His word had gripped him and had transformed his life. He encouraged his hearers to let it do the same for them. The whole tenor of the readings and the closing sermon was upbeat, full of challenge but also full of hope and goodness all through.

As Daniells concluded the readings, he commented with a sober sense of the high significance of the fact that he had just read "the last word that has come to us in the form of a message to us." Its final paragraph was a solemn closing admonition that without "the transforming power of God," His church would not be able to accomplish its task. Ellen White would not be attending any more General Conference sessions or sending Daniells any more communications to guide him or his fellow leaders gathered in session like this. A sadness and sense of nostalgia swept over everyone in the pause that followed. Then a voice called, "Please read that last thought again." The congregation wanted to savor the moment and hear the voice one last time. Daniells took time to slowly read the paragraph again, noting as he did that when delegates returned to their homes it was vital to keep drinking "at the fountain of spiritual life." Then he turned to the words of Jesus about the water of life in John 10 and urged his listeners to drink of the life-giving water of the Spirit. He concluded with a reference to the gospel story about Jesus' parents losing their boy as they returned from the feast, and Daniells urged his audience to make sure that Jesus returned with them from the feast. And then it was over. Soon the delegates would break camp and return to their posts of duty. Daniells would continue exercising his extremely valuable gift of leadership. But from here on out, the gift of leadership, as it met with the community of faith in General Conference session, would not be dealing with the living voice of prophecy. It would need to learn to relate to the writings of someone who had been specially gifted, but who was no longer there to clarify, explain, repeat, strengthen, soften, or modify what had been said or written. But that is the subject of another volume.

In the broad sweep of the previous chapters we have seen that Ellen White was closely involved in the selection of leadership during this long but critical period in the church's development. We have observed that she also participated in guiding and counseling those called to leadership. It was not always an easy partnership. Presidents not only faced the challenge of leading colleagues and the wider church through the difficult processes of decision making, they also experienced the often uncomfortable prospect of being second-guessed by the prophet. Every president that this study has reviewed recognized this challenge and tried to avoid the problem by genuinely seeking counsel and advice before they had to make major decisions, if at all possible. Sometimes this was not possible, and sometimes, as happens in all organizations, some decisions had to be made at short notice when available information was rather inadequate. And sometimes decisions made with the best of intent and with the widest advice from those who might be expected to know still might have been less than the best decision. Corrective counsel and rebuke often came after such decisions. This aspect of the reality of leadership in the General Conference required that presidents needed a robust spirituality, a healthy sense of self-esteem, and a humble confidence in their own relationship with God, along with an attitude of meekness that was ready to accept both personal and public criticism. The individuals we have studied all recognized the value of the special charisma that exhibited itself among them in the ministry of Ellen White. They were blessed and challenged by it as well as being hurt, annoyed, and frustrated by it. And they were grateful for the opportunity of exercising their own gifts in what was a unique and richly profitable partnership

CHAPTER 11

A HERMENEUTICAL PARADIGM for UNDERSTANDING ELLEN WHITE in the 1890s

Readers of the manuscripts and the letters Ellen White wrote during the 1890s find themselves struck by the fact that much of her correspondence to the General Conference presidents and to their associates in church leadership has a distinctive tone and character compared to that from other periods of her life. As this study has already pointed out (for example in the discussion on Olsen's presidency), much of her material takes on a noticeably somber hue and is characterized by a passionate, provocative intensity that on many occasions has echoes of the severity and force of the biblical, eighth-century B.C. prophets such as Amos and Joel. Arthur L. White, grandson of Ellen White, observes that the 1890s era was a difficult period and consequently resulted in a substantial body of distinctive letters and manuscripts that he describes as "dramatic," "extensive in volume," and "severe in its terminology."[1] Why is this so?

Arthur White suggests that Ellen White generally targeted these particular communications at church administrators at headquarters in Battle Creek and at several conference presidents perceived as comprising "a hard core of resistance" to the message of righteousness by faith with which she had linked her influence and charismatic authority. Much of the resistance she faced at this time resulted directly from the innovative theological positions she encouraged or adopted. The concept of theological change and development was little understood at this period, and many church leaders had difficulty responding to new theological insights and emphases such as those advocated by E. J. Waggoner and A. T. Jones. Ellen White's endorsement of such positions created resistance, and sometimes as a result her opponents manifested skepticism regarding her claim to authority in the community. This was probably the most difficult period for Ellen White in the exercise of her leadership role in the church. It was a period that required extraordinary exertion and resulted in significant distress as she sought to exercise her influence effectively. In many respects, one could view her influence at this time as unsuccessful—at least in numerous short-term encounters. Some leaders chose not to change and simply withdrew from their roles and in some cases from their involvement with the church itself. In other cases, institutional change did not occur as she had desired. The resistance Ellen White encountered, it is implied, required numerous determined strategies, high-volume communication, and persistent effort in order to achieve the long-term outcomes she wanted.

The extent and seriousness of the problems she encountered comprised other factors that occasioned stronger language than she commonly used. In his foreword to Albert Olson's treatment of the period, Arthur White notes that while in some ways the years 1888 to 1901 were "the most progressive" in the development of the church up to that time, those thirteen years were also "fraught with conflict and clashes over organizational ideas and theological views." The literature on conflict in religious communities notes that it is not unusual for theological conflict and church fights to involve high-decibel discussions, because theological ideas are held so deeply and are generally linked to a person's or a community's core belief system at a deep emotional level.[2] George Knight concurs that the 1890s were "one of the most formative and controversial" periods in the development of Adventism and notes that the issues that raised their heads at that time have remained focal points of discussion in the church ever since.[3]

Identifying and understanding the specific issues and carefully considering the "time, place, and circumstances" of the messages given by Ellen White has been recognized as a fundamental hermeneutical principle in the study and use of her writings. She herself establishes this principle. "Regarding the testimonies, nothing is ignored; nothing is cast aside; but time and place must be considered."[4] The "time and place" principle is usually considered to include the nature of the problem being addressed and the specific historical circumstances and context of the problem—factors that must be allowed to moderate the application of a specific instruction. The general intent of the principle is to establish whether a particular instruction is applicable to other times and places. A specific counsel may or may not necessarily have universal relevance—relevance to other places or problems or even to similar situations at other times. The nature of the problem and the historical context of the recipients of the counsel are usually considered to be the necessary aspects of the "time and place" principle one must take into account in order to understand and interpret correctly the material Ellen White has left us. But one might ask if there were other circumstances that also help to explain the occurrence of such a distinctive body of material as we have been examining in this book. This chapter will seek to demonstrate that the hermeneutical concept of "time and place" needs to be broadened to include consideration of the personal experience—the emotions, health concerns, and specific life circumstances—of the writer of the counsel at the time she wrote. Such an expansion will provide richer insights and help in understanding and interpreting the counsel given.

What follows in this final chapter is a discussion of Ellen White's personal circumstances and life situation, including the physical and emotional journey that forms an important and previously overlooked part of the background from which she wrote. To some extent, the discussion will involve rehearsing some of the historical episodes and details already discussed earlier in this volume, but we will review the material here in a different context. The purpose is to provide a summary and contextual background for a more comprehensive hermeneutic for understanding the Ellen White of the 1890s. It will be argued that the unusually dark hue and severe intensity that characterizes a significant portion of her correspondence of this period can be better understood in the light of her own personal circumstances and experience. Several important considerations color the background of this period of her life and provide a helpful framework for understanding and interpreting these letters and manuscripts.[5] We highlight the background and life context of Ellen White not to suggest that there were not, in fact, serious problems in the structure and administration of the church. There clearly were. Nor is the purpose to diminish the problems of those who consciously took a position of resistance and skepticism toward her work or who apparently intentionally attempted to limit the exercise of her influence. Rather, we seek the background in order to obtain a more complete understanding of why Ellen White, as a writer, so frequently used such hyperbolic and even severe language. Understanding this background also helps to explain why she sometimes saw the problems of church organization in personal terms as the fault of individual leaders, rather than primarily in systemic structural terms arising from the natural stresses generated by the rapidly expanding activities of the denomination and the inadequacies of the existing structures to accommodate them.

Consciously chosen language

In this section, to illustrate the style of Ellen White's writing, we will first consider samples of expressions indicating her increased levels of frustration. Our purpose is to survey briefly the topics that caused such concern and the intensity of expression that they called forth as well as the reactions they produced in the recipients. We will then explore her view of the language that she frequently chose to use during this era. Was the language simply a subconscious reflection of the depth of emotion she felt at the time, something that helped her to feel better for having expressed herself thus? Or did she consciously choose the many strong expressions to convey the seriousness of a problem or even, perhaps, for the effect they might have on the reader?

During this period, she frequently used hyperbole to communicate the significance of her many concerns. For example, in 1893, she wrote of the Lord sending "a scourge" to drive church members out of Battle Creek to correct the problems of overcrowding and the developing of an Adventist ghetto mind-set.[6] In the context of recurring cholera and scarlet fever epidemics, the terminology caused many people to panic. And protesting the animosity at the headquarters' church toward her ministry, she spoke of "a malaria of disbelief" among church leaders and of certain leaders actually "cultivating hatred" against some others.

During this time, the marketing policies and other business practices of the church's flagship publishing house repeatedly ignited within her an intense indignation. This topic in particular occasioned the use of super-heated language. "A leprosy of cunning and double dealing" pervaded the Review and Herald office, she alleged. Publishing leaders had been designing "act after act of complicated robbery" for the purpose of defrauding authors and employees.[7] She feared that such "robbery and dishonesty" had begun spreading to the General Conference from the Review and Herald. An attitude of either "control or crush all that cannot be controlled" had manifested itself in management as administrators widely practiced "cruelty and injustice." The Review's insincere and dishonest approach to adopting resolutions and making agreements was corrupt.[8] She herself had been on the receiving end of royalty negotiations that convinced her that the Review management was obtaining "terms of royalty" "by fraud."[9] Business practices adopted by the publishing house were "specious inventions" and involved "unlawful schemes." Though they might be clever secular business practices and though they might have been occasioned by the fact that the publishing house was in serious financial difficulties, nevertheless, such strategies for dealing with the problem were "in direct opposition to the work which God has specified as his."[10] The publishing program needed "cleansing," she declared. The proposed plan to consolidate the church's publishing houses under one administration would be a colossal mistake. "The sooner this bubble blown by Satan is burst, the better it will be."[11]

Ellen White seemed to focus her sharpest and most direct language on the finance and the treasury people, some of whom, she lamented, had "padlocked their hearts against evidence" so that the Holy Spirit could not find entrance. Individuals such as the manager of the Review and Herald publishing house and the General Conference treasurer should probably not have been appointed in the first place, but certainly, she insisted in the mid-1890s, they should now be removed from their positions without further ado. She said that the publishing men were greedy, were seeking high wages, were not consecrated to God, and needed genuine conversion. This kind of poison had been at work for a long time, and now others were drinking of the cup and being corrupted.[12]

The level of spirituality and loyalty among conference presidents also distressed her deeply. She had not much confidence, she suggested, in many of them. "Many presidents of conferences," she believed, "needed to be replaced." They "do not answer to the measurement of God" and were therefore "unfit for the work and should be dismissed." "If the men who bear responsibilities" would not make known to the people the statutes of God and His laws, then leadership "must be committed to others."[13] Ellen White perceived in such leaders a willful resistance to new theological understandings, but even that was not as much a problem as their antagonism toward her influence and authority.

She put her litany of complaints about Olsen in terms that were just as strong. She disagreed with his policy of diplomacy through which he had tried to build bridges of understanding to those of his fellow officers who had difficulty with the 1888 theological emphasis and thus with her ministry. Mrs. White asserted that his strategy was a mistaken policy from the beginning. Olsen had become "blinded," was "confused," and was more influenced by his fellow administrators than they by him. He had "failed" in his duty as a president in not reading her letters of warning and rebuke to them. Thus he had become a party to the dictatorial spirit at headquarters and was guilty of "oppressing" his fellow leaders through sanctioning the resolutions made by his committee. Olsen had been silent or had uttered only a "feeble protest" at things on which he should have stood firm. His central committee, consisting of only a few individuals, "supposed they could take the place of God and order and dictate and lord it over men's minds and talents." It made her "indignant" just to think about it.[14] Regarding Olsen's presidency as a failure, she publicly denounced and rebuked him for his weaknesses.

She aimed what probably was her most dramatic language and her strongest protest at the institution of the General Conference itself. She struggled to conceal her disillusionment when she asserted that the General Conference committee could no longer be relied on to provide safe leadership for the church. "The General Conference—what is it?" she asked. "Is it a General Conference, or is it something wrapped up and called by that name?" The leaders at the center of the work had lost the sense of the "sacred character" of the cause of God. "The voice from Battle Creek, which has been regarded as authority in counseling how the work should be done, is no longer the voice of God; but it is the voice of—whom?"[15] The answer to her rhetorical question was obvious as she acknowledged that she had lost confidence in the General Conference and its leaders. "We cannot therefore present before the people that the voice of the General Conference in its decisions must move and control them; for its propositions and decisions cannot be accepted."

It had been some years, she reported in 1898, since she had "considered the General Conference as the voice of God."[16] Why? The "councils" at Battle Creek were not "converted." Leaders at Battle Creek "bind about the conscience of others" in order to "achieve their purpose."[17] Those appointed to lead the church were no more qualified "than are children to guide the steamships over the broad ocean," she observed. "What reason have we to have implicit confidence in decisions in these councils?" she challenged. In fact, she said, "have I not every reason to believe if they could manage to place me in trying places they would do it? They have done it," she declared emphatically. Therefore, she said with prophetic defiance, she would not "feel under restraints which they wish to impose." With regard to arrangements for her book publishing, she was "sick and disgusted with the management of those things."

So disillusioned was she that she found herself tempted at times to administratively bypass the General Conference. For example, in inviting E. J. Waggoner to visit Australia from his post in England, she explained that because she no longer had confidence in the General Conference, "therefore I feel no desire to write" to make the arrangement following the official protocol. So, she wrote directly to Waggoner, urging him to come to help her in her work. "Cannot you do this? Please write us whether you can." In addition, she explained that she thought his magazine, *Present Truth,* was the best periodical that the church produced. It was better than the *Review*.[18] To her friend Jenny Ings, she reflected on her rationale for bypassing the official leadership: "As one whom the

Lord has chosen to lay great burdens of the cause of truth upon, I must not consent to be led in all things by the counsels and decisions of my brethren, when I know there are times they are moving blindly." Occasionally, she urged such civil disobedience on others. To C. H. Jones she wrote in 1895, "You are not to hold yourself to seek permission of the authorities in Battle Creek whether you shall or shall not pursue a line of work that seems impressed upon you to do. The Lord is the one to whom you are to be amenable."[19]

To the reader even at this distance more than a century later, the highly charged language still breathes her intense passion, and it still effectively communicates the level of concern that she felt about the extremely serious nature of the threat posed at Battle Creek. Today's reader is left with the overriding impression that there was corruption on every hand and that the church was rapidly sliding into apostasy and collapse. So strong were Ellen White's condemnations that some, such as the spiritually sensitive Prescott, felt they had no option but to resign and not participate in church administration at all. Prescott was a regular member of the boards and committees to whom she addressed her warnings. "I dread to go back to America," he explained to her, because he did not want to get tied up in the system as it was.[20] Later, in 1897, when Prescott was appointed to work in Great Britain as the result of a highly unusual and irregular action from the floor of the General Conference session, he took it as a good sign that he had not been assigned to the task by any officially appointed committee or board. The implication was that an appointment by such a committee would have been invalid, or highly suspect at best. Leaders at the time struggled to know how best to relate to the strong doses of rebuke and condemnation in Mrs. White's letters.

Olsen could not understand many parts of her admonitions and felt helpless and uncertain as to what he could do to untangle the complex organizational mess in which he found himself trapped. In January 1896, he explained to W. C. White, "Above everything else I am desirous to do the right thing, as far as I know it. One of my greatest embarrassments is that I find myself much of the time so worn under the continual pressure of the work that I am not in a fit condition to deal with intricate matters, which call for the keenest discernment and the most deliberate judgment. It is impossible for a man who is under continual pressure and in constant hurry to always be prepared to properly discern and take right action on important questions. Being in this condition I have felt many times that I did not dare to touch some of these matters, feeling myself so utterly unfit to deal with them properly."[21] Two months later, he again confided to Willie that he felt "very weary" and worried about his nervous health. "At times it seems as if I must go under," he reported.[22]

As the years passed, Olsen responded to Ellen White with a developing maturity of spirituality and self-awareness. "The last mail from Australia brought a large amount of matter from your pen," he told her in August 1896. He had read "with care" the "faithful warnings and admonitions," stating that he accepted them "heartily" and thanked her. "It grieves me deeply," he went on, "to realize how greatly I have come short in the work I have been given to do and how I have failed to meet the mind of the Lord." The General Conference president indicated that he would not only receive the counsel but would act upon it to the best of his ability. The counsel had "thrown a flood of light" on his way, and he now grasped some things that he had "not understood before." As a result, he apologized for being "so blinded."[23]

Ellen White, on the other hand—before she received Olsen's August 14 letter—complained to Oscar Tait, the Foreign Mission Board secretary in Battle Creek, that the General Conference president had not understood things for years and had "given unmistakable evidence that he does not regard the testimonies which the Lord has seen fit to give his people as worthy of respect or as of sufficient weight to influence his course of action." The situation distressed her "beyond any words my pen can trace."[24]

In an attempt to explain things to Ellen White, Olsen had noted, "But as U [*sic*] see the situation, and my duty made so plain, I never before felt myself so unfit and so utterly incapable of moving forward and doing the work that needs to be done. . . . I am surrounded with exceedingly great perplexities. I do want to do what is right. . . . As I look upon the failures of the past, I am not only filled with grief, but sometimes a feeling of depression comes over me, to the effect that there is but little hope for my future improvement." He felt it important to explain to her that his motives were clear. "When you speak of the underlying principles that have actuated in some of these moves, I can truly say that I have not knowingly had any selfish purpose in any action as far as I know." Because of his "blindness," he acknowledged that he did not see the full ramifications of the actions on individuals and the work, but these things he would seek to "correct as far as God will give grace to do so." Furthermore, he acknowledged that his soul was "sorely burdened for the work. This you know and appreciate."[25]

Although many of her letters employing strong language are addressed to specific individuals and apparently refer to specific problems, nevertheless, many also exhibit a certain vagueness and imprecision. Often recipients would be quite confused as to what she expected, and it would take some time for them to process the letter. Mrs. White frequently employed metaphor and quoted numerous biblical passages from the prophets on social justice issues and righteousness. Sometimes the problematic decisions or moral issues about which she specifically protests become lost or obscured in the middle of paragraphs of general spiritual counsel. Many of the complaints are generalized ones about the apparent lack of spirituality among leaders and unacceptable "dictatorial" attitudes. It is often difficult from this distance in time to determine from the letters themselves the particular malpractice that she had in mind. The administrators at the time who received these strongly worded letters would undoubtedly have been in a better position to know more clearly what she referred to, but even the first-intended recipients often struggled with uncertainty about what the letters sought from them, and significant misunderstandings arose about what they needed to do by way of correction. Sometimes sharp differences of opinion developed among leaders as to what a testimony actually meant, but even when there was a relatively clear understanding of its intent, just how to implement the counsel within the existing system and within the context of the prevailing organizational and legal parameters was often not obvious.

When a letter dealt with personal matters, the recipient sometimes felt that Mrs. White needed to take into account a larger picture. But replying to give a different interpretation or explanation of events was not an easy or safe option. In March 1895, for example, A. G. Daniells received a letter that Ellen White sent to him following a conversation they'd had at a camp meeting at Ashfield in Sydney. He reports that he read the letter many times during a period of weeks in an effort to comprehend it fully. In his reply to the letter several months later, he commented, "Some portions as yet, I do not understand." He indicated that while parts were plain, some sections he would have "liked to write about." It seems clear that not only did he feel he did not understand her letter fully, but also that perhaps some further explanation on his part would have enabled Ellen White to more fully understand the situation. Daniells appears to have come to terms eventually with the realization that discussing particular issues further, by way of adding explanation, would perhaps be seen as some form of self-defense or justification that would not help the situation. Therefore, he resolved to humbly accept the letter, uncomfortable though it was, pray for grace and wisdom to adjust to it and profit from it, and move on. "Oh! may God give me a submissive spirit," he wrote.[26]

Although some prominent leaders in the church obviously had grown cold spiritually, and became overbearing in manner, many others were spiritually alert and sensitive.

Committee meetings regularly commenced with prayer. Members of nominating committees prayed sincerely and believed that the Spirit was leading them in their decisions. Leaders such as Olsen were people of prayer and daily devotion and struggled to understand what Mrs. White sought to tell them. It seems that they were committed to doing their best to try to address issues in spiritual ways. They had reasons for the different practices they adopted—maybe not always good or sound reasons in the light of her later comments, but within the information available to them and within the parameters of the financial, time, and personnel constraints of the situation, they felt that it was the best they could do.

As the 1890s wore on and Ellen White saw little change in the problematic circumstances developing at headquarters, she acknowledged that she found herself struggling to find language to express the intensity of her anxiety and concern. Thus, as Arthur White observes, her warnings came "with growing frequency and accelerating force."[27] For example, on one occasion when she was troubled about problems at Battle Creek, she confided to Professor Prescott, "My spirit burns within me as these things are revealed to me." As a result, she experienced "agony of remorse" and "intense agony of soul" as she anguished over the "perils" at Battle Creek and lamented that she could not "find language to describe" things adequately.[28] She felt strongly that there needed to be shifts in personnel and in the policies they implemented. But when she saw little forthcoming response, she then fretted that matters simply went on "accumulating in their objectionable features" until she perceived the problems as having an increasingly "aggravated character." Because she could not see changes taking place, she found herself trying to exert her influence through adopting a more forceful tone of writing. When she described some of her letters as "earnest, decided testimonies," she meant that they were quite direct and blunt in portraying spiritual weakness, personal failings, or poor decisions.[29] Mrs. White explained that she adopted such a frank style because she felt so intensely and was so convicted. "I desire the meekness of Christ; and yet, when I see men interposing their unsanctified decisions in the way of the Lord's work, I shall not be clear in holding my peace. I shall speak decidedly; . . . I dare not be silent."[30]

On occasion she wrote so strongly and directly that after she had unburdened herself in writing, she feared to send the letter because she thought she might have expressed her feelings and concerns too intensely. Sometimes on these occasions she would lay the letter aside for a time, possibly never even mailing it. Other times she worried that she might tend to overstate things, and experience had taught her that while spiritually casual people might not respond to the letter at all, people who were more spiritually sensitive would "hear things with too strong a spirit" and either become greatly discouraged or overreact in seeking to put things right.[31] She commented to O. A. Olsen, for instance, "I would have sent this letter long ago: but after writing it, I have drawn back from sending it" because she feared that he could not cope with the things she had said.[32] On the other hand, at times she feared that she could not present things strongly enough. In 1895, still worried about the trends at Battle Creek, she anguished, "I have now no words of sufficient force to describe the situation that has been steadily carried forward."[33]

As noted already, the problems arising in the 1890s clearly were serious and had long-term implications for the welfare of the church. But since then, the church has accepted quite a number of the practices that Ellen White opposed. This suggests that the church has decided that while her counsel in the 1890s meant that such practices were not helpful or appropriate for the church at that time, these practices do not violate universal ethical principles. The strong language with which she protested against them in the 1890s was, in part, an indication that they were clear dangers then, but the degree of her opposition to them at that time had also been influenced by her own experience as a church employee. So, the background to her personal experience during that period needs to be explored, for it casts helpful light on what else must be considered as subject to the principle of "time and place" in interpreting her writings of the 1890s.

The difficult Australian sojourn

During the final decade of the nineteenth century, Ellen White lived in Australia, moving about from city to city until finally settling at Cooranbong near Newcastle in New South Wales. Right from the start she felt very ambivalent about Australia. For the first several years, she struggled with the fact that she was there and had mixed feelings about it all. There were times when she lamented that she had been sent, blamed O. A. Olsen personally for allowing it to happen, and to a large degree regarded the difficulties and perplexities she encountered in the southern colonies as being the result of the corruption and mismanagement that she saw occurring at denominational headquarters.

When it was proposed that Ellen White go to Australia, she was sixty-four years old—very near today's retirement age. The proposal, first made in 1890, came just after she had purchased a piece of land and taken the effort to construct a small summer cottage in the resort area of Petoskey near Harbor Springs in northwestern Michigan, about

260 miles north of Battle Creek. The idea of going to Australia did not excite her at all, because she had her heart set on using the cottage as a retreat for writing a large book on the life of Christ as well as books on other topics.

Her close friend Stephen N. Haskell had first raised the idea of her going to Australia following his own recent tour of South Africa, Australia, and the South Pacific region. He was convinced that she would bring strength and inspiration to the denomination in Australia and that her presence would help in establishing a training school. When the March 1891 General Conference Session discussed the suggestion informally, others also saw value and wisdom in it. The idea gained wider currency until eventually the Foreign Mission Board formalized the request in the following resolution:

> "*Whereas,* In our judgment it would be a great blessing to the cause in Australia and adjacent colonies for Sister White to visit that field; Therefore,
>
> "*Resolved,* That we hereby invite her to do so, as soon as the coming autumn, if her own judgment, and the light she may have in the matter, shall be in accordance with this request; it being understood that W. C. White shall accompany her on this visit."[34]

The action of the Foreign Mission Board took care to leave the decision as to whether or not to go in Mrs. White's own hands. It clearly indicated that this was an invitation they were leaving to "her own judgment, and the light she may have in the matter." Church leaders evidently wanted to be careful that they did not appear to be dictating a course of action or imposing their will in the matter.

For her part, as various groups in the church discussed the matter, she personally hoped no invitation would materialize, for she did not want to leave America. She had her heart set on getting some rest and "quietude," and she wanted time to "get out the 'Life of Christ.' "[35] Her diary of August 1891 reveals her inner struggles as she confided to its pages that she was troubled in regard to her duty in the matter. Was it "the will of God that I go to Australia?" She did not seem to have any "special light" on the matter. Ellen White noted her awareness that "some who are bearing responsibilities in America seem to be very persistent that her special work should be to go to Europe and to Australia"; however, she did not identify those she had in mind. Previously, when she had gone to Europe for two years "to work with all the power of influence" that God had given her, it had been at some serious disruption to her domestic affairs. Her personal effects had become scattered; she had not obtained a good price on the sale of her house to Kellogg; and she had sustained other losses. Now, on this occasion, she was sure that if she "knew it was the voice of God," she would go. But her mind was not clear. Her diary entry hints that she suspected some leaders "wished to carry the work in America in their own way."[36]

Two weeks later she was just as uncertain. Others were talking much about the proposal, but still she could not "see" her way "clear to go." Some advised that she would have fewer burdens to carry in Australia and could thus give more time to her book writing, but she knew different. She realized that it would mean hard and strenuous work. In fact, she was reluctant even to indicate that she knew of the troubles that existed in the church's Australian publishing house in Melbourne, for she knew that the leaders would then probably "firmly conclude" that she "must go."[37] At times, she feared that her "unwillingness to go" was "the reason why I had not more evidence on the point."[38]

But in spite of her ambivalence and uncertainty and her natural reticence because of the disruption and difficulties involved, in the absence of any specific contrary light convicting her otherwise, Ellen White decided to respect the system and respond favorably to the request of the General Conference. However, even as late as October she was still uncertain. She confided to O. A. Olsen, "I am considering, can it be my duty to go to Australia?" Some of the doctrinal objections that she might have to deal with while there especially troubled her. But she had presented the case to the Lord. "I believe he will guide me," she noted.[39] It was only later, after she had arrived, that she realized she had made a terrible mistake—an assessment shaped by a long stretch of painful experience and reflection. But could God use mistakes?

As noted earlier, Ellen White's decade-long sojourn in the antipodes was not a comfortable one—at least not until the latter years. Not long after she arrived in Melbourne, she became ill for almost a year with inflammatory rheumatism and recurring bouts of malaria that gave her severe and prolonged pain. The illnesses confined her to bed for extended periods and restricted her ability to write much. It was "the most terrible suffering" of her whole life, she recounted later. The ill health compounded the effects of the significant culture shock she experienced as she struggled to adjust to her new environment. Her inability to get good rest and her worries about the state of the church both in Australia and in America also compounded the effect of the illness as it extended into a long depressing Melbourne winter in a house that, typically for Australia, was not properly heated. The result was that she experienced extended periods of deep discouragement. Later she recounted that she could not "bear" the "inactivity," "fretted in spirit over it," and felt the darkness gather around her. She questioned whether it had ever been her duty to "come to this far-off country" and "deeply regretted having crossed the broad waters."[40] Furthermore, she reported that she had spent "many sleepless hours of the night . . . in going over our experience since we left America for Australia."[41] Worn out by lack of sleep, she at times "felt very much depressed."[42] Nevertheless, she willed herself not to be despondent and chose to look at the experience positively. In 1892, in the midst of the discouraging situation and in spite of being unable to "explain why or how," she desperately wanted to understand that somehow her being in Australia was "a part of the Lord's great plan" for the good of Australia, America, "and for my good."[43] She believed God had His hand over it all, and that was a conviction she clung to. But it wasn't always easy to maintain her hold on that conviction, and as the problems at Battle Creek loomed larger and darker in the mid-1890s, she was as sure as she ever could be in the deep recesses of her inner self that her being in Australia was a mistake, the result of a mistake, and that the blame for her plight lay squarely with General Conference president O. A. Olsen.

At the end of 1896, just before Olsen stepped aside from the presidency, she attempted to explain what she saw behind the desire to have her go to Australia in 1891. Her letter indicates that in times of difficulty she was still processing the fact that she was in the southern climes. "I have not, [previously] I think, revealed the entire workings that led me here to Australia," she commented. Lamenting that Olsen would probably "never fully understand the matter," she affirmed forcefully that "the Lord was not in our leaving America. He did not reveal that it was his will . . . did not plan this . . . but let you all move after your own imaginings."[44] Observing that not a person in Battle Creek in 1891 really understood the position in which she had been placed (hinting at her financial embarrassment), she said there was much "haggling over matters" (referring, it seems, to what she believed it was her right to receive by way of fair royalties). The "burdens" she had had to bear that others should have shared with her, she recalled, "nearly cost me my life."[45]

By 1896, she was sure that the Lord had really wanted to have her and her son and her staff "remain in America." "We were very much needed at the heart of the work, and had your spiritual perception discerned the true situation, you would never have consented to the movements made," she lamented to Olsen. In hindsight, Ellen White perceived that there was a "great willingness to have us leave"—particularly, it seems by "those who were weary of the testimonies borne." "Relief was felt by many" she alleged, although not so much by Olsen himself. Ellen White felt so alone on these issues because there was no one she dared to speak to about it. She felt "that no one would discern the matter in all its bearings." Her separation from America and from Battle Creek "was to let men have their own will and way" and "the result is before you." She considered the fact that E. J. Waggoner had been sent off to England because people felt uncomfortable with him and wanted him out of the way to be another vivid example of the problem at Battle Creek, where "the power of dictation over the conscience of others" had been assumed.[46]

Mrs. White had no illusion about the added burdens she had to carry. Being in Australia had increased her workload immeasurably. It expanded the amount of writing she had to do as she rushed each month to prepare large packets of mail and other communications to send by steamer. It impoverished her, because the needs around her were always greater than her income, and the reluctance of the publishing authorities to promote her books deprived her of royalty income. Above all, it set back her book writing project by years, because she had to attend to more immediate, more urgent problems all the time. As she considered the matter at the end of 1896, coming to Australia seemed all just a big mistake.

If Olsen had been a different kind of leader, it would not have happened, she said, laying the blame squarely at his door. "Had you stood in the right position the move would not have been made at that time. The Lord would have worked for Australia by other means," and a "strong influence" would have been maintained at Battle Creek. She and Olsen should have stood "shoulder to shoulder" in order to create "a healthful atmosphere to be felt in all our conferences."It was not the Lord who "devised" her Australian sojourn, she declared categorically. Rather, it was the "result of man's devising." She reminded the General Conference president that she had written to him at the time about her view that God had really designed that they should work together, but he had not recognized its importance.[47] "If ever then you had discerned the matter, and said, I must have you, or I dare not stand in this position [as General Conference president], we would have answered the call. Had you said, I cannot bear these responsibilities alone, we would have responded, and returned." She concluded emphatically, "The sum of the matter is proved, and its figures are before you. We are here." In words tinged with frustration and perhaps just a touch of bitter regret, she added, "I do not suppose I shall ever revisit America, I shall be seventy years old next November. . . . I desire quietude.

And yet here I am in Australia with funds low, and straining every nerve and muscle to establish the work here. What will be our future destiny no man can know."[48]

We have related the background to how Ellen White viewed her Australian sojourn in some detail, because of the importance of its connection to her oft-repeated and provocative statements during this period that she did not recognize decisions of the General Conference as representing the "voice of God." She had gone to Australia without a clear personal sense of duty but with a willingness to accept the judgment of her fellow leaders at the General Conference. But her experience there seemed so wrong and so painful and so financially disastrous for her (as noted previously, it was no small thing not to be able to pay for grocery items and to have to run up her account with her long-suffering grocer for six months) that she knew it to be a decided mistake. She felt that her own conscience had been "bound" by denominational administrators. Now she knew from experience that "no man is a proper judge of another man's duty."[49] "If I knew it was the voice of God," she had written in 1891, "I would go." As she looked at things later through the prism of her experience in the colonies down under, it came home to her in a highly personal and costly way that what she had heard from the General Conference was not the voice of God. On the other hand, theologically, in the larger perspective and in less distressed, more reflective moments, Ellen White was able to see that in God's overall sovereign providence, good would eventually come from the experience. But this lessened the sting only a little and certainly did not diminish the issue—that a word from the General Conference was not the voice of God. Her writings and her expressions on this particular theme were undoubtedly shaped and colored emotionally by the intensity and the pain of her own personal experience.

PERSONAL TROUBLES WITH THE PUBLISHERS

Mrs. White directed many of the strongest letters she wrote during this period to the leadership of the church's publishing program. The litany of protests was long, because, on a principled basis, she objected strenuously to much that was happening in the church's publishing arm—and it reflected more than just her own personal experience. She argued that the marketing policy adopted by the publishing house in Battle Creek in an attempt to reverse its financial losses by pushing onto the Adventist market cheaper and more popular books that door-to-door salespeople found easier to sell was wrong-headed. She also objected to the pressure to reduce royalties to authors in order to increase the margins needed to operate the publishing business in the black, something that she considered as amounting to "highway robbery," and she thought the managers' attempts to pit one author against another in order to reduce royalty rates was nothing other than "fraud."

She also protested against the church's publishing houses taking in "commercial" non-religious print jobs to achieve economic sustainability. When fire destroyed the Review and Herald publishing plant in 1902, the first resolution of the board after the event was that they not resume doing commercial work.[50] Ellen White recognized, however, that because of the financial realities at the moment, the publishing houses might not survive without such work, and that in at least one way, doing commercial print jobs fit the mission of the church in that it provided opportunities to witness to people in the business community who were not Adventists. But there were complications. If there were scheduling conflicts between the commercial jobs and the in-house religious work, usually the external customer was given priority. That, she argued, was wrong. But the production managers at the publishing houses found the counsel to give priority to church work difficult to implement, particularly if they had already agreed with the commercial client upon deadlines for the delivery of the work. The content of the commercial work was also a concern. Ellen White insisted that at the least, the commercial jobs should always be consistent with the religious mission of the publishing house.

Ellen White vigorously disapproved of the publishing houses' attempts to retain skilled managers and key production people by paying them market rates—often double the wage of ordinary pastors. She protested strongly the injustice thus done to pastors and other church employees, who at that very time were having their wages reduced because of the financial difficulties both in Australia and elsewhere. The printing plant in Battle Creek had become too big, and the need for large buildings to house it all and to create a favorable "impression" in the business world was out of keeping with the spirit of the denomination. (By the end of the 1890s, the Battle Creek plant had become the largest and best-equipped publishing plant in the state of Michigan, consisting of a four-story building encompassing 80,000 square feet of floor space with 275 employees.)[51] Many foremen were not Adventists, and according to the estimate of General Conference president George A. Irwin, approximately 80 percent of the annual sales income of half a million dollars came from commercial non-religious production.[52]

Ellen White protested loudest of all about the lack of spirituality of the managers, about the harsh dictatorial attitudes they manifested toward their workers, and about their appalling employment practices on the factory floor. On every hand she saw only the philosophy of secular business, driven only by its rationale of economic survival. It appears that this goal had permeated the entire enterprise, corrupting the religious dimensions and the core mission of the publishing program. And, as she stated repeatedly, the administrators deliberately resisted her advice and counsel because they had become skeptical of her prophetic authority.

The attempt to consolidate the various church publishing plants into a unified whole in order to achieve more efficient economies of scale and at the same time reduce the debilitating competition that was emerging between them also met with Ellen White's complete and utter condemnation on moral and religious grounds. She regarded it as a diabolical plot of the devil and considered that those who fostered and promoted the idea were unquestionably in league with Satan, though they might not know it. In her view, it was not only bad business practice but also a policy that would result in the managers at Battle Creek having absolute control over editorial content and that this would stifle completely any new voice or new response to the Spirit. Furthermore, it would more sharply curtail the ability of the local plants to respond flexibly to local needs.

The general tenor of the severe and persistent rebukes from Ellen White, which reached their crescendo in the late 1890s, gives the impression of someone shouting and shaking her finger as vigorously as she could, trying to make herself heard and understood all the way from Australia. Eventually, her warnings and objections resulted in major personnel changes at headquarters, although much later than she had urged. Among the men disconnected from the publishing and/or treasury work were Archibald Henry, Harmon Lindsay, Frank Belden, Captain Clement Eldridge, Leroy Nicola, and Henry Kellogg, and Ellen White was positive that others should also have been let go. These dismissals resulted in much bitter feeling and even led for a while to the floating of a countersuit for libel and unfair pay practices.

In attempts to redress the situation, the church instigated numerous weeks of prayer, scheduled revival meetings among the apprentices and factory hands, and considered a program for the proper training of apprentices. In 1897, a comprehensive review of human resource management practices at the Battle Creek publishing house, which involved a panel of three talking to every employee in the factory, led to a more comprehensive understanding of the reforms that needed to be implemented—as did another review in 1899. But not until the Review plant burned down in 1902 and the work relocated to Washington, D.C., was the church able to reform the publishing program completely and set it up on a basis that more fully met her expectations.[53]

But the problems were not just at Battle Creek. It seemed the whole church system had become more or less infected with the commercial spirit of the time. In 1899, for example, W. W. Prescott, who was president of the tiny publishing enterprise in England in addition to his other church leadership responsibilities, wrote several letters that strenuously protested W. C. White's heavy-handed business practices and what Prescott considered to be his unjust, harsh, and demanding attempts to manipulate, control, and dominate others. At the time, W. C. White was the manager of his mother's publishing interests and apparently was also representing the Bible Echo publishing house in Australia. Prescott resigned his chairmanship in protest at the soured relationships that developed between the press in Great Britain and the church's publishing houses in America and Australia.[54]

On the other hand, in keeping with the thesis of broadening the concept of "time and place" as a way of understanding her communications about publishing problems, we need to consider still another dimension. It is clear that much of the criticism and highly wrought language that Ellen White directed at the publishing work through her letters and manuscripts was colored to some extent by her own frustrations and what she had experienced at the hands of the publishing managers. It would seem that the problems caused by church publishing policy mingled in her mind with the ongoing attitude of resistance both to theology and to her influence and prophetic role. Merging with the difficulties arising from her personal financial distress, they eventually all became of one piece.

Already in 1890, the year before leadership approached her about going to Australia, Ellen White had experienced deep frustration with the publishing personnel of the church. The reluctance of the publishing house managers, the state tract societies, and the canvassing agents (door-to-door salespeople) to promote the sale of *The Great Controversy* (published in 1884 as volume four of the Spirit of Prophecy series and revised in 1888) distressed her greatly. She believed deeply that the themes of this book needed to be read and grasped by church members and by the public at large. It was "special light"—vital information necessary to interpret correctly the developments occurring in society around them and to prepare the saints for the end times. She had invested three thousand dollars (equivalent to four years of her salary) to enlarge the book. Not only did she own the plates, she had paid for the publishing expenses herself, but she received only twelve-and-a-half cents per copy in royalties.

Then, she noted, "our people [the canvassing leaders?] shoved in the *Bible Readings*," a cheaper book that was much easier for the door-to-door salespeople to sell. (The publishing house had already recouped its development costs on this product, which originally had been a periodical.) As a result, nearly every canvasser dropped *The Great Controversy,* and it lay on the shelves "scarcely touched" for almost two years. Mrs. White argued that the salespeople should have been trained to handle both books so that *Bible Readings* would not be so "all absorbing." The fact that the information in her book was not being read, "burdened" her "beyond expression," and she interpreted the action of the administrators as a deliberate attempt to sideline her. "I have to confess that I have not felt that my work has been understood or appreciated." How could they so easily "come in and close the door to the very special light for this very time?" And she had waited a long time for the situation to be remedied! What hurt her most was that she knew her publishers tended to deal with her "as though I was the one to be enriched," and therefore they tended to view her projects primarily as commercial products. "This they have done," she said, "because their understanding is darkened."[55]

It is true that royalty rates often figured largely in her letters. After all, it was an issue that came very close to home for her. She needed the royalties to help recoup her investment. Furthermore, she also desperately needed the income to enable her to contribute to the development of the church and to pay off some of the loans she had taken (at 7 percent interest) in order to donate to important new church projects. "I am going deeper into debt," she anguished to Olsen, and because nothing was changing, she figured that she would probably have to "take my books in my own hands." Her sons wanted to do something to help but felt constrained to hold their peace because they feared they would be "charged with having selfish interest." Ellen White was in a serious financial bind and could not even obtain a loan in order to buy back her own books from the publishers.

She had considered many approaches to promoting and selling the books herself. For a time she thought about doing the marketing herself, shipping boxes of her books to camp meetings at her own expense and employing her own agents to sell them—in effect bypassing the canvassers and retaining the profits herself "after all expense is met." It had become a necessity, she explained, to "plan and devise" and then "change my plans and devise again" just to see how she could meet her everyday operating expenses. Eventually she declared to Olsen, "I refuse to live in this way any longer." Worrying about it all robbed her of sleep. "What am I to do, Elder Olsen?" she exclaimed in frustration. "I have no rest day or night in spirit."[56] It was at this time, in the midst of these perplexities, that arrangements were made with the non-Adventist religious publisher Fleming H. Revell to produce the twelve-chapter *Steps to Christ.* Supportive ministerial friends at the 1891 Harbor Springs meetings had suggested the idea. It was hoped that a wider circulation of the work could be achieved in this way. The venture was successful, and beginning in 1892 the volume quickly went through several printings, but in 1896, pressure from the church's publishing authorities persuaded her to transfer the rights back to the church.[57] Publishing affairs were complicated and stressful.

Foreshadowing the intensifying conflict to come and warning administration, she asserted, "If my brethren allow me to carry this burden longer in this way I will certainly know that God does not lead [both] them and me. One of us is not moving in God's order." Having made her case, she declared, "I will say no more on this point. But be assured I shall not much longer wait for my brethren in positions of trust to do their duty." And then she warned, "I shall not let the matter rest."[58] Eight years later, she confided to an old-time pioneer friend, "Just at this point his satanic majesty was in the management of my books published at the Review and Herald Office."[59]

The problem still remained unsolved when Ellen White was settling into Australia. It had, in fact, become worse, because her financial plight had grown more desperate. Church projects, such as the fledgling Avondale College, demanded assistance. Congregations had to build new houses of worship. Causes such as camp meetings and evangelistic campaigns required support; denominational employees' salaries had to be paid; and students needed scholarship money. She also felt obligated to entertain the constant streams of visitors who passed through her home. And to make matters worse, the deep economic recession affecting America had rippled its way across to Australia, causing severe hardship and cutting church income drastically.[60] Ellen White felt the impact of the economic collapse over an extended period.[61]

Against this background of poverty and extreme financial distress, the proposal at headquarters to reduce her royalties from twenty cents a copy to ten cents a copy seemed indeed to be outrageous robbery. It brought from her the strongest of protests.[62] And she was not the only one affected. Her son Edson White, her nephew Frank Belden, and her colleagues W. H. Littlejohn and Uriah Smith all had been dealt with, she felt, unjustly. The publishing house had pitted one author against another in an attempt to force them to accept lower royalty payments. "Anyone . . . who would not be robbed without making a protest" found themselves treated as trouble-makers, she reported, and members of boards whom it was suspected would not go along with the "exaction and double dealing" were not invited to the meetings that discussed and approved the plans.[63]

Ellen White had reluctantly agreed to accept less royalty, but on condition of the publishing leaders' assurance that they would vigorously promote both *The Great Controversy* and *Patriarchs and Prophets,* thus compensating her by increasing the volume of sales. But the Review broke its promises. *Bible Readings* was selling well and more easily, and management decided to keep the book in the field. Ellen White felt the change of policy bitterly. She believed she had been lied to and became convinced that those on the book committee were fraudulent.[64] "By cutting off this revenue," she argued, "men were cutting off the possibilities of establishing new plants in all parts of the world."[65] The way that publishing leaders had treated her over royalties left her feeling extremely humiliated. And she knew that others had suffered similarly. Some authors, it seems, had actually found themselves in debt to the publishing houses because management had persuaded them to sign over their royalties to help cover the cost of publishing the manuscript. The fraudulent obtaining of copyright for the Edson White book *The Gospel Primer* also cut close to home. It likewise deprived the developing church in the southern states of much needed income.[66]

The financial downturn in the economy led to reductions not only in operating allocations in every area, but also in salaries as well. It struck W. C. White particularly hard since he had to support part of his family back in the United States. His mother tried to appeal the decision, given the particular difficulties he faced. In the light of the increases in salary given to the managers of the publishing houses to retain their services, the decision seemed perverted to her, and as already noted, she protested in the strongest language. She knew from intimate personal acquaintance how difficult it was to work in new fields without adequate financial income or support. At the end of the decade, she was still feeling the pinch. "On every hand we are cramped for means," she wrote to a donor in America who was offering to lend her money to invest in developing the church in Australia. Ellen White agreed to pay him 5 percent interest. "Any money you can spare will be gladly received . . . for some time I have been greatly straightened for want for means." She noted that her salary and what she received from her books "does not come in fast enough to meet the demands." By 1900, she was in debt to various organizations and individuals in America to the amount of almost ten thousand dollars, and she owed various people and entities in Australia nearly five thousand dollars, most of the debt undertaken to promote her publishing activities and various branches of the church. "This will show you how Sister White is getting rich," she concluded with a wry sense of humor. But she protested that she did not worry over the matter. "The work must go."[67]

In truth, however, she did worry frequently. And as she reports in numerous other places, she lost much sleep to anxiety about how to stretch herself to cover the many commitments she felt obliged to assume. To some degree, it was natural that she should feel that leadership did not fully identify with her needs in Australia. In certain ways this was also a natural tension in the intense competition for scarce resources. The demands of the work in England, in Europe, and in South Africa were also very great, and church employees were crying out for more assistance in many places. But Ellen White felt as if denominational administration was ignoring her. She complained to her old friend Haskell about being left "high and dry." "Thousands of dollars have been appropriated in Europe that we greatly needed in this field. Will they [the people in Battle Creek] ever take it in?" she wrote—meaning, will they ever understand the needs of the mission field in Australia?[68] By year's end, she was still in financial difficulties, and she told Irwin that because of the debt, there was no way she could afford to travel to the 1899 General Conference Session in the United States.[69] It was not until 1899 or early 1900, that, under the continuing pressure of her relentless criticism, the new management of the publishing work sought to reverse some of the earlier decisions and pay royalties that were in arrears.

Management at Battle Creek, of course, needed to balance the various demands for resources, which meant that they had to negotiate through the competing interests and wrestle with complex financial perplexities. They were individuals who seemingly were trying to do the best they could with the information they had and within the constraints of the time and the personnel resources available. As a result, marketing policies and publishing house competition became very murky. Hindsight shows that undoubtedly, some decisions they made in their attempts to get out of their difficulties were faulty. And the domineering attitude manifested by some business managers and treasurers who were aggressively promoting the interests of their own organizations, were not appropriate for a church entity. They were able to reverse some. Others they couldn't. But the overriding concern for Ellen White was that the church's publishing program was not an ordinary business motivated simply by the bottom line. It was first and foremost a mission enterprise, and business must of necessity come second. But it was through the framework of her own intense personal frustrations, painful circumstances, and sleepless nights that Ellen White viewed the unacceptable practices in the publishing houses. The intensity of the language with which she painted a picture of corruption and malpractice in Battle Creek reflected not only her protest for the rights of others who had been wronged, but to a significant degree her own experience of injustice.

Seeing through the clouded prism of insomnia

Another significant dimension of Ellen White's experience in Australia that helps us understand the language she employed during the 1890s is her chronic insomnia. During much of her life, she had difficulty getting regular sleep. Whether this problem became worse during the 1890s is not clear, but the letters and manuscripts clearly indicate that insomnia was a persistent health problem for her and a dominant pattern of her experience in Australia. It is not uncommon, of course, even for people who have slept well throughout their lives to develop insomnia in their seventies. In any case, many of her letters refer to the fact that she had slept for only one or two or sometimes three hours, and that she had awakened anywhere between 12:30 and 3:00 A.M. in the morning. It seems that for her, a full night's sleep was a rare event.

Sometimes she could not get to sleep easily because her mind was active during the night that followed an evening preaching appointment. For example, in early 1898, she told her friend Ellen Gotzian that after speaking at the Ashfield church in Sydney she left before the meeting closed and tried to get to sleep at 11:00 P.M., but her mind had brought to bed with her "the burden of the souls of the church members" in Ashfield. "Oh how my heart ached!" she wrote. "I felt at times in an agony of spirit. I could not obtain sleep until 2:00 am." The next night, after preaching again, this time in a tent, she could not sleep until 1:00 A.M. and then awoke at 3:30 again, this time not because she was burdened but because she was "so grateful to God." She went on to say that she had resolved to give up speaking in the evenings because her mind would not slow down in time for her to get to sleep afterward.[70]

Sometimes the sleeplessness went on for months. "My heart burns with desire to engage more fully in the work, but I find I am not able to do so. For four months I have been unable to obtain sufficient sleep. Last Friday night I passed through the most severe suffering that I have had for years. For months it has been impossible for me to sleep after the hours of twelve, one and two and three o'clock in the morning. I rise at these untimely hours, light my fire, and begin writing. I work the entire day, and often speak three times in the week."[71]

The lack of sleep and the excessive exertion of the week caught up with her on this particular Friday night and brought on physical distress. She experienced what she called "an attack" that caused her severe shortness of breath, her heart skipping beats, and a feeling of such weakness that she could not sit up.[72]

Ellen White was aware of the problems posed by these episodes and this pattern of life. They seemed to be a recurring part of her life. Was the temperament she had inherited as further shaped by the pressures of life and work to blame in part? She worked at managing her sleep troubles better.[73] She consciously tried to avoid unnecessary anxieties and worries so that she could sleep better. But in spite of her efforts, she had little success, and she often lay awake with her mind churning away over problems, though she also recognized that lack of sleep tended to make things look worse than they were.

If getting more wholesome sleep was a frequent concern of Ellen White's and was something that she worked at, nevertheless, she also reports that she interpreted much of the interruption as being part and parcel of the distinctive spiritual gift given to her. She regarded "being awakened" as evidence of the Holy Spirit's influencing her. The spiritual nature of the ideas that came to her in such circumstances and the serious nature of the matters and the sense of urgency associated with them were clear evidence to her that these thoughts were "a message from the Lord." In 1902, for example, she commented that night after night she had been "awakened at eleven, twelve, and one o'clock with a message from the Lord." Her response was to "arise at once and begin to write, fearing that if I do not, I shall forget the instruction given me."[74] Waiting until morning just would not work for her.

In 1901, Mrs. White alluded to her concern for her son Edson because of his overwork and difficulty sleeping. She counseled him to "preserve" his "vitality," going on to note that "when one becomes very weary and unable to sleep, there is danger that he will not look at things in a right light." In the darkness of night, when the mind focuses on the problems one faces, they seem to grow larger and sometimes present themselves in exaggerated detail. She had also written to Kellogg about his sleep patterns a few years earlier: "Give yourself proper time to sleep. They who sleep give nature time to build up and repair the weary waste of the organism."[75]

Insomnia was a problem that Ellen White faced continually, and it is a context that we need to keep in mind as we hear her dramatic portrayal of circumstances in Battle Creek. It must be reiterated that this is not to say there were no such problems in Battle Creek or that she didn't need to address them. But this factor in her circumstances helps us to understand the perspective that so consumed her and burdened her spirit at times.

Other background factors could also help us interpret the dark hues of this particular strand of Ellen White's writings. One is that she was a spiritually and emotionally sensitive person. It was her nature to experience things intensely and to communicate them as she felt them, even when preaching. At times she remonstrated with herself about it, on one occasion, confiding to her son, "I cannot stand before a congregation but the burden comes on me with overwhelming force . . . and I carry the burden which others cannot realize. It seems to consume me. If I can avoid these pressing agonizing thoughts in behalf of souls I shall preserve my strength better."[76]

Second, some scholars in the field of communication studies have reported that there are documentable differences in the communication styles and patterns of men and women. While generalizations can capture commonalities, they can also obscure differences, and stereotyping is neither helpful nor desirable. Nevertheless, the studies have given rise to the question of whether women writers may be more inclined to give priority to expressing the affective aspects of matters under consideration. The astute use of hyperbole and overstatement may well aid in communicating the dimensions and seriousness of a problem.[77]

Does taking into account the factors that may have shaped Ellen White's communication style allow us to place the language she used more precisely in its context? Are there insights to be gained by taking into consideration this dimension of Ellen White's humanness? Did her personality and makeup undergird and facilitate her unique gift of spiritual insight? Did these aspects of her mode of communication enhance her effectiveness as a handmaiden of the Lord? Does awareness of them help the reader to understand and interpret the relational and affective aspects of her writing?

Prescott, who was aware of Ellen White's spiritual sensitivity and understood her intensity of feeling, was also a member of many church boards and committees and understood the problems they were wrestling with and the complexities they faced. When he was visiting Australia and Ellen White knew with certainty his spiritual sensitivity and understanding, she ventured to share with him some of her anxieties. She wrote, "I was so troubled that in conversation with Brother Prescott I told him my feelings. Both he and W. C. White tried to dissipate my fears; they presented everything in as favorable a light as possible. But instead of encouraging me, these words alarmed me. If these men cannot see the outcome of affairs, I thought, how hopeless the task of making them see at Battle Creek. The thought struck to my heart like a knife."[78]

Sometimes she felt intensely because she disagreed strongly with administrative decisions, such as the appointments made by those entrusted with the task of leadership, and she vigorously expressed her opinion from the sidelines. For example, her comments about the appointment of the president of the British field in 1898 are highly critical. "When I learned that Brother [H. E.] Robinson and his wife had been sent to England, I said, 'It is a mistake.' He has not the qualifications that would be of use and benefit in Europe; for unless he can rule, he would ruin." Her comments about Robinson's wife were even more cutting. She noted bluntly, "His wife's influence would be a very wrong one. There is no light in her. She is a body of darkness, a channel through whom the enemy works, and that continuously." Concluding her observations with some amazement, she asked, "Who placed him in power? Why did they place him in that position?" And then she sympathetically commiserated with Waggoner, who would have to work with him: "The Lord help and strengthen you against all such influences."[79] Sometimes such forceful statements could express a spirit of bewilderment and frustration perhaps not meant for public circulation. Could such letters, sent to close friends, perhaps reflect a need to "let off steam"—something normal and understandable? This letter to E. J. Waggoner reacting to the appointment of his new president appears to be just such a case.

Yet another dimension of Ellen White's personal experience in Australia involves the relative levels of her emotional resources. It is clear that the threshold of her sensitivity, and therefore of her ability to cope adequately with distressing news and discomforting situations, rose and fell with the state of her physical health, her age, and also probably because she was a normal human being struggling with the effects of inadequate sleep. On some occasions she seemed to stress out easily, surprising even her domestic staff. A clear instance of a low threshold of sensitivity to distressing news, for example, occurred in 1894, when one of her helpers asked if she had read a two-part series of articles on the dangers of extremism that were written by W. H. Littlejohn and published in the *Review*.[80]

Viewed from our distance time-wise from the 1840s and in the light of today's journalistic expectations, we would consider these articles to be a carefully worded, discreet piece of writing acknowledging that in its earliest years the Adventist movement had experienced some fanaticism, as have all young movements. Littlejohn had noted that at times Adventists had taken some odd stands, such as the early opposition to any form of organization, resistance to the need for education, and a position against voting. However, in all these things Adventism had matured and developed beyond such inadequate perspectives.

The two articles provoked a strong response in Ellen White, perhaps because she had been so closely linked with the pioneers anonymously referred to in the articles and had a large emotional investment in the period. Or perhaps the articles had such a large emotional impact because they came at a time when she and her colleagues were emotionally drained from their struggle to establish the credibility of the Adventist church in a skeptical and irreligious Australia. To one who was already vulnerable, they appeared to have the potential to undo much of her hard work. In these circumstances, she suffered an emotional and physical collapse when she read the articles.[81]

During the night after she read them, she felt herself descend into "an agony of distress both of mind and body" and she feared that she would not live. For the following two days, her "feelings were so intense" she could not write or do anything. The second night, also, she later reported, she "felt crushed as a cart beneath the sheaves."[82] Some considerable time after she had recovered, she responded with a rebuke to Littlejohn, saying that he had not presented the full picture by not emphasizing "the fact that the power of God worked in connection with their labors even though they had made some mistakes." And she bemoaned the fact that she would now have "to put forth labor" to call up the circumstances that would vindicate the pioneers. "I would not for my right arm have given to the world that which you have written," she said.[83]

On another occasion, the problem of jealousies and difficult relationships in the North Fitzroy Church in inner Melbourne caused her such intense anxiety that she was again physically sick. "Some things have been urged upon my mind about which I felt so deeply, and suffered such agony of soul that I became very sick. I could not sleep through the night for more than two hours after this matter was brought before me; for I could not see in what way it could be treated. But light came to me in the night season."[84]

Frequently during the night, Ellen White woke up because her mind was, in modern parlance, "stressed out" by worries or anxious thoughts about problems in the denomination. Sometimes she would try to go back to sleep, but most times as she lay in bed, the issues churned around and around, and she found it easier to get up and write. Often the churning itself gave insights into the problems, while at other times she sensed that the Lord was working through such thoughts to help her see things more clearly. And at still other times, she had the clear sense that she was elsewhere in dream or by the spirit attending meetings, speaking to gatherings, or listening in on committee discussions. But through all this the worrying and the anxieties gave her much agony because she felt so keenly, so intensely, about things.

Recalling her experience following the Minneapolis General Conference, she wrote, "I was able to sleep but a few hours. I was writing all hours of the morning, frequently rising at 2:00 and 3:00 a.m. and relieving my mind by writing upon the subjects that were presented before me."[85] In 1899, as the looming Kellogg problem began to create much anxiety, she noted to Irwin, "I cannot sleep past two o'clock a.m., and I may as well take up my pen as to be so full of thought."[86]

The pattern was a common one. "The intensity I have felt as I have written these things can never be expressed," she commented to Irwin.[87] "Morning after morning I awake at 2:00 a.m. and often at 12 p.m. [midnight] . . . My spirit burns within me as these things are revealed to me and I cry to God in an agony of remorse. . . . At this time above all others the paths of life are beset with perils that I cannot find language to describe," she related to Prescott.[88] "As I consider the past history of our people in Battle Creek, I suffer intense agony of soul." To the young Camden Lacey, she commented, "There are many things to write of; but I have such an intensity of feeling that it is consuming me. May God help me is my prayer."[89]

Her "intensity of feeling" led to an intensity of expression and a heightened sense of injustice, frustration, and fear of the eventual outcome if the policies or people did not change. As noted previously, much in her writing from this period echoes the kind of language that the eighth-century B.C. prophets used. They wrote in a way that was forceful and filled with passion because of perceived injustices and wrongdoing. The parallel becomes complicated, however, because generally we do not have many responses from the people who were being addressed by the Old Testament prophets. In the situation in Battle Creek, however, we have an abundance of letters and other documents that portray how individuals responded to her letters and the reasons they gave for some of the practices Ellen White rebuked—practices that, in some cases, the church has now accepted as normal. Realizing the intensity of emotion she experienced helps to provide a framework for us to understand the communications in their "time and place."

The conditional prophecy paradigm

A further helpful dimension to consider in seeking to understand this strand of Ellen White's 1890s writing is that, at least on some occasions, she realized that she was often addressing what might be or what could be rather than what actually was the case. This pattern of portraying things in a worst-case scenario was a common practice of biblical prophets. As Ellen White pondered the problems, thought about the long-term implications of decisions, or was taken in spirit into committee discussions, she often saw potential outcomes of the decisions almost as a present reality when it was not yet reality. "This anticipation of terrible difficulties need not be," she commented to Olsen in the run-up to the 1897 General Conference.[90]

On another occasion she declared, "I present the above picture for your consideration, for it has been presented to me as a representation of the state of things which Satan is seeking shall exist at Battle Creek."[91] Undoubtedly, much of what Ellen White protests against at Battle Creek in the 1890s concerned actions that had already occurred. But one must keep in mind that much of what she wrote was also penned as word portrayals of worst-case scenarios—what the situation would be like if things continued unchecked. Clearly, in some situations, her communications were presented with the conditional element not stated but implied or sometimes simply assumed, which is similar to what we often observe in Scripture. Readers, therefore, need to exercise discrimination in the judgments they make about individuals mentioned in her letters and about the actions that had been or might have been taken. At times, the distinction was not clear to Ellen White herself. Sometimes she wrote out her impressions and thoughts and then felt that she could not, or should not, send them. On other occasions she was moved to hold her letters and send them later. Sometimes their arrival was timely, but occasionally they came too late. But in all cases it is helpful to try to establish what response the recipient gave to the communication received and what changes were or were not implemented because of certain circumstances.

It is also clear that when Ellen White perceived deliberate resistance to her communications or sensed a lack of confidence in her authority, the next time she wrote, she tended to express herself more pointedly. She "turned up the heat" to overcome the resistance and to bring about the desired outcome. Sometimes it worked, but sometimes the recipients responded by becoming more stubborn. Occasionally, they sought to explain themselves by pointing to the circumstances.

The problem of apparent contradictions

During this period what seemed to bother Ellen White most about the resistance to the exercise of her influence that she encountered from such men as Uriah Smith, George Butler, Archibald Henry, Harmon Lindsay, and even John Harvey Kellogg was their claim that they had lost confidence in the reliability or validity of what she wrote. They blamed their waning confidence, in turn, on the inconsistency of the counsel she gave.

During the period leading up to and immediately following 1888, for example, they claimed that she had changed her position on the law in Galatians, first advocating one viewpoint and then the other. To a mind-set that regarded a prophet's utterances to be "infallible" or dogmatically true for every situation, the apparent shifting of Ellen White's position presented genuine problems.

She herself stressed that the "time and place" principle must always be considered in identifying and understanding the principles in what she wrote. In this setting, the "time and place" principle is really another way of saying that, to a significant degree, her prophetic ministry was conditioned by pragmatic factors. Ellen White clearly had a flexible understanding of what she wrote and of the guidance that she gave to her colleagues in the church. What firm and unchanging principles underlay the flexibility or the pragmatic application then?

Barry Oliver's observation about the core principle unifying all that she offered by way of counsel on church organization leading up to, and during, the structural reforms of 1901 is instructive and may serve as a useful illustration. He notes that she did not have any fixed view of the particular form of organization that the church should adopt. With regard to administrative practice, she could at one time advocate one position or a particular strategy and then at another time a different method that might even be an opposing strategy. The reason for this, he observes, is that where there was no clear moral principle involved and where the matter concerned practical implementation at an operational level, the guiding concept was that whatever action "best facilitated the achieving of the mission of the church at that particular time and place" was the right one. This flexible, pragmatic approach was necessary, because circumstances and conditions constantly change. The role of the prophetic voice was to read and understand the times and then offer guidance in particular contexts. Of necessity, it often required a humble and teachable spirit on the part of those exercising the gift of administration. Logic there was, but consistency there might not always be—at least at the level of governance by policy and precedent. But at the level of governance to achieve the mission of the church in the best and most effective manner given the time and place, Ellen White was consistent.[92]

Those who operated on the basis of precedent could find fault with her, and unfortunately, if they didn't have a submissive spirit, they would find themselves in difficulty. The apparent inconsistencies and what might appear to be flip-flops could become stumbling blocks. This, apparently, was most difficult for the rational and objective business types involved in leadership. Oliver suggests that this is the most reasonable way of interpreting what otherwise would appear to be irreconcilable conflicts in the kinds of counsel she gave from time to time.

For example, she could vigorously urge the need to pay workers fairly and equitably and become seriously upset at the injustice of publishing house employees not receiving fair remuneration. The core principle of distributive justice was the underlying consideration when it came to payment of employees in the church's various institutions. This was intuitive with her. On this basis, therefore, she could urge that Avondale principal C. B. Hughes be granted continuing salary during the year-end holiday period. It was something he was entitled to on the principle of justice. How could he not be paid during his holiday?

On the other hand, just a few years later, as the Sydney Sanitarium was being established, she criticized Dr. Edgar Caro and his colleague, Mr. Sharman, for drawing salary during their annual holiday period, because the institution's finances were in a desperate state and the cost could not be afforded. Furthermore, Sharman had shown himself to be somewhat of a dilatory worker. Perhaps if he had worked with more energy, she may have felt differently. But the overriding principle involved what was best for the survival of the institution and the accomplishment of its mission at a particularly critical period of its development.

The same hermeneutical principle may explain the tension between the positions she espoused in another matter. She insisted that writers of books for the church should receive an appropriate level of royalty because they had invested significantly in the product and their intellectual effort should be remunerated so they could continue to produce other such works for the benefit of the church and thus contribute to the development of its various causes. On the other hand, she did not feel Kellogg's claim of patent rights for his health-food inventions was valid because the foods had been produced on behalf of, and for, the church and because the need of funds for Union College at the time was critical to its very existence. Without the income from the bakery, it might not survive at all.

Ellen White's counsel about printing commercial work in the church's publishing houses at first seemed to be that it was not appropriate under any circumstances. But her later counsel on the matter seemed to be more pragmatic. The right kind of commercial jobs might actually be acceptable and even beneficial because they would provide the opportunity to meet and witness to people from the business world. The qualifications were that the commercial work must not take priority over the church's own publications, and the content of the material to be printed must be appropriate. The publishing houses could not have stayed afloat in their early years without the commercial work, and their survival so they could fulfill their mission was the overriding consideration.

This hermeneutic of pragmatism, focused as it was on whatever would best facilitate the achievement of the church's mission, also provides part of the paradigm for understanding why the church has come to accept some of the things that stirred Ellen White's protests in the 1890s. In the circumstances of the twenty-first century, the leadership of the church has apparently decided that such courses or practices enable it to accomplish its mission more effectively. This appears to be true, for example, of the remuneration of church employees; the salary scales used to determine the pay of those who work in the various branches of the church—pastoral, educational, medical, publishing, and so forth—differ. In many places of the world, in fact, such changes are now necessitated by social or legislative environments.

Conclusion

The years between 1888 and 1901 are widely recognized as constituting a unique period in the development of the Seventh-day Adventist Church. Most of the scholarly discussion and analysis of this period has focused on the theological issues that grew out of the 1888 General Conference and their significance for Adventist theology. The process of organizational development that played such an important role during the period has also attracted considerable attention. But understanding the tensions that developed between Ellen White and those responsible for administering and leading the organization has not received as much thought and study.

Ellen White's role is crucial to understanding this critical period of the church's development, because she was so vocal about the problems. Much of the material she wrote during this era takes on a noticeably more somber hue and exhibits a provocative intensity not present to the same degree in what she wrote at other times. We can understand the reason for her passion and intensity better when we adopt a broad interpretive framework that includes consideration of her circumstances at the time she wrote as well as the persons to whom she wrote and the circumstances surrounding the problems they faced. This broad hermeneutic not only allows a more enriched understanding of Ellen White and her charismatic ministry, but also provides helpful new insights into the way that Providence led in the growth and development of the church through a particularly challenging and difficult period.

As we noted at the beginning of our journey with the prophet and these three presidents, this is a believers' study. It is an attempt to understand more fully the role and function of Ellen White's extraordinary prophetic charisma that contributed so much to the survival and growth of Adventism and to the molding of its distinctive shape. For the author, the study has involved careful reading and reflection upon a wide range of correspondence between Ellen White, her colleagues in leadership and ministry, and her family. It has involved also a careful reading of the articles that expressed her concerns in church publications and thoughtful reflection upon the manuscripts that were summaries of the talks and sermons she gave in a wide span of times and places. It is the experience and conviction of the author that as one engages with these documents, listens in on the conversations, feels the passion and conviction, connects events, and observes responses, one cannot help but be impressed that here was a woman whom God gifted and used in truly extraordinary ways—in ways that differed from those He used with other church leaders. Hers was a distinctive call and a unique experience. In these pages, one meets Ellen White as a risk-taker, an innovator, and a powerful, outspoken communicator whose voice carried prophetic authority. The presidents we have studied and the community they led recognized that.

Ellen White's radical commitment to sharing the love of God, her hope in the return of Jesus, and her call to readiness for that event shaped her life and that of her community, inspiring generations to lives of service and witness. The Seventh-day Adventist Church—with its distinctive emphasis, its lifestyle, its institutions, its publications, and its breadth of mission—would not be what it is today without the ministry of this gifted person working in partnership with those who were entrusted with the gifts of administrative skills. Appreciating more fully the colorful patterns in the rich tapestry that is the history of the Adventist Church deepens an appreciation of the mysterious ways of the Providence that led in its development. Such an appreciation also leads to gratitude and a confident hope that the same Spirit of truth who was so distinctly manifested in the ministry of Ellen White will continue to lead the church in fulfilling the gospel commission.

APPENDIX

SUMMARY of FINDINGS of the 1897 COMMITTEE of INVESTIGATION Into the AFFAIRS of the REVIEW and HERALD OFFICE

The major findings of the investigation committee (submitted to the Review board on August 9, 1897) revealed a distressing lack of good human-resource management practices that had led to poor morale among employees. The major issues are listed below:

1. Inadequate payroll and wage scale system

The publishing house did not have a regular system for handling wage increases and promotions. As a result, it tended to deal with granting raises to apprentices and other employees rather erratically and subjectively. Management did not follow through on probationary periods and promised raises, which led to complaints from the apprentices and repeated requests to foremen, who had the power to grant the requests. When finally approved, raises were often not retroactive. Relationships between foremen and employees suffered as a result. The performance review system was not working systematically, which led to a demoralized work force, inefficiency, and incidents of sabotage. By the time of the inspection in July 1897, the new management had completed a wage audit of the entire workforce several weeks previously and felt that the system had been rectified and most problems settled.

2. Technical education and training for apprentices

The publishing house had no systematic approach to ensuring proper training for apprentices. Even board members disagreed on the best approach. At least one advocated self-learning. A good apprentice, this individual felt, would pick up the skills needed through observation and practice. Others felt that direct instruction was necessary and that the foremen in each of the different departments should provide it. Some believed that the Review needed an overall trainer—and perhaps a general chaplain as well. The committee suggested conducting some kind of night school to teach the principles of the printing trade, the theory of electricity, and some aspects of metallurgy. Could Battle Creek College provide such instruction?

3. Cross-training of employees

The publishing house needed cross-trained employees who could move from department to department as required in emergencies. But some apprentices wanted to become specialists in areas in which they could earn more money. Mobility across departments was difficult to achieve, moreover, because of salary differentials granted for different skill sets. Employees were unwilling to take a drop in salary just to learn a new skill in a different department. Managers also had to cope with employee ambitions that were not always easy to deal with. As an extreme example, the "messenger boy" could not be allowed to edit the *Review and Herald*, even if he wanted to.

4. Employee discipline

Relationships between foremen, regular workers, and apprentices had deteriorated to the point at which there had developed "a system of actual terrorism." Many employees were scared of their bosses. The publishing house needed a way to discipline employees who failed in their duty or who made costly mistakes, but achieving "Christian discipline" in the context of deadlines and work pressures was difficult. Apparently, harsh exchanges were common.

5. Promotion opportunities for employees

The system of bringing in outside personnel when vacancies opened disturbed those already working at the Review. Management must consider "promotion from within." But management faced difficulty in finding appropriately qualified employees and sometimes had to recruit non-church members. Staff turnover, with good leadership people being called to other publishing houses, evidently created some problems.

6. Issues of hygiene and cleanliness

A system of using the last hired apprentice as the cleaner for the department needed better supervision. Spitting on the floor and in other inappropriate places was a hygiene problem and particularly distressing to female employees. Janitorial services were inadequate, and some rooms were dusty and unkempt. The night cleaner was apparently ineffective, and the house needed to adopt a better system. Public areas were also untidy and uncared for.

7. Piecework agreements vs. hourly paid work

Difficulties achieving equitable agreements over piecework in some departments led to dissatisfaction among employees and a sense of injustice. The committee felt that it would be more efficient to use the piecework system generally, rather than hourly paid work, but it would require closer supervision. Rates for piecework needed to be equitable for the employee and affordable for the institution. Piecework was not always easy to manage.

8. Production foreman on important church publications

Both management and the investigating committee believed that the production foreman on the weekly *Review* definitely should be a Seventh-day Adventist. The present foreman was not.

9. Employment of non-Adventists

The management should not move in a slash-and-burn manner to remove non-Adventist employees. Rather such individuals should have opportunity to study denominational beliefs. If an employee was overtly hostile to the religious atmosphere that management was endeavoring to create, then he or she should be discharged. The difficulties in managing relationships in this area were challenging, as they have always been. Some non-Adventist employees did not want to convert, because it might be perceived that they were doing so just to keep their job. Sometimes nominal church members had poorer attitudes and work practices than did their non-Adventist colleagues. There was uncertainty about whether "cleaning up the institution" meant discharging non-Adventist personnel. Many on the committee expressed discomfort with this approach unless attempts were first made to properly labor for the employees.

ENDNOTES

Foreword

1. Edward J. Young, *Zondervan Pictoral Bible Dictionary*, ed. Merrill C. Tenney, (Grand Rapids: Zondervan, 1963), s.v. "Prophets," 685.

2. Gerhard von Rad, *Old Testament Theology* (New York: Harper & Row, 1962, 1965), 2:36, 37.

3. Ellen G. White, *Selected Messages* (Washington, DC: Review and Herald®, 1958), 1:32.

4. Abraham J. Heschel, *The Prophets* (New York: Harper Torchbooks, 1962), 1:5.

5. John Goldingay, *Old Testament Theology* (Downers Grove, IL: IVP Academic, 2003–2009), 3:760.

6. Heschel, *The Prophets,* 2:256–259.

7. See George R. Knight, *Angry Saints: Tensions and Possibilities in the Adventist Struggle Over Righteousness by Faith* (Washington, DC: Review and Herald®, 1989), 15–115.

8. Jerry Allen Moon, *W. C. White and Ellen G. White: The Relationship Between the Prophet and Her Son* (Berrien Springs, MI: Andrews University Press, 1993).

Introduction

1. Ellen White's first visionary experience occurred in 1844, not long after the disappointment of her Millerite Advent hopes on October 22, 1844.

2. The term *charisma* is often used to convey the idea of charm, appeal, and a certain allure that attracts followers to a leader. In the context of this work I use the term rather to denote an inspiring quality of leadership that carried in itself a certain appeal and a giftedness in exerting influence effectively so that, with time, it gathered an informal authority. Ellen White understood this giftedness as involving insights and understandings that came from beyond herself. In this sense, early Adventists accepted that she was not only "inspiring" but "inspired" in a technical, theological sense. There is a connectedness and a continuum between the uses of the term.

3. Ellen White's role in doctrinal formation was "confirmation," not "initiation," as George R. Knight points out in *Anticipating the Advent: A Brief History of Seventh-day Adventists* (Boise, ID: Pacific Press®, 1993), 28.

4. In "Charisma, Sectarianism and Institutionalization: Identity Issues in Seventh-day Adventism" (PhD diss., Sydney College of Divinity, 2006), Rick Ferret provides an insightful sociological analysis of the factors that provided the basis for the confidence of early Sabbatarian Adventists in the distinctive charisma evident in Ellen White using Weber's model of charisma and routinization. See particularly chapter 2, 82–136. Ferret points out that his study is not a disparagement of divine involvement in Ellen White's experience, but that "a prophet has neither function nor legitimacy without a willing audience," and the study of the social processes involved is "an attempt to recognize the validity of human experience in legitimizing the charismatic gift" (86). "The source of her visions, dreams and revelations is not the central concern in this study; of more interest is the legitimacy that her followers would afford her due to those extraordinary experiences" (111).

5. Uriah Smith, George Butler, W. C. White, and A. G. Daniells, for example, all needed to grapple with the problem of seeming inconsistencies at times. Francis D. Nichol in *Ellen G. White and Her Critics* (Washington, DC: Review and Herald®, 1951) provides probably the most comprehensive denominational discussion of the dissenters' responses to and interpretations of Ellen White's charisma. Herbert E. Douglass's *Messenger of the Lord* (Boise, ID: Pacific Press®, 1998) provides a more contemporary treatment.

6. A December 1855 meeting was the first formal gathering of Adventist believers to examine in detail and reflect theologically on the phenomenon of Ellen White's visions. The concluding report supported an official authentic status for her. "We regard them [the visions] as coming from God and entirely harmonizing with His written word, we must acknowledge ourselves under obligation to abide by their teachings and be corrected by their admonitions." See Arthur L. White, *Ellen G. White: Messenger to the Remnant* (Washington, DC: Review and Herald®, 1969), 53. Robert Wolfgramm points out that this decision represented "the first in a continuing series of formal, bureaucratic approvals" of her leadership and exercise of her spiritual gift. See "Charismatic Delegitimation in a Sect: Ellen White and Her Critics" (master's dissertation, Chisholm Institute of Technology, 1983), 62.

7. The first general meeting of believers she attended was in 1845. The last General Conference Session she attended was in Washington, D.C., in 1909.

8. In contrast, Catherine Booth (1829–1890), mother of the Salvation Army, and Mother Ann Lee (1736–1784), leader of the earlier Shaker movement, both eventually occupied formally appointed offices in their movements.

9. Her credentials were regarded as "honorary," not by the "laying on of hands by men." See Arthur L. White, *Ellen G. White: The Lonely Years: 1876-1891* (Washington, DC: Review and Herald®, 1984), 3:337; *General Conference Bulletin,* November 27, 1887. Apparently, the Michigan Conference had given her credentials before this.

10. Remuneration for Mrs. White was set at the level of that of a pastor, but she was informally contracted to provide a regular supply of articles and reports for the church's journals and magazines. See E. G. White, letter to O. A. Olsen, May 12, 1895.

11. The term adopted for the leadership of the movement was not "bishop" or "elder," but "president," following the terminology and governance model common to the North American cultural setting in which the movement took root. The eight presidents with whom she worked

and the periods of their leadership of the General Conference of Seventh-day Adventists were John Byington 1863–1865; James White, 1865–1867, 1869–1871, 1874–1880; John Nevins Andrews, 1867–1869; George Ida Butler, 1871–1874, 1880–1888; Ole Andres Olsen, 1888–1897; George A. Irwin 1897–1901, and Arthur G. Daniells, 1901–1922.

12. A detailed schedule of General Conference sessions can be found in the *Seventh-day Adventist Encyclopedia* (Washington, DC: Review and Herald®, 1976), 502. The number of sessions is forty-three if allowance is made for five specially called sessions. Ten General Conference sessions convened between 1887 and 1903, the focus of this study.

13. The 1913 episode is discussed more fully in chapter 10.

14. W. C. White, letter to A. G. Daniells, December 31, 1913. I am indebted to Bert Haloviak for drawing my attention to this correspondence. His research paper, "Ellen White and the SDA Church: Sligo Series" (1980), which also explores these matters, is available at http://www.adventistarchives.org/doc_info.asp?DocID=57.

15. Gerald Wheeler's recent biography highlights James White's entrepreneurial initiatives so effectively applied in publishing and institution building. See *James White: Innovator and Overcomer* (Hagerstown, MD: Review and Herald®, 2003).

16. For example, J. N. Andrews's wife, Angeline (neé Stevens), was a sister of *Review* editor Uriah Smith, and a very close friend of Ellen White.

17. In the 1930s, for example, W. C. White pointedly objected to members of President Charles Watson's administrative team and complained about what he considered their "imperialist" tendencies. See Gilbert M. Valentine, *The Struggle for the Prophetic Heritage* (Muak Lek, Thailand: Institute Press, 2007), 32; W. C. White, letter to C. H. Watson, July 19, 1933.

18. For example, W. C. White argued the importance of staffing the new college at Avondale in 1899 through placing calls for W. W. Prescott, E. J. Waggoner, Hattie Andre, and C. C. Crisler on the basis that Australia was a far more needy mission field. The same kind of arguments were made for funding both the development of Avondale and the Sydney Sanitarium as opposed to funds needed for the establishment of a school or sanitarium in England or at Boulder, Colorado, or in Mexico.

19. Even for writers other than herself, Ellen White's view was that it was unethical for publishing houses to expect authors to contract copyright of their manuscripts to publishers.

20. Knight considers this "myth of the inflexible prophet" to be one of the most destructive in Adventist thinking. See *Myths in Adventism* (Washington, DC: Review and Herald®, 1985), 17; Barry Oliver, "Principles for Reorganization of the Seventh-day Adventist Administrative Structure, 1888-1903: Implications for an International Church" (PhD diss., Andrews University, 1989).

21. Gilbert M. Valentine, *W. W. Prescott: Forgotten Giant of Adventism's Second Generation* (Washington, DC: Review and Herald®, 2005), 208.

Chapter 1

1. 1 Kings 1:11–14, 22ff, NIV.

2. "Amphictyonic" here describes a set of neighboring or contiguous territories united loosely in a league or confederacy in the purposes of common interest. See John Bright, *A History of*

Israel (Philadelphia: Westminster Press, 1976), 179ff.

3. The spiritual gifts exercised by Timothy were recognized by the elders of his community through a ceremony involving the body of elders laying their hands on him. First Timothy 1:18 and 4:14 associate the occasion with the spontaneous utterance of a prophetic message about his work. The apparent spontaneity of the prophetic message would seem to indicate that it was understood not as being a directive of the need for the church to recognize Timothy's gift (this seemed to be already happening), but rather a descriptive narrative of the kind of work challenges he would face. It was not the normal pattern for the prophetic gift to designate what gifts the community should recognize in others. Paul, as an apostle, participated in the recognition ceremony mentioned in 2 Timothy 1:6.

4. Donald Guthrie, *New Testament Introduction* (London: InterVarsity Press, 1976), 666. Other New Testament authorities suggest A.D. 53 for the approximate date of the episode.

5. Paul came to attach great importance to "the collection" as a token of fellowship between the churches of the Gentiles and the mother church in Palestine. Some scholars suggest there is reason to believe that certain Jewish believers in Palestine viewed the collection as an acknowledgement of the Jerusalem church's right to receive a sort of tribute from Gentile Christians in a similar way as the Jerusalem temple received an annual contribution from Jews throughout the world. See F. F. Bruce, *The Spreading Flame* (Exeter, England: Paternoster Press, 1976), 93, 126.

6. William Neil in *The Acts of the Apostles: New Century Bible Commentary* (London: Oliphants, 1973), 216, suggests that the expression "through the spirit" means that the Tyrean Christians were simply "expressing their judgment as responsible Christians." It is noted that the prophecy was not precisely fulfilled as Agabus described, but that it ultimately did come to pass in Rome.

7. *The New Interpreter's Bible* (Nashville: Abingdon, 2002), 10:289, suggests that the reader knows that Paul alone possessed the correct motive of Agabus's prophecy, which is not designed to warn him away but actually to quicken his resolve to go to Jerusalem. "Agabus has authority to receive and deliver God's revelation, and others to interpret it according to their own lights. Only Paul, however, possesses additional revelation that enables him to interpret its normative meaning." Paul firmly corrects the misinterpretation of the prophecy.

8. John Polhill, *The New American Commentary: Acts* (Nashville: Broadman, 1992), 26:433–436, adds, "Ultimately individuals are left to themselves to determine God's will for them. On the other hand, the understanding of others is significant input in seeking to determine the purposes for oneself."

9. See Valentine, *W. W. Prescott,* 235. See also Valentine, *The Struggle for the Prophetic Heritage,* 57–60; E. G. White, letter to Conference Presidents and Counselors, August 1896.

10. To see parallels between Ellen White and biblical prophetic figures does not thereby imply, of course, that we should list her writings among the canonical prophets of Scripture. Canonicity acknowledges the universal applicability of inspired texts. It is helpful to realize, however, that what we call inspiration in recognition of the unique prophetic charisma functions the same in an individual prophet whether they are canonical or non-canonical. To speak of degrees of inspiration is inadequate and unhelpful. We simply must respect the complexity of the mystery of inspiration.

CHAPTER 2

1. K. E. Clark and M. B. Clark, eds. *Measures of Leadership* (West Orange, NJ: Leadership Library of America, 1990), 493–504; R. J. Sternberg, "Managerial Intelligence: Why IQ Isn't Enough," *Journal of Management* 23 (1997): 475–493.

2. Daniel Goleman, *Emotional Intelligence* (New York, Bantam Books, 1995). Practical intelligence is seen as resting on a basis of what is called tacit knowledge—knowledge that is procedural in nature, relevant to the attainment of goals and acquired through interaction with people during a period of time through a variety of experiences.

3. H. Mintzberg, *Power In and Around Organizations* (Englewood Cliffs, NJ: Prentice-Hall, 1983).

4. R. Jackall, *Moral Images: The World of Corporate Managers* (New York: Oxford University Press, 1988). See also F. R. Ferris, D. B. Fedor, and T. R. King, "A Political Conceptualization of Managerial Behavior," *Human Resource Management Review* 4 (1994): 1–34, and Joel DeLuca, *Political Savvy: Systematic Approaches to Leadership Behind-the-Scenes* (Horsham, PA: LRP Publications, 1992).

5. Ms. 2, 1888.

6. Lack of a clear consensus on the location of denominational colleges such as Avondale College (1897) and Emmanuel Missionary College (1901), the establishment of publishing house organizations, and the adoption of marketing policies for the church's publishing work in the 1890s were all contentious and may serve as examples.

7. F. R. Ferris, D. B. Fedor, and T. R. King, "A Political Conceptualization of Managerial Behavior," *Human Resource Management Review* 4 (1994): 1–34. See also Joel DeLuca, *Political Savvy*.

8. See Richard Daft, *Organization Theory and Design* (St. Paul, MN: West Publishing, 1983).

9. Daft, 399. Dan L. Madison, et al., "Organizational Politics: An Exploration of Managers' Perception," *Human Relations* 33 (1980): 79–100.

10. E. G. White, letter to W. W. Prescott, October 2, 1893. See Valentine, *W. W. Prescott,* 88–89, for a more extended discussion of this episode.

11. E. G. White, letter to Brother and Sister Maxon, February 25, 1887. The new *Seventh-day Adventist Encyclopedia* has an entry for a Doctor Maxson, but not for anyone named Maxon. However, Maxon is the spelling in the letters referenced here.

12. E. G. White, letter to Brother and Sister Maxon, April 16, 1887. The letter reveals Ellen White's perceptive insights into human relationships and her philosophy of servant leadership. "A man, in order to bear responsibilities with success, must show an aptitude to take any department of the work, and make himself the master of the situation wherever he has duties to do. He must put his powers to the tax; he must make his aim high, and be willing to place himself in any position that he may gain his object. . . . If you make up your minds to be missionaries for God, and are willing to endure something in the path of duty, willing to be anything or nothing, then you will be a blessing in California, and God's hand will exalt you in due time. If your great anxiety is for the exaltation to the highest place, you will, in God's providence, find yourselves in the lowest place. If you are willing to work anywhere, rise by your own merits, and let others testify to your value, then I know you will be exalted in due time. I am so thoroughly disgusted

with this striving for the supremacy that I will not hold out the least encouragement to you, or any one, as any inducement to exalted positions. Your own merits will exalt you, far more than words or position can do. If you are willing to work for God, wherever he in his providence places you, then the Lord will reward all such humility. But there is so much child's play in regard to the Christian life and duty, that I am pained to the heart."

13. E. G. White, letter to Brother and Sister Maxon, March 24, 1887.

14. Ibid.

15. E. G. White, letter to Brethren Rice, Gibbs, and Loughborough, March 16, 1887. In order to avoid the difficulty of having Maxon go to Ohio, Ellen White proposed an alternative that she discussed with Kellogg. Relating that she had been surprised to hear that the Maxons had left the Battle Creek institution, she wrote to Kellogg "in confidence," suggesting that the potential results of the Maxons connecting with the Ohio institution disturbed her. "I fear the results with you and with them." She knew it would be "just one sore difficulty between the two institutions."

16. E. G. White, letter to JHK, February 23, 1887.

17. E. G. White, letter to Brethren Rice, Gibbs, and Loughborough, March 16, 1887.

18. E. G. White, letter to Brother and Sister Maxon, May 20, 1887. The use of her publications and correspondence in influencing the restructuring of church organization in 1901 or in the allocation of greater resources to the work among African Americans in the American South in the decade following 1901 are examples of this legitimate political dimension. She employed her influence to help persuade people to agree to action.

19. *The Seventh-day Adventist Encyclopedia* provides a detailed listing of dates and places General Conference sessions were held. See article "General Conference."

20. E. G. White, Letter 82, 1888. On this occasion she related that both she and her son had to "watch at every point lest there should be moves made, resolutions passed, that would prove detrimental to the future work" (cited in Arthur L. White, *Ellen G. White: The Lonely Years 1876-1891* [Washington, DC: Review and Herald®, 1984], 3:409. In 1887, for example, there were the issues related to the workload of the president and the need for providing appropriate assistance. But in the 1901 and 1903 sessions, much discussion concerned defining the role and position of the president.

21. E. G. White, Ms. 25, 1899; Arthur L. White, *Ellen G. White: The Lonely Years,* 3:417.

22. Details about the various editions and publications of Ellen White can be found in appendix D of *The Comprehensive Index to the Writings of Ellen G. White* (Mountain View, CA: Pacific Press®, 1963), 1:3, 193.

23. It appears to have been generally understood and accepted that such letters might be acceptably circulated to others who might need to be informed. In 1896, for example, she sent a copy of her letter to S. N. Haskell to Professor W. W. Prescott so that Prescott might know just what she had said to Haskell. Haskell was somewhat suspicious of the professor, and the professor was on his way to meet him. To G. A. Irwin, in 1900, she dispatched copies of letters and manuscripts that she had written to J. H. Kellogg. See also E. G. White, letters to Brother Steed, S. N. Haskell, and Brother Farnsworth (Ms. 112, 1897) and E. G. White, letters to Brethren Irwin, Sisley, Smith, and Jones, March 11, 1899.

24. For example, in late 1896, she gave to Prescott numerous letters and manuscripts that she had been sending to Olsen and others in Battle Creek. See W. W. Prescott, letter to W. C. White, September 5, 1896; W. W. Prescott, letter to E. G. White, October 6, 1896; E. G. White, letter to J. H. Kellogg, May 26, 1896.

25. E. G. White, letter to Bro. Steed via W. L. H. Baker, 1898. O. A. Olsen noted, "A short time ago I wrote a letter to some of the leading brethren, and sent them copies of the testimony from Sister White, addressed to them." "I inclose [*sic*] in this a copy of my letter to them. Will you please show it to your mother, and also to Brother Prescott? I send it to you in order that you may be fully conversant with all my moves." O. A. Olsen, letter to W. C. White, January 28, 1896.

26. For example, markings on such a letter written on July 1, 1896, indicate that it was given to W. W. Prescott on July 3 and then mailed to O. A. Olsen, the General Conference president, and C. H. Jones, the manager of Pacific Press®, and her son, James Edson White, three days later on July 6.

27. E. G. White, letter to O. A. Olsen, November 26, 1894; E. G. White, letter to O. A. Olsen, December 1, 1896.

28. E. G. White, letter to O. A. Olsen, May 31, 1896.

29. E. G. White, letter to Bro. Salisbury, November 5, 1898. Apparently she did not follow such a practice frequently. Sometimes it caused considerable misunderstanding, because it gave the impression that W. C. White was manipulating the advice being given as, for example, when she wrote a short note to Prescott in 1904 at a very difficult time in the church's relationship with J. H. Kellogg. The note was given to W. C. White to deliver at an appropriate moment. W. C. White either chose not to deliver it or forgot to deliver it, resulting in a major confrontation between Prescott and Kellogg's supporters. See Valentine, *W. W. Prescott: Forgotten Giant,* 179, for a discussion of this episode.

30. E. G. White, letter to G. A. Irwin, June 20, 1900; E. G. White, letter to Brethren Smith and Jones, April 22, 1898.

31. E. G. White, letter to Mrs. R. Anderson, June 8, 1896. The reference to Mrs. Anderson's name occurred in a *Review* article of July 30, 1895.

32. E. G. White, letter to J. E. White, June 1, 1901. Ellen White reports in a June [n.d.] 1901 letter that she has received letters from Daniells and Kilgore, and in a June 5, 1901, letter (see endnote 33) that she has received letters from Daniells, Kilgore, and Smith, but she doesn't specify which of these letters she is referring to.

33. E. G. White, letter to J. E. White, June 5, 1901.

34. Ibid.

35. See Valentine, *W. W. Prescott: Forgotten Giant,* 226, for a discussion of this problematic episode.

36. E. G. White, letter to A. G. Daniells, November 17, 1902.

37. E. G. White, letter to A. G. Daniells, February 24, 1897. See also Milton Hook, *Experiment on the Dora* (Cooranbong, Australia: Avondale Academic Press, 1998), 37.

38. E. G. White, letter to Metcalfe Hare, August 17, 1897; E. G. White, letter to Edson, Emma, and W. C. White, August 29, 1897; *Diary,* Ms. 127, 1897.

39. E. G. White, letter to C. H. Jones, July 8, 1895. "You are not to hold yourself to seek

permission of the authorities at Battle Creek whether you shall or shall not pursue a line of work that seems impressed upon you to do. The Lord is the one to whom you are to be amenable."

40. E. G. White, letter to G. A. Irwin, October 14, 1902.

41. E. G. White, Ms. 21, 1888. See also Arthur L. White, *Ellen G. White: The Lonely Years,* 3:406.

42. E. G. White, letter to A. G. Daniells and E. R. Palmer, June 27, 1897.

43. E. G. White, Ms. 30, 1889; Ms. 16, 1889.

44. E. G. White, Ms. 9, 1888, "Morning Talk," 5:30 A.M., Wednesday, October 24, 1888.

45. E. G. White, letter to O. A. Olsen, May 8, 1890.

46. E. G. White, letter to J. E. White, May 6, 1896; E. G. White, letter to O. A. Olsen, May 25, 1896; Valentine, *W. W. Prescott: Forgotten Giant,* 93.

47. E. G. White, *The Writing and Sending Out of the Testimonies* (Mountain View, CA: Pacific Press®, 1913).

CHAPTER 3

1. The nominating committee was composed of three members: J. B. Goodrich, J. Fargo, and Daniel T. Jones. It is not clear who served as chairman. See *General Conference Bulletin,* October 23, 1888, 2.

2. Nash had been requested to stay by for a few minutes apparently for the purpose of escorting Mrs. White to her residence following the discussion. Nash's duty at the session was to saw wood between meetings to keep the dining tent cook stove well fueled. See R. T. Nash, letter to A. L. White, July 9, 1955.

3. *General Conference Bulletin,* October 23, 1888, 1.

4. E. G. White, Ms. 21, 1888; Letter 2a, 1892.

5. George R. Knight, *Angry Saints: Tensions and Possibilities in the Adventist Struggle Over Righteousness by Faith* (Hagerstown, MD: Review and Herald®, 1989), 15–39, provides a helpful analysis of the context of the 1888 meetings in Minneapolis. See also E. G. White, letter to E. J. Waggoner and A. T. Jones, February 18, 1887; E. G. White, letter to G. I. Butler and U. Smith, April 5, 1887.

6. G. I. Butler, *Review and Herald,* March 22, 1887, 182–184; E. G. White, letter to G. I. Butler, April 5, 1887. Butler did not see any justice in this letter. See G. I. Butler, letter to E. G. White, October 1, 1888.

7. W. C. White, letter to G. I. Butler, August 14, 1888; E. G. White, letter to Brethren who shall assemble in General Conference, August 5, 1888; G. R. Knight, letter to G. M. Valentine, February 16, 2008.

8. G. I. Butler, *Review and Herald,* August 28, 1888, 560; G. I. Butler, letter to E. G. White, October 1, 1888; E. G. White, Ms. 13, 1889; E. G. White, letter to Mary White, October 12, 1888. Ellen White commented to Mary that Butler's letter was "a most curious production of accusations and charges against me."

9. *General Conference Bulletin,* October 25, 1888, 1; G. I. Butler, letter to E. G. White, October 1888; E. G. White, letter to Mary White, October 12, 1888.

10. E. G. White, letter to Mary White, November 4, 1888.

11. W. W. Prescott, letter to O. A. Olsen, July 15, 1894.

12. *General Conference Bulletin,* October 31, 1888, 1.

13. E. G. White, letter to J. Fargo, May 2, 1889.

14. Olsen had given an extensive report on progress in Scandinavia and had recommended the acceptance of the newly organized Norway conference by the General Conference. *General Conference Bulletin,* November 14, 1887, 1.

15. Arthur L. White, *Ellen G. White: The Lonely Years,* 3:237, 374. The *General Conference Bulletins* during the mid-1880s document the increasingly prominent role Olsen played at General Conference sessions. His role was not that of a prominent popular speaker. Rather, he offered important public prayers, served as a member of an increasing number of standing committees, and regularly chaired the committee on resolutions. His speeches were noted, and he filled in frequently for absent chairs of various committees and boards. He was re-elected to the executive committee in 1884 (*Review and Herald,* November 18, 1884, 729). Olsen served as chair of three standing committees at the 1885 session (ibid., November 24, 1885, 738). In 1886, he was re-appointed to the General Conference executive committee even though he was not present at the session (ibid., December 7, 1886, 763). See also *General Conference Bulletin,* November 16 and 21, 1887, 2.

16. Kristine Dahl, letter to E. G. White, August 1886. O. A. Olsen's younger brother, E. G. Olsen, and his wife had also gone to Scandinavia with O. A. Olsen. E. G. Olsen was also an ordained pastor. They worked together in Moss. See D. A. Delafield, *Ellen G. White in Europe, 1885-1887* (Washington, DC: Review and Herald®, 1975), 298.

17. Delafield, *Ellen G. White in Europe,* 314.

18. Ibid.

19. W. C. White, letter to G. I. Butler, November 6, 1886. See also Delafield, 222.

20. Ellen and James White visited the Wisconsin camp meeting in June 1879 while Olsen was president. See *Review and Herald,* June 12, 1879. See also Arthur L. White, *Ellen G. White: The Lonely Years,* 3:119.

21. Daniel A. and Grace Lillian Ochs, *The Past and the Presidents* (Nashville: Southern Publishing Association, 1974), 80.

22. I. H. Evans, "Elder O. A. Olsen: Obituary," *Review and Herald,* February 25, 1915, 14.

23. Denominational leadership asked Olsen to "go to Europe as soon as consistent with other duties, to assist in the work of the old world, particularly in the Scandinavian Mission for a period of one year or more" (*Review and Herald,* December 1, 1885, 745).

24. Edwin Torkelsen, "Ellen G. White in Norway 1885-1887," in *Centennial Symposium: Ellen G. White and Europe 1885-1887* [Oud Zandbergen, Netherlands, April 16–19, 1987], ed. Pierre Winandy (Bracknell, England: Ellen G. White Research Center), 215.

25. E. G. White, letter to G. I. Butler, Letter 117, 1886. Matteson had commenced the publishing program in Norway and also started a church in Oslo, but in sending his children to school on Sabbath, Ellen White felt that he had not been able to set a good example concerning Sabbath observance and as a result others in the church had also adopted compromising positions concerning Sabbath keeping. See Torkelsen, 163.

26. O. A. Olsen's diaries for the period are located in the General Conference archives in Silver

Spring, Maryland. They largely record his movements and activities and tell little of the writer himself.

27. E. G. White, letter to Mary White, November 4, 1888; Ochs, *The Past and the Presidents,* 83.

28. Ibid.

29. O. A. Olsen, letter to W. C. White, December 20, 1888.

30. W. C. White, letter to O. A. Olsen, November 29, 1888; E. G. White, letter to Mary White, November 4, 1888.

31. Knight, *Angry Saints,* 31.

32. O. A. Olsen, "The Progress of the Work in Scandinavia," *Review and Herald*, April 16, 1889, 251.

33. E. G. White, letter to W. C. White, March 7, 1890; E. G. White, letter to W. C. and Mary White, March 1890, (Letter 83); Dan T. Jones, *Review and Herald,* April 1, 1890.

34. E. G. White, letter to O. A. Olsen, August 25, 1889. If there were other handwritten letters, they have not been preserved.

35. O. A. Olsen, letter to E. G. White, August 13, 1891.

36. O. A. Olsen, letter to W. C. White, January 1, 1892.

37. *General Conference Bulletin,* November 21, 1887, 1.

38. *General Conference Bulletin,* November 25, 1887, 3.

39. The action was taken on November 18, 1888. W. C. White, letter to O. A. Olsen, November 1, 1888; O. A. Olsen, letter to W. C. White, December 20, 1888. See also Barry D. Oliver, *SDA Organizational Structure: Past Present and Future* (Berrien Springs, MI: Andrews University Press, 1989) 70, 71.

40. *General Conference Bulletin*, 1889, 152, 153. A helpful, detailed analysis of these developments appears in Oliver, ibid. Richard W. Schwarz and Floyd Greenleaf provide a broader overview in *Light Bearers: A History of the Seventh-day Adventist Church* (Nampa, ID: Pacific Press®, 2000), 252ff.

41. E. G. White, letter to O. A. Olsen, June 9, 1890; Arthur L. White, *Ellen G. White: The Lonely Years,* 3:461.

42. E. G. White, letter to O. A. Olsen, July–August 1894. Having expressed her frustration and complaints to Olsen, she felt much better. "Since writing these communications, which ought to have been done some time ago, freedom has come to my soul." She felt she could get back to her work. "And now I think, as I have thought a few hundred times, I shall be able after this mail closes, to take the 'Life of Christ' and go ahead with it, if the Lord will."

43. E. G. White, letter to F. E. Belden, June 8, 1895. In later discussions, Ellen White quoted Belden as arguing "that he did not like to promote E. G. White books lest others should say it was because I was your 'Auntie.' " Ellen White "was disgusted at this talk" and at "the flimsy excuse offered." She believed her nephew was stating things that he "may have imagined were true but they were false." The unwillingness to promote *The Great Controversy,* she said, had caused her "to suffer," but she was more distressed that "God's message could not come to the people."

44. E. G. White, letter to O. A. Olsen, June 21, 1891.

45. E. G. White, letter to O. A. Olsen, August 27, 1890.

46. E. G. White, letter to O. A. Olsen, December 15, 1890.

47. E. G. White, letter to O. A. Olsen, June 21, 1891.

48. Ellen White was not sure, for example, that it was the correct thing for her to go to Australia and was not sure that the General Conference Committee had the right wisdom for her on that. E. G. White, letter to O. A. Olsen, July–August 1894 (O-55-94).

49. On reflection, Ellen White expressed significant disquiet about the overall tone of the 1891 General Conference Session. "The Lord did not preside in many meetings. There were loud voices and urgent pressing of things . . . more of the common fire than the sacred." In her view, the general setting in which the suggestion that she go to Australia was decided upon was dominated by a few "who were misleading the Conference," and who were "blinding" Olsen's eyes. See E. G. White, Ms. 33, 1891.

50. Valentine, *Struggle for the Prophetic Heritage,* 32, 83, and *W. W. Prescott: Forgotten Giant,* 301, 302.

51. W. W. Prescott, letters to O. A. Olsen, January 4 and 5, and November 1, 1893. See also "Report of Righteousness by Faith Committee," February 18, 1893.

52. E. G. White, letter to O. A. Olsen, November 26, 1894.

53. O. A. Olsen, letter to W. C. White, February 1, 1892.

54. O. A. Olsen, letter to W. C. White, March 23, 1892.

55. O. A. Olsen, letter to E. G. White, May 23, 1892.

56. O. A. Olsen, letter to E. G. White, June 15, 1892.

57. O. A. Olsen, letter to W. C. White, July 12, 1892.

58. E. G. White, letter to O. A. Olsen, September 22, 1892.

59. O. A. Olsen, October 6, 1892.

60. E. G. White, letter to O. A. Olsen, November 25, 1892.

61. Ibid.

62. Ibid.

63. Ibid.

64. W. C. White, letter to O. A. Olsen, December, 21, 1892; May 8, 1893; July 9, 1893. *Seventh-day Adventist Yearbook, 1894,* 60, 61. After the church gave approval for the establishment of the sub-unit, it assigned A. G. Daniells the task of chairing a committee to draw up an appropriate constitution, which was approved on January 19, 1894. The initiative was not without its critics in the church, who, according to a later report by Daniells, feared that a "secession" was under way "out there in the South Sea Islands" (*General Conference Bulletin,* 1913, 108). See also Barry D. Oliver, *SDA Organizational Structure,* 105.

Chapter 4

1. Harmon Lindsay, letter to E. G. White, August 16, 1894; *General Conference Bulletin,* 1895, 401.

2. O. A. Olsen, letter to L. T. Nicola and J. I. Gibson, November 21, 1895; O. A. Olsen, circular letter to "Leading Brethren," November 28, 1895.

3. *General Conference Bulletin,* January 29, 1893, 2; Schwarz and Greenleaf, *Light Bearers,* 246.

4. W. H. Edwards, letter to O. A. Olsen, October 5, 1893.

5. E. G. White, letter to O. A. Olsen, June 10, 1894; Harmon Lindsay, letters to E. G. White, September 13 and November 28, 1894. Ellen White's desperate search for cash is evident in this correspondence. She had asked Lindsay to track down a cooking stove, because she wanted him to sell it on her behalf. When he finally located it in someone's house, it turned out to be worthless. Lindsay was also unable to find a tenant for the small office building on her Battle Creek property. But he was trying "to realize something from it" for her.

6. E. G. White, letter to O. A. Olsen, June 10, 1894.

7. Ellen White had given up the regular consumption of meat on principle decades earlier, and it appeared on her table only occasionally thereafter. A. L. White, *Ellen G. White: The Australian Years, 1891-1900,* 4:118, 119; E. G. White, letter to O. A. Olsen, (O-54a-1894).

8. E. G. White, letter to O. A. Olsen, June 10, 1894.

9. Ibid.

10. Ibid.; E. G. White, letter to W. H. Littlejohn, June 3, 1894. She had written out the letter on June 3 but had delayed sending it for fear that he, too, like others in Battle Creek, would react negatively to it. But she eventually mailed it several weeks later. "Could you see the harm that the articles may do, you would, I should hope, have sincere repentance before God." Mrs. White was as much worried about what might happen as a consequence of the articles as about the damage they had actually caused.

11. E. G. White, letters to O. A. Olsen, June 10 and July–August 1894 (O-55-94).

12. E. G. White, letter to C. Eldridge, January 9, 1893.

13. Ibid.

14. E. G. White, letter to C. Eldridge, June 9, 1893.

15. E. G. White, letter to O. A. Olsen, undated, but about July–August 1894 (O-55-1894).

16. E. G. White, letter to O. A. Olsen, June 10, 1894.

17. O. A. Olsen, letter to W. C. White, June 19, 1894.

18. O. A. Olsen, letter to E. G. White, January 2, 1895.

19. Ibid.

20. O. A. Olsen, letter to W. C. White, January 3, 1895.

21. *General Conference Bulletin,* 1895, 341, 373, 374.

22. O. A. Olsen, letter to S. N. Haskell, February 26, 1895.

23. O. A. Olsen, letter to W. C. White, March 28, 1895.

24. *General Conference Bulletin,* 1895, 341, 374, 385, 401, 422, 425, 444.

25. E. G. White, letter to Brethren, October 21, 1894.

26. E. G. White, letter to O. A. Olsen, May 1, 1895.

27. E. G. White, letter to O. A. Olsen, May 12, 1895.

28. Schwarz and Greenleaf, *Light Bearers,* 248–349.

29. Ibid., 262.

30. E. G. White, June 19, 1895.

31. E. G. White, letter to O. A. Olsen, September 19, 1895.

32. G. A. Irwin, letter to E. W. Farnsworth, March 8, 1903.

33. E. G. White, Ms. 57, October 12, 1895; E. G. White, letter to O. A. Olsen, May 22, 1896;

E. G. White, letter to Book Committee, October 26, [1896]. A more extensive discussion of this episode is provided in Valentine, *W. W. Prescott: Forgotten Giant,* 116.

34. O. A. Olsen, letter to W. C. White, April 18, 1895.

35. Ibid.

36. Ibid.

37. O. A. Olsen, letter to E. G. White, January 6, 1896.

38. O. A. Olsen, letter to W. C. White, January 28, 1896. The matter of L. R. Conradi's illicit liaison with a woman in Chicago and the care of the mother and child was one such delicate situation.

39. E. G. White, letter to O. A. Olsen, November 26, 1894.

40. E. G. White, letter to O. A. Olsen, March 18, 1896. This letter has a more formal mode of expression in the discussion of Christian business principles as opposed to secular business practice and is set out in a clear list of points, suggesting that it was the transcription of an address or chapel talk that Ellen White may have given.

41. O. A. Olsen, letter to E. G. White, April 24, 1896.

42. Ibid.

43. O. A. Olsen, letter to W. C. White, April 23, 1896.

44. E. G. White, letter to O. A. Olsen, April 24, 1896.

45. E. G. White, letter to O. A. Olsen, May 22, 1896.

46. Ibid. Ellen White, of course, did not in any way endorse infanticide. But the allusion is a troubling one. In the heat of her passion of the moment about the wrongs being allowed to develop in the publishing house she grasped at an apparently common literary device that reflected the attitudes and values of her time about the betrayal and disloyalty represented in the social phenomenon of illegitimate birth and the social stigma that was a burden for life. "Better not to have been born" was the general idea.

47. E. G. White, letter to O. A. Olsen, May 22, 1896.

48. In 1898, Henry recalled that on the subject of royalty rates, nothing that Ellen White had said to him on the matter had been sufficient to persuade him to change his mind. Testimony of A. R. Henry before the Review and Herald® board in the matter of arbitration, February 22, 1898. Schwarz and Greenleaf, *Light Bearers,* 266.

49. Ibid.

50. Ibid.

51. E. G. White, letter to O. A. Olsen, May 31, 1896. Which of the letters and manuscripts were not sent at the time they were written is not clear.

52. O. A. Olsen, June 28, 1896.

53. O. A. Olsen, June 28, 1896.

54. E. G. White, letter to O. A. Olsen, May 26, 1896. Olsen immediately set up a commission of inquiry headed by A. T. Jones.

55. O. A. Olsen, letter to E. G. White, March 9, 1896.

56. G. A. Irwin, letter to E. G. White, March 26, 1899; Schwarz and Greenleaf, *Light Bearers,* 264.

57. O. A. Olsen, letter to W. C. White, November 6, 1896. See also Terry W. Carlisle,

"O. A. Olsen's Contribution to the Seventh-day Adventist Church's Organizational Structure and Other Related Areas of Church Growth From 1888 to 1897 as Seen in the 'General Conference Bulletin' and in Olsen's Personal Correspondence to Other Church Leaders," unpublished term paper, Andrews University, March 11, 1974, 35.

58. O. A. Olsen, letter to E. G. White, December 9, 1896.

59. E. G. White, letter to A. O. Tait, August 27, 1896.

60. E. G. White Manuscript, August 1896.

61. Ibid.

62. Ibid.

63. O. A. Olsen, letter to E. G. White, August 14, 1896.

64. Ibid.

65. O. A. Olsen, letter to E. G. White, November 6, 1896.

66. E. G. White, letter to I. H. Evans, November 27, 1897. Robert J. Wieland pointed out the significant correction in 1974. See the memorandum by A. L. White attached to the letter.

67. E. G. White, letter to O. A. Olsen, December 1, 1896.

68. W. C. White, letter to W. W. Prescott, June 2, 1896.

69. O. A. Olsen, letter to W. C. White, May 25, 1895.

70. E. G. White, letter to O. A. Olsen, May 25, 1896.

71. W. W. Prescott, letter to E. G. White, July 16 and August 9, 1896.

72. The letter is referred to in W. W. Prescott, letter to E. G. White, July 16, 1896.

73. E. G. White, letter to W. W. Prescott, September 1, 1896.

74. For the reaction to his attempted implementation of the basic reform idea of including the Bible as a required part of the college curriculum, see Valentine, *W. W. Prescott: Forgotten Giant,* 97–109.

75. W. W. Prescott, letters to E. G. White, July 30, October 6, and November 10, 1896.

76. E. G. White, letter to Brother and Sister Waggoner, August 26, 1898. "I was surprised that he did not remain in Battle Creek when he returned. It may be in the providence of God that he is where he is but I do hope and pray that the Lord will adjust the work so that proper ones will take hold of it in Battle Creek."

Chapter 5

1. "Life Sketch and Funeral Service of Elder George A. Irwin," *Review and Herald,* June 5, 1913, 543.

2. *Union Conference Record,* July 28, 1899, 14. The remarks were made as part of a farewell speech for Irwin at the 1899 Australasian Union Conference meeting he attended at Cooranbong in July 1899.

3. The district included Kentucky, Tennessee, North Carolina, South Carolina, Georgia, Florida, Alabama, Mississippi, and Louisiana.

4. W. W. Prescott, letter to E. G. White, November 15, 1897.

5. O. A. Olsen, letter to W. C. White, March 27, 1896.

6. *General Conference Bulletin,* February 12, 1897, 1.

7. Although the General Conference Session proper started officially in mid-February, the executive committee, with a number of other invited individuals, began meeting on the ground

about February 1. A ten-day pre-session Bible Institute for leaders and delegates followed on February 9 and focused on the issues that the session would address. The session itself began February 19 and continued to March 10, when, for legal purposes, it adjourned in Nebraska and reconvened in the state of Michigan, where it met for a further week to complete its business about March 19.

8. *Nebraska State Journal,* March 4, 1897, 8.

9. Ibid. To complaints about the lack of reporting of business actions from readers of the *Bulletin,* the editors responded that for those who were at the session, the reason was obvious. They tartly observed that "the *Bulletin* does not *make up* business proceedings. Less business has been transacted than at any previous meeting for years" (*General Conference Daily Bulletin,* 1897, 320).

10. "President's Report," *General Conference Bulletin*, 1897, 107–110.

11. E. G. White, Ms., August 1896 (sent in December).

12. *Nebraska State Journal,* March 5, 1897, 8.

13. W. W. Prescott, letter to E. G. White, August 4, 1897.

14. E. G. White, letter to W. W. Prescott, cited in W. W. Prescott, letter to E. G. White, November 15, 1897. The September 12 letter is not extant.

15. W. W. Prescott, letter to E. G. White, November 15, 1897. His letter asking about his future work was written in July 16, 1896. He wrote on October 6, 1896, thanking her for what she wrote about his "future work" and said that he had "committed it all to the Lord and shall leave it with him."

16. See G. M. Valentine, "Conflict of Interest: An Impediment to Reform, 1897-1901," *The Adventist Professional* 3, no. 3 (September 1991): 7–10.

17. W. W. Prescott, letter to E. G. White, November 15, 1897.

18. E. G. White, letter to Brother and Sister Waggoner, August 26, 1898.

19. E. G. White, letter to Brother and Sister Prescott, August 27, 1898.

20. Irwin planned to undertake this at the end of July when A. T. Jones returned from a preplanned itinerary in the American West. G. A. Irwin, letter to W. W. Prescott, June 21, 1897.

21. W. W. Prescott, letter to E. G. White, November 15, 1897.

22. The Henry case absorbed much attention in mid-1897. Irwin reported that the General Conference had set up a committee of five leaders to try to arbitrate the claim and settle it out of court. After laboring for many days, the committee felt that there was little hope of arriving at anything satisfactory because, as they studied the situation, it became clear that to arbitrate the matter would unfortunately compromise the spiritual authority of the testimonies. The two issues, they felt, could not be separated. To compromise or arbitrate the testimonies would mean a "denial of our faith in them." Ellen White took the view that in no case should the matter be settled "by buying A. R. Henry's silence with money" (E. G. White, letter to A. R. Henry, April 20, 1898).

23. Alta Robinson, "From Soldier Boy to President," *Guide,* May 3, 1967, 2–6, 20. Alta Robinson was a great-granddaughter-in-law of Ellen White.

24. G. A. Irwin, letter to E. G. White, June 6, 1897.

25. Ibid.

26. Ibid. The explanation of the rationale for W. C. White's appointment might seem to imply

a gentle rebuke. Irwin does not refer to the previous discussions and tentative agreements between Ellen White and Olsen about W. C. White's role prior to the 1897 session. Had he not yet caught up on these tacit arrangements?

27. See *General Conference Bulletin,* 1897, 1.

28. Herbert Lacey had just returned to Cooranbong from America with a degree in the classics from Battle Creek College. Ellen White felt that once back in the field, such graduates needed "to go through another process of education, and unlearn many of the things they have acquired." Why could not Adventist schools teach the Scriptures in "pure, unadulterated simplicity," keeping out "argumentative, debating methods." The years of study at Battle Creek cultivated "many habits and methods in the students that will cripple their usefulness." She later acknowledged that Lacey had changed, "had broken his heart before the Lord," and had "manifested a good contrite spirit." She defended him against S. N. Haskell, who had also been critical of the new graduate and who thought he could run things all by himself (E. G. White, letter to A. G. Daniells, June 6, 1898; E. G. White, letter to Bro. and Sis. Haskell, March 3, 1898).

29. Ibid.

30. G. A. Irwin, letter to E. G. White, October 13, 1897. A. T. Jones chaired the committee, composed along with him, of G. A. Irwin and J. H. Loughborough. They began their study July 25 and finished on August 8. The investigation involved extensive site inspections and interviews with almost the entire work force of about two hundred employees. A short report had been given to the employees during a chapel service. The publishing house board received a more extended, but still informal, verbal report on August 8 that was recorded stenographically. Titled "Informal Report of Committee on Investigation of Affairs in Review and Herald Office," it is still the only extant document on the results of the investigation. A handwritten note on the stenographic record dated October 20 by A. T. Jones indicates that a follow-up visit had occurred in October to confirm that the publishing house had implemented the recommendations. "I am glad to be able to state that Bro. Sisley and Bro. Gibson are making honest endeavors to reform all these evils. As to the terms and c[onditions] of apprentices and hands generally, Bro. Gibson keeps a regular account in his diary when each hand enters and when his first term expires—to the very day. This has worked just as we said it would; the boys are encouraged and work well, and take an interest in things. I believe Bro. Sisley and Brother Gibson are both conscientiously doing all that they can to bring things into the right channel in the publishing house and to keep all things moving to the better." A summary of the study's major findings appears in the appendix.

31. G. A. Irwin, letter to E. G. White, October 13, 1897.

32. R. W. Schwarz, "The Perils of Growth, 1886-1905," in Gary Land, ed., *Adventism in America* (Grand Rapids: Eerdmans, 1986), 127.

33. G. A. Irwin, letter to W. W. Prescott, April 8, 1898; L. A. Hoopes, letter to W. C. White, March 30, 1899.

34. G. A. Irwin, letter to W. W. Prescott, April 8, 1898.

35. W. W. Prescott, "Notes From Great Britain," *Review and Herald,* September 13, 1898; *Union Conference Record,* July 28, 1899, 13.

36. I. H. Evans, letter to E. G. White, March 17, 1898.

37. E. G. White, "Bible Principles to Govern SDA Institutions," Ms. 66, 1898.

38. E. G. White, letters to G. A. Irwin, May 19 and October 30, 1898.

39. E. G. White, letter to Brother Irwin, December 18, 1898. (Some copies of this letter had initially been dated December 8 with "1" being added by hand to correct it to 18 afterwards). Ellen White complained that it was the unbelief she met in her colleagues that made it hard for her. They were "men of intelligence, men of excellent ability, but headstrong, that, when we make an attempt to advance, [they] build up thin walls, [saying] 'It can't be done.' I move right ahead, with them blocking the way at every advance."

40. It bothered Ellen White that she had not been paying her secretaries their regular wages. "I have, in order to advance the work donated the wages that should be paid to them; and [at] the last call [for donations for a special project] for the first time my name was not on the list. I must be just as well as liberal" (ibid.).

41. Ibid. See also *General Conference Bulletin,* March 1, 1899, 129.

42. E. G. White, letter to G. A. Irwin and U. Smith, June 6, 1898; G. A. Irwin, letter to E. G. White, January 20, 1899.

43. G. A. Irwin, letter to E. G. White, January 20, 1899.

44. Ibid.

45. E. G. White, letter to "Those Occupying Important Positions in the General Conference," January 24, 1899.

46. E. G. White, letter to S. N. Haskell and G. A. Irwin, April 25, 1900.

47. E. G. White, letter to Bro. and Sis. Olsen, August 26, 1898. Robinson had been working in New England and had been assigned by the Foreign Mission Board to go to England in October 1895. He served only a short term there, but later in the United States continued "in various capacities through the years and was a faithful efficient worker." He died September 10, 1935, in Florida ("Death of H. E. Robinson," *Review and Herald,* September 26, 1935, 24).

48. *General Conference Bulletin,* February 24, 1899, 75.

49. Richard A. Schwarz, "The Perils of Growth, 1886-1905," in Gary Land, ed., *Adventism in America,* 128.

50. *General Conference Bulletin,* February 24, 37.

51. E. G. White, letter to Brother and Sister Waggoner, August 26, 1898.

52. *General Conference Bulletin,* February 24, 1899, 75.

53. Ibid., 77.

CHAPTER 6

1. E. G. White, letter to S. M. I. Henry, June 21, 1899.

2. Alta Robinson, "From Soldier Boy to President," 6.

3. *Union Conference Record,* July 28, 1899, 13.

4. E. G. White, letter to S. M. I. Henry, June 21, 1899.

5. E. G. White, letter to J. E. White, May 6, 1896; E. G. White, letter to O. A. Olsen, May 25, 1896.

6. See, for example, Julia Buckner et al., "Social Anxiety and Insomnia," *Depression and Anxiety,* November 2006; Luigi Specchio et al., "Insomnia, Quality of Life and Psychopathological

Features," *Brain Research Bulletin* 63, no. 5 (June 2004): 385–391.

7. E. G. White, letter to S. M. I. Henry, June 21, 1899.

8. G. A. Irwin, letter to E. G. White, March 26, 1899; L. A. Hoopes, letter to W. C. White, June 7, 1899. Arthur L. White has a good discussion of this episode in *Ellen G. White: The Australian Years, 1891-1900,* 410–419.

9. The school reported that "the larger part of the great trees which stood in front of the school buildings" were removed in this way and later turned into firewood. Delegates during the "work hours" had used spades, grub-hoes, axes, and the "forest devil" (an apparatus for uprooting large trees) ("The Union Conference," *Union Conference Record,* September 1, 1899, 7).

10. "Organization," *Union Conference Record,* July 26, 899, 3. "It is the sense of this meeting, that the Australasian field be more adequately represented at the session of the General Conference than in past years" (*Union Conference Record,* July 16, 1899, 16).

11. E. G. White, letter to "My Brethren in Responsible Positions in the Work," February 22, 1899.

12. E. G. White, letter to G. A. Irwin, W. Sisley, U. Smith, and A. T. Jones, March 11, 1899; E. G. White, letter to A. T. Jones, May 1, 1899. The committee was a representative group of thirteen leaders and included J. N. Loughborough, C. H. Jones, W. C. Sisley, S. H. Lane, A. J. Breed, W. T. Knox, E. J. Waggoner, J. O. Corliss, J. H. Kellogg, A. T. Jones, I. H. Evans, L. R. Conradi, and H. P. Holser.

13. S. N. Haskell, letter to E. G. White, October 24, 1899. The amount was to compensate for the damage done to the circulation of his book.

14. General Conference leaders thought bankruptcy the best option for the publishing house located in Christiana (Oslo). But local leadership, fearful for the reputation of the young Norwegian church, persuaded the General Conference to undertake a special fund-raising drive among the membership in order to pay the creditors. The rescue was hugely expensive as well as being an embarrassment and a huge worry for the church. Daniells thought the exercise was a total waste of financial resources. See Schwarz and Greenleaf, *Light Bearers,* 5.

15. E. G. White, letter to G. A. Irwin, W. Sisley, U. Smith, and A. T. Jones, March 11, 1899. See also follow up letters to *Review* editor A. T. Jones, May 1, 1899.

16. E. G. White, letter to G. A. Irwin, W. Sisley, and U. Smith, March 11, 1899. This lengthy letter rehearses many of the irksome publishing problems.

17. W. C. White, letter to W. W. Prescott, October 6, 1899. The correspondence included copies of several letters sent to Irwin and Haskell several weeks earlier.

18. W. C. White, letters to W. W. Prescott, August 22 and October 6, 1899; W. W. Prescott, letter to W. C. White, October, 26, 1899.

19. Ibid. "Officialism," which Prescott put in quotation marks, was the same term he used in a vigorous speech at the 1899 General Conference Session, when he protested the unethical misappropriation of donations by the General Conference treasury that had hurt Ellen White's work so badly. A year previously, Prescott had alerted Ellen White to the convoluted financial arrangements between the Australian Bible Echo publishing house and the office in London. The Foreign Mission Board and General Conference sent money to London to pay for the printing of books. The London office sent the books to Australia for sale by colporteurs. The income from

the book sales served to pay General Conference workers' salaries in Australia. Trouble occurred when the Foreign Mission Board announced that it no longer had money it could send to London, but debts had already been incurred on its behalf. London could not ship any further books to Australia unless they paid for them in cash. And who was going to pay the General Conference workers in Australia? See W. W. Prescott, letter to E. G. White, February 21, 1898. Ellen White herself had not been claiming her General Conference salary for more than a year as an economy measure.

20. Ellen White was thus aware of the developing tensions. In the midst of Prescott's dispute with W. C. White, she expressed her fears and cautioned about rivalry and competition between publishing houses (E. G. White, letter to "Managers," September 24, 1899). She spoke of managers of institutions getting the advantage over another and of deals being done secretly and in an underhanded manner.

21. E. G. White, letter to "My Brethren in Responsible Positions in the Review and Herald Office," January 16, 1900.

22. E. G. White, letter to G. A. Irwin, January 16, 1900. The depth of indignation and the strong position that Ellen White took over this issue in 1900 made it extremely difficult for General Conference leaders to see the consistency when in 1905 she instructed that money specifically raised in an advertised fund-raising drive to build a new publishing house in Washington should be sent instead for the support of activities in the South. If such a diversion had been "robbery" back in 1900, Prescott did not know how a similar one could be made to "look straight" when it occurred in 1905 (W. W. Prescott, letter to W. C. White, July 31, 1905). W. C. White replied that he was just as much perplexed by the inconsistency. Again, the dispute involved a disagreement over the allocation of scarce resources. The incident may perhaps be seen as another example of Ellen White's role as an umpire. Leadership was prepared to go along with it in the sense of accepting the decision of an umpire even though they may not have agreed with it. The rationale that enabled them to do this was a spiritual willingness to submit for the good of the wider cause. They expressed it as "believing that the Lord knows more about his work than we do" (W. C. White, letter to W. W. Prescott, August 11, 1905).

23. E. G. White, letter to G. A. Irwin, January [n.d.], 1900.

24. Ibid.

25. Ibid.

26. Ibid.

27. E. G. White, letter to A. T. Jones, February 26, 1900.

28. E. G. White, letter to G. A. Irwin, August 29, 1899.

29. G. A. Irwin, letter to E. G. White, April 12, 1900.

30. E. G. White, letter to General Conference Committee, February 13, 1900.

31. G. A. Irwin, letter to E. G. White, April 12, 1900.

32. E. G. White, letter to G. A. Irwin, April 25, 1900.

33. G. A. Irwin, letter to E. G. White, July 2, 1900.

34. G. A. Irwin, letter to E. G. White, April 12, 1900.

35. E. G. White, letter to H. T. Kellogg, November 1, 1900. W. C. White released his claim on the book, and Ellen White needed to ask others to relinquish their claims on the book, in

order to have the profits go exclusively to projects in the American South.

36. G. A. Irwin, letter to E. G. White, January 30, October 3, and November 10, 1898.

37. *Union Conference Record,* July 28, 1899, 12.

38. *Union Conference Record,* July 31, 1899, 18.

39. E. G. White, *Diary,* August 15, 1899.

40. Hetty Haskell, letter to E. G. White, September 12, 1899; S. N. Haskell, letters to E. G. White, October 19 and 25, 1899. According to Haskell, his wife had begun to counsel him that perhaps he was too burdened with the need to secure aid for Australia. The church had other needs as well.

41. S. N. Haskell, letter to E. G. White, November 10, 1899.

42. S. N. Haskell, letter to W. C. White, October 25, 1899.

43. S. N. Haskell, letter to E. G. White, October 24, 1899.

44. W. C. White, letters to G. A. Irwin, September 18 and October 6, 1899.

45. W. C. White, letter to W. W. Prescott, October 6, 1899.

46. E. G. White, letter to J. H. Kellogg, December 14, 1898.

47. E. G. White, letter to J. H. Kellogg, March 10, 1900 (sent March 24).

48. E. G. White, letter to J. H. Kellogg, February 27, 1900.

49. E. G. White, letter to C. H. Jones, March 9, 1900. She explained to Jones that this and the need for her to support Irwin in the investigation of the related legal issues was what required her personal presence in America.

50. Richard W. Schwarz, *John Harvey Kellogg, M.D.*, (Nashville: Southern Publishing Association, 1970), 68, 69.

51. E. G. White, letter to W. W. Prescott, February 17, 1890.

52. "Transfer of the Medical Missionary Work to the Union Conference," *Union Conference Record,* May 1, 1900, 14, 15.

53. G. A. Irwin, letter to E. G. White, February 15, 1900. See also R. W. Schwarz, "The Kellogg Schism: The Hidden Issues," *Spectrum* 4 (Autumn 1972): 23–39.

54. E. G. White, letter to J. H. Kellogg, *Diary,* March 12, 1900.

55. E. G. White, letter to J. H. Kellogg, February 27, 1900. She expressed similar sentiments in an undated letter probably written early March 1900 and in a further letter composed at midnight on March 12, but not sent at that time.

56. E. G. White, letter to C. H. Jones, March 9, 1900.

57. E. G. White, letter to G. A. Irwin, March 23, 1900.

58. E. G. White, letter to S. N. Haskell, April 5, 1900.

59. W. W. Prescott, letter to E. G. White, April 26, 1900.

60. G. A. Irwin, letters to E. G. White, April 12 and 26, 1900.

61. E. G. White, Letter 170, January 1900.

62. G. A. Irwin, letter to E. G. White, April 12, 1900.

63. E. G. White, letter to S. N. Haskell and G. A. Irwin, April 25, 1900.

64. E. G. White, letter to J. H. Kellogg, written in May, but sent June 16, 1900.

65. G. A. Irwin, letter to E. G. White, June 11, 1900.

66. E. G. White, letter to J. H. Kellogg, July 2, 1900.

67. E. G. White, letter to Brother Braught, July 14, 1900; G. A. Irwin, letter to J. H. Kellogg, July 19, 1900.

68. The "Cats of Kilkenny" is a proverbial reference to a willingness to fight to the death. An old limerick expresses the thought well:

"There once were two cats of Kilkenny
Each thought there was one cat too many
So they fought and they hit
And they scratched and they bit
'Til (excepting their nails
And the tips of their tails)
Instead of two cats there weren't any!"

69. G. A. Irwin, letters to E. G. White, July 2 and 19, 1900.

CHAPTER 7

1. E. G. White, letter to S. N. Haskell and G. A. Irwin, February 7, 1900.
2. *Union Conference Record,* April 1, 1900, 16.
3. *Seventh-day Adventist Encyclopedia,* s.v. "Claremont Sanitarium." The sanitarium never recovered from the heavy losses caused by the war. Members of the Wessels family took over management of it in 1901 in an attempt to restore its patronage, but the post-war depression made that difficult. Although operated for a time as a hotel, it finally went bankrupt. Fire destroyed the building in 1905.
4. *Union Conference Record,* May 1, 1900, 18; July 1, 1900, 15; and "A Visit to Africa," *Union Conference Record,* August 1, 1900.
5. "My Visit to Europe," *Union Conference Record,* October 1, 1900, 2, 3.
6. A. G. Daniells, letter to G. A. Irwin, cited in G. A. Irwin, letter to E. G. White, July 2, 1900.
7. G. A. Irwin, letter to E. G. White, July 2, 1900.
8. Ibid.
9. Ibid.
10. Ellen White was also stating to others that it would have been better if the Wesselses had not given the $40,000 to Kellogg for his Chicago projects. At the same time, she had advised that the health food work then being established in New Zealand should not link up with Battle Creek, especially since Kellogg sought to patent his health foods in such a way as to claim all profits. This had caused great distress at Union College. E. G. White, letter to Brother Braught, July 14, 1990.
11. G. A. Irwin, letter to E. G. White, July 2, 1900.
12. Ibid.
13. G. A. Irwin, letter to E. G. White, July 19, 1900.
14. Ibid.
15. Ibid.
16. E. G. White, letter to G. A. Irwin, August 12, 1900.
17. Ibid.

18. E. G. White, letter to S. N. Haskell, August 13, 1900.
19. E. G. White, letter to G. A. Irwin, August 12, 1900.
20. E. G. White, letter to the Officers of the General Conference, November 1, 1900.
21. E. G. White, letter to Edson and Emma White, August 14, 1900.
22. W. C. White had given this to the church membership in Australia as the specific reason for her return. See "Returning to America," *Union Conference Record*, September 1, 1900, 16.
23. E. G. White, letter to G. A. Irwin, October 16, 1900.
24. Ibid.
25. D. H. Kress, letter to E. G. White, October 18, 1900.
26. E. G. White, letter to Officers of the General Conference, October 24, 1900 (but typed November 1).
27. E. G. White, letter to H. T. Kellogg, November 1, 1900; Arthur L. White, *The Early Elmshaven Years*, 43.
28. E. G. White, letter to E. W. Farnsworth et al., December 12, 1900.
29. E. G. White, letter to G. A. Irwin, November 13. The balance of the letter sets out at length good practical advice on meeting planning. But it also illustrates Ellen White's tendency to elevate a local and specific problem into a large-canvas issue. One could get the impression that she regarded holding meetings in winter as a significant moral issue.
30. E. G. White, letter to G. A. Irwin, December 4, 1900.
31. G. A. Irwin, letter to E. G. White, December 11, 1900.
32. Ibid.
33. E. G. White, letter to G. A. Irwin, December 28, 1900.
34. *General Conference Bulletin,* April 25, 1901, 464.
35. W. W. Prescott, letter to E. J. Waggoner, June 15, 1902.
36. E. G. White, "Verbatim Report," Library Meeting, 1901. Three versions of the speech are extant, each recorded by a different stenographer. Kellogg took his own stenographer to the meeting, while Daniells had C. C. Crisler as his personal stenographer. The parties wanted to make sure they were not hearing different things.
37. Ibid.; *General Conference Bulletin,* April 3, 1901, 24–27.
38. *General Conference Bulletin,* April 3, 1901, 27.
39. "Life Sketch and Funeral Service of Elder G. A. Irwin," *Review and Herald*, June 5, 1913, 544.
40. Ibid.
41. W. W. Prescott, letter to W. C. White, October 26, 1900; A. G. Daniells, letter to W. C. White, July 1, 1901.
42. *Union Conference Record,* July 1, 1900, 16.
43. E. G. White, letter to G. A. Irwin, June 30, 1902.
44. Ibid.
45. Ibid.
46. E. G. White, letter to G. A. Irwin, October 14, 1902.
47. G. A. Irwin, letter to E. G. White, cited in Alta Robinson, "From Soldier Boy to President."
48. G. A. Irwin, letter to A. G. Daniells, October 10, 1901.

CHAPTER 8

1. W. W. Prescott, letter to A. G. Daniells, January 25, 1903.

2. W. W. Prescott, letter to A. G. Daniells, January 26, 1903.

3. A. G. Daniells, letter to E. G. White, March 13, 1903.

4. Ibid.

5. A. G. Daniells, letter to W. C. White, October 29, 1903.

6. Other biographical details appear in Percy T. Magan, "Life Sketch of Arthur Grosvenor Daniells," *Record,* June 3, 1935; Everett Dick, "Arthur G. Daniells, Organizer," *The Youth's Instructor,* October 24, 1944, 4; and John J. Robertson, *A. G. Daniells: The Making of a General Conference President, 1901* (Mountain View, CA: Pacific Press®, 1977), 13–23, 99.

7. A. G. Daniells, letter to E. G. White, October 10, 1892.

8. See Gilbert M. Valentine, "A. G. Daniells, Administrator, and the Development of Conference Organization in Australia," in Arthur J. Ferch, ed., *Symposium on Adventist History in the South Pacific: 1885-1919* (Wahroonga, Australia: South Pacific Division of Seventh-day Adventists, 1986), 76–91.

9. Milton R. Hook, "The Inter-relationships Between A. G. Daniells and E. G. White During Their Years in Australasia," ibid., 92–104.

10. W. C. White, letter to A. G. Daniells, October 20, 1892.

11. W. C. White, letter to O. A. Olsen, January 20, 1893.

12. Milton R. Hook, in *Symposium on Adventist History in the South Pacific: 1885-1919*, 103.

13. Australian Union Conference Minutes, January 18, 19, 25, 1894.

14. W. C. White, letter to Foreign Mission Board, February 20, 1895. See Valentine, "A. G. Daniells," in *Symposium on Adventist History in the South Pacific: 1885-1919* for a more detailed discussion of the organizational developments during Daniells' time in Australia.

15. W. C. White, letter to O. A. Olsen, June 3, 1896.

16. W. C. White had not had the opportunity of a furlough, was under financial strain supporting his two young daughters back in the United States, and had been overworking. He was approaching burnout. For a fuller discussion of the problem and the sensitive but spiritually mature way in which it was resolved, see Valentine, "A. G. Daniells, Administrator, and the Development of Conference Organization in Australia," in Arthur J. Ferch, ed., *Symposium on Adventist History in the South Pacific: 1885-1919,* 82–86.

17. O. A. Olsen, letter to W. W. Prescott, August 10, 1896.

18. A. T. Robinson, "Autobiographical Sketch," cited in Barry D. Oliver, *SDA Organizational Structure,* 74

19. *General Conference Bulletin,* April 7, 1901, 90.

20. A. G. Daniells, letter to E. G. White, March 3, 1895. Hook notes that Daniells's reply reads like "the words of a man groping his way back from a fractured relationship," and that the statement "some portions I do not as yet understand" could be a euphemism for his feeling that some of the criticisms may have been unjustified (Hook, in *Symposium on Adventist History in the South Pacific: 1885-1919,* 97).

21. E. G. White, letter to A. G. Daniells, March 12, 1897; A. G. Daniells, letter to E. G. White, April 18, 1897.

22. A. G. Daniells, letter to E. G. White, January 19, 1897.

23. E. G. White, letter to A. G. Daniells and E. R. Palmer, June 27, 1897.

24. A. G. Daniells, letter to E. G. White, May 17, 1900.

25. A. G. Daniells, letter to W. W. Prescott, July 21, 1901.

26. A. G. Daniells, letter to W. W. Prescott, June 24, 1901.

27. This freewheeling approach to voting constituencies did not last. It backfired when the Annual Council of 1902 threw open committee meetings to the church public and controversy became very public indeed. The 1903 session also highlighted the need for a firm basis for delegate selection.

28. A. G. Daniells, letter to W. C. White, July 1, 1901. It seems that Ellen White was reluctant to have the address circulated publicly for fear that it could be libelous. Some had apparently advised her that others might challenge it on legal grounds (A. G. Daniells, letter to R. A. Underwood, March 21, 1902). Kellogg had produced his own version of the address taken down by his own stenographers.

29. With regard to the locating of the college, Ellen White did reply that "as far as she had any light regarding the general principles, she could not see any objection to the place and advised us to take it." As it happened, time constraints meant that the committee had to reach a decision before her letter arrived. In this case the response served as affirmation of something made on the basis of the best information then available to the committee. See A. G. Daniells, letter to W. W. Prescott, July 21, 1901.

30. E. G. White, letter to A. G. Daniells, June 24, 1901.

31. The problematic sentence occurs on page 29 of *Special Testimonies for Ministers and Workers* (College View, NE: College Press, 1897): "It is not wise to choose one man as president of the General Conference." It had earlier appeared in "E. G. White to Conference Presidents and Councilors," August 1896, a manuscript that Ellen White had given to Prescott to take with him to the 1897 session. Jones, Waggoner, and Prescott had opportunity to study the extensive body of material at length prior to the meetings. The sentence became a rallying cry for reform and resulted in the 1897 session creating three General Conferences and three presidents. W. C. White recalled that after the 1897 session "we had no president of the General Conference," but that the title crept back in "within a few months." The sentence was eventually re-interpreted through a focus on the spirit and intent behind it rather than on the formal wording itself. It came to be understood that "the president should not be the one person to whom the details in the various parts of the field should be referred." See A. G. Daniells, letter to W. C. White, May 30, 1901; Barry D. Oliver, *SDA Organizational Structure,* 186ff.

32. A. G. Daniells, letter to W. C. White, July 1, 1901.

33. *General Conference Bulletin,* 1903, 151, 158. Jones had expounded to delegates at length on the importance of the earlier statements.

34. U. Smith, "The Cause," *Review and Herald,* January 7, 1902.

35. A discussion of Prescott's diplomatic handling of the troubling change in editorship appears in Valentine, *W. W. Prescott: Forgotten Giant,* 195ff.

36. A. G. Daniells, letter to W. W. Prescott, February 25, 1902.

37. A. G. Daniells, letter to G. A. Irwin, December 12, 1902.

38. E. G. White, letter to A. G. Daniells, September 6, 1902.

39. A. G. Daniells, letter to C. W. Flaiz, November 6, 1903. Dr. Flaiz was the medical director for the newly created North Pacific Union.

40. In 1901, the total institutional debt totaled $1.25 million. Using a minister's salary for 1901 ($950.00) as a benchmark, the debt was 131,572 times a pastor's annual salary.

41. E. G. White, letter to H. W. Kellogg, January 13, 1903.

42. E. G. White, letter to H. W. Kellogg, January 13, 1903. It was the second letter that she had written to Kellogg on the same day. "I think that after having written these letters to you my mind may be at rest." Two years later, she would describe her general approach to the president of the East Pennsylvania Conference, W. J. Fitzgerald. "We just raise every penny possible from the friends in the locality where the institution is to be, and then we pray, and then we feel clear to borrow at low interest from our brethren who have money to lend, and I have worked this way in Australia and since coming to this country." She would not encourage Fitzgerald "to look to the General Conference to take the responsibility of paying the debts of the Sanitariums that are being established." Instead, independently "when we take up the burden of purchasing buildings, we lay the whole matter before our own people in the Conference . . . and let them share the burden. We have done this with much success" (E. G. White, letter to W. J. Fitzgerald, June 8, 1905). The strategy was not always successful, and it caused severe tensions with administration when it did not work.

43. E. G. White, letter to "My Brethren in Positions of Responsibility," December 26, 1902.

44. E. G. White, "Special Testimonies to Ministers and Workers," 1895, 50, 51. See also General Conference Committee Minutes, July 19, 1895. During the 1894 economic depression, C. H. Jones had complained that S. N. Haskell was also too inclined to this approach of "reaching out on borrowed capitol [*sic*] and then pressing for means to relieve the strain every little while." Jones felt that this approach discouraged the churches (C. H. Jones, letter to O. A. Olsen, June 26, 1894; Barry D. Oliver, *SDA Organizational Structure,* 148–154).

45. Magan observed that church members were in the lending business and the General Conference was in the borrowing business. Daniells later lamented that the $60,000 that had to be raised by donations from church members to solve the bankruptcy of the Christiana Publishing House had been done simply in order to be honest. Absolutely no assets remained after it was all over (Oliver, *SDA Organizational Structure,* 151).

46. "Report of a Portion of a Council Meeting held at Mrs. E. G. White's home, Elmshaven, 8 am October 19, 1902," 11.

47. Ibid.

48. E. G. White, letter to Edson White, January 5, 1903. Ellen White's deepest fear was a spiritual one—that she might die "and leave you and Willie standing in your present attitude to one another." She entreated Edson to be reconciled to his brother.

49. E. G. White, letter to A. G. Daniells, November 17, 1902. "The statements I made must not be held but retracted." Nor did she want the transcript of the interview distributed. "I had not a clear knowledge of the facts that make it safe to make such statements." She apparently felt uncomfortable by the directness of the questions that had been put to her and felt that she should not put in writing statements "drawn out by questions such as were asked me at that

time." See also E. G. White, letter to Judge Jesse Arthur, January 14, 1903. Ellen White stated that she had been wrong in endorsing the plans of W. C. White and A. G. Daniells. C. C. Crisler had circulated the transcript of the lengthy interview session, and when Ellen White read it she felt most uncomfortable with what she had said.

50. For example, fitting out part of the publishing house with good (but expensive) carpet and furniture had been done in a hurry in order to have the place ready and with the particular intent of having the facilities comfortable and appropriate in time for the use of delegates from the north who would be attending meetings—not for the use of the regular employees. Criticism had arisen over this "unwise" expense.

51. E. G. White, *Diary,* November 7, 1902. See also E. G. White, letter to "My Brethren in Positions of Responsibility," December 26, 1902. The personnel problems in Nashville perplexed Ellen White for some weeks. She had second thoughts about the whole situation in late October, composed some reflections on the issue in her diary in early November, but did not write to Daniells and Palmer on the issue until late December.

52. P. T. Magan, *Diary,* August 9, 1908. Magan discusses an interview with Ellen White in which she reportedly stated that "the Southern Union Conference is not to own you or control you. You must not turn things over to them." "In the matter of the Madison school, there has been a standing off from them because they were not under the ownership and control of some conference. This is a question that should sometimes be considered . . . The attitude that some of our brethren have assumed toward this enterprise shows that it is not wise for every working agency to be under the dictation of conference officers. There are some enterprises under certain conditions, that will produce better results if left standing alone" (E. G. White, letter to A. G. Daniells and I. H. Evans, September 23, 1907).

53. W. W. Prescott, letter to A. G. Daniells, July 16, 1902.

54. W. W. Prescott, letter to A. G. Daniells, October 13, 1902.

55. E. G. White, letter to Edson White, January 5, 1903.

56. Kellogg felt that he needed to also count on Dr. David Paulson, Dr. Daniel Kress, Edson White, A. T. Jones, P. T. Magan, and E. A. Sutherland to help get his perspectives across.

57. G. A. Irwin, letter to A. G. Daniells, November 3, 1903.

58. *General Conference Bulletin,* 1903, 32.

59. In the midst of a heated debate on the constitution at the 1903 session, G. I. Butler and A. T. Jones in a public disagreement lightheartedly agreed that they would not "quarrel" even though they disagreed with each other. The exchange seems to be an allusion to Ellen White's counsel and that they could still shake hands though their perspectives were opposed on the issue under debate ("Recording Secretaries Minutes," April 9, 1903, 163).

60. Ibid.

61. A. G. Daniells, letter to G. A. Irwin, December 12, 1902.

62. Ibid. Daniells summarized the conflict at this stage as revolving around two issues. "Whether we have abandoned the debt-making policy or not, and whether or not every man shall have the privilege of exercising the divine right to use his thinking machine as it seems best to him, and to express his convictions freely." According to Daniells, Kellogg "wished to create a $30,000 debt in England. USA brethren to pay 20,000 and British brethren 10,000." "Because

I chose to think differently from him, and to state my views as freely as he chose to state his, he held me up as an obstructionist, and represented to others, especially the medical fraternity, that I was unsympathetic and unfriendly with the medical work and unwilling to cooperate with them."

63. General Conference Committee Minutes, April 18, 1901.

64. A. G. Daniells, letter to G. A. Irwin, December 12, 1902.

65. George R. Knight, *From 1888 to Apostasy: The Case of A. T. Jones* (Washington, DC: Review and Herald®, 1987), 189; General Conference Committee Minutes, November 15, 1902; A. G. Daniells, letter to C. C. Nicola, July 30, 1906.

66. J. H. Kellogg, letter to F. M. Wilcox, January 5, 1903. Prescott had earlier reported to Wilcox that the rumors that Daniells and Prescott were against the institution and its work were simply not true. They just did not believe the new building or the one in England should be built on borrowed capital (W. W. Prescott, letter to F. M. Wilcox, December 7, 1902).

67. G. A. Irwin, letter to E. W. Farnsworth, March 8, 1903. How many others she talked to in this vein is not clear, but she intended it as a clear political and economic statement designed to exercise maximum leverage on the decision.

68. The tabernacle's heating system depended on the steam provided by the Review boilers, which had been destroyed. W. W. Prescott, letter to A. G. Daniells, January 18, 1903.

69. W. W. Prescott, letter to A. G. Daniells, January 25 and 26, 1903.

70. E. G. White, letter to Judge Jesse Arthur, January 14, 1903.

71. E. G. White, letter to E. R. Palmer and A. G. Daniells, January 8, 1903.

72. E. G. White, letter to A. G. Daniells, January 23, 1903.

73. E. G. White, letter to J. E. White, January 11, 1903.

74. E. G. White, letter to A. T. Jones, C. H. Jones, and M. C. Wilcox, January 27, 1903. In the letter, Ellen White lamented the stressful time she had experienced at the 1901 General Conference and felt as if her efforts were of "none effect." "The testimonies are speculated upon, and do not reform existing evils," she complained. Earlier she had written to Edson White that she was resolved "to throw off as far as possible the burden of the work in Nashville. It is too great for me to carry. I must drop it from my soul . . . I shall have to lay it off, else I shall be unfitted for my writing" (E. G. White, letter to J. E. White, January 5, 1903).

75. W. W. Prescott, letter to A. G. Daniells, January 18, 1903.

76. E. G. White, *Diary,* February 13, 1903. Following the Jones visit, Ellen White commented to herself about the severe pain she was experiencing in her head and in her eyes. On the sensitive path ahead, she wrote, "May the Lord lead us and guide and direct us that we shall not make one false step that will injure the precious cause of truth."

77. E. G. White, letter to A. G. Daniells, January 5, 1903.

78. E. G. White, letter to Dear Children, Edson and Emma, January 29, February 1, 1903.

79. E. G. White, letter to S. N. Haskell, February 28, 1903.

80. E. G. White, letter to Sister Hall, February 29, 1903.

81. Butler alludes to this apprehension of Ellen White in a speech toward the end of the session. *General Conference Bulletin,* 1903, 161.

82. E. G. White, letter to Sister Hall, March 6, 1903. A letter from an attorney named Green,

reporting public criticism that Ellen White was getting rich and that "among our people there is great dissatisfaction as to how her money is obtained," traumatized her badly and exacerbated her hypertension. She had been unable to "have any matter of perplexity, requiring thought" brought before her for two or three weeks. But she reported that Clarence Crisler had been able to put her mind at rest by reading to her some earlier effective responses to the financial allegations.

83. G. A. Irwin, letter to E. W. Farnsworth, March 8, 1903.

Chapter 9

1. A. G. Daniells, letter to E. G. White, March 13, 1903.

2. Ibid.

3. A. G. Daniells, letter to W. C. White, December 24, 1903.

4. J. H. Kellogg, letter to E. G. White, February 15, 1903.

5. J. H. Kellogg, letter to W. C. White, March 18, 1903.

6. A. G. Daniells, letter to W. C. White, March 11, 1903; J. H. Kellogg, letter to W. C. White, March 18, 1903.

7. J. H. Kellogg, letter to E. G. White, March 27, 1903. Whether W. C. White actually read this letter to her or not is not clear. Along with it, Kellogg sent a package of potato flour and offered his service in any way if it would make her more comfortable.

8. W. W. Prescott, letter to A. G. Daniells, January 26, 1903.

9. She was listed as a delegate in 1901. Her name was not listed at the 1905 General Conference. While preliminary materials listed 139 delegates, a significant number did not arrive. Only eighty-eight had registered by the first meeting. A few others later joined them. Apparently by an oversight, the list of delegates was not published in the *General Conference Bulletin.* The names are available only in the stenographic record of the meeting.

10. *General Conference Bulletin,* 1903, 169.

11. Arthur L. White, *Ellen G. White, The Elmshaven Years, 1900-1905* (Washington, DC: Review and Herald®, 1981), 5:241ff. Ellen White had complained that the acoustics in the Oakland church were not good. Even in the social meetings, which she did stay for, it was exceedingly difficult for her to hear what people were saying from the floor.

12. E. G. White, letter to E. A. Sutherland and P. T. Magan, 1904, cited in the Spalding-Magan Collection, 361–363.

13. J. H. Kellogg, letter to E. G. White, April 8, 1903.

14. A. G. Daniells, "How the Denomination Was Saved from Pantheism," (1935), 16, 17.

15. A. G. Daniells, letter to W. C. White, February 15, 1932.

16. J. H. Kellogg, letter to E. G. White, March 27, 1903. Kellogg mentioned that he had "reason to think that my letters seldom reach you on account of the great press of burdens and your feeble health," but he hoped that "this line may come to you," and so he added a defense of his course, suggesting that "both my work and myself have been misrepresented to you" as was done with Edson.

17. E. G. White, letter to A. T. Jones, April 19 and 22, 1903. Other letters addressed issues dealing more with policy. Of particular interest is that in adopting this strategy, Ellen White was

bypassing the General Conference leadership group even though she was expecting them to be informed about such expenses in advance.

18. E. G. White, letter to F. C. Gilbert, March 28, 1903.

19. "General Conference Proceedings," March 27, 1903, 12–19.

20. Ellen White, Irwin, Daniells, Conradi, Waggoner, Jones, and Prescott (twice), all delivered lengthy sermons during the first Sabbath and Sunday of the session. Two lengthy social or testimony meetings were also included in the program.

21. E. G. White, "Lessons From the Sending Out of the Spies," *General Conference Bulletin,* 1903, 10, 11.

22. "General Conference Proceedings," 3:00 P.M., March 30, 1903. There had been some disagreement among the delegates as to what should be the official minutes. Were they to be found in the *Bulletin* published every morning? Or were they embodied in the "Proceedings" that functioned as a kind of *Congressional Record* or *Hansard* and caught every word said on the floor? A number of the speeches made by Kellogg from the floor of the conference were mentioned, but not reproduced in the *Bulletin,* though stenographically recorded in the "Proceedings."

23. "General Conference Proceedings," 6:00 P.M., March 30, 1903.

24. *General Conference Bulletin,* 1903, 67. The clarification was highly significant given the context of the discussion, and some delegates insisted that the minutes be amended to properly reflect what had been said. When it was realized that the content of Ellen White's talks was not handled by the *Bulletin* editors, but by her own editorial staff, proponents of the amendment had to be content with a simple publishing of the additional comments in a highlighted section of the next issue of the *Bulletin.*

25. "General Conference Proceedings," April 3, 1903, 10. The editors omitted his comments from the *Bulletin.*

26. "General Conference Proceedings," April 6, 1903, 44. Waggoner's comments do not appear in the *Bulletin.*

27. *General Conference Bulletin,* 1903, 78.

28. *General Conference Bulletin,* 1903, 216. The meeting that approved the action took place on Sunday evening, April 12, at 8:00 P.M., just hours before the session concluded.

29. When the sanitarium first legally incorporated in 1867, the only act under which it could do so was a law for commercial companies. The state of Michigan did not yet have laws for charitable enterprises. The thirty-year limit on its charter meant that it had to be re-incorporated in 1897 under difficult circumstances, and the insertion of terminology in the constitutional documents that the institution was to perform acts of "an undenominational, unsectarian, humanitarian and philanthropic nature" led to a change of mission, loss of control, and considerable confusion over its identity. For further details, see *Seventh-day Adventist Encyclopedia,* 138.

30. *General Conference Bulletin,* 1903, 146, 147.

31. "General Conference Proceedings," 11:00 A.M., April 9, 1903.

32. "General Conference Proceedings," 2:00 P.M., April 9, 1903. His implied threat did not make it into the pages of the *Bulletin.*

33. *General Conference Bulletin,* 1903, 159–161.

34. "General Conference Proceedings," April 10, 1903, 24.

35. *General Conference Bulletin,* 1903, 195.

36. It is not clear which Sunday morning it is that Ellen White refers to. She does not identify it by date. The letter was written on Sunday, April 12. Thus it seems likely that the Sunday she has in mind is the previous one, April 5, which occurred in the middle of the debate over ownership and the finances of the sanitarium. Kellogg had said highly provocative things during that weekend. Furthermore, he did not stay in Oakland for the final meetings of the session but returned home early. Ellen White was back home in Elmshaven by late evening on the twelfth.

37. E. G. White, letter to Elder Daniells and His Fellow Workers, April 12, 1903. Ellen White reported that she had been interrupted many times in the process of writing the letter, but that when she got back to finishing it she still had the same impression that she had when she "began to write."

38. G. A. Irwin, letter to E. G. White, December 18, 1903. Irwin reports that George Tenney from the Battle Creek Sanitarium had written to a host of friends and colleagues in the Australasian Union Conference expressing Kellogg's side of the story. Supporters also circulated Ellen White testimonies in defense of the Battle Creek position.

39. E. G. White, letter to A. G. Daniells, W. W. Prescott, and W. C. White, August 3, 1903.

40. E. G. White, letter to "Leaders in Our Medical Work," August 4, 1903; E. G. White, letter to A. G. Daniells, August 4, 1903.

41. J. H. Kellogg, letter to A. T. Jones, August 27, 1903.

42. E. G. White, letter to David Paulson, October 14, 1903.

43. E. G. White, letter to S. N. Haskell, November 28, 1903.

44. G. A. Irwin, letter to A. G. Daniells, November 3, 1903.

45. *General Conference Bulletin,* 1903, 156.

46. G. A. Irwin, letter to A. G. Daniells, December 19, 1903.

47. A. G. Daniells, letter to C. W. Flaiz, November 6, 1903.

48. Ibid.

49. A. G. Daniells, letter to W. C. White, December 24, 1903.

Chapter 10

1. 1919 Bible Conference Transcript, July 3, 1919. The transcript of the discussions on the gift of prophecy also appears in *Spectrum* 10, no. 1 (May 1979): 27–57.

2. Ellen White had cautioned Paulson prior to the Oakland General Conference about associating himself too closely with Kellogg and supporting him in his disagreement with Daniells and the church. After the 1903 Annual Council in Washington, she wrote to him protesting his linking of her writings and *The Living Temple.* "I am obliged to make a denial of this," she wrote. She could see that Paulson's assertions would seriously mislead and confuse church members (E. G. White, letter to D. Paulson, October 14, 1903).

3. A. G. Daniells, letter to E. G. White, October 20, 1903; E. G. White, letter to A. G. Daniells, November 1, 1903. Letters 211, 1903, and 216, 1903, were the ones she sent to be read at the council meeting. Daniells related the story frequently. See *The Abiding Gift of Prophecy* (Mountain View, CA: Pacific Press®, 1936), 336, 337, 342. Daniells's view of providence would likely suggest that the expression "exactly at the right time" did not necessarily mean that that

was the only, or even the best, time for the letters to arrive. If Ellen White had read the book earlier or written the letters after her first sleepless night and if they had arrived a few days earlier, they would probably have been just as useful and had as much impact and may have saved him and his colleagues significant anguish and distress. But second-guessing Providence is not just difficult and unreliable, it is unprofitable. What is done is done, and the eye of faith sees the hand of God and is grateful.

4. Valentine, *W. W. Prescott: Forgotten Giant,* 225.

5. W. W. Prescott, letter to J. W. Watt, February 18, 1904. For an analysis of the final stages of the Kellogg conflict, see Valentine, *W. W. Prescott: Forgotten Giant,* 171–191.

6. One of the more tragic events of the conference was the death of Percy Magan's wife, who had been struggling with lapses in nervous health. Late in 1903, the rumor mill in Battle Creek reported that Ellen White had turned against Magan, one of her "sons." Magan's wife became distressed over the report, suffered a collapse, and died on May 19, when the Berrien Springs meetings had reached its fevered worst. Accusations as to the source of the rumors fueled high emotion, for many attributed them to Daniells and Prescott. In fact, an anti-Magan faction in Battle Creek had spread them. Ellen White felt obliged to write a letter to be read to the conference before it closed to correct the misunderstanding, but no one wanted to read it. See Valentine, *W. W. Prescott: Forgotten Giant,* 179.

7. J. S. Washburn, "An Open Letter to A. G. Daniells and the General Conference," May 1, 1922.

8. W. C. White, "The Influence of Sister White's Helpers Over the Testimonies," in *The Sending Out of the Testimonies* (Mountain View, CA: Pacific Press®, 1913), 30, 31.

9. *Review and Herald,* May 18, 1905, 27. The 1905 session produced no *General Conference Bulletin.* The publishing enterprise in temporary quarters in Washington was stretched to the limit just trying to survive. Reports of the General Conference appeared in the regular *Review.*

10. Voted at the first meeting of the session on May 11 (*Review and Herald,* May 18, 1905, 23, 27).

11. *General Conference Bulletin,* 1903, 2.

12. *Review and Herald,* May 18, 1905, 6, 27.

13. E. G. White, letter to A. G. Daniells and I. H. Evans, September 23, 1907.

14. A. G. Daniells, letter to E. G. White, October 11, 1907.

15. Ibid.

16. $600,000 spent in the United States compared to only $150,000 overseas.

17. A. G. Daniells, letter to E. G. White, October 11, 1907.

18. E. G. White, *Early Writings* (Battle Creek, MI: Review and Herald®, 1882), 74.

19. General Conference Committee Minutes, May 31, 1905. The review committee for the book had comprised Olsen, Westphal, Thompson, Haffner, and Prescott.

20. W. C. White, letter to A. G. Daniells, October 6, 1910.

21. Valentine, *W. W. Prescott: Forgotten Giant,* 214–238, has a comprehensive discussion of the controversy over the interpretation of "the daily."

22. S. N. Haskell, letter to W. C. White, October 22, 1908; S. N. Haskell, letter to E. G. White, December 15, 1908.

23. W. C. White, letter to A. G. Daniells, March 22, 1908, cited in A. G. Daniells, letter to W. C. White, June 25, 1908.

24. *General Conference Bulletin,* May 28, 1909.

25. E. G. White, letter to J. E. White, June 16, 1909.

26. The continuing low-level personal attacks combined with remarks reportedly made by Ellen White and circulated by her older friends such as G. B. Starr, stung Prescott's wife, Sarah, who not long afterward succumbed to cancer. Her last days were darkly clouded not only by the unkind things said about her husband by others, but by the reported loss of confidence of Ellen White in her husband (W. W. Prescott, letter to W. C. White, April 15, 1915). Prescott's second wife, Daisy, aware of the distress caused to Sarah, because she had nursed the woman in her last illness, destroyed most of the professor's correspondence after his death for fear that his critics would continue to be unkind.

27. Valentine, *W. W. Prescott: Forgotten Giant,* 239–248.

28. E. G. White, letter to A. G. Daniells, 1910. If understood within a fully developed biblical formulation of the doctrine of salvation, Ellen White could not have been suggesting that Daniells at that point was outside the pale of God's grace. The General Conference president's relationship with God was much stronger than that. What seems to have been happening is that Ellen White felt that she needed to shout in order to get his attention. Suggesting that he needed to be reconverted was more a way of saying he needed to re-order his spiritual priorities at that point. She certainly got his attention. But she was not suggesting, it would seem, that Daniells had actually departed from the Christian faith and that if his life had ceased at that point he would have died unredeemed. Daniells acknowledged years later, in 1928, in a lighter homiletic moment, that "he did not have as much light on the matter of conversion as I now have." The 1910 letter, he related "cut me severely at the time," but he did not reject it. It led him to pray, he said, for "the understanding I seemed to lack" (*Australasian Record,* August 13, 1928).

29. C. C. Crisler, "Report of an Interview," June 19, 1910.

30. A. G. Daniells, letter to W. C. White, July 5, 1910.

31. A. G. Daniells, letters to W. C. White, January 3, February 11, and July 5, 1910; A. G. Daniells, letter to E. G. White, May 26, 1910; E. G. White, letter to A. G. Daniells, June 15, 1910. An extensive discussion of the exchange of correspondence appears in Arthur L. White, *Ellen G. White: The Later Elmshaven Years, 1905-1915,* 6:221–230.

32. A. L. White, *The Later Elmshaven Years,* 6:364.

33. *General Conference Bulletin,* 1913, 5, 6.

34. Almost 30 percent of the delegation came from overseas mission assignments.

35. *General Conference Bulletin,* 1913, 275.

36. See Greenfield and Schwarz, *Light Bearers,* 313ff.

37. *General Conference Bulletin,* 1913, 218.

38. See Valentine, *The Struggle for the Prophetic Heritage,* 32, 94, for a discussion of the Whites' difficulties with Evans.

39. General Conference Committee Minutes, January 21, 1913.

40. General Conference Committee Minutes, April 13, 1913.

41. Loma Linda University Constituency Minutes, March 28, 1912; Ms. 14, 1912; *Review*

and Herald, September 28, 1916; A. L. White, *The Later Elmshaven Years,* 6:368, 369.

42. General Conference Committee Minutes, January 22, 1913.

43. *General Conference Bulletin,* 1913, 129; General Conference Committee Minutes, January 22, 1913. S. E. Wight took care to report that the closure had the "full consent" of the union committee and the sanitarium board after receiving advice from the General Conference Finance Committee, which had "carefully investigated it."

44. W. C. White, letter to A. G. Daniells, December 31, 1913.

45. *General Conference Bulletin,* 1913, 218–221.

46. E. G. White, *The Writing and Sending Out of the Testimonies* (Mountain View, CA: Pacific Press®, 1913). Some of the statements were drawn from letters Ellen White had written in 1906. Others were personal reflections written in her diary and some from letters written in Australia, when W. C. White first connected with her work.

47. W. C. White, letter to O. A. Olsen, June 3 and 8, 1896; W. W. Prescott, letter to O. A. Olsen, May 4, 1896.

48. General Conference Committee Minutes, November 5, 1913.

49. What particularly troubled the leaders was a letter that Ellen White had sent to G. F. Watson in 1905 in which she had described in some detail her strikingly independent approach to the use of tithe monies as well as a letter written about the same time to W. J. Fitzgerald. The latter advocated the irregular practice of bypassing denominational channels in the developing of institutions. Such documents did indeed present problems for those called to exercise their gifts of leadership within a regulated organization. The letters were quite anti-establishment in tone. While W. C. White felt that it might seem easier to "repudiate" the letters or perhaps regard them as "forgeries," the best way, in his view, was to "tell the truth" and to deal with matters "just as they are." Ultimately, the unique charisma recognized in Ellen White was being exercised in her as a person, and inevitably, then, this was also processed through her distinctive temperament and her personality, one shaped by her whole life experience. She was a normal human being in that regard, flawed, struggling, striving for high ideals, sometimes failing, but totally committed in her faith and in her conviction of God's providence (see W. C. White, letter to A. G. Daniells, December 31, 1913).

50. Ibid.

51. For an extended discussion of these issues, see Valentine, "The Church 'Drifting toward a Crisis': Prescott's 1915 Letter to William White," *Catalyst* 1, no. 2 (2007).

52. W. C. White, letter to A. G. Daniells, December 31, 1913.

53. A. L. White suggests that only two were sent (*The Later Elmshaven Years,* 387), but Daniells cites three messages from which he read extracts (*General Conference Bulletin,* 322).

54. *General Conference Bulletin,* 1913, 150.

55. *General Conference Bulletin,* 1913, 14.

CHAPTER 11

1. Arthur L. White, *Ellen G. White: The Lonely Years,* 3:412. Cf. A. V. Olsen, *Through Crisis to Victory: 1888-1901* (Washington, DC: Review and Herald®, 1966), 7. The book was later reissued as *Thirteen Crisis Years.*

2. See, for example, Speed P. Leas and Paul Kittlaus, *Church Fights* (Westminster-John Knox, 1973), and Kenneth O. Gangel and Samuel L. Canine, *Communication and Conflict Management in Churches and Christian Organizations* (Wipf and Stock, 2002).

3. George R. Knight in *From 1888 to Apostasy: The Case of A. T. Jones,* 11, identifies the issues as "the meaning of the 1888 General Conference session, the problem of 1893 and the delay of Christ's return, the nature of sanctification, the Adventist holiness movement, charismatic gifts, the role of Ellen White, the human nature of Christ, the Adventist crusade against a Christian America, church and state relationships, and the proper function of church organization."

4. E. G. White, *Writing and Sending Out of the Testimonies,* 25. The chapter titled "Counsel on How to Study and Use the Writings," authored by T. H. Jemison, in Arthur White's *Ellen G. White: Messenger to the Remnant* (Washington, DC: Ellen G. White Estate, 1969), 88–91 has a helpful discussion of this hermeneutical principle among others.

5. The correspondence often included manuscripts that she intended to be read as letters to various groups of people.

6. E. G. White, letter to W. W. Prescott, October 2, 1893; *Review,* October 17, 1893, 660.

7. "To the Men Who Occupy Responsible Positions in the Work," July 1, 1896. The robbery was complicated, she explained, because "everything seemed to have reference to some other line and some other interest."

8. "They have made rules and resolutions and agreements with their fellow men, only to change and break them, to promise and not perform" (Ellen G. White, Letter 7, 1896).

9. "To the Men Who Occupy Responsible Positions in the Work," July 1, 1896.

10. Ibid.

11. Ibid.

12. A series of strongly worded letters raises these problems. See E. G. White, letter to O. A. Olsen, June 10, 1894; O-56-94, which is undated but was probably sent in July or August of that year; E. G. White, letter to O. A. Olsen, November 26, 1894; E. G. White, letter to O. A. Olsen, May 1, 1895; and E. G. White, letter to O. A. Olsen, June 19, 1895.

13. Letter C 24, 1896.

14. E. G. White, letter to J. S. Washburn, July 5, 1896.

15. "To the Men Who Occupy Responsible Positions in the Work," July 1, 1896.

16. Ms. 66, 1898.

17. Ibid.

18. E. G. White, letter to Brother and Sister Waggoner, August 26, 1898.

19. E. G. White, letter to Jennie Ings, December 4, 1894; E. G. White, letter to C. H. Jones, July 8, 1895. Mrs. White wrote the latter letter to protest the consolidation of the publishing program under one organization.

20. W. W. Prescott, letter to E. G. White, July 30, 1896.

21. O. A. Olsen, letter to W. C White, January 28, 1896.

22. O. A. Olsen, letter to W. C. White, March 9, 1896.

23. O. A. Olsen, letter to E. G. White, August 14, 1896.

24. E. G. White, letter to A. O. Tait, August 27, 1896.

25. O. A. Olsen, letter to E. G. White, August 14, 1896; O. A. Olsen, letter to W. C. White, April 18, 1895.

26. A. G. Daniells, letter to E. G. White, March 3, 1895. Daniells prayed that God would give him "a tender, responsive heart to all His warnings, reproofs and promises."

27. A. V. Olson, *Through Crisis to Victory,* 7.

28. E. G. White, letter to W. W. Prescott, August 27, 1898.

29. E. G. White, letter to O. A. Olsen, November 26, 1894.

30. E. G. White, letter to O. A. Olsen, 1894 (O-55-94).

31. E. G. White, letter to W. W. Prescott, December 22, 1893.

32. E. G. White, letter to O. A. Olsen, October 21, 1894.

33. E. G. White, Ms. 57, October 12, 1895.

34. *General Conference Bulletin,* 1891, 256.

35. E. G. White, Ms. 29, 1891.

36. E. G. White, *Diary,* August 5, 1891 (Ms. 44, 1891).

37. E. G. White, Ms. 29, 1891.

38. E. G. White, Ms. 75, 1893.

39. E. G. White, letter to O. A. Olsen, October 12, 1891.

40. E. G. White, Ms. 75, 1893; E. G. White, letter to J. H. Kellogg, July 5, 1892 (Letter 18a).

41. E. G. White, Ms. 75, 1893.

42. E. G. White, Letter 10, 1892.

43. E. G. White, letter to J. H. Kellogg, July 5, 1892.

44. E. G. White, letter to O. A. Olsen, December 1, 1896.

45. Ibid.

46. E. G. White, letter to "All Ye Are Brethren," March 8, 1895.

47. Ellen White's reminder was in the context of explaining why she had written him a strong letter of rebuke twelve months previously. In it she recounted how she had left manuscripts with Olsen when she left Michigan and had enjoined him to read them to his colleagues on the committees and boards "in order to correct the existing evils." But he had not felt able to carry out this instruction directly as she specified, thinking that he would deal with the matters in his "discourses by dwelling upon general principles," thus hoping that "this would prove the best method of correcting the wrongs." She criticized him severely for giving "such a feeble protest" and stated bluntly, "You failed to do your duty as President of the General Conference" (E. G. White, letter to O. A. Olsen, November 26, 1894).

48. E. G. White, letter to O. A. Olsen, December 1, 1896.

49. E. G. White, letter to "All Ye Are Brethren," March 8, 1895.

50. SDAPA board minutes, January 4 and 29, 1903.

51. *Seventh-day Adventist Encyclopedia,* 1213.

52. "The Publishing Work," *General Conference Bulletin,* February 16, 1899, 8; A. L. White, "The Story of the Review and Herald Fire," *Review and Herald,* December 8, 1977, 5, 36.

53. See my discussion of the difficulties in reforming the publishing program in *W. W. Prescott: Forgotten Giant,* 192ff.

54. W. C. White, letter to W. W. Prescott, August 22, October 22, 1899; W. W. Prescott,

letter to W. C. White, October 26 and December 28, 1899; January 15 and March 16, 1900.

55. E. G. White, letter to A. G. Daniells, June 28, 1901.

56. E. G. White, letter to O. A. Olsen, June 21, 1890. See also E. G. White, letter to O. A. Olsen, July–August 1894 (O-55-94).

57. The reason given for the transfer of the publishing rights to the church was to satisfy some who were disturbed that a non-Adventist concern published the popular book. See *The Comprehensive Index to the Writings of Ellen White,* vol. 3.

58. E. G. White, letter to O. A. Olsen, June 21, 1890.

59. E. G. White, letter to J. N. Loughborough, February 19, 1899.

60. In 1893, the Australian Federal Bank collapsed as the international depression affected the country. The authorities implemented a five-day bank holiday to address the panic. During the previous year, 133 companies went into liquidation in Victoria, the state where Mrs. White lived at the time. Although the crisis bottomed out in 1894, it took the rest of the decade to rebuild business confidence and a healthy economy. See Michael Cannon, *The Land Boomers* (Melbourne University Press, 1966), 197.

61. "For the last six months I have not been able to pay my workers. A heavy grocery bill has been accumulating in Newcastle, the place where we trade, but the merchants have waited patiently for me to see [to] the account" (E. G. White, letter to "Brethren in California," December 28, 1898). She resolved to sell two of her houses in Battle Creek, asking J. H. Kellogg to take them off her hands (E. G. White, letter to J. H. Kellogg, December 29, 1898).

62. The July 1, 1896, letter, "To the Men Who Occupy Responsible Positions in the Work," is one of her most emphatic letters, employing frequent hyperbole.

63. Currently, Seventh-day Adventist denominational policy sets royalty rates at 12 percent of the wholesale price of softcover books and 14 percent for hardcover books. Royalties increase to 16 percent for sales above fifteen thousand copies. Royalty rates are lower for certain high-volume items such as devotionals and textbooks. See, e.g., pacificpress.com/index.php?pgName=newsBookSub#Contracts.

64. E. G. White, letter to J. N. Loughborough, February 19, 1899.

65. E. G. White, letter to A. G. Daniells, June 5, 1901.

66. She argued that the publishing house should have absorbed the costs of publication for those kinds of books written for the purpose of raising funds for developing the church in new places (E. G. White, letter to A. G. Daniells, June 5, 1901).

67. E. G. White, letter to Brother and Sister Hart, February 19, 1900.

68. E. G. White, letter to S. N. Haskell, March 27, 1898.

69. E. G. White, letter to G. A. Irwin, December 18, 1899.

70. E. G. White, letter to Mrs. Gotzian, February 11, 1898.

71. E. G. White, letter to O. A. Olsen, May 12, 1895.

72. Ibid.

73. E. G. White, letter to Edson and Emma White, June 26, 1901.

74. E. G. White, Ms. 41, 1902. See also, Letter 114, 1896.

75. E. G. White, letter to Edson and Emma White, June 26, 1901; E. G. White, letter to J. H. Kellogg, December 1, 1898.

76. E. G. White, letter to W. C. White, August 1898.
77. See for example, Deborah Tannen, *You Just Don't Understand* (New York: Ballantine Books, 1990).
78. E. G. White, letter to O. A. Olsen, May 25, 1896.
79. E. G. White, letter to Brother and Sister Waggoner, August 26, 1898.
80. W. H. Littlejohn, "Danger in Adopting Extreme Views," *Review,* April 3, 10, 1894.
81. Maybe it was the quote from Joshua Himes that during the years following the 1844 disappointment "fanaticism was seven feet deep" that proved so cutting to Ellen White's sensitivity, but Littlejohn acknowledged that it was undoubtedly an exaggeration.
82. E. G. White, Ms. 27, 1894.
83. E. G. White, letter to W. H. Littlejohn, June 3, 1894.
84. E. G. White, letter to Brethren/North Fitzroy Church, 1898.
85. E. G. White, Ms. 24, 1888.
86. E. G. White, letter to G. A. Irwin, W. W. Prescott, E. J. Waggoner, and C. H. Jones, February 21, 1899.
87. E. G. White, letter to G. A. Irwin, June 15, 1902.
88. E. G. White, letter to W. W. Prescott, August 27, 1898.
89. E. G. White, letter to H. C. Lacey, December 20, 1896. The letter has had a section added in May 1897. Ellen White wrote it when she felt obliged to tell the young Lacey that he was not experienced enough to serve as the principal of the Avondale School, even though the board had appointed him to the role. She had to countermand the board action and obviously found the situation quite stressful. "You have perceptive faculties, Bro and Sis Lacey. God has given you talents, and you must use them to a purpose. May the Lord help you."
90. E. G. White, letter to O. A. Olsen, August 11, 1896, with seven copies circulated to other general leaders in December 1896. Letter C 24, 1896.
91. "To the Men Who Occupy Responsible Positions in the Work," July 1, 1896.
92. Barry D. Oliver, *SDA Organizational Structure,* 52, 53, 56.

INDEX

More about Ellen G. White

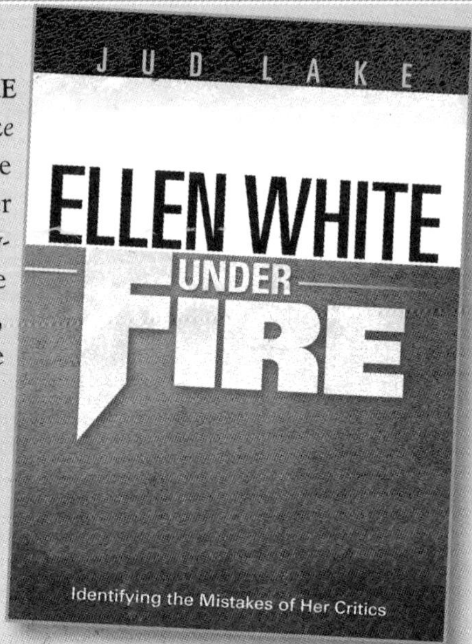

Ellen White Under Fire

by Jud Lake

During her lifetime, Ellen White withstood wave upon wave of personal criticisms. Yet the historical records confirm her as a person of integrity, and her writings confirm her loyalty to the Bible. In ***Ellen White Under Fire***, Dr. Jud Lake provides a comprehensive assessment of Ellen White critics, past and present, as well as her defenders—all the while building confidence in her prophetic gift.

Hardcover, 352 pages
ISBN 10: 0-8163-2408-5

Ellen White on Leadership

by Cindy Tutsch

If Ellen White wrote a book about how to be a good leader, what would she say? In this new compilation with commentary, author Cindy Tutsch answers that very question. She carefully examined the writings of Ellen White and made some surprising discoveries about who is a leader, what a leader thinks, and how a leader behaves.

Hardcover, 160 pages
ISBN 10: 0-8163-2270-8

101 Questions About Ellen White and Her Writings

by William Fagal

Every day the White Estate receives questions about Ellen White: her writings, her life, and her beliefs. Her books have been translated into dozens of languages, printed by the millions, and distributed around the world. In this book, thought-provoking answers are provided to 101 of the most frequently asked and often most controversial inquiries.

Paperback, 224 pages
ISBN 10: 0-8163-2378-X

Pacific Press®
Publishing Association
"Where the Word Is Life"

Three ways to order:

1 Local	Adventist Book Center®
2 Call	1-800-765-6955
3 Shop	AdventistBookCenter.com